Advance praise for

Robert E. Sherwood

"This biography of Sherwood brilliantly demonstrates the complexity of pacifism as a personal belief system. . . . The writing is wonderful, the chapters are nicely balanced, and the organization of the material on both the personal life and the writings is excellent."

—Melanie Gustafson, Department of History, University of Vermont

"This reader-friendly book written in lucid, accessible prose is an extraordinary accomplishment. . . . Alonso's handling of Sherwood's journey provides pleasure, joy, and engagement for anyone interested in pacifism, war, peace, politics, theater, history, and culture."

—Howard Stein, emeritus, Center for Theatre Studies, Columbia University

Robert E. Sherwood

Also by Harriet Hyman Alonso—

Growing Up Abolitionist: The Story of the Garrison Children (2002)

Peace as a Women's Issue: A History of the U.S. Movement for World Peace and Women's Rights (1993)

The Women's Peace Union and the Outlawry of War, 1921–1942 (1989; rpt. 1997)

Robert E. Sherwood

The Playwright in Peace and War

Harriet Hyman Alonso

UNIVERSITY OF MASSACHUSETTS PRESS   Amherst and Boston

Copyright © 2007 by University of Massachusetts Press
All rights reserved
Printed in the United States of America

LC 2007022047
ISBN 978-1-55849-619-4 (paper); 618-7 (library cloth)

Designed by Dennis Anderson
Set in Adobe Garamond Pro with ITC Caslon 224 display by dix!
Printed and bound by The Maple-Vail Book Manufacturing Group

Library of Congress Cataloging-in-Publication Data
Alonso, Harriet Hyman.
Robert E. Sherwood : the playwright in peace and war / Harriet Hyman Alonso.
    p. cm.
Includes bibliographical references and index.
ISBN 978-1-55849-618-7 (library cloth: alk. paper)—
ISBN 978-1-55849-619-4 (pbk. : alk. paper)
1. Sherwood, Robert E. (Robert Emmet), 1896–1955.
2. Dramatists, American—20th century—Biography.
I. Title. PS3537.H825Z55   2007
812'.52—dc22
[B]
                    2007022047

British Library Cataloguing in Publication data are available.

Photograph sources abbreviated as "Houghton" are reproduced by permission of the Houghton Library, Harvard University; as "NYPL" are by permission of Billy Rose Theatre Division, The New York Public Library for the Performing Arts, Astor, Lenox and Tilden Foundations.

Title page: Robert E. Sherwood and the tools of his trade, 1940. Houghton.

For my mother, Clara Hyman,

and

in memory of my father, Joseph Hyman,

for instilling in me a love for the theater

And for my great-niece Leah McComb,

who is carrying on the tradition

Contents

Act One

Prologue

In June 1901, when Robert Emmet Sherwood was just five years old, his mother, Rosina (or Posie, as her loved ones called her), visited a fortune-teller. She was skeptical of fortune-tellers, spiritualists, and other seers of the unknown, but her sister Lydia, an avid fan of such practices, insisted that she go, and Posie's curiosity and sense of fun allowed no other option. After giving Posie a perfunctory description of her four other children, the woman zeroed in on young Bobby and refused to discuss the others any further. "She was simply inspired and prophetic about Bobby," Posie told Lyd. "She described his appearance and said that if there was one thing I could count upon utterly in the universe it was that child and his great nature and his great genius. She fairly laughed over the sureness of Bobby's success and achievement. I must never doubt him, never fear for him. In spite of numberless risks and hairbreadth escapes, nothing could harm him. She said he is a great old soul in a child's body. . . . I have not half told you her ravings about Bobby and his wonderful power. It was very strange." [1]

Posie wondered if these predictions could have the least bit of truth in them. Of course, in 1901 she could only ponder these things, but years later she realized just how accurate the fortune-teller's words had been. By then her son had eluded death from gassing and wounds in World War I and from enemy fire in World War II. By the age of twenty-six he had become the country's leading film critic. Over the next eighteen years he also proved to be a great success as a playwright, scripting such audience favorites as *Idiot's Delight*, *Abe Lincoln in Illinois*, and *There Shall Be No Night*, for which he won Pulitzer Prizes, as well as *The Road to Rome*, *The Queen's Husband*, *Waterloo Bridge*, and *Reunion in Vienna*. In addition, he was among the highest-paid screenwriters in Hollywood, where he turned some of his own Broadway hits into films, including *The Petrified Forest*, *Idiot's Delight*, and *Abe Lincoln in Illinois,* and created new stories or adaptations, such as *Rebecca* (one of Alfred Hitchcock's major successes), *The Scarlet Pimpernel*, *The Adventures of Marco Polo*, *The Bishop's Wife*, and *The Best Years of Our Lives*, for which he won an Academy Award. There were a number of other plays and films that Sherwood authored for eager audiences, who considered him one of the top writers of the day.

But Robert Sherwood also became a well-known public figure. Like many peace proponents appalled by the inhumanity of Italian and German fascism, he moved away from his post–World War I pacifism to embracing intervention and then, much to his chagrin, another war. For a leader he chose Franklin D. Roosevelt, the man he believed most capable of addressing increasing world tensions. He developed a close friendship with the president— campaigning for him, writing speeches, and then, in a most unusual role for a show business personality at that time, becoming involved in foreign policy. During World War II Sherwood served as director of the Overseas Branch of the Office of War Information, the propaganda arm of the U.S. war effort, where he created the Voice of America radio network. He also took on other war-related assignments throughout Europe, North Africa, and the Pacific. Although many writers and performers became deeply involved in the war, Sherwood was one of the first to be welcomed into the higher echelons of the world of politics. Initially he was simply a master wordsmith, but within a short time he became someone whom others sought out for ideas, especially about issues of war and peace. After the death of Roosevelt and the end of World War II, Sherwood returned to his other life, that of a writer. As such, he took on the task of sorting through the papers of the recently deceased Harry Hopkins, Roosevelt's friend and close adviser on both New Deal politics and foreign affairs. From that project grew *Roosevelt and Hopkins*, a seminal history which garnered him several honors including both the Pulitzer and Bancroft prizes. It is a book that to this day is cited in almost every work on Roosevelt, Hopkins, the New Deal, or World War II.

Sherwood's entire career as a writer and political adviser evolved around his personal search for what the suffragist and peace organizer Carrie Chapman Catt termed "the cause and cure of war."[2] His internal debates found their way into almost every play, film, and article he wrote, even if in just a few lines of dialogue. His was a life of constant reflection and evaluation. An avid reader, he absorbed thousands of philosophical and historical facts and ideas about war and peace and weighed them against the political world that he was living in and reading about in newspapers. Then, rather than merely speaking through the characters he created, he acted upon his ideas, so that in his case reality and fiction became intertwined.

As the fortune-teller predicted, in many ways Robert E. Sherwood achieved great heights in his professional life, but in his personal life he faced the same trials and frustrations as anyone else. He loved, lost, and loved again— finding unhappiness with his first wife, Mary Brandon, and new life with his second, Madeline Hurlock. He also tried, with only moderate success, to be a good father to his daughter, Mary, and an attentive son to his mother. He suffered the pangs of near bankruptcy, ill health, writer's block, and tensions with theatrical producers, the last leading to the creation of the Playwrights Producing Company, a truly collaborative venture in theater history. But he was unusual in that he was often afflicted by an inner turmoil over the responsibility he felt to protect the world from fascism and war.

Sherwood's combination of personal commitment, artistic talent, and sense of civic responsibility set him apart from many other playwrights of his day. His was a unique voice that simultaneously echoed public opinion while challenging people to think about the world beyond the borders of the United States. Passionate and outspoken about his politics, he became a literary activist, one who took on the multiple issues facing the American people from World War I to the early years of the Cold War. In many ways, his life was shaped by the larger world—by his involvement in international affairs, his passion for human rights, and his desire for world peace.

1

Being an Emmet and a Sherwood

ROBERT EMMET SHERWOOD was born into two illustrious families, the Emmets and the Sherwoods, both with long histories in the United States and with shared common values. First, they were patriotic, loved the nation they lived in, and supported their government's positions in both domestic and foreign policies as long as they deemed them fair and honest. Second, they were committed to social justice—to standing up for individual freedoms and protecting civil liberties. Third, they valued the printed word, and several family members engaged in some sort of writing themselves. Fourth, they also loved the arts, especially literature, theater, painting, architecture, and music. While he was growing up, Robert E. Sherwood's family (especially his mother, Posie) made him aware of his heritage and imbued in him the values that had driven generations of Emmets and Sherwoods into politics and the arts.

The Emmets had by far the more dramatic family history.[1] As one descendant expressed it, the entire family from as far back as could be remembered suffered from "Emmetry," the sense of being "Irish, proud, and romantic and thinking you're just a bit better than anyone else."[2] Certainly, as a young child Robert Sherwood heard stories about the fighting Emmets, especially his namesake Robert Emmet and his brother Thomas Addis, who left a legacy of rebellion against Britain's tyrannical hold on Ireland in the late eighteenth and early nineteenth centuries.[3] Their story of heroism and martyrdom was one that any family would romanticize as it was handed down from one generation to the next. By the time it reached the ears of young Robert Sherwood, it was so huge that it became part of his personal identity. He was always quick to refer to his namesake whenever he had the chance and to imagine himself as emulating his strong values and valiant behavior.

What he learned was this. The brothers (Thomas Addis, born on April 24, 1764, and Robert, born fourteen years later on March 4, 1778) were very close, so much so, in fact, that the actions of the elder sibling had a disastrous effect on the younger. A 1782 graduate of Trinity College, Dublin, Thomas went on to study medicine and then law and was admitted to the bar in Dublin in 1790. Two years later, his story took a dramatic turn. Greatly affected by the success of the U.S. War of Independence, the ongoing French Revolution, and the abundance of literature that espoused liberal ideas about government, nature, and science (including works by John Locke, Thomas Paine, Thomas Jefferson, and Jean Jacques Rousseau), Thomas joined the crusade for Irish self-rule. He was a man who believed deeply that Ireland should be autonomous, for when he looked at the so-called Irish House of Commons, he saw hypocrisy. How could a parliament exist that banned Catholics from participating and barred them from voting? How could commoners have a voice when only sixty-four out of three hundred seats were determined by fair elections, the others remaining under the firm control of landowners and government leaders? Being Protestant did not prevent the Emmets and others from sympathizing with the Catholic population in the interests of justice and freedom. Nor did it prevent them from supporting the idea of the separation of church and state. As a result, on December 14, 1792, Thomas joined other Dublin Protestant and Catholic men in the Society of United Irishmen, whose purpose was to achieve parliamentary reform to ensure democratic representation in government and whose members embraced the concept of self-sacrifice as a national honor.

Seventeen ninety-two, however, was not a good year in which to express one's desire for national sovereignty. Having lost its American colonies, and fearing a revolution like the one in France, Great Britain did not want to hear any words of protest from the mouths of its Irish colonials. Therefore, the Irish colonial government set out to intimidate and disband the United Irishmen by planting spies and informers within the group's membership. But the most drastic action occurred after the Irish Uprising of 1798, which consisted of many small skirmishes. In order to close down the organization permanently, the British arrested Thomas, now one of the group's leaders, and a number of other members for expressing traitorous ideas. After being imprisoned in Dublin, the men were shipped to Fort George prison in Scotland, where Thomas's wife, Jane Patten, and their children joined him. Unable to obtain a conviction of treason, the British authorities eventually offered the Irishmen freedom as long as they agreed to emigrate to the United States. To protect his family, Thomas accepted the deal, and in October 1804 he left Europe for New York, taking some of his family with him and arranging for the others to follow.

Although it began in such a negative way, Thomas's immigration story would be one of complete success. His expectation that the former independence fighters in the United States would welcome an Irish compatriot was destroyed when, in the same year he arrived, the more conservative federalists in New York took steps to prevent men of his ilk from being admitted to the bar by getting the New York Supreme Court to adopt a ruling prohibiting revolutionaries from countries other than the United States to practice law. A clever man, Thomas was able to overcome this obstacle by befriending DeWitt Clinton and other anti-federalist leaders who desperately needed a lawyer and orator with his talents to speak against the federalists' desire for a strong central government. He agreed to work for them in exchange for admittance to the bar. Within a short time, Clinton and his associates persuaded the New York State legislature to pass a special act entitling Thomas Addis Emmet to practice in all the courts in the state. After several years of practicing law, Thomas took a break to serve as colonel of an Irish regiment organized to protect New York against a possible British invasion during the War of 1812. He was rewarded by being appointed attorney general of New York State, an office he left after two years in favor of returning to his busy and profitable law practice. Meanwhile, his family quickly became part of the social elite and married well. His son Robert became a judge in a New York court; another son, John, studied medicine; and yet another, Thomas Addis, became a prominent New York physician.[4]

The elder Thomas Addis had good reason to hate the British apart from his own imprisonment and forced emigration, and that reason was the sad fate of his younger brother, Robert Emmet. By the time he entered Trinity College, Dublin, in 1793 at the age of sixteen, Robert had two major interests—science and Irish freedom. Following in his brother's footsteps, in 1796 he was sworn in (by Thomas himself) as a member of the college branch of the United Irishmen; but soon after Thomas was arrested in 1798, Robert and eighteen of his fellow activists were expelled from the university on the grounds that they were subversives. For a while, Robert continued working with the organization, visiting prisoners, rebuilding the society, and planning the next move against the English. But when a warrant for his arrest was issued soon after Thomas was shipped to Scotland, Robert fled Ireland and stayed briefly in England, then Switzerland, Holland, Spain, France, and Belgium. Upon his return home, Robert's every move was monitored by government informers. In spite of this, he worked with others on a plan to seize control of Dublin Castle. Even falling in love with Sarah Curran, the daughter of a well-known Dublin lawyer, could not alter his path.

The planned uprising took place on July 23, 1803, but had little chance of success, as British informers had carefully filled in the authorities on every aspect of the scheme. Still, it involved scores of people, more than two hundred of whom were arrested and imprisoned within a week and countless others within the next month. Robert himself remained in hiding in Dublin until August 25, when a spy told the government where he could be found. When he was arrested, the police confiscated a cache of Sarah's letters from Robert's jacket pocket and threatened to expose her if he refused to finger other rebels then in hiding. For five nights and days his jailers tortured and interrogated him, but to no avail. Although he feared for Sarah's reputation and safety, he would not betray the cause of Irish freedom. Finally, on August 30, Robert Emmet was quickly tried, found guilty, and sentenced to be hanged on September 10. At his execution, his head was severed from his body and held aloft for the public to see. "This is the head of Robert Emmet, a traitor," the hangman shouted out several times.[5] Soon after a simple burial at Hospital Fields, a public burying ground, the headless corpse disappeared. No one knows for sure where it was taken. Robert Emmet became a hero and a martyr in Ireland. His portrait is said to hang in every pub in the country. According to one of the Emmet descendants, "If a young woman is married, she hopes to receive two portraits—one of the Virgin Mary and one of Robert Emmet."[6] Whether this is true is debatable, but there is no question of Robert Emmet's romantic image in Irish history—and in the mind of his namesake, Robert Emmet Sherwood.

The deeds of other Emmet ancestors with reputations as the great protectors of freedom and national independence (this time in the United States) set equally high standards for the following generations. Elias Boudinot, a patriot with a sense of social justice, and a writer, was the most notable.[7] Born in 1740 into a wealthy family of French Huguenot immigrants to the West Indies whose grandsons settled in Philadelphia, as a young man of twenty Elias studied law with his brother-in-law, Richard Stockton, in New Jersey. Once licensed, he moved to Elizabethtown (now Elizabeth), New Jersey, where he set up a successful law practice combined with a bit of commercial trade and some real estate investment. By the time he reached his early thirties, Elias was a wealthy, influential man who, like the Emmets of Ireland, saw the value of the English colonies' becoming autonomous and then gaining their independence from the mother country. In 1774, during the pre-Revolutionary struggle in the United States, he joined the Essex County Committee of Correspondence and chaired its Committee of Safety. His main objective was to seek a compromise with the British that would not lead to violent conflict. When war broke out, however, he did not flinch from the fight. In 1776 he spent a brief period as aide-de-camp to William Livingston, brigadier general of the New Jersey militia.

It was George Washington who involved Elias more deeply in the war effort. At Washington's urging, he agreed to serve as commissary-general of prisoners captured by the British. In the course of this work Elias came to see the other face of war, describing it as "unnatural and [a] disrelishing state of . . . slaughter," an opinion his future descendant, Robert Sherwood, would share.[8] Still, Elias admired Washington, and even though he abhorred the violence of war, he became committed to the establishment of an independent nation and so continued to support the war effort. He served two terms as a New Jersey delegate to the Continental Congress, from 1778 to 1779 and again from 1781 to 1783, and was elected president of the congress on November 4, 1782. For the Emmets, one of the most outstanding features of Elias Boudinot's life was that on April 15, 1783, he joined in signing the provisional peace treaty with Great Britain that ended the War of Independence and established the United States as a sovereign state. He was then elected to the first Congress, which met in New York City on March 4, 1789, where he became an ardent federalist. He remained in Congress until 1795, when he left to direct the U.S. Mint, a position he held until 1805.

In addition to his government activities, Elias Boudinot was a great philanthropist. He gave generously to charity, and in the spirit of social justice he spoke out against slavery and the oppression of Native Americans. So admired was he by Galagina, a young Cherokee, that Galagina adopted his name before becoming chief of his nation. A religious man, Elias Boudinot was also one of the founders and first president of the American Bible Society. The Boudinots and the Emmets became joined when Thomas Addis Emmet's grandson William Jenkins Emmet married Boudinot's granddaughter Julia Colt Pierson. Among Julia and William's children was Robert Sherwood's mother, Rosina (Posie).

While the Emmet side of Robert Sherwood's family certainly had illustrious roots, the Sherwood side could boast a similar distinction.[9] The Sherwoods' English ancestors were among the original European settlers of Stratford, Connecticut, and their descendants claimed that all U.S. Sherwoods could trace their ancestry back to Stratford-upon-Avon, England. "So I guess," Robert Sherwood later noted, "that all of us Sherwoods on this continent are related to each other—and we may also be related to the Shakespeare family."[10] The Hubleys, the Huguenot branch of the family, settled in Pennsylvania and became early supporters of the American Revolutionary movement.

Robert Sherwood was most familiar with his Sherwood ancestors who came to the United States from Ireland in the eighteenth century. His great-grandparents, James and Mary Wilson, who settled in Keene, New Hampshire, were the parents of Sherwood's paternal grandmother, Mary Elizabeth, born in 1826, a woman Sherwood remembered quite well as "a sort of dilettante writer" and "the Emily Post of her day." Her subject, "etiquette," he jokingly lamented, was something about which he was "woefully ignorant."[11] Some of the books Mary Elizabeth Wilson (M.E.W.) Sherwood wrote as an older woman include *Home Amusements* (1881), *A Transplanted Rose, A Story of New York Society* (1882), *Etiquette, The American Code of Manners: A Study of the Usages, Laws, and Observances* (1884), *Manners and Social Usages* (1884), *Amenities of Home* (1884), *Royal Girls and Royal Courts* (1887), and *The Art of Entertaining* (1892), all of which earned her a considerable amount of money. Her autobiography, *An Epistle to Posterity: Being Rambling Recollections of Many Years of My Life,* written in 1897, in which she vividly described her family's earlier years, also provided some family role models for her grandson. In her father, James Wilson, whom Robert Sherwood never met, he nevertheless discovered another ancestor committed to law and politics: Wilson represented New Hampshire in the U.S. Congress. Her mother's early death at age fifty opened a wider world to M.E.W. as her father called upon her to act as his companion and hostess in Washington, D.C., and other places where he served the government. It was during one of her trips with him that she observed the institution of slavery for the first time, an experience that made her an ardent, though not active, abolitionist. Her memories of the Civil War and her opposition to slavery impressed her grandson Robert, who as an adult was equally disturbed by racism and xenophobia in his twentieth-century world.

In 1851, while M.E.W. was in Washington, she met and married the lawyer John Sherwood. Together they left Washington, the city M.E.W. described as having "plenty of time and plenty of sunlight," for New York, where "we have annihilated both." [12] Living in Washington, however, had given her a taste for high society and fashion which she continued to pursue in New York, where during the Civil War she also helped the New York Sanitary Commission raise money to feed and clothe Union soldiers. Over the postwar years she wrote hundreds of poems, articles, essays, and books, which publishers eagerly bought. The money came in handy, as her tastes were more extravagant and her social life more expensive than her husband could afford to support. At times John could not pay the bills, and the family fell into debt. But M.E.W.'s gossipy, humorous writings gained steadily in popularity. When John suffered from health problems, her income became more than just a luxury; it was a necessity. In addition to working and socializing, the Sherwoods raised four sons, two of whom died early—one in infancy and the other, Philip, at the age of twenty-five. Of the sons who survived to maturity, Samuel and Arthur Murray, it was Arthur who married Rosina Emmet in 1887.

These brief portraits of family members illustrate how well the Sherwoods and the Emmets complemented each other. Both families were firmly situated in the middle class, and though their incomes were not always lucrative, all had some inherited family wealth, good education, and social standing.

They had common ties to the colonial era and the War of Independence. They were literate and artistic and shared the values of patriotism and sympathy for the underdog. Both families included members who had served in the U.S. Congress. Both had been involved in the Civil War, though much to the family's chagrin, one of Thomas Addis Emmet's grandsons fought for the South. As Robert Sherwood later wryly put it, "He felt it was his . . . duty as an Emmet to serve on the side of the rebels." [13] In later years the combined Emmet-Sherwood family produced young men and women who aided in both the World War I and World War II efforts. They were two families that fit like a pair of gloves.

The blended Emmet-Sherwood family came into being with Rosina (Posie) Emmet and Arthur Murray Sherwood's marriage, but their story begins before that, first with Arthur, then with Posie. There is little surviving information about Arthur's childhood. Although his parents' incomes were not steady, he and his brothers grew up among some of the wealthiest families in New York City. Their father, John, spent most of his time trying to earn money, not in enjoying the pleasures of playing with his children. M.E.W., it appears, relied on nannies to tend to them before they were old enough to be sent off to private boarding schools. In her memoir, *An Epistle to Posterity*, she mentions her children only twice, leading one to suspect that they were not her primary concern. After completing their boarding school educations, the Sherwood boys moved on to Harvard University, where Samuel and Arthur helped found the satirical *Harvard Lampoon,* for which Arthur served as first president. They also participated in the Hasty Pudding Club, where Arthur stretched his acting and singing wings, performing the role of "King Henry the Two" in the burlesque *Fair Rosamund.* He also wrote poems, theater pieces, parodies of ballets, and limericks, which entranced Posie Emmet. For a while, it seemed that Arthur's talents might lead to the career his son later took on; but because of his experience of growing up in a home where money was a constant point of contention, he chose to study business instead. After graduating in 1877, he concentrated on earning a good income as a Wall Street stockbroker and member of the New York Stock Exchange, a life that did not suit him very well and seemed to take some of the spirit out of him. His son later recalled: "I believe that he hated it. He always urged my brothers and sisters and me to keep away from Wall Street. . . . He never expressed any desire to pass along his business to any of his children." [14] Arthur did, however, find a good amount of happiness in his home life. In fact, perhaps the best thing to happen to him was his marriage into the indomitable Emmet family, a clan he knew to be artistic, energetic, and just plain fun.

By the time Posie was born on December 13, 1854, the Emmets had proliferated in the United States, several producing larger families than was the average at the time. Posie's parents, Julia Colt Pierson and William Jenkins Emmet, spawned ten children: Robert Temple and Posie (who were twins), Julia Colt (who died young), William Le Roy, Richard Stockton, Devereux, Lydia Field, Christopher Temple, Thomas Addis (who died at the age of sixteen), and Jane Erin.[15] Several of the children went on to become prominent, at least two of them in the military, including Posie's twin, Robert, who graduated from West Point in 1877. As a colonel in the U.S. Cavalry, he was awarded the Congressional Medal of Honor for his service in the campaign against the Apaches in the early 1880s. William Le Roy, after graduating from the Naval Academy in 1881, became an electrical and mechanical engineer in an era when science and technology were just taking hold in the industrial and urban sectors of the U.S. economy. As an employee of Thomas Edison's General Electric Company, he pioneered research in alternating current. He also spent ten years designing and planning the Niagara Falls Power Company. In 1909 William lobbied for the construction of ships driven by electricity. As a result of his efforts, at least three hundred ships powered by turboelectric drives were afloat by the end of World War I. Less is known of the three other Emmet sons—Christopher, Richard, and Devereux—except that the last, after becoming a successful real estate investor in Suffolk County, Long Island, turned to designing golf courses, of which he created 160.

The three Emmet sisters, Posie, Lydia, and Jane, all became respected artists. Though considerably separated in age, they were as close as any sisters could be, and their frequent correspondence during their adult years presents a portrait of love and devotion. Posie, the eldest, was twelve years older than Lydia, who was born in 1866, and nineteen years older than Jane, born in 1873. Like their mother, Julia, who had studied illustration with Daniel Huntington, the girls showed both an early talent and a desire to pick up sketchpad, pencils, and then paints. Indeed, over the years, more than a dozen Emmet women from various branches of the family became painters, sculptors, and sketch artists—skills they cultivated in their offspring as well.[16] Like other Emmets and Sherwoods, Posie's parents were not exceptionally wealthy, although they had some inherited resources and they owned land. William, who came from an educated family, had eschewed college in favor of going into the Brown family's sugar refining business in Portland, Maine. When the business was sold after the Civil War to a larger competitor, William was left without a place to work. Afflicted throughout his adult years by ill health and poor business sense, he never amounted to much, and hence William and Julia faced innumerable financial problems. Nor was Julia, an intelligent and stately woman, much help at earning income. She had her hands full with caring for the couple's large family and their home on a small, pastoral island connected by a causeway to the north shore of Long Island Sound near Pelham, about eighteen miles north of New York City. Nearby was the Bolton Priory, where all the Emmet children got their early education.

Posie grew to womanhood in an era that favored women's advancement more than any other in the country's past. Before her time, the artwork produced by the Emmet women remained in the attics or parlors of their families' homes. Posie's generation, however, benefited from a blossoming of opportunities for women. There were several reasons for this social change. The women's rights movement, which officially began in July 1848 in Seneca Falls, New York, had gained both momentum and supporters for women's suffrage, education, job opportunity, and a voice in the public and private spheres. Many educational institutions had opened their doors to women, including art schools. Also, with the deaths of approximately 620,000 in the Civil War, mostly men, there were many women who might otherwise have chosen marriage but for whom there were no partners. During the Gilded Age that followed the war, a time of growth in industry and personal wealth, middle-class women in particular sought out other options, such as professional or charitable work, which would give their lives meaning. Many were thrilled with the results. For Posie, Lydia, and Jane, this meant that the Emmet talent for art could be cultivated and advanced in a professional way rather than merely for private enjoyment.

A lovely, tall young woman with dark brown eyes, the calm and serene Posie had a penchant for independence, which showed itself when, at the age of thirteen, she sent an illustration for a joke to *Harper's Weekly,* which promptly sent her a check for twelve dollars. Julia and William were horrified that this young woman they were raising had taken such an unorthodox step, but after much hesitation and discussion, they decided to allow her to keep the money. Encouraged by her first success, Posie continued to draw, producing at least one known sketchbook in 1873 and another dated 1876–77. (It is possible that there were others that were lost over time.) Although there was no shortage of men who wished to court her, including Andrew Carnegie, Posie felt no inclination to settle down with a husband, children, and household responsibilities. Rather, she actively pursued a career as an artist, in 1878 becoming one of the American impressionist William Merritt Chase's first pupils at his Tenth Street Studio in Manhattan. For two years she worked with Chase and then set up her own space in his building, seeking projects that she would find meaningful. One was to illustrate a children's book, *Pretty Peggy and other Ballads*, and a spin-off, *The Pretty-Peggy Painting Book*, both published in 1880.

That same year Posie entered a Christmas card contest sponsored by L. Prang and Company, a British firm that wanted to establish a Christmas card market in the United States, which at the time imported its season's greetings from England. Posie's design of a group of choristers with archaic instruments surrounded by flowers and a scene of an angel appearing to the shepherds took first prize, the princely sum of $1,000. The next year another of her designs won fourth prize. The first-prize money would have been enough to send Posie and Lydia to Paris for the winter, but as an anonymous author later put it, when one of her brothers did not have "the necessary money for his college tuition," Posie, in a gesture common among women, gave him the prize money.[17] Posie's reputation as an artist grew quickly after that. In 1881 she exhibited works at the National Academy of Design in New York. The next year she showed paintings at the Boston Art Club. In 1883 she joined Candace Wheeler's design firm, Associated Artists.[18] Wheeler was one of the most famous designers, craftswomen, and needle artists in the country, and her Manhattan firm was an unusual operation, for it included only women. Everything—all business, all designs, and all work—was done by American women artists and craftswomen. The talented group produced tapestries, curtains, and wallpaper but was best noted for embroidering with silk thread on silk canvas in a technique Wheeler termed "needle-weaving." Posie became Wheeler's second assistant designer, and with Wheeler's daughter Dora was largely responsible for drafting the figure designs while other artists translated them onto fabric. By the end of her time with the firm, Posie had become a very well rounded artist, but she still wanted to explore more artistic avenues, especially in paint.

In the fall of 1884 Dora Wheeler, Posie (then thirty), and young Lydia (then eighteen) left for Paris, where they spent six months in the segregated women's class in the Académie Julian studying with Frederick MacMonnies, and then at Vitti's Academy. Posie had a wonderful time in Paris, just as she had in New York, doing the work she loved, socializing with women artists such as Elizabeth Boott, Annie Dixwell, and Ellen Day Hale, drinking coffee while sketching in cafés, meeting a few times and corresponding with her distant cousin Henry James, and generally living the life of an artist. In all of this she was joined by Lydia, somewhat of an opposite type to Posie, with flashing blue eyes and an endless amount of energy. "Lyd," as she was called, began studying art at an early age, perhaps as a result of her older sister's persistence and success. At first she had private lessons but then enrolled at the Art Students League in New York. After the three young women returned home from their Paris sojourn, Lydia studied with William Merritt Chase, as Posie had done, while the more artistically advanced Posie was immediately invited to become a member of the Society of American Artists, founded by Chase, Abbot Raye, John Singer Sargent, and others as an alternative to the more conservative and traditional National Academy.

Though set on a career, Posie could not resist the attentions of Arthur and Philip Sherwood. On the one hand, she had great fun with Arthur, spending hours one afternoon in January 1881 at the Sherwood home as Oscar Wilde "cavorted & performed for our special benefit." Posie was prepared to enjoy the performance because Arthur had been "going on like mad" about it, reducing her to "hysterics" even before Wilde himself came on the scene.[19] On the other hand, Posie adored the more serious Philip. The two enjoyed the same classical music, talked endlessly about all kinds of subjects, and accompanied each other to the theater and opera. When she took a trip to Pueblo, Colorado, in the summer of 1882, it was Philip who was on Posie's mind. She wrote emotionally about how much she missed him: "I want to see you dreadfully, Pandy. We will have so much to tell each other that we will out do ourselves. Our former feats of conversation that Arthur was so much struck with were simply nothing to what we will do."[20] M.E.W. was most enthusiastic about the prospect of one of her sons marrying Posie. After all, she came from good American stock, was well educated, seemed to have some family wealth (at least in land), and was both sociable and socially connected. In an effort to lure Posie, the attentive M.E.W. took care to share her famous advice and constantly invited Posie to their home. When Posie and Lydia were in Paris in 1884–85, M.E.W. kept in touch, sending a list of her friends in Paris and advising Posie to invite them all to tea, a ludicrous idea to the rather bohemian sisters and their friend Dora Wheeler.

For some time it appeared that Posie might choose to spend her life with Philip, but when he died at age twenty-five from a lung condition, she gravitated to Arthur for support. Four years after Philip's death, on June 1, 1887, the thirty-three-year-old Posie married the thirty-one-year-old Arthur. Within eleven years, she gave birth to five children and gradually moved away from being a full-time artist to being a wife and mother who happened to paint on the side. This transition did not take place overnight, however. Until 1900 Posie continued to work in various ways. In 1887 she illustrated *The Old-Fashioned Fairy Book* by Mrs. Burton Harrison. Then in 1889 she exhibited some of her paintings abroad, receiving the silver medal at the Paris Exposition. The following year she and several other artists showed their work in a "Painters in Pastel" exhibit held in the Wunderlich Gallery in New York

City. She later received two bronze medals at the Pan-American Exposition in Buffalo in 1901 and another silver medal for work at the St. Louis Exposition in 1904. Posie's art also appeared in publications such as Harper's *My Golden-Haired Laddie,* and by 1891 she had become a regular illustrator for *Harper's Weekly* and *Century Magazine,* often using her children as models. She wrote a story, "Wool Gathering," which appeared in *Harper's Second Reader.* She and Arthur even collaborated on a small volume, *Out of Town* (1896), which poked gentle fun at their lives as suburban dwellers in New Rochelle, New York. In 1891 Posie was named a member of the executive committee of William Merritt Chase's Shinnecock Summer School of Art, located on 3,800 acres of land outside the town of Southampton on Long Island, the first major summer art school in the United States. Up to 150 students from all over the country and Canada who wanted to learn Chase's principles of plein air painting, an impressionist technique which he used most effectively, especially in landscapes, attended the school until its closing in 1902.

One of the highlights of Posie's career up to this point was creating a piece for the Women's Building at the 1893 Columbian Exposition in Chicago.[21] Lydia, too, was asked to design artworks, and the project touched the sisters' feminist side, which yearned for independence and political equality, especially the right to vote. Lydia, the more outspoken of the two on the issue of suffrage, was a member of the Women's Political Union, an organization founded by Harriot Stanton Blatch (Elizabeth Cady Stanton's daughter) in 1910 out of her 1907 Equality League of Self-Supporting Women. Both sisters, however, were part of the community of women engaged in self-expression at the time, and the Women's Building, a unique feature of the world's fair, was a natural way for them to combine their artistic and political interests.

The Board of Lady Managers for the fair, which oversaw the Women's Building, wanted the entire project to be created by women. Therefore, they chose Sophia Hayden, a young architect in her early twenties, to design the building and Enid Yandell, a mere twenty-two years of age, to sculpt the caryatids on the building's façade—the figure of a woman repeated twenty-four times. Mary Cassatt painted a mural depicting "Modern Woman" and Mary MacMonnies, a mural depicting "Primitive Woman." Others whose work was represented in the building included Rosa Bonheur, Harriet Hosmer, Edmonia Lewis, Ann Whitney, Vinne Ream Hoxie, Adelaide Johnson, and Cecilia Beaux, the crème de la crème of women artists and sculptors. Candace Wheeler was also involved in the project, taking on the assignment of director of the applied arts exhibit and "color director" of the Women's Building itself. It was she who recommended Posie and Lydia to the committee. She also recommended that her daughter Dora paint the ceiling's mural, which she did. When the building was completed, Wheeler called it "the most peaceably human of all the buildings. . . . [I]t is like a man's ideal of woman."[22]

Posie's mural, which was hung on the west side of the art gallery, was titled *The Republic's Welcome to her Daughters.* It portrayed a woman playing a guitar, a mother and child, and three classical figures, one holding a laurel wreath, one a small statue, and one a scrolled document. Lydia's mural, a pastel in the southwest rotunda titled *Art, Science, and Literature,* portrayed a violist, a sculptor, a scholar (in robes) with a book, and a painter. Posie was also represented by a watercolor of a mother gazing at a child sleeping in a hammock. For their efforts the Emmet sisters were asked to donate their labor as a display of their patriotic fervor. Granted, the two came from a family steeped in love of country, but they also knew that other artists were being paid lucrative sums. Both wrote more than once to the committee requesting payment. In the end Lydia received about $500, but there is no record that Posie ever received anything. After the fair ended, several of the artworks, including Posie's and Lydia's, were placed in a warehouse, never to be seen again. No one seems to know what happened to them.

By 1893 Posie and Lydia were both recognized as successful artists and illustrators. Lydia was especially well known for her portraits of children, a talent that provided her with a substantial income throughout her adult life as a single woman. She was so successful that she established her own portrait studio in New York City and in 1905 had a summer home built in Stockbridge, Massachusetts. Robert Sherwood and his siblings spent many happy times there with Lydia, one of their favorite aunts. Existing records show that after 1912, Lydia earned an average of over $20,000 a year, a considerable amount at that time. She charged her wealthy customers about $2,000 to $5,000 for each figure she painted.

Jane, only twenty years old at the time of the Columbian Exposition, trailed behind her sisters. Like them, she studied with William Merritt Chase, at the Art Students League, and in Paris. Her life, however, took her in a different direction. In August 1903 Jane announced her engagement to Wilfrid Gabriel Von Glehn, an English impressionist. The sisters were stunned by the engagement, believing that the thirty-year-old Jane would remain single, as Lydia had. Besides, this meant that after the couple's marriage the following year, their sweet younger sister would most likely spend the rest of her life in Europe. The Von Glehns (who changed their name to de Glehn in 1919 so as not to be taken as Germans after World War I) were good friends of the famed artist John Singer Sargent, and between 1905 and 1914 spent a great deal of time traveling through Europe with him. Sargent painted several works portraying the couple. Best known is *The Fountain* (1907), which depicts a white-clad Jane sitting on a marble pillar painting in the gardens of the Villa Torlonia in Fascati, Italy, while a casually posed Wilfrid looks on. *In a Gondola* (1904) shows an elegantly dressed Jane in Venice and *In the Generalife* (1912) shows Jane gazing at Sargent's sister Emily. Jane herself was never as well known as her sisters, choosing to keep her painting more of a private affair than a public career.

The Emmet sisters remained close throughout their lives. Until her marriage, Jane was a constant presence in the Sherwood children's lives. Lydia, too, was a permanent fixture. Because she and Posie lived near each other and at times with each other, Lyd was involved in all aspects of the children's upbringing from birth to adulthood. Both of the sisters helped in many ways with Posie's large family, making it possible for her to continue painting. Indeed, all three sisters taught the children to draw and paint and exposed them to the world of art, literature, and culture, in the process inculcating a spirit of artistic independence in them. Although the sisters enjoyed each and every one of the children, they were especially taken with Robert, who at an early age proved to be delightfully spirited and, oftentimes, quite naughty.

2

Born to Be a Ham

OVER FORTY YEARS after his birth on April 4, 1896, Robert Sherwood's mother still recalled how happy she was on the day he arrived, when her artist's eye took in the heaps of white snow on a maple tree "covered with scarlet tassels" outside her window and heard the doctor say, "This is the biggest baby I ever saw."[1] Indeed, even in his adulthood, Sherwood's height, thinness, and slight stoop were noted in almost every newspaper article, memoir, or speech in which he was mentioned and remained a cause of his constant self-consciousness. As a small child entering the Jay Kindergarten in Westport, New York, his height already marked him. Posie wrote her sister Lydia that it was amusing to see her little boy tower over all the other "little Jays," unable to fit his long legs under the classroom tables but looking "perfectly happy" nonetheless.[2]

Just two years later, at the age of seven, Bobby (as he was affectionately called) was insecure about his height, despite the example of his own father, a tall six feet two inches. Upon hearing about the "freaks" in the sideshow of a visiting circus, he stunned his mother by saying: "I do hope to goodness I'm not going to be a freak. I suppose the only kind of a freak I *could* be would be a giant, & I hope I'm not going to be that." Young Bobby felt "sorry for the poor French Giant" he had seen. It frightened him to think that this man whom everyone laughed at "was once just a simple boy—quite big for his age, but just a simple French boy going out with his sled to slide down hill like any other boy!"[3] An average boy, just like him.

Being a member of a financially successful family presented Bobby with enough opportunities so that not every waking moment was consumed by worrisome contemplation about his height. His attentive and artistic mother encouraged his obvious talent and interest in literature and the arts, and he was a quick learner. After his first year in New Rochelle, the family moved to Manhattan, where his world was filled with relative luxury. Arthur made sufficient money on Wall Street to support a house, a nanny (Delia Gilligan), housekeeping help, private boarding schools, a social life that included appreciation of all the arts, and then, for the boys, college at Harvard. Within a few years, it also included a summer home near Lake Champlain in upstate New York. There was nothing the Sherwood children lacked in terms of material needs, and the free-spirited Posie saw to it that their days were filled with interesting and pleasurable learning experiences.

Arthur Jr., born in 1888, was the first Sherwood child, followed by Cynthia in 1889 and Philip in 1891. Fourth came Bobby, and then, finally, Rosamund about three years later, in 1899. For a woman of thirty-three to begin such a large family and not complete her childbearing until the age of forty-five must have been exhausting. This was certainly not a common pattern at that time, but Posie was never one to follow custom or to lack energy and enthusiasm for life, and she had lots of help. Not only were there Delia, Lydia, and Jane, but also the sisters' mother, Julia, did as much as she could until her death in 1908, and Arthur proved a happy and lively father in spite of his long, boring hours as a stockbroker and his busy social role as a prominent Harvard alumnus.

It would almost be an understatement to say that Bobby Sherwood was an active child. Even when he was a mere seventeen months of age, his Aunt Jane, then a young and strong twenty-four-year-old, found it difficult to keep up with him. "He is without exception the most vigorous manly child I've ever seen of his age," she wrote Lydia. "He runs me off my feet and is perfectly tireless and tumbles down and violently bumps his head and struggles up again without turning a hair." Jane likened Bobby to "a young lion cub, an infant Hercules."[4] Whenever Delia had a day off from tending the Sherwood family, Posie would practically collapse from exhaustion, largely from running after Bobby. Jane told Lydia that Posie was "almost dead" by the time she arrived to help out with her "troublesome" nephew, who constantly tried to keep Posie from working on her paintings or doing chores.[5]

Some of the curly-haired toddler's need for attention was the result of his slowness in developing language skills, an irony considering that his later fame would come from his use of language. In 1898, however, Posie lamented that he was "divine but woefully backward about talking although smart as paint."[6] The previous May, on a visit to the country, Bobby had pleased her by dragging a flowerpot full of dandelions over to her and shouting, "A flower," but since then he had not mastered many words or phrases.[7] He did know his brother Philip's name, though. "Lip," he called him. When Philip's crib was replaced by a cot to mark his passage from babyhood into childhood, little Bobby could not understand and threw a tantrum. He mistakenly believed that "Lip" was leaving their shared bedroom, a child's haven full of toys and a menagerie of stuffed animals, where he and his siblings played contentedly for hours at a time. Posie's worries about Bobby's lack of speech eased as he neared the age of three. By that time he could greet his father with "Good morning my gate big tall handsome Daddy," and Posie with "Mudder

or the city, he kept up a constant flow of writing and drawing, creating his own childhood publishing companies and printing his material with his own hands. His Second Artists Club Co.'s S.A.C. Press "published" his "Story of the Awful Daughter and Here [sic] Good Father" and "The Bad Man and the Good Man and the Woman," both with illustrations by the "Auther [sic]." At age eight he wrote his first play, *Tom Ruggles' Surprise,* and soon after an unfinished work on the American War of Independence, complete with intrigue and romance as well as illustrations.

In early 1904, at the age of eight, Bobby was sent away to boarding school to start his formal education, largely because his father felt that he needed to learn discipline. Posie did not necessarily agree, as she had wanted to keep this particular troublemaking but highly creative son with her a while longer. Nevertheless, she acquiesced to her husband's plan to send Bobby away to school, as they had done with his older siblings. The institution, which Arthur, Phil, and Bobby all attended at one time or another, was the Fay School in Southborough, Massachusetts. Founded as a day school in the early 1860s by Eliza Burnett Fay and her sister Harriet, it became a boarding school in 1866. By the time Bobby was enrolled as a student, the school had grown from only two boarders to (in 1908) approximately seventy-seven young scholars in residence. This small establishment was run by Waldo B. Fay, the headmaster, and seven "masters," or teachers. There were a few classrooms, a gymnasium, a study hall, a music room, recitation rooms, a sports field, and tennis courts. A library was added during Bobby's years there.[20]

Bobby's departure was a crushing blow for Rosamund, whom Posie described as "a little widowed thing."[21] Left all alone with her mother and her toys, Rosamund sulked, missing Bobby. One day Posie found her eating breakfast with Bobby's napkin ring beside her, just because it reminded her of him. Posie, too, missed her son a great deal. Lyd commented to Julia that she felt "very sorry for poor Posie" but that the experience would "be the making of Bobby."[22] Lydia was sure he would love boarding school—and for the most part, he did. It seemed, however, that nearly every year he was at the Fay School he became ill and had to spend part of the term at home to recover. Posie suffered each time she had to let him go, and Bobby did not make it easy for her. At dinner the day before he left for school in January 1906 after a pleasurable holiday, Posie reported that "he suddenly buried his face in his napkin and cried to break his heart because he had to leave us," but when morning arrived, "he went off cheerfully."[23] He also left in great spirits the next fall, but after being at school for just a few days, he wrote her, "Come and take me away from this place or I shall kill myself tomorrow!" Posie was so upset that she cabled Waldo Fay and then her son Arthur, by now a student at Harvard, asking him to go over to the school, but no sooner had she sent her urgent messages than Bobby decided that everything was fine. Bobby was "such a tempestuous character," Julia wrote Jane. Posie had been "really alarmed." [24] Apparently he loved both school and home, and wished to be at both simultaneously.

In the fall of 1907 Posie had good cause to hold Bobby back from school, for he was convalescing from a long bout of whooping cough. To help in his recovery, she took him and a private tutor to Westport. Her intention was to allow her son to rebuild his strength until after the Christmas break. But when the time came to plan for his return to the Fay School, Posie faced yet another problem. That November reckless business speculation had resulted in a national economic panic. Some New York banks had to close in order to prevent a run by depositors wanting to withdraw money, and Wall Street went into a slump. During the downturn Arthur lost so much money that rumors circulated in Westport that the sheriff was about to seize Skene Wood. Within a short time things returned to normal, but the strain on Arthur was palpable. Out of sympathy for their hard luck, Waldo Fay offered the Sherwoods a break. Bobby could return after Christmas as planned, and though his time away from school would require another year of attendance, Posie and Arthur would be asked to pay for only half a year. Posie still hesitated to send her son back. She felt that he was not only gaining in strength but also learning sufficiently with her. "He is just now steeped up to his eyes in Scots novels," she told Julia, "and very much interested in theatrical matters." [25] Nevertheless, in January he did indeed return to the Fay School.

On the whole, Bobby enjoyed the institution, whose headmaster showed the boys warmth and consideration. He enjoyed the walks that Waldo Fay took them on in the woods, often followed in the winter with hot cocoa, cookies, and apples. Bobby liked the available sports and games, which included football, skating on the neighboring reservoir, and tobogganing down the hills. On the whole, he did well at the Fay School, especially in his writing assignments, and sent home many samples of his poetry and long letters about his adventures in the nearby countryside. His aunts Lydia and Jane and his grandmother Julia all wrote to him in the hope of receiving one of his entertaining yarns. When Arthur's brother Sam died in 1905, Bobby's letter with "the mourning bow at the top," astonished Julia, who thought it "remarkable" for so young a child to write so sensitively about his uncle's death.[26] She also found a poem he sent her "too absurd" for words and declared herself just "wild" to hear more of his adventures.[27]

Writing, drawing, and performing were important parts of young Bobby's life all through his school years. Perhaps because he was so big and "funny

looking," as Lydia put it—and so painfully aware of it—he presented himself
as an entertaining clown. "I wish I had the look of Phil . . . & the voice of
Caruso & the taste of Mamma," he told Posie when he was just nine years of
age.[28] Figuring that he would never appear "normal," he often dressed in a
manner he considered unique, even showy, when going into town or visiting
his parents' friends. On one occasion he donned a clean white shirt and one
of Philip's light blue jackets with a scarf pin, a pair of riding breeches, and
shiny tan shoes. Then he parted his hair perfectly and put hair cream on it to
make it glossy and straight. Posie was proud of his "most stylish" appearance
as he "sallied forth on horseback for the village" to deliver some messages
for her. She described Bobby himself as being "very much amused" and not
taking himself seriously at all.[29] His ostentatious behavior became a way for
him to deal with the staring eyes that found his tall, skinny body comical. By
making himself other than ordinary, he tried to beat people to the punch.
How else could he draw attention away from such features as his feet, which
grew so quickly that Posie had to resort to cutting the ends of his sneakers
to give his toes more room so that the family would not go broke constantly
purchasing new shoes.

In addition to his height, thin frame, long face, and big nose, Bobby was
given to oversized movement. He was always on the run, making faces to
express his emotions, and appearing quite awkward. The theater in particular seemed to offer him an outlet, and the works he created illustrated his
natural instinct for imitating the sentimental melodramas and outrageously
flamboyant music hall and vaudeville styles of the day. At the Fay School he
was constantly involved in plays and musical events. When he was twelve,
he wrote Posie that he was rehearsing in a play, his part being that of "a
perfect fool." Could his mother, as the person who always helped make his
performances and his writing better, come to the school and assist him with
"little things in the play which I need coaching on"?[30] Like all "amateurs,"
Posie claimed, he went through "the usual period of depression . . . as the
time of the performance draws near."[31] That New Year's Eve she helped
him and Rosamund prepare their production, *How the King Was Saved: A
Rotten Play*, in which they acted all the parts except the "Witch," who was
not identified in the hand-drawn program. On another occasion Bobby and
two schoolmates prepared to perform a play about his famous namesake, the
original Robert Emmet. Not wishing to turn him into a comic figure (his
Irish accent was not very good), Bobby gave the role to his friend Archer.
Posie promised to send him a small picture of the family hero, and Bobby
was so anxious to receive it that he requested it twice, saying that he would
rather have that likeness than all the other treats Posie was putting together

to mail. At the same time, inspired by a comment that his teacher Mr. Boyer had made about Posie's name appearing in an international encyclopedia of artists, he requested a copy of the book, telling her how very proud he was to have a mother who had been so acknowledged.

In all the many times he appealed to her for help, Posie never turned her son down if she could help it. In fact, it was she more than any other person who enabled him to develop his creativity. In early November 1907, when he was home ill, she encouraged him to give "an exclusive entertainment" which included several neighbors. A few of them he organized into "The Royal Band of the Kahedive of Egypt" with an appropriately costumed "Mrs. James Still" playing the banjo to his drumming. (Mrs. Still was the Sherwoods' cook and Bobby's favorite actress and musician.) Following this act came "The Great Wizard Fortune Teller and Juggler," a magician, and finally a play involving a tramp, "an automobile crank," and a policeman.[32] Posie later reported to her mother that she "could not have believed that he could do what he did. He was really wonderful."[33] The children were kept busy by following up this evening with plans for the Christmas holiday entertainment. Bobby told Posie that he and Rosamund would be "in *Repertoire*," reviving plays they had staged previously as well as a new play he was writing, titled *The Curse of Bacchus,* in which eight-year-old Rosamund would play the barmaid.[34]

Summers in Westport offered time for the boy's most active theatrical development and outdoor pleasure. Each year Bobby mounted home entertainment, participated in local fairs, and played a key role in the town's annual musical, a vaudeville-style concert which many of the vacationing families developed into a sort of friendly competition. Gretchen Finletter, the daughter of the famed pianist and conductor Walter Damrosch, described such an event in her memoir *From the Top of the Stairs.* Her story can be placed in 1909, when Bobby was thirteen years old and dominated the Sherwood family contribution to the yearly festivities, with Posie acting as his artistic director. Gretchen, a youngster herself, heard that Bobby's skit was going to be more exciting than her family's and decided that she wanted to be part of it because, as she put it, "People would say, 'Hot Stuff, oh boy!'" after seeing it.[35]

She described how Bobby came up with his ideas by going off on his own to brood and dream, never writing a scene down or explaining to the actors what he had in mind. "If he saw a drama perfect and whole in his head," she wrote, "it was unbelievable to him that a few muttered words through his nose in the way of plot, dialogue, and direction would not immediately create a snappy and sparkling scene." It seemed to her that if people could not read Bobby's mind, he would become "indignant, then furious . . . give up in despair and look elsewhere for actors who weren't so dumb."[36] Posie, however, often sensed what her son was unable to express and gave him a helping hand. She created scenery as she thought he had envisioned it, cut out masks, designed costumes, and experimented with lighting effects. Rarely did she prohibit him from expressing his vision, except when he tried to cut down one of her favorite trees. "You can't have that one!" she shouted, but only after some arguing did she get her way.[37]

"Pop Concert," as the evening was called, was attended by friends, parents, guests staying at the local inn, and boys from Camp Dudley, a local summer camp. It was such a popular event that neighborhood businesses took the opportunity to advertise, placing photos and text on the curtain. On the night Gretchen Finletter describes, Bobby was at his finest, creating his own version of a "coon song," a minstrel number using dreadful racial stereotypes that were at the time popular with both black and white performers.[38] After a musical introduction and an improvised musical accompaniment, a "vamp," which was played twice, the curtain rose on a drop painted with a street scene. A young white youth entered in blackface makeup, carrying a bag. He was followed by Mrs. Still (also in blackface) with her banjo. The two represented a married couple, the wife sadly bidding the husband farewell as he left on a journey. "During the vamp," wrote Finletter, "they discussed this [his leaving] with a series of remarkably sophisticated jokes on marriage which were greeted uproariously by the younger members of the audience."[39] The jokes were of course written by Bobby, and the insinuations behind them were most likely way over the heads of the campers (and perhaps even Bobby himself). As the vamp grew louder, there were a few drum rolls, followed by a voice calling from off stage, "Porter, porter!"[40] As Mrs. Still began to strum her banjo softly, Bobby made his grand entrance in his usual musical attire (Phil's long white trousers, a checked jacket, a striped tie, a stiff straw hat, and a cane), and the audience broke into waves of applause in anticipation of his performance.

Like a true thespian, Bobby paid this enthusiastic reception no mind. Instead, he acted his role to perfection, turning to the porter and asking him why he was so slow. In what today would be considered racist dialogue to go along with the blackface, Bobby told the porter to "shuffle along," while Mrs. Still cried out, "Where yo goin', Massa?" Bobby then turned toward the audience, leaned dapperly on his cane, and with a "tortured" look on his face sang Irving Berlin's "When the Midnight Choo-Choo Leaves for Alabam."[41] As his singing grew more energetic, so did Mrs. Still's playing, until Bobby was pacing up and down, belting with great force at the audience. But the best was yet to come. At the conclusion of the chorus, as he sang out, "All a-board for Al-a-bam," the street-scene drop curtain rose, revealing a most realistic train he and Posie had built from the trees Bobby had so happily cut down.

Bobby and Posie did not stop there, however. While the colorfully costumed chorus sang, the stage lights blacked out, allowing the train's windows to light up from within. Although the lighting was produced by flashlights held in the singers' hands, the effect was extremely convincing. At this point, the train began to move across the stage. As it neared stage right, Bobby and the porter carrying his bag jumped on, Bobby, holding his hat at a rakish angle, singing at the top of his lungs. After the next-to-last "All a-board," a musician blew a real train whistle, the last line was sung, and the audience once again broke into wild applause. "Those harsh critics from Camp Dudley" whom Finletter had earlier described with disdain gave the number their greatest tribute: "They pounded their feet."[42] Finletter was sorry not to have been there the summer Bobby staged *Aida*. Unfortunately, no descriptions of that or any other Pop Concerts exist to tell us what other great theatrical performances this young prodigy produced. What is clear, however, is that from his youth, Robert Sherwood had a love for Irving Berlin. He later socialized and even collaborated with the composer, never losing his initial awe of Berlin's work.

Late that same summer that Finletter recalled, Posie related to Lydia an amusing incident in which her son saved the day. In this case he ensured that the annual fair in Westport took place in spite of the fact that nobody had taken the time to organize it. With his unlimited energy and creative spirit, Bobby took the task in hand until he had "the whole village by the ears and everyone a gog." In fact, he "dominated" his mother's time and attention to such a degree that she felt as if she had "worked like a galley slave for two days" for him. As usual, Bobby dressed himself in a flamboyant style, then mounted the family's mare and, "performing the Paul Revere act," rode from house to house asking for help in organizing the event. Posie tried to advise him about how best to approach his neighbors, but he responded, "Don't worry, I can captivate the ladies all right." And so he did, creating a fair as well as a vaudeville show in which he, Mrs. Still, Cynthia, and his mandolin-playing neighbor Earl Braman put on "a most frightful assortment of vulgar songs and dances."[43] Posie sent out a hurried call to her husband advising him to postpone a planned meeting and return home for an event she knew he would hate to miss. Bobby organized several of these fairs, donating any money earned (usually between one hundred and two hundred dollars) to the *Life* magazine Summer Camp Fund for poor children.

All through his youth, Bobby thought—and lived—theatrically, providing endless entertainment for his family and community. Even refusing to attend a wedding reception became an opportunity to be creative. When Posie tried to convince her then eleven-year-old that he would have a "fine lunch" at the affair, he simply responded, "Fancy eating a lunch in one's best clothes."[44] Then he danced around the house singing his own lyrics to George M. Cohan's "Give My Regards to Broadway":

> Give my regards to Reddy
> Remember me to old Hyde Hall
> Tell Anne and all her pretty Bridesmaids
> That I can't Join them all
> Whisper of how I'm Yearning
> To sail along Otsego Lake
> Give my regards to old Hyde Hall
> And bring me back some wedding cake.[45]

What was a mother to do?

In September 1909 Bobby was enrolled in Milton Academy in Milton, Massachusetts.[46] Founded in 1798, Milton has long been one of the most esteemed private academies in the country and one of the first coeducational day (and then boarding) schools with preparation for college as its primary goal. After the institution's centennial in 1898, in response to pressure from concerned parents, the administration divided the academy into a separate boys' school and girls' school, which was the arrangement when Bobby attended. (Today it is once again a single, coeducational establishment.) Sending Bobby to Milton, though deemed essential, was difficult for the Sherwoods, for that same year Arthur suffered a heart attack, which required a hospital stay followed by bed rest, and which resulted in bouts of nervousness and depression. Posie, under great emotional stress, needed Bobby to behave himself. But though his housemaster Albert Weeks Hunt, a friend and former tutor at Westport, was someone he liked enormously, the boy did not fare as well at Milton as he had at the Fay School. As he reached adolescence, he was far more interested in the arts and sports than in his academic subjects, and he often misbehaved and underachieved; most of his grades hovered between C's and D's. Posie and Arthur both recognized the great intelligence and creativity that resided in this special child, but they also became increasingly frustrated by his attitude. Bobby barely tolerated the four-hour stretch each morning when he had to attend classes, while he relished the two hours after lunch devoted to sports. Of course, he also thrived on any extracurricular activity that involved writing or the arts.

Milton had a practice of giving its students "marks" for bad behavior and then issuing what headmaster Frank Edward Lane deemed appropriate punishment. Bobby excelled at gaining marks.[47] At Milton, once a student accumulated over five marks in half a week, he had to report to a classroom for detention and sit quietly for ten minutes a mark. If he received more than nine marks, he had to report to the track on Saturday afternoon to walk one quarter-mile lap for each mark. Bobby was usually the lone student to be seen walking that track. Hunt finally came up with the solution for getting Bobby to behave, even though it took two years to prove successful (and was far outside the school's accepted policy on discipline). Hunt asked a few of the older boys to take the recalcitrant student in hand. They did so with threats and then whacks on his behind. According to his biographer John Mason Brown, Robert Sherwood recalled the beatings without rancor. In fact, he claimed to have deserved them as much as he had his parents' "share with hairbrush and shingle."[48] It was during this period that Bobby, in an effort to destroy the reports of his bad behavior, accidentally set fire to a classroom, causing just enough damage to close the room for half a day.

In spite of his many "marks" and punishments at Milton, with Posie's encouragement, Bobby tried to adhere to the rules. After two years she reported to Lydia, with some exaggeration, that he was doing "very well, getting no marks, doing splendidly in his studies."[49] In spite of his actually less than stellar academic performance, he was wildly popular with the other students, having played hockey, tennis, baseball, and football until an injury forced him to stop. He was president of the Glee Club and the New Civics Literature Club and was on the advisory committee of the Athletic Association. In 1913 Bobby was elected one of four monitors by the first and second classes, a great honor at the school, and served as writer and then managing editor of the *Milton Orange and Blue*, the student publication, until the school's administration required him to resign because of bad grades. He also continued his theatricals, incorporating his reputation for being a leader in that field into a poem titled "Prologue" for the *Milton Orange and Blue*:

> The stage is set, the play's begun;
> The curtain rises on Act One;
> The actors come in bright array,
> All have their little parts to play:
> The athlete with o'erbearing looks;
> The scholar deep in study books.
> Each, as the call-boy's cry he heeds,
> Does his short turn, and then recedes.
>
> There'll come a day when you'll be there
> Bathed in the foot-lights' blinding glare,

Then do not falter, don't delay
Prove that you're ready, come what may.
Show them that you're a man, and own
Power to win, though placed alone
That, when this schooltime drama stops,
And when the final curtain drops,
Those of your audience may tell:
"He played the man, and played it well." [50]

Most notable of all his endeavors at Milton was Bobby's election as vale-dictorian of the class of 1914, the irony being that because of poor grades he never officially graduated. Instead, he received a certificate indicating that he had completed his time and was simply "clear" for moving on. [51] His speech, the usual thanks and references to future accomplishments, was short and well received .

In spite of his bad behavior and poor grades, Bobby loved Milton Academy, and as an adult kept in touch with the institution. In fact, contrary to what anyone at the time would have expected, he returned to the school in 1940 and 1954 as an honored guest speaker, and the administrators proudly claimed him as one of their own. In his teens, as he struggled with his loathing for academics and his father and siblings wondered how such a willful child could ever amount to anything, he found support in Albert Weeks Hunt, Frank Edward Lane, and Posie. Later in life he was grateful for what the institution had given him, writing, "I don't believe there are many boys at any school who received so much in the way of tolerance, understanding, and superhuman forgiveness as I did at Milton." [52] In the end, Arthur and Posie pressured Bobby into an intensive program of tutoring until a path to Harvard University opened for him and he could follow in the Sherwood men's footsteps.

3

From Soldier to Pacifist

THE MONTH after war broke out in Europe in 1914, Robert Sherwood entered Harvard University as a freshman. His father, Arthur, had graduated from Harvard in 1877, his brother Arthur in 1910, and Philip, now a senior, was scheduled to complete his degree in 1915. Sherwood's experience at Harvard duplicated those at the Fay School and at Milton Academy. He excelled in the arts and creative writing while turning his back on academics. Still, his two and a half years at the university exposed him to the wider world, especially as the war in Europe moved closer to home. In 1917, when the United States entered the conflict, the still immature Bobby found himself drawn to the romance of military service. As a soldier in the Canadian army, he would come face to face with the reality of war, and its sobering effect would change his life forever.

When Bobby left home for college, his mother worried that he might find the attractions of wealth that he would be exposed to in Cambridge and Boston so appealing that he would not be able to "practice the most rigid economy" required by his family's financial problems.[1] Before he entered Harvard, everything he needed had been provided for him, and Posie was naturally concerned that this freewheeling child might easily become distracted, even overwhelmed, by his independence. Bobby, however, immediately proved her wrong. Because of an initial delay in receiving Posie's first check, he spent several days in the cheapest hotel he could find, Mooneys Pleasure Palace, eating hardly any food except for an occasional cup of coffee and a sandwich. Having been told that he must conserve money, he hesitated to ask for any. Finally, exhausted, hungry, and somewhat depressed, he cabled home. Posie was appalled. "Such an ordeal," she told Lydia. "The last thing I wanted to do was to starve the poor thin overgrown tired child! . . . He is so uncomplaining."[2] Once settled into his comfortable dormitory room in the then new James Smith Hall, he evaluated the Harvard scene, and as his parents feared, he immediately worked his way into sports, literature, writing, and the arts, while giving his courses a casual shrug.

In today's terms, one might say that for Bobby Sherwood, Harvard University was a party school. His outgoing personality won him immediate popularity with his classmates, as did his skill at sports and his eagerness to join organizations such as the Signet Society, the Stylus Club, Delta Kappa Epsilon (D.K.E.), the Hasty Pudding Club, and the *Lampoon*, all of which demanded a great deal of time. His Harvard records show that at the midpoint of his first year, after he received D's in Greek, Latin, history, geography, and algebra, the college's administrative board considered placing him on probation but decided to hold off because he had begun the term on a good footing. Midway through the second term, however, Bobby was placed on probation because of his continued poor grades (2 D's and 3 E's, the latter the equivalent of today's F) and a request from his German instructor that he be removed from the course because of his slipshod performance and innumerable absences.

His son's failures prompted Arthur to begin writing to Henry A. Yeomans and other deans, a correspondence that lasted until 1917, when Bobby left the school. Arthur, and to a much lesser extent Posie, were used to intervening with deans on behalf of their sons, as Arthur Jr. and Philip had also performed poorly during their first two years there. To Arthur Sr., seeing his sons graduate from Harvard was of utmost importance, and he was determined that nothing, not even failing grades, would undermine his goal. His initial approach in Bobby's case was to issue a plea for leniency on the grounds of his son's various physical ailments—including colds, sore throats, viral infections, and "extreme growth . . . [which] retarded his power of concentration and ability to work."[3] Yeomans was most sympathetic, offering Bobby a friendly ear, recommending tutoring with members of Phi Beta Kappa, and emphasizing that only "perfect attendance . . . and the most faithful attention to business" would get him out of his mess.[4] Posie added her voice as well. She had "no excuses to offer" for her son's unsatisfactory start to his advanced education, except that he was only eighteen "and fresh from the restraint of boarding school" and so a bit wild.[5] Despite their pleas, in June the administrative board voted to "sever" Harvard's "connection" with Bobby unless he attended summer school and received passing grades in those subjects in which he had not performed well.[6] This he did. Arthur was profuse in his thanks to the dean, assuring him that although Bobby had been "careless and lazy and did a lot of idiotic things," he had finally "come to his senses."[7] By October, Bobby had been readmitted to his class (now sophomores), but with severe warnings about possible expulsion if he did not cultivate a more studious nature.

While his little sister Rosamund excelled at her school in Catonsville, Bobby continued his downward slide. During his second year at Harvard he frequently cut classes, refused to hand in assignments, and continued to miss exams. If he wished to avoid a course entirely, such as German or government, he simply went on strike against it until the instructor requested that he withdraw. By the end of the year he had improved somewhat, receiving only one D (in English) and the rest all C's. His exclusion from German class, however, remained at the request of his instructor, F. S. Cowley, who complained that Bobby's delinquency was "particularly flagrant."[8] At one point he met his student walking through Harvard Yard on his way to a lecture after having skipped Cowley's exam that very morning. Again, Bobby and Arthur received letters threatening expulsion (or a request for Bobby's voluntary withdrawal), and once again Arthur jumped into action. His son had a cold which had badly affected his head, and his growth had also "seriously impaired his physical condition."[9] The plea to save his son's academic career was repeated the following spring. "Bob is suffering from a malady which always accompanies rapid growth and takes the form of a certain kind of indolence both physical and mental," he wrote Dean B. S. Hurlbut. "I know what it is because I suffered from it myself when a young man and found hard concentrated work very difficult."[10] Hurlbut countered that if Bobby suffered so, why was the poor child not under a physician's care. Indeed, many of his absences were *not* due to illness. Hence, in May, Bobby found himself suspended from Harvard until a physician could vouch for his good health.

As a means of strengthening his physical condition, Arthur and Posie approved of Bobby's participation in two summer Civilian Military Training Camps sessions in Plattsburg, New York. Established by General Leonard Wood, chief of staff of the U.S. Army, the program was an expression of Wood's belief that every citizen ought to be prepared to defend the nation if necessary, and that such training also benefited the individual. To the administrators at Harvard, such a program could only help Bobby in adopting a constructive work ethic toward his college studies. Indeed, the rigid course of study and physical exercise suited him surprisingly well. Bobby never missed a drill or received a demerit, and he even added some bulk, gaining almost ten pounds. In fact, he was so well regarded that during the second session he was promoted to the rank of corporal and later was given the unofficial title and duties of a sergeant, although for some reason the official designation was never authorized.

Harvard readmitted Bobby for the fall 1916 term, but his academic performance did not improve very much. Even though he was passing five courses, his sixth, German, remained a problem. By February he was once again on probation, having done poorly on his oral examinations. Although Posie and Arthur continued to plead his supposedly weak health, in fact Bobby was far from bedridden. While his days were spent avoiding classes and claiming fatigue and illness, his nights were filled with attending movies, plays, and musicals, drinking and carousing with friends in local pubs, or writing stories and drawing cartoons. Bobby's problem was not his health but the simple fact that he was more interested in extracurricular activities than in doing the usual college coursework. As he later recalled, he spent so much time working for the *Lampoon* and writing shows for the Hasty Pudding Club that he "overlooked the dreary duties involved in getting an education."[11] Indeed, he was so popular with his fellow students that they elected him president of the *Lampoon* on January 19, 1917, a point of great pride for his father.

The year 1917 in general did not start out propitiously for the Sherwood clan. Arthur's health was a primary concern. Early in the year, at sixty-one, he suffered a second, more severe heart attack than in 1909, which was followed by a debilitating bout of pneumonia. To his and Posie's great dismay, he had to retire from the world of business. A few months later his firm, Tower and Sherwood, which had provided well for the family for over thirty years, shut its doors. During this period Arthur fell into a deep depression. For more than a month he refused to get out of bed unless it was absolutely necessary; he slept long hours and would not even look at his favorite books or newspapers. Instead, as Posie wrote to her sister-in-law Nelly, he was "like a child living in the land of counterpane. He shrinks from knowledge of anything going on outside of the four walls of his room."[12]

Arthur's incapacity put all responsibility on Posie's shoulders. Not only did she have to attend to his every need, but also, at the age of sixty-three, she had to deal single-handedly with the family's financial crisis. When Tower and Sherwood went out of business, the firm had a deficit amounting to almost $400,000. Posie felt that it was her duty to pay off half of it. She soon decided that in order to do so, she would have to sell both of the family homes—in Westport and in New York City—and support the family by taking on as many portrait commissions as she could. Arthur was "bitterly offended" by her making such a huge unilateral decision and hardly spoke to her for some time. But, knowing her husband well, Posie took his behavior in stride, believing that he would "come around gradually."[13] Meanwhile, absorbing all the family's responsibilities wore her down to the point of emotional exhaustion, finally requiring a summer away from one and all in Maine.

These difficulties at home seemed to wash right over Bobby, who found plenty of time and energy to work on the *Lampoon* and write two plays for the Hasty Pudding Club. In order to avoid attracting the attention of the administrative board, he had kept his association with *A White Elephant*, produced in 1916, anonymous, though the planned 1917 production of *Barnum Was Right* listed him as both a writer and a performer. The open admission of his participation was a mistake, as the board took the opportunity to penalize him for his poor grades by forbidding him to continue with the Hasty Pudding Club at all. Posie immediately appealed to Dean Yeomans on her son's behalf. Would the board consider allowing his name to appear as the author and perhaps reconsider his participation in the production if his schoolwork immediately improved? "He will always be careless and odd," she noted, "but he has lots of ability which will probably someday be turned to journalism or playwriting perhaps." [14] The board members would not budge, except to assure Posie that out of respect for Arthur and their concern over his weakened health, they would not insist that Bobby also abandon the *Lampoon*.

In March, Bobby consistently missed classes—six during the week of March 17 alone. His brother Arthur, a former classmate of college administrator C. C. Little, tried a last-ditch effort to help out. Bobby, he told Little, was "the most one-idead character" he had ever known. The Hasty Pudding Club and the *Lampoon* constituted the "one idea" and "college work . . . a bad second." With Arthur Sr. ill and Posie extremely upset about her youngest son's "defection," Arthur Jr. had decided to take his brother in hand "to preclude any further monkey business." [15] He also met directly with Little, assuring him that he had scared Bobby enough to guarantee his presence in classes. But Arthur had negotiated conditions that Bobby could not possibly meet. The board allowed him to remain at Harvard, but only with the promise of perfect attendance and no outside activities, including the *Lampoon*. Expulsion from the Hasty Pudding Club became a moot issue when the premiere of *Barnum Was Right* was canceled in light of the threat of war looming over the nation.

Bobby had been following events in Europe ever since the assassination on June 28, 1914, of Archduke Franz Ferdinand of Austria-Hungary and his wife, Sophie, had sparked the conflict. The slaying was not the only cause for the conflagration that followed, but it was the most dramatic. For years, numerous undercurrents had been roiling among the European nations. Nationalists in eastern Europe, including Slavs, Croats, and Bosnians, had been pushing for autonomy and eventual independence, but the royalty of the Austro-Hungarian Empire would hear none of their arguments, especially after secret societies such as the Black Hand began to take guerrilla-type actions against the crown. Nationalism could also breed hatred of one group toward another, the most frequent scapegoats at the time being Jews and Gypsies, who suffered no end of segregationist and exclusionary laws, hate crimes, and government-sponsored terrorism. Added to this were day-to-day tensions such as overcrowding, periodic droughts and famines, and economic cycles of relative prosperity followed by depression. Millions of people had already left Europe to avoid these circumstances; many ended up in the burgeoning cities of the United States, including Bobby's hometown, New York. At the same time, growing international conflicts among the European powers took the form of border disputes, competition over trade and colonial development, and an arms race which fostered the growth of a war mentality.

For the eighteen-year-old Bobby Sherwood, the pressing issue of 1914 was a romantic one. His was a youth spent in the remembered glow of patriotic, nationalistic ancestors, heroes like Robert Emmet, Thomas Addis Emmet, and others who had fought for U.S. and Irish independence and served in the American Civil War. Two wars had already occurred during his brief lifetime, and he knew his family's views on each. In 1898, when he was turning two, the three-month Spanish-American War broke out, the result of which was the U.S. colonization of Puerto Rico, the Philippines, and Guam and the protectorate status of Cuba. To many in the United States who favored it, the war was about two issues: Spain's human rights violations against the Cuban people and the desire of the United States to take its place among the world powers in trade and expansion. For other Americans, however, the war was a defamation of the principles put forth in the Declaration of Independence and the Constitution, both of which spoke of the right of people to decide their own form of government. Before the actual fighting began, the Sherwoods and Emmets were split over the war. Bobby's aunt Lydia, then in Paris busy painting portraits, felt "sick with worry," not believing that the folks back home would let themselves "be duped into an unnecessary humbugging, hypocritical war."[16] Her mother adopted the opposite viewpoint, wanting the U.S. Army to help the Cuban people. With the debacle of the explosion aboard the battleship *Maine* (which most historians believe was caused not by Spain but rather by an internal accident) and President William McKinley's request to Congress for a declaration of war, Lydia changed her mind, though she still hoped that the country would move slowly enough to give Spain a chance to back off and negotiate. Arthur Sr. proved to be the most enthusiastic about the war. He believed it to be a question of national pride and human rights, and he was proud of both McKinley and the American people and felt that Lydia had every reason to be proud of them as well. As for the Spaniards, "We shall sooner or later lick the tar out of them," he assured her. "I would give anything if I could go. Hooray for the United States."[17]

By the time he was a mere eight years old, stories about war had imbued Bobby with a military spirit. He enjoyed listening in on conversations about international conflicts, and even if he did not comprehend the situation correctly or chose the wrong side, he eagerly joined the fray. In the case of the 1904–5 war between Japan and Russia, in which Japan was clearly the aggressor, young Bobby sided with the Japanese. He was delighted when the empire of the Rising Sun trounced the Russians in 1905, not understanding it as an effort to keep the European nations at bay in Asia. The family favorite, President Theodore Roosevelt, played the mediator in the conflict and won a Nobel Peace Prize for his success in bringing an end to hostilities and maintaining the balance of power. In his fervor to participate in this international event, Bobby drew the flags of both Japan and the United States and made up a language that sounded to him like Japanese.[18] He also wrote an illustrated story titled "A Japanese and a Russian," showing a Japanese soldier standing over a kneeling Russian while holding a sword directly over the Russian's head. At the same age he reflected on the Spanish-American War with a similar creation called "How the Fire Started," which included a drawing of the battleship *Maine* with a flag reading "Peace" on the stern.[19]

Bobby's fascination with the First World War (the European conflict, or the Great War, or the War to End All Wars) grew out of this family tradition of paying close attention to global conflicts, discussing them, and finally expressing one's opinion, and oftentimes taking action. In this case he was also influenced by his feelings for England, especially London, where his aunt Jane and uncle Wilfrid de Glehn had their home and art studio. Bobby had had the opportunity to visit England in the summer of 1912, a trip that included a visit to Skibo Castle in Scotland, where Posie's friend Andrew Carnegie hosted them. In addition, his mother and aunts had told him many stories about their years in Paris, when they studied art and painted professionally, and where they still returned from time to time to complete a commission or visit friends. Lydia practically commuted between the United States and the continent. Letters between Posie, Lydia, and Jane were constant reminders that his mother and her sisters were of one heart, no matter how far apart they might reside. Finally, there was the family's commitment to human rights and equality. What Bobby read and heard about the European conflict convinced him that for many people, democracy and freedom were indeed in danger.

During the latter half of 1914 and throughout 1915, Bobby experimented with writing stories and drawing cartoons dealing with the politics of Europe, but he had no reason to feel compelled to participate in the war himself. In fact, that avenue was cut off by President Woodrow Wilson's stance of neutrality. Although between 1914 and 1916 he authorized military interventions in Haiti, the Dominican Republic, and Mexico, Wilson was not eager to lead the nation into this raging European war if peaceful methods were available to resolve it. He was worried that conflicts might break out among the many immigrant groups entering or already residing in the country if neutrality were abandoned, and he wished to protect U.S. trade with all nations willing to engage in it. In addition, public opinion at the time was overwhelmingly in favor of neutrality, and Wilson did not want to anger his political allies. With the heads of large corporations such as Andrew Carnegie, Edwin Ginn, and Henry Ford choosing the path of neutrality and peace, Wilson felt assured that his efforts to keep the country out of the war were sound.

By 1916, however, the situation had changed. Although President Wilson continued to avoid involving the United States in the war, popular opinion was shifting. In May, Congress passed the Army Reorganization Act, which allocated a huge amount of money for upgrading the military in terms of both munitions and personnel. Almost unbeknownst to the public, a section of this bill, known as the Hayden Joker, instituted military conscription by stating that if not enough volunteers signed up in case of a war, the government could draft members of the National Guard to fill the army ranks. In August, Congress passed the Naval Appropriations Act, which allocated more money to build battleships. All over the country, school systems were mandating military exercises for young boys through their physical education classes, creating a furor among those parents who opposed this training.

Meanwhile, the savagery of the war in Europe intensified. Soldiers representing both the Allies and the Central Powers were stalemated in trenches; hundreds of thousands had been killed in battle, and entire towns and villages had been totally destroyed. Austria-Hungary was a weak enemy, soon to fall, but Germany grew stronger and more belligerent by the day. Newspapers trumpeted rumors that German soldiers were cutting off the hands of little Belgian children, a story that was later disproved. But civilian injuries and the rape of local women (by both sides) were common. Throughout the year, public opinion in the United States fluctuated. Some felt that it was urgent for the country to take up what they understood to be the cause of freedom and democracy; others saw no sensible reason to become involved. Bobby Sherwood fell into the former category. With his background, there was almost no question that he would be attracted to war as a possibility for adventure, an attitude handed down through his family line; but he would enter that war believing that he was fighting for a just cause—to protect freedom and democracy in the world, even if the United States itself was not threatened.

Bobby took his 1916 summer preparedness course at the Plattsburg camp very seriously and began to contemplate what his role might be in the ongoing horror in Europe. But once back in Cambridge, he spent more time than ever at the *Lampoon* and continued surreptitiously to work on plays for the Hasty Pudding Club. Several articles in the *Lampoon* addressed the issue of the war. Since they are unsigned, it is impossible to discern which ones Bobby himself wrote, but they all echoed his ideas and shared his sense of humor. One favored universal conscription, especially for pacifists; another excoriated the United States for its cowardly neutrality. Bobby's interest in politics took him, on the night of the November election that year, to a torchlight parade through the streets of Boston in support of the presidential candidacy of Charles Evans Hughes. Woodrow Wilson, however, was re-elected on the slogan "He Kept Us Out of War." This was a grave disappointment for Bobby, who had come to believe that for the United States, war was imminent. Small nations were being terrorized by the large and aggressive Germany, and the United States had to give up its neutrality to help preserve democracy throughout the world.

At around this time Bobby took on a songwriting partner, fellow student Samuel Powers Sears. Together they created their own informal company, Sherry & Powers, which they believed would lead to great fame and fortune. In 1916 Bobby wrote a poem which Sam put to music and the two then sold to a Boston music publisher. The lyrics, which may have been a *Lampoon*-ish comment on President Wilson's move from neutrality to preparedness, illustrate an early cynicism about war that none of Bobby's other writings at the time expressed. Would not getting ready for war lead directly to it?

> In Europe they've taught us the mean-ing of war,
> Bat-tle with-out cease;
> The burst of the shrap-nel, the can-non's roar,
> Teach us the les-son of peace.
> We have seen the fire and pil-lage
> In ev'-ry Bel-gian vil-lage,
> We've heard the call for help a-cross the sea—
> But now that we have seen
> What war may real-ly mean
> Let us pre-pare to keep our na-tion free.
> *Chorus*
> Put your gun on your should-er, be ready for war—
> That's the bat-tle cry of Peace
> For we can't stand back when the foes at-tack
> Striv-ing for our home and coun-try
> We need an arm-y to fight for our flag—
> And a larg-er nav-y too—
> With Peace for-ev-er
> We'll still be able to shout out
> The Bat-tle cry of Free-dom.[20]

The two had such faith in another of their songs, "Yokohama Bay," that they persuaded some friends to donate one hundred dollars to send Bobby to New York City to try to sell it to the great showman Florenz Ziegfeld for his famous *Ziegfeld Follies*. Somehow, Bobby managed to get in to see the producer, who rejected the tune. With only five dollars in his pocket, the aspiring lyricist returned to Cambridge with an "itemized" bill charging, "For getting Flo Ziegfeld in Receptive Mood—$95." [21] Still, Sherry & Powers persisted, signing an agreement to share all profits equally, even after graduation. Sears, who became a Boston lawyer, was later asked if he ever tried to collect his share of Robert Sherwood's lucrative income. "I couldn't collect," he quipped. "Sherwood was under twenty-one when he signed it." [22]

As the European conflict progressed, Bobby spent an increasing amount of time thinking about it and less time on the threats to his career at Harvard. He was excited by the war news and the accompanying rumors. He liked to share these with Posie, who was happy to have his company during her difficult times with Arthur, although she also worried about the fate of her three sons should the United States become involved in Europe's problems. Bobby was especially obsessed with submarines, telling Posie that a friend of his in the Naval Reserves had experienced a German submarine attack upon his destroyer. To Bobby, submarine warfare was a horror. Indeed, it was the key issue for Woodrow Wilson as well. Although submarines had been in existence (albeit in a primitive form) since the U.S. War of Independence, they were not seriously used as weapons until World War I, when the Germans instituted their U-boat campaign. (U-boat was an abbreviation for the German *Unterseeboot,* or "undersea boat.") During the war, the British had anywhere from 74 to 203 operational submarines, the French 75, and Russia and Italy a smaller number, but only the Germans chose to capitalize on their technological advances. During their struggle with the Allies, German submarines sank a total of 5,554 battle and merchant ships.

The United States felt greatly threatened by Germany's use of submarines and expected that nation to honor Uncle Sam's stance of neutrality by making its U-boats surface to warn neutral ships of their presence. The Germans felt that this was just another way for the United States to protect its unfair trade balance with the Allies. Indeed, between 1914 and 1916, U.S. exports to England and France grew by 365 percent, whereas exports to Germany dropped by more than 90 percent. The U.S.-German disagreement on neutral shipping came to a head on May 7, 1915, when a German submarine attacked and sank the British luxury liner *Lusitania,* resulting in the death of 1,198 people, 128 of them from the United States. Wilson angrily charged the Germans with abusing the rules of war, even though the ship was carrying 4.2 million rounds of ammunition and other war materiel. Still, in order to avoid bringing the Americans into the conflict, Germany temporarily halted attacks on passenger ships. For nearly two years, however, the United States continued to protest various U-boat incidents that took its citizens' lives. Then, early in 1917, Germany acted to stop the flow of U.S. supplies to the Allies by declaring unrestricted submarine warfare in its self-designated war zone, then attempted to win Mexico to its side. This finally moved Wilson to take an aggressive step. He asked Congress to declare a state of "armed neutrality" so that he could protect American trade and travelers, which included the arming of commercial ships. When German attacks continued, Wilson asked Congress on April 2 to vote for a declaration of war. Citizens who opposed bringing the United States into the melee filled the balcony of the congressional chambers and lined the streets outside to protest the action. But four days later, on April 6, the resolution passed the Senate 86 to 6 and the House 373 to 50.

Robert Sherwood, who had no tolerance for pacifists, lost little time in planning his participation in the war. His enrollment in the Reserve Officers Training Corps (ROTC) after the Plattsburg summer program had already provided him with six months of training. Once Congress declared war, he immediately thought of enlisting in the U.S. Army. Harvard students were actually encouraged to do so, as the college allowed those with ROTC training to complete their coursework immediately after war was declared. In his usual manner, however, Bobby ignored the authorities, choosing not to bother to appear for the specially arranged finals. Posie and Arthur, who thought he had completed his work, were shocked when he was suspended in July, but with the unofficial assurance that once the war was over, his readmission would be seriously considered. Years later Robert Sherwood expressed chagrin that he never took Harvard up on its offer. As he told a young college student in 1950, "I . . . spent the rest of my life regretting how stupidly and lazily I had wasted those two and a half years at Harvard, and of all the time I had expended subsequently educating myself to make up for my failure to take advantage of the wasted opportunities at college."[23]

In any case, Bobby returned to Plattsburg in the spring of 1917 to sign up for overseas duty, but the army (and then later the navy) rejected him, deeming him, at 6 feet 6½ inches, too tall in proportion to his weight of 167 pounds for military service. Arthur felt particularly bitter about his son's rejection, accusing the U.S. government of "sticking on a few technicalities instead of finding out what kind of fighting stuff a man possesses."[24] Bobby himself was not a young man to accept no for an answer. He therefore turned his eyes to the Canadian Expeditionary Force, which rated him as " 'A' Fit for General Service" on July 3, finding that he had excellent vision and hearing, with only a scar from his childhood appendectomy marring his appearance.[25]

He was immediately assigned to the rank of private in the Second Reinforcing Company of the Fifth Royal Highlanders of Canada, the famous Canadian Black Watch.

Of course, the first question that must have gone through Posie's mind was why, if the U.S. military had rejected her son, would the Canadians accept him. In addition to concerns over his height and weight, Posie feared that his constant illnesses and a chronic knee inflammation sustained while playing football at Milton Academy would endanger him in a combat situation. But Canada, under orders from England to recruit men, was desperate for soldiers, and Bobby was eager to sign up, as were thousands of young Canadians. Entire towns and provinces, especially in the West, saw their young men, many only of high school age, leave for the war in Europe. These were, in large part, men of the land—farmers, lumberjacks, hunters—who were not used to the group discipline demanded by the military. The British, who oversaw Canadian military units, thought of these colonials as troublesome, even unmanageable, but they needed the manpower. Bobby found them to be the friendliest, happiest, and most compatible men he had ever met. Once in Montreal, he felt no remorse about another failing performance at Harvard and quickly put his college years behind him.

Though happy to be in the service, Bobby did experience a few minor problems in basic training. First, F. Maurice Child, the soldier responsible for supplying his uniform (including a loose-fitting tunic, tartan kilt, and a large furry sporran), could not find boots big enough for Bobby's feet, so for months—in fact until he reached France—he had to wear his own size 13D shoes. Second, because of anti-draft protests in Canada, soldiers were restricted to their barracks. Because Bobby, already too thin, complained about the quality and quantity of army food, Child arranged to take him to the tailor each day at lunchtime for special fittings—and then for a more tasty and substantial lunch. Third, within a few weeks of his arrival he was admitted into Montreal General Hospital for "synovitis," or inflammation, of the knee.[26] There, Posie later claimed, a surgeon who looked at his x-rays told Bobby that while he was unfit for the trenches, he could serve the military in some other way. Months later, when he was sent for combat duty, Posie saw it as a double-cross on the part of supposedly responsible officers who were about to "force someone into the trenches by a subterfuge."[27]

Meanwhile, Bobby was most in his element when he obtained the position of drum major for his company. "It was one of the sights of Montreal," Maurice Child later recalled, "to see Bobby swinging a gigantic stick and turn a corner. It was the spirit of Harvard and the Black Watch."[28] People stopped and stared as this young man, who towered a good foot above the pipers and drummers, strutted dramatically through the fashionable parts of town to the main streets and then to the training grounds on the McGill University campus. Bobby's letters at the time were like those of so many Canadian soldiers—optimistic, cheerful, and uncomplaining, except about any delay in pay. His father, meanwhile, derived some pleasure from the fact that all three of his sons were about to prove their manhood. Arthur Jr., who was working in a shipyard in Portland, Oregon, was accepted the following October for the Artillery Officers Training Camp at Camp Zachary Taylor in Kentucky, and Philip held the rank of first lieutenant in the Seventeenth U.S. Cavalry, stationed in Douglas, Arizona. For Posie, however, it was a time of "fearful anxiety." Between dealing with Arthur's precarious health and his anger over the loss of his business and their houses, and her worries over Bobby's enlistment, she felt "knocked . . . up a good deal." [29]

Bobby's regiment sailed from Halifax, Nova Scotia, on October 4 on board the *Carpathia* and arrived in Liverpool, England, almost two weeks later, on the seventeenth. He was now part of the Twentieth Canadian Reserve Battalion of the Royal Highland Company, stationed at the Bramshott army camp. While there, he took the opportunity to visit his aunt Jane in London, about fifty miles to the northeast, where he was just in time to witness a bombing of that city by a hydrogen-filled airship, the *Zeppelin*, another German invention. Since Jane's husband, Wilfrid, was on the front line in France, she was very much alone and was especially happy to have Bobby's company, even for short visits. It also gave Posie great comfort to picture her gentle giant of a son in the safety of her sister's home.

Bramshott was actually not a very pleasant place. Thomas Dinesen, brother of the Danish author Isak Dinesen, was another foreign national in the Canadian Expeditionary Force and knew Robert Sherwood quite well. In his memoir *Merry Hell!* he described Bramshott's sprawling camp situated on the slopes of a large ridge in the English moor country. Its late fall chill and dampness required warm pants rather than kilts, which in any case could "be slung round one's waist in a jiffy." [30] More than twenty battalions and detachments were housed in row upon row of makeshift huts and trained in the parade grounds, muddy trenches, and ditches quickly assembled for their use. There, Private Sherwood learned how to march, to protect himself against gas warfare, and to slouch and duck down in the trenches, which usually measured a mere six feet in depth. He also faced the ignominy of being assigned menial labor, such as overseeing the working of the camp incinerator and whitewashing posts. Bobby felt that he was given these jobs because of his health problems, height, and low weight. His friend Maurice Child wrote Cynthia that he had heard "from a reliable source" that his friend would "never see a trench."[31] In late January 1918, however, Bobby was shipped out with all the others. As he later recalled, when he landed in France on February 23, he was "full of a spirit of high adventure—I was a Crusader."[32] Two days later he was with his new unit, the Seventh Infantry Brigade of the Forty-second Battalion of the Third Division of the Canadian Expeditionary Force. The fact that he had finally reached the battle zone terrified his mother, who had been told that "the tradition of the Black Watch" was "to fight like Highlanders hand to hand in the forefront of the battle & never stop even when they are told to."[33] Phil tried to comfort her by saying that just because Bobby was in France did not necessarily mean that he would see any action. If he did, the family needed to remain "stoical," because Bobby's main reason for enlisting was to be sent to France."[34]

At Étaples, the newly arrived Canadian troops spent several days passing time by playing baseball and cards and socializing with one another. Then orders came for a train ride and march to Avion, which took place over dusty lime-soil roads, causing much coughing and choking. The contents of Bobby's seventy-pound pack, quite heavy for his wire-thin body, consisted of "a thick greatcoat, an equally substantial sweater, a leather buff coat—as solid and stiff as a breast plate; a haversack with our polishing and toilet kit; a steel helmet; a bayonet; a spade with a long wooden handle; gas mask; mess tin; blanket and rubber sheet, and, last, but not least, 120 rounds of ammunition."[35] Along with all of this he carried his rifle slung across one shoulder, a water bottle, and two spare ration bags. When the men finally reached Avion, they found it totally in ruins and with German snipers on the prowl. On his third night there, when Bobby heard the thunderous sound of a German artillery barrage and saw the fireworks that accompanied it, for the first time he doubted his decision to go to war and wondered what would become of him. "As I looked at this awful sight," he later told a group at Canada's Bishop's University in 1950, "my youthful enthusiasm was drained out of me. I was scared stiff. I thought, 'In a few days—or maybe, a few hours, how do I know?—I'll be up in that terror. Let's face it—I'm going to be killed in this war. And that's the end of me.'"[36]

For several weeks Bobby served as part of the working party digging trenches. This was usually done at night, when each man was responsible for enlarging the trench by three or four yards. He also joined in foraging through village ruins for food and performing other types of manual labor. By the time he left Avion as part of the "Big Push" to Vimy Ridge and Arras, he had been appointed acting quartermaster, replacing a man who had been arrested for grand larceny. En route, the transport system broke down, and he and a few others were left behind to watch over the equipment until replacements could be sent. For three rather luxurious days he was billeted in what he described as "an exquisite Louis IX chateau and high living." Much to his delight, during that same time King George V of Great Britain and Sir Douglas Haig arrived to inspect an imperial battalion fresh off the battlefield. As Bobby and his peers, dirty and tired, looked on, one of the staff officers encouraged them to come forward. Naturally, the king spotted the lanky American and asked how tall he was. "I wised him up," Bobby wrote his father. When his majesty asked if he was Canadian and Bobby responded, "No, sir, a Yank," King George was moved to "merriment." Bobby was "enjoying all this to the utmost"—the variety, the excitement. It all appealed to him "immensely." [37]

Bobby's unit was ultimately assigned to defend Vimy Ridge in northern France not far from the Belgian border and right on the famed Western Front. It was a big, broad, barren hill in the midst of flat, devastated fields. By the time the men arrived, the ridge was strewn with "rusty heaps of barbed wire, rotten sand bags and bits of wood and stumps," as Dinesen recalled.[38] The trees had either been destroyed or left as mere trunks with blackened branches, and the ground was pitted with shell holes. Vimy was just another front in a gruesome war, but it was already well known in the annals of Canadian history. There, in April 1917, under British command, the Canadians had defeated the Germans in a series of dramatic battles that cost 78,000 Allied lives. The result, however, was possession of Vimy Ridge, from where they could look out over the fields to detect any movements on the part of the enemy. When Bobby arrived, the Germans were still in their trenches, intent on taking Vimy Ridge back. And he was in the Allied trenches, one speck in the 250 miles of "ditches" (as the Canadians called them), with their accompanying 300 miles of barbed wire entanglements. He was but one infantryman out of 1.48 million Allied forces. Part of the army's work in the Arras area was to complete and maintain the trenches as well as to build additional machine gun emplacements and battery positions behind which ammunition could be stacked. The intricate defense system had to be constantly tended while artillery attacks continued to harass each side.

Life in Arras and on Vimy Ridge was difficult, to say the least. Trench life, in particular, was one of the most wearying experiences of the war. The physical conditions alone were very hard. Thousands of men were packed together for weeks and months at a time in what were basically narrow gullies without permanent tops. Interconnecting branches led to sections where officers might have makeshift quarters, supplies could be kept, and the injured might be cared for. Men in the trenches were exposed to all of nature's wrath—rain, snow, cold, fog, and intense sun. Day and night they lived outdoors, the only relief being provided by cave-like dugouts where they took breaks to sleep, eat, play poker, and tell stories of their trysts with Frenchwomen while on leave in Paris. At its best, trench life was excruciatingly boring as soldiers waited for their next foray into enemy territory or the enemy's into theirs. At worst, it was wet, muddy, and constantly damp. Death could come quickly from illness, a sniper's good shot, a poison gas shelling, or an attack, and corpses could not always be removed immediately.

In his letters home, Bobby presented the war as one great adventure. Like many men, he did not want to alarm his loved ones. But he was also aware that the censors read every piece of mail that went in either direction, so discretion was the key to receiving and sending news. Because of the great discrepancy between his letters and his actual experiences, it is not always easy to figure out exactly what war was like for him. For example, trench life, which has been painted by historians and veterans alike as hell on earth, for Bobby (at least publicly) was "tough," but "somehow or other one doesn't mind" it. All the men he was serving with were optimistic and took their situation as "merely a matter of course," as people do in the most difficult situations. They sat around and roared with laughter at one another's comments; indeed, the Canadians, as far as Bobby was concerned, were "certainly the most cheerful and utterly happy-go-lucky crowd" that he could ever imagine, with humor to spare even after three years of "dodging whizz-bangs and minnies." He claimed to be having "the time of my young life" and said that he would not think twice about doing it again.[39]

In truth, trench life was not grand for Robert Sherwood. One of its worst aspects was rat infestation. Black rats were bothersome, particularly at night, when they crept over sleeping soldiers to reach their often meager and spoiled food supplies. But brown rats were the most frightening, as they liked to gnaw on the corpses which had not been removed; and because they had a constant source of nourishment, they grew to be quite large. There was no avoiding them. The rats multiplied quickly in the hospitable environment of the trenches and reciprocated for their good fortune by passing disease and food contamination to their hosts. Bobby, who had developed an aversion to mice and rats when he was growing up, hated these pests. At times he used his rifle to shoot them; at other times he slept on the muddy fire step in the trench with nothing but his rubber sheet to lie on in order to avoid them. This left him directly in the line of sniper fire. He still considered this preferable to being among the rats. The vermin, however, were not confined to the trenches. Much to his horror, one day under heavy German fire Bobby and others took shelter in a ruined house, where every time a shell struck, the rats were shaken off the rafters and fell on top of them, and where a stove in the cellar revealed hordes of the rodents. As he wrote to his aunt Lydia: "No words can express my loathing and disgust for them . . . the most forward and nerviest rats you ever saw—absolutely afraid of nothing. Besides running over us and frightening us out of our skins, they ate the rations, our candles, chewed the shoes on our feet and our leather equipment." [40] After he returned home, he had nightmares about them and could not bring himself to look at a mouse or rat, even if it was enclosed in a cage in a pet store window.

Bobby's second trench annoyance was lice, another constant among soldiers. Filthy, wet clothing welcomed these pests, where they lodged in seams and caused constant itching. Many men also had head lice, which drove them to shave their heads, for no matter how often they washed and deloused their clothing and hair with creosote and carbolic soap, as Bobby did, they could not remove the louse eggs, which quickly hatched, starting the cycle all over again. Other trench annoyances included frogs, horned beetles, and slugs, which proliferated in the hospitable muddy environment.

Bobby was among a group who reported to Vimy Ridge on April 7, 1918, to replace those who had fallen in a bout of intense fighting in March. His commander, General Arthur Currie, was a dynamic Canadian leader—a working-class man who proved to the elite British officers that a Canadian was capable of making the most difficult decisions, coming up with the most insightful military strategies, and inspiring his men. Many a time he argued with the British commanders for his right to head the Canadian divisions; in 1918 he won that right and, in the end, the respect of the British. Currie's Canadian troops, including Bobby's division, had relieved a British one and taken an additional 3,000 yards in the Acheville-Arleux sector of the battle zone just before Bobby's arrival. By mid-April they held more than 29,000 yards of the front. For sixty-three days the men remained in the trenches, an interminable stay of tense, boring, and uncomfortable confinement. Perhaps that is why, on the evening of May 1, Thomas Dinesen, Bobby, and some friends had a bit of an adventure "of a more peaceful nature," as Dinesen described it. After some foraging, each drank an entire bottle of champagne. No sooner had they finished the last gulp than they were called to march all night with their full packs. One of Bobby's closest friends, a man named Chris, had sprained his ankle, so tipsy Bobby and Thomas Dinesen took turns carrying his rifle and pack. [41]

Luckily the Canadians were relieved the next day by British replacements, and for almost two months the men remained near the village of Caucort "out on rest," taking long hikes, drilling eight hours a day, and generally entertaining themselves. [42] As Robert Sherwood told a reporter soon after his return home, "Believe me, close order drill is the greatest tonic in the world for men just out of the trenches; after a few days of that the men just pray to go back to the front line again where they can rest."[43] To his great delight, Bobby also caught sight of some U.S. soldiers, the first he had seen in the war. He was so ecstatic that he ran out into the street, jumped onto the running board of their truck, and began shaking hands.

On July 1, the Canadian national holiday of Dominion Day, the men released some pent-up tension by enjoying sports, games, entertainment, and refreshments provided by the YMCA War Volunteers. Nearly fifty thousand Canadian soldiers of every rank gathered at Tinques, a village fourteen miles west of Arras. The weather was perfect, sunny and mild with none of the dreaded mist that often gathered in the valley, but as a precaution, airplanes circled overhead to defend them from possible German attack. Bobby's assignment was to organize and stage-manage his unit's contribution—a float which he fixed up to resemble a ship supposedly returning in 1950 from this seemingly endless war, its still active soldiers then aged and white-haired. The carpenters of the battalion secured a French farm wagon, on which they built an authentic-looking smokestack that belched out real smoke, thanks to some grenades of the type used to create a smokescreen during an advance. The flag- and banner-festooned "ship" was pulled by six transport horses and held various "trophies," including a German prisoner of war in chains, a goat which some French locals claimed had belonged to the Kaiser himself, and several soldiers in full senior citizen makeup.[44] For Bobby, it was like being back at a Pop Concert or summer fair at Westport. The unit took first prize in the float competition—a large keg of beer. At the end of the second day, after the staging of a traditional Highland gathering, the games ended with the playing of "Retreat" by 184 bagpipes and 164 drummers of the combined Canadian and Scottish bands. For Bobby and his comrades, the music paid respect to the more than nine thousand Canadians who had suffered casualties during the March and April campaign.

On July 5 Bobby's battalion returned to the Arras-Vimy area directly across from the Wotan switch line, which ran from Dracourt to Quéant. In the heat of the trenches, he continued to write cheerful, not always truthful, letters home. In one he explained how much safer it was to be in the infantry than in a tank, which was extremely dangerous at the time. Small, terribly hot, liable to tip over, and impossible to escape from once attacked and in flames, they were, in Bobby's opinion, "crawling coffins." As for their crews, "for sheer heroism and nerve they can give everyone else cards, spades, and the Big Casino," he declared. "And incidentally I should hate to get into an argument with any of them."[45]

In another letter he announced the happy news that he had finally gotten that desk job Posie had hoped for. Bobby claimed that the censors, while reading his letters, had alerted the officers in charge that he might be a good candidate for some kind of work other than digging trenches. Hence, he told Posie, they had assigned him to "intelligence work," just the sort of thing he had hoped to do in the U.S. Army. He felt "immensely pleased and proud" because his new assignment entailed responsibility and called for "mental alertness." Bobby claimed to be in charge of writing reports on everything that occurred within his battalion's area as well as making observations of "happenings in the enemy's lines." For instance, he explained, "I have to report every shell that lands in our area, stating its calibre, the approximate direction from which it came, and the exact map location where it landed. . . . If any of our men see or encounter any of the enemy, I have to state whether any marks were observed which would identify them as Prussian Guards, or Bavarians, or Brandenburgers or what not. I have to get these bits of information from all ranks—officers, non-commissioned officers, machine gunners, etc." [46] Bobby reported that he was now excused from all working parties and trench life, had new quarters with good rations, and occasionally received a nip of Scotch, a cigar, or a cigarette from a friendly officer. Since he averaged ten to fifteen cigarettes a day, any contribution was gladly accepted.

The news of Bobby's privileged position was a great relief to his mother, but his description was entirely fabricated. Posie learned this only after his return home and blessed him for sparing her from suffering and worry. What Bobby had actually volunteered for (not been invited to participate in) was assignment to one of the patrols that were often sent out into No-Man's-Land, that area between the opposing sides' trenches which Dinesen described as "one maze of shell holes: dark, silent, desolate." [47] There he stopped at listening posts, where he attempted to pick up information from the enemy lines. It was hoped that such data would educate the commanding officers about hostile plans and movements. This was dangerous work, for any patrol entering the dreaded No-Man's-Land was vulnerable to attack, being shot by snipers, or possibly being taken prisoners of war.

It is unclear from his medical records and existing letters just when in July it was that Robert Sherwood experienced some sort of gas attack. World War I was the first to witness extensive use of chemical warfare. Even though such early efforts as the Second Hague Peace Conference of 1907 prohibited the use of "poison or poisoned weapons," Germany instituted gas warfare in 1915, claiming that gases were not poisonous. [48] Once the Germans began using chemicals, the other nations followed. The one most commonly used in 1918, when Bobby experienced the attack, was mustard gas, but he might also have inhaled one of the other chlorine-phosgene mixtures, of which there were many. He later remembered the gas as phosgene, although his records do not specify its content. Mustard gas, developed in 1917, became the gas of choice. Made up of dichlorodiethyl sulfide, it was also known as "Yellow Cross" because of the yellow markings on the German shells. The chemical was caustic and resulted in large numbers of casualties. From July 1917 to November 1918, 4,086 soldiers died from its effects and another 160,526 were treated for it. Mustard gas was known largely to affect the eyes and the respiratory tract, but it could also create skin blisters and cause severe vomiting.

While at Bramshott training camp, Bobby had participated in gas drills, in which he was taught to slip on his mask, securing the strap behind his head and the clip on his nose within six seconds. He learned that he could live on a small amount of oxygen inhaled through a long tube from a copper holder filled with chemicals which he wore on his chest. He drilled in rooms filled with supposedly harmless teargas, whose residue on his clothing later made his eyes water. Yet in spite of his training, on that hot July day in 1918 something went terribly wrong. Perhaps he did not put the mask on correctly or quickly enough, or perhaps he ripped it off too soon, finding the heat inside it suffocating. In any case, Bobby reported to the hospital barracks, an old cart shed which had been equipped with two tiers of wire bunks, after having vomited for approximately two hours. He seemed to recover fairly rapidly, indicating that the attack had not been severe. The medics released him with the recommendation that he be assigned only "light duty" for a while.[49]

Bobby was eager to get back into action quickly, as he had heard rumors that a large offensive was to take place, and he wanted to be a part of it. In the final weeks of July, General Currie and his divisional commanders had indeed completed plans for a surprise attack on Amiens. In order to keep it under wraps, open plans were made for an attack in another area, complete with decoy troop movement and overt word of mouth. In the meantime, the secret attack plans were also put into place—their object, to protect the railway lines linking the Arras area to Paris. The men in the corps were warned that anything they were told or heard through rumors was not to be repeated. In each individual's service and pay book was pasted the words "KEEP YOUR MOUTH SHUT" and the advice that if taken prisoner in the ensuing battle, to give only one's name and rank. The order concluded, "Though the enemy might use threats, he will respect you if your courage, patriotism, and self-control do not fail."[50] In early August, in the dark of night, the Canadian Corps began to move by train and bus to the concentration area southwest of Amiens. At the same time, a false move was staged during the day to an area northwest of Arras involving a great deal of noise, dust, and some false wireless communication for the Germans to intercept.

On the moonless night of August 7, fully equipped with his rifle, ammunition, and gas mask, Bobby and the rest of the Forty-second Battalion moved silently to their assembly position. By four a.m. they were in place, waiting for that one all-important order, "NOW!" Meanwhile, a thick ground mist had formed in the valleys. Even after the sun rose, it was difficult to see very far ahead. Once the men were ready, the supporting tanks moved into position about a thousand yards behind the front. In order to cover the sound of their engines so German ears could not hear them, a constant "harassing" artillery fire was maintained, and a "large bombing plane droned noisily up and down above the forward trenches."[51] Because this was to be a surprise attack, the usual preliminary bombardment was canceled. Instead, the infantry had to depend on the barrage and the tanks to damage German machine guns and barbed wire.

The attack began at exactly twenty minutes after four, when nine hundred guns opened fire and the infantry, including Bobby, pressed forward. The noise was almost unbearable, the shells, gas, and mist adding to the confusion. It was one of those surreal experiences in which one does what is expected without really registering its happening. The barrage lasted a mere four minutes and then the infantry was on its way. Bobby was excited, his adrenalin transforming his usual calm state into one of readiness. He was surprised to find himself less frightened than he had expected, although he remembered wishing that he had been offered a small shot of rum, as he felt "a bit green around the gills." But "Oh! how sweet!" he wrote home. "One cannot conceive the frightful intensity. The enemy's lines looked like a stormy sea of molten lead, the showers of red-hot shrapnel appearing like clouds of spray."[52] The mist remained a problem, making it difficult for many of the men to keep up with their comrades and causing some to lose their way. The tanks had a particularly hard time dealing with the reduced visibility and the marshy ground they had to cover. Trying as conditions were, they also affected the Germans, who quickly counterattacked, but not with the expected ferocity.

The Canadians took the lead in the action, while the French, Australian, and English troops followed—approximately 200,000 men in all. The Third Division, covering the right wing of the attacking force, had the difficult task of crossing the Amiens-Royce road at Hourges, a village about nine miles from Amiens, continuing in a northeasterly direction for half a mile to the river Luce, then north for 4,500 yards before bending to the east again to reach the Amiens-Chaulnes railway line a mile beyond Villers-Bretonneux. By 7:30, three hours and ten minutes after the battle began, the division as a whole had achieved one of its goals, and an ever-increasing flow of German prisoners crossed the battle line. Bobby's battalion had traveled approximately seven and a half miles, at least half of that distance behind enemy lines. Resistance was not strong; gunfire and shelling were only sporadic. Dead bodies lay everywhere; yet the victory was fairly easy, like "an ordinary stroll through intensely interesting surroundings," or so he told Posie.[53] After a brief pause, the battle began again. This time the Forty-second Battalion overran two German batteries firing at them point-blank. It was most likely at this point in the battle that Bobby was hurt.

What exactly happened is a bit fuzzy because Robert Sherwood himself gave different accounts of the incident. What is clear is that the young soldier sustained injuries to his legs, which were badly cut by barbed wire. He wrote Posie that he had been a long way from the original front line when he and his comrades ran up against a nest of machine guns. Although four of the men were wounded, the rest succeeded in overcoming their enemy. As far as he could remember, it was at this point that he "stepped" into a German booby trap. He downplayed the seriousness of his trauma by telling her that there had been "no charging at breakneck speed with bayonets fixed and concentrated hate and passion exuding from every nerve and fibre."[54] Rather, there was just a stumbling fall and then unconsciousness. Bobby, to his great embarrassment, was the victim of a simple enemy ploy. In an effort to stop the charge of the cavalry, the German army often dug pits about three feet deep and ten feet wide, which they lined with sharp stakes and filled with tangles of barbed wire. These booby traps were cleverly covered over with sticks and twigs so that the horses and riders, or even the infantrymen on foot, could not detect them. Bobby simply did not see the trap and fell into it.

Robert Sherwood's biographer John Mason Brown embellished the story, saying that Bobby was also gassed, this time quite badly, and his "protruding feet and legs" sticking out of the pit were further "lacerated by shrapnel."[55] At various times, Bobby gave his mother conflicting accounts of his injuries. In one version he said that he had not been aware of the leg lacerations until he and his buddies turned over control of the captured territory to the Salvage Corps. He then noticed that the tops of his socks were "suffused with a sample of New Rochelle's 'bluest blood.'" Thinking that he had been hit, he stashed his rifle and equipment in the deepest and wettest shell hole he could find and then "beat it to the rear."[56] Then he told her that he had sustained a minor wound that he could just as easily have suffered at home. Later on he said that he had been wounded by bullets, not barbed wire, and that he had been "suffering horribly from gas" before the fall.[57]

The Canadian military records lay out a somewhat different scenario. According to them, on August 1 Bobby was treated for multiple boils on his arms. He explained that he had been gassed in July and was not feeling well.[58]

Apparently he reported that he "could not hold out on route marches" and was suffering shortness of breath and heart palpitations. He also complained that he felt "nauseated and vomited on any over exertion." [59] Then on August 8 he was treated for barbed wire cuts on his right ankle and bruises, and for at least two weeks afterward he suffered from boils and ulcers on his legs. All of these reports are consistent with his being gassed and the fall into the booby trap. In all likelihood, Bobby had inhaled the fumes from "friendly" fire, for on August 8, the Number Five Squadron of the Royal Air Force was assigned the task of laying down smokescreens to supplement the artillery fire. The R.A.F. dropped forty-pound phosphorus bombs on the Canadian and Australian front lines, supposedly in order to protect their forward movement from being detected by the Germans. Thomas Dinesen remembered that their friend Chris had lamented Bobby's gassing and subsequent hospitalization, exclaiming somewhat enviously that "Poor Bob has gone West!" (meaning to England and then home). [60]

One other condition also showed up on Robert Sherwood's medical charts. Labeled "D.A.H.," it stood for "Disordered Action of the Heart." The records state that Bobby had a heart murmur, causing shortness of breath during periods of exertion, but that otherwise his heart was normal. His physicians agreed that it was a "result of service" rendered in Arras. [61] On the day of his injury he was one of 3,868 Canadian casualties—1,036 killed, 2,803 wounded, and 29 taken prisoner. There is no mention in the charts of his being shot or cut by shrapnel. Bobby often exaggerated the truth in writing to his family, and he may have done so in this case. He also seems to have felt humiliated by his less than spectacular war injury, telling his sister Cynthia that he "experienced the same shock" to his "self respect which one sustains after finding out that there was a brick inside the silk hat which one kicks on April Fools Day." [62] In the end, the discrepancies are of little matter when measured against the young man's overall experiences and the effect they had on the direction of his life.

The battle of Amiens began what historians often refer to as the "Last Hundred Days of the War." British Field Marshall Julian Byng, who commanded the Canadian Corps at Vimy Ridge, called the colonials' performance "the finest operation of the war." [63] General Eric Ludendorff, the German commander, termed it "the blackest day . . . in the history of the war" for the German army, which suffered major defeats and the capture of thousands of prisoners, already discouraged and depressed, many of them relieved to be taken away from the fighting. On August 10, when he reported the defeat to the Kaiser, the German ruler reportedly said that it was time for the war to end. [64] Unfortunately, it did not. This particular action lasted through

August 11, and the war itself did not come to an end until November 11 at 11 o'clock in the morning. By that time, 8,020,780 military men had lost their lives and another 21,228,813 had been wounded. Approximately 6,642,633 civilians also lost their lives.

For Bobby Sherwood, however, the fighting was over. After his immediate treatment, he spent four weeks in French hospitals in Rouen and Trouvelle. Again, he tried to soothe his mother. Without disclosing his exact whereabouts in the Seine Valley (again because of the censors), he related that he was in a British general hospital in a beautiful setting that had formerly been a seminary for young girls. It was fully equipped with a cloistered courtyard, dormitories, baths, kitchens, dining halls, and a gym. His life there was leisured, with nothing for him to do except eat and rest. With so much free time, he took to drawing in an École normale notebook he found, using black charcoal pencils his aunt Jane had sent him. He filled the pages of the book and other loose sheets of paper over the next months with sketches of soldiers and civilians going about their every day lives: a fisherman, a French official, a young soldier, a sailor on board ship, a local woman selling something to a tall soldier, and a man on board ship tied to a stretcher snoring while other men in hammocks make a fuss. He produced "half decent stuff," in his own estimation, when he drew specifically to please Posie. Being safe, however, made him feel cut off and lonely, and being wounded and away from the action and his friends were worse hardships than any other he had experienced. He received no mail and no pay, so he could not buy cigarettes and candy or hear news from home, "which three factors constitute the breath of life to me."[65] Worse still, he was not allowed to leave the hospital grounds, which were enclosed by barbed-wire fences. Consequently, he spent many hours sitting on a bench near the boundary watching people pass by, hoping beyond hope that he would see someone he knew. Boredom, the worst fate of all, had set in.

Finally, Bobby was placed on a stretcher and shipped to England to be treated in Reading, Bexhill, and finally Bushy Park, outside London, where he remained as an ambulatory patient from September 14 until his release on December 14. There were worse cases than his at the various hospitals where he was treated. At one a horribly burned Australian soldier lay in a bed on one side of him while on the other was a Jewish South African soldier permanently paralyzed by a bullet in his spine. Bobby's own pus-filled boils, ulcers, and infection from the gassing and cuts took some time to heal, but of more concern was his heart. His pulse was checked every day, his heart rate constantly tested, and a regimen of mild exercises prescribed to increase his strength. One of the pleasures of Bushy Park was that the recovering soldiers were able to go out in the afternoons and early evenings and once again become acclimated to civilian society. Unpleasantly for them, however, they had to wear regulation blue hospital uniforms, which identified them as convalescents and by law prevented those on the outside from serving them alcohol.

Bobby took some time during his convalescence to reflect on his experiences with the Canadians. He wrote his brother Phil that of course he was "naturally a dilettante and a loafer as you say, and I didn't make much success at the rough life," but neither did he "make the mess of it" that had usually characterized his past undertakings, particularly his education.[66] He credited his Canadian comrades for this improvement. Furthermore, while it was true that he was the only one of the Sherwood "boys" not to have received a commission, he was also the only one to go overseas and get "his hands on a Hun—outside of the Hofbrau Haus Rathskeller on 37th Street" in Manhattan.[67] While at Bushy Park, Bobby was able to see family and friends in London. Even when the de Glehns were away in France, he stopped by their home, where their elderly cook, Ellen, made him meals and gave him her delicious gingerbread to take back to the hospital. Ellen also kept his mail for him, which he had sent to his aunt's address, and on occasion she would lend him ten shillings, which she claimed he always paid back. He saw his cousins Mamie and Florence, and friends Buddy and Dorothy Cross, who took him for an auto ride and then in a punt on the Thames, and to tea and lunch at an old wayside inn. He also tried his hand at writing, and found one of his letters, titled "The Tank," in a copy of Life magazine which he purchased at Waterloo Station. A few others were published in various periodicals, while still more which he deemed unpublishable he tore up for being "rotten and crude."[68]

In 1930 a more mature Robert Sherwood remembered that on November 11, 1918, when the inmates of Bushy Park lined up as usual for mail call, an elderly, invalid chaplain asked them to join him in a prayer of thanks because the war was over. The Amens said, "God Save the King" sung, and General Currie cheered, a group of men sneaked out through the barbed-wire fence surrounding the hospital grounds, climbed aboard a Hammersmith bus, and rode into the frenzied bewilderment of London's celebration. Bobby remained "absent, missing and unaccounted for" for four days. It was a wild and uninhibited time for all, as the recuperating men celebrated their relief that the war had ended before they could be designated as "fit" and returned to the front, and Bobby was not sorry to be AWOL. He wrote Posie about the "wild conglomeration of Tommies, Jocks, Australians, Yanks, sailors, wounded men, Italians, Belgians, Indians, French, Portuguese, Land-girls,

'WAACS,' 'Wrens,' Munition Girls, and everyone else in uniform parading and howling and hooting and dancing through the streets and breaking things, and hurting each other. It was much worse than New Year's Eve in New York." [69]

The mobs had seized a massive number of German guns, which were on exhibit all along the Mall to Buckingham Palace, and carted them to Trafalgar Square, where many were torched at the base of Nelson's statue. Flags from all the Allied countries were on display, but for some odd reason Old Glory was hung upside down. Too weak to stay for very long among the crowds, Bobby spent every afternoon and evening going to musical variety shows, where the crowds were exuberantly boisterous. When he returned to Bushy Park, he was soundly reprimanded and assigned to kitchen duty. That Thanksgiving Day the one thing he had to be thankful for was that there were only three hundred patients in the hospital to wash dishes for. It was a time that young Bobby Sherwood would never forget. Almost two months later, on January 3, 1919, he was shipped home on board the *Scotian*.

Soon after he arrived in Montreal, Bobby took a train to New York. When he arrived early in the morning at Grand Central Station, he immediately called Posie, who quickly woke up Ros and Lydia. The three of them met him at the door of Lyd's apartment at 535 Fifth Avenue—a pathetic-looking, gaunt, and thin young soldier wearing an old khaki army shirt his much shorter uncle Wilfrid had given him, a pair of shabby khaki trousers, and his khaki cap with a red feather on the side. He told his welcoming party that he had slept on the floor of the ship because the hammocks were too short for him, but to his horror, a rat kept running around his tired body. The ship crossing and the long train ride that followed had given him a cold, and as he told his mother, just the day before his heart had experienced a "bad turn." [70] Posie quickly put her son to bed for a much-needed rest. A few days later Lydia remarked how quiet he was. "He talks so little"—not like his previous self, she noted—but she felt reassured when, after some time, Posie was able to "worm" his experience out of him. [71]

What Bobby told his mother may or may not have been exactly true. He did confess to having whitewashed the truth so as not to alarm her and lying about the nature of his so-called intelligence work. But he also told her that during his seven months in France, the personnel in his company had changed twice because *every* officer and enlisted man had been either killed or wounded during the unrelenting fighting. He told her that one day he and another man had made a small dugout outside the trenches and were about to have breakfast when a shell hit the road and blew his comrade to pieces. He related how he was one of six volunteers who served on a party to draw

German attention away from twenty-five others on a surprise attack mission. During the operation he killed a German officer who was pointing a revolver at the twenty-five approaching from the other direction. (He told Phil that the officer was facing him, not away from him.) Bobby's party brought back eleven prisoners, but when medals were awarded the next day, he did not receive one. He accounted for this lapse by claiming that the others deserved them, as they had been at the front for three years. Then he told Posie about a toothache which had been so painful that he walked six miles over the top of Vimy Ridge, which was being shelled, to a dentist, who was not there. Instead, his sergeant assistant removed first the wrong tooth, then the right one. Then Bobby walked the six miles back to his world of no water and no toothbrushes. Finally, he related that just four days after being gassed, he had marched with full equipment before being shot through his legs. He could not remember being shot, as he had fainted, but he did remember falling into the booby trap.[72] Posie believed that it was this final stressful march which had damaged his heart.

Bobby remained at home, withdrawn and sick with a cold, until early February, when he had to return to Montreal for his formal discharge from service. Soon after he arrived, he cabled home asking that Cynthia join him. He said that he needed some medicine he had left behind, but more likely he did not want to be alone. On February 5, Robert Sherwood was handed his discharge papers, which stated that he was "Medically Unfit" for service, that he had left the army with a scar on his back and two on his right ankle which he had not entered with, and that he was six-tenths disabled, with the prognosis that he would recover within six months.[73] But in fact he left the military a very different man, one who had lost the innocence of being "Bobby" and who now entered a more mature phase of his life as "Robert," "Bob," or "Mr. Sherwood." For all his cheerful bravado and boasting, he had learned that war was not just about love of country or adventure; it was about incomprehensible politics, horror, and untimely death. The somber young man who returned from war was not the same one who had written his letters home. Much remained unspoken and would remain so. World War I, however, became the defining experience for the rest of Robert Sherwood's life. He had entered it a militarist and left it a pacifist.

4

Life after the War

FOR ALMOST a decade after his war experience, Robert Sherwood went through a series of changes. For some time he suffered from a case of moderate postwar trauma with nightmares and sweats, fear of rodents, and general restlessness and bouts of undisciplined behavior. In seeming contradiction to his wildness and hyperactivity, he was also often withdrawn, pensive, and silent, never wishing to discuss his military service. During the same period, he pushed forward in his pursuit of a career in writing—at first as a feature writer, essayist, and film critic; then as a short story author and screenwriter (neither very successful at the time); and, finally, as a playwright. Throughout these years, his gut reaction of anger toward war evolved into a pacifist ideology, which he then expressed in many of his plays and articles, and ever so gently in his film scripts.

Sherwood's pacifism became the key to understanding most of his work. His definition of the term, however, was purposely broad. Like so many others who had lived through the World War I era, he considered a pacifist to be anyone who was opposed to war based on his or her first- or secondhand knowledge of the violence and bloodshed that the conflict had created. But pacifism is also a very personal phenomenon, a position that can range from refusing to support war in any way, including serving as a medic, to simply protesting a specific war but not war in general as a means of resolving conflicts. Sherwood's specific brand of pacifism grew out of his abhorrence of the injuries, death, and destruction of World War I, which he could make no sense of. The entire enterprise, which at first appeared to be an adventure in "saving the world for democracy," had ended in chaos and despair. Having been raised a Christian (though delinquent in observing its rituals), Sherwood expressed his antiwar fervor in terms of Jesus' Sermon on the Mount. "Blessed are the peacemakers, for they will be called children of God," and "Blessed are the meek, for they will inherit the earth," became the principles that undergirded his pacifist convictions. In addition to this was the Emmet and Sherwood families' history of defending civil liberties, which Sherwood came to believe could be accomplished through nonviolent actions and protective laws. Although at first he struggled with his postwar anger, gradually his opposition to war, greed, unbridled power, and censorship emerged in a clear artistic expression.

It is hardly surprising that when young Bob returned home from the war, he suffered something close to culture shock. When he left the United States for Canada in 1917, the nation was just gearing up militarily. During the years he was away, the wartime economy boomed, thanks to the close collaboration between business and government. Wages were relatively high, industrial and government clerical jobs plentiful, and for many with no loved ones in danger in Europe, life was better than it had ever been before. At the moment Bob arrived back in New York in January 1919, the city was still flush with excitement and prosperity, and plans were being made to shift to an equally lucrative peace economy, which came to fruition by 1922 after the usual postwar deflation and depression had passed. Indeed, for many Americans the 1920s proved to be a period of peace and prosperity. But a good overall economy does not mean that every individual is enjoying a prosperous life. Indeed, with the family economically dependent on Posie while Arthur convalesced in Savannah, Georgia, the Sherwoods' situation was far from its comfortable prewar level. Bob would have noticed quickly that things had changed drastically for his parents while he was away. The couple was suffering from a sharp decline in income at a time of skyrocketing costs. When he arrived home a sick and skinny veteran, Bob was faced with the shocking reality that the price of clothing had tripled. Even with a generous bonus and back pay from the Canadian government, his money did not go as far as it would have in the years before he left. Posie, ecstatic to have her son back at home, still had to face the fact that even a quart of milk, which had cost only nine cents in 1914, now cost seventeen cents. Bread, cheese, meat, flour—indeed, any item she wanted to buy to bring up Bob's weight—had doubled or tripled in cost.

On top of this, Posie feared that her weakened son might fall victim to the flu, which reached pandemic proportions during 1918–19, killing as many as 40 million people. She tried hard to keep him under her watchful gaze so he could recuperate from his wounds and rebuild his strength. Indeed, she insisted that he go to Savannah to be with Arthur and the professional nurse who cared for him. There she felt he would have the attention he needed. Bob, in fact, did join his father, and Posie arrived soon after. Immediately, his father, too, noticed his son's markedly different behavior, especially his fitful nights and his quiet demeanor. He remained pensive, often refusing to talk about his personal war experiences, though he was willing to present a detached, factual description of events, as he did for a group of students at Harvard a month after his return and for a reporter from the *Boston Herald*. But at his twenty-third birthday celebration, when Posie asked him to describe that day a year before, when he was in France and "the Germans attacked in force & Hell broke loose," he declined her request, saying that "he did not want to mar the day by talking of it." [1] This was so unlike the Bobby who had gone off to war, the child whose life had revolved around weaving stories and acting them out, that it gave Posie cause to worry. Her only relief at the time came when the pulmonologist Dr. James Alexander Miller announced that Bob's lungs were healing nicely from the gas attacks and that he would be back to normal by autumn. In the meantime, though, he startled his mother each time he gasped loudly for air.

For Bob and others, withdrawing from the war meant more than just not talking. They wished neither to remember nor to be reminded of their experiences. Hence, it also meant seeking out ways to distract themselves and to keep focused on the here and now. As Bob wrote in 1949, this period was "one of the most sordid" of his life, a time when he was "seeking escape" from the memories that refused to leave him in peace. [2] Soon after returning home to New York, he apparently sought solace with the wrong crowd, as Lydia portrayed his friends. In actuality, it seems that at first he simply reverted to his prewar behavior—carousing with friends, staying out late, singing, and trying to recapture the carefree days before he learned what death in war looked like. Lydia apparently criticized him too harshly for Posie's taste. "You speak as if you blamed Bobby for going to any entertainment or spending any money," she reprimanded her sister. "But you must remember that he has spent nearly two years practically in Hell." [3] Posie felt that her son deserved a period of time simply to enjoy himself.

Because Posie would not indulge her harping, Lydia turned to Jane instead. She told her that Bob, who was staying in Posie's small apartment in New York while his mother was out of town, was acting like "he was four years old." He apparently had invited six of his "rough neck" friends to stay with him, and together they had destroyed the place. "All that pretty furniture of Posie's had to be done over, tables smashed as well as defaced and chairs with the backs broken off," Lydia related to Jane. Curtains had been pulled down and linens had been "dragged off the lounge & thrown in heaps on the floor & then walked over." It took Rosamund and a helper a full two weeks to get the apartment cleaned up. Lydia had no doubt that Bob, usually a responsible young man, would pay for the damages and repairs, but still, how awful that Posie, who worked so hard for everything she had, would have to start all over again to set up her "lovely little home." Lyd thought that Posie should force Bob to "take a room somewhere by himself," though it was highly unlikely that her sister would do so. [4]

For Bob and the thousands of other veterans who suffered some form of psychological or physical trauma, the 1920s offered many distractions. The appellation "the Roaring Twenties" characterized an exciting era of technological development, consumerism, and cultural explosion. The burgeoning advertising industry persuaded consumers to purchase cars, radios, phonographs, washing machines, telephones, and a vast array of luxury items. Movies, sports, music, dancing, and theater all witnessed expansion and artistic experimentation. New York City was, as usual, a center of frenetic twenty-four-hour-a-day activity. The Harlem Renaissance burst forth with jazz, art, literature, and nightclubs that attracted patrons from all over the world, and the New York theater and film scene offered equally enticing fare. Numbers of single men and women moved to the city or refused to leave it after having found work there during the war. It was no coincidence that one of the best-known songs of the era was "How Ya Gonna' Keep 'em Down on the Farm After They've Seen Paree?" So many people decided not to return to their farms and small towns that when the Bureau of the Census concluded its 1920 calculations, it revealed that for the first time in U.S. history, more people lived in urban areas than in the countryside. Bob joined the mobs who spent their days looking for and often finding work and their nights throwing around the money they had just earned. He also turned to a number of his favorite prewar activities, which offered him a frenzied escape from his memories. But he soon decided that a job, not just for the money but also to engage his mind, was what he needed. So he contacted a family acquaintance, Frank Crowninshield, the editor of *Vanity Fair* magazine, who took him on at twenty-five dollars a week for an initial three-month probationary period. Who could resist a young veteran who showed up for his interview in his full Canadian army regalia, kilt and all? The job lasted from May 1919 to January 1920.

At the time, *Vanity Fair* was a slick 120-page monthly which published mostly literary essays, articles, short stories, and poems. The magazine featured the writings of Robert Benchley, Dorothy Parker, P. G. Wodehouse, and John Jay Chapman, and newcomers such as Willa Cather. Articles on literature, the arts, opera, theater, photography, antiques, society events, dog shows, and horse racing were intermingled with advertisements for Tiffany's, Franklin Simon's Fifth Avenue store, expensive cars from Thompson Custom-Built Bodies, and pedigreed dogs. The tone of *Vanity Fair* was one of urban sophistication. Bob's job, however, had no pretensions to sophistication or high culture at all. As he later described it, he was "a sort of maid of all work." He ran errands, edited articles, selected photographs, and did anything else he was asked to do. Perhaps the best part of the job was getting to know twenty-eight-year-old Robert Benchley, an enormously creative humorist, and twenty-five-year-old Dorothy Parker, a cynically funny essayist and poet, both of whom opened up worlds of fun and diversion for him as well as giving his career what he called a "miraculous start."[5]

Benchley was a man whom Bob had admired since first seeing him at Harvard, where Benchley was a student in the class of 1912. At Bob's freshman smoker he gave the featured speech and then spent time with the new students, drinking beer, smoking, and generally joking around. Benchley also served as president of the *Harvard Lampoon* and wrote scripts for several of the Hasty Pudding shows. "It gave me a particular thrill to see Benchley," Bob recalled of his college years, "because I had every intention of stepping into his boots." Benchley had become Bob's role model, "a shining objective toward which to strive as an undergraduate," though one he felt he "never even approached" throughout his entire career.[6] After World War I ended, Bob had another reason to admire Benchley; he had been raised by his mother to be a pacifist after his brother Edmund, thirteen years his senior, was killed in action during the Spanish-American War.

It was exciting for the young veteran to find himself at *Vanity Fair,* sharing an office with these two up-and-coming authors. "As I got to know them and watched them at work," he remembered in 1954, "I realized that I had already landed in the major leagues."[7] During the summer of 1919, when editor Frank Crowninshield and publisher Condé Nast took a trip to Europe, they left their managing editor, Benchley, in charge. He decided that young Bob Sherwood should fill out several articles that were not quite long enough. "If an article by G. K. Chesterton ran 27 lines short, I had to fill it," Bob explained to Benchley's son Nathaniel thirty-five years later. "Or it might be a sports article by Grantland Rice."[8] When the author of the "For the Well-Dressed Man" column went on vacation, Bob had to write a good half of his piece. He proceeded to exaggerate the usual snobbish tone of the columnist, who, when he saw the result, complained loudly to those in power. Although Nast and Crowninshield were annoyed at Bob's efforts and those of Benchley and Parker to turn the high humor of *Vanity Fair* into the low humor of the *Lampoon,* they appear to have forgiven at least Bob, whose talent they now noticed for the first time, for his inaugural signed article appeared in the October issue of the magazine. Titled "The Wanderings of a Column Hound," it was a humorous description of those readers who became obsessed with following the writings of certain newspaper columnists. As he noted, the addiction had taken hold of him at an early age, "with the result that, today, I spend all my leisure time reading the special columns and never have time to turn to the news section."[9]

When Bob's first article proved successful, Crowninshield gave him the opportunity to write his second, "The Bloodlust of Broadway," which appeared in December. In this piece he joked about the great popularity of murder mysteries on Broadway. Bob noted that there was nothing like "a good, rousing murder" to put the audience in "an amiable and receptive frame of mind." Accidents and suicides were also crowd pleasers, and any actor who yearned for "dramatic honors" had to "step forth and die" if he hoped to reach stardom, no matter how good a performer he was.[10] In the same vein, Bob wrote "If Shakespeare Were on Broadway," another humorous piece, this one about how difficult it was for an aspiring playwright to have a play produced unless it was rewritten "by every manager, press-agent, doorman, usher and wardrobe mistress" in town. Unlike in Shakespeare's time, he claimed, authors no longer had total control over their work. To illustrate, Bob put Shakespeare's *Macbeth* through the proverbial wringer until he had turned it into a melodramatic murder mystery complete with exaggerated emoting and theatrical trickery.[11]

When Benchley and Parker first met Bob, they were struck by his seemingly quiet nature and the fact that he looked ill and constantly had trouble breathing. Benchley thought he was simply shy, and Bob's manner of speaking—slow and pausing "like a glacier," as S. N. Behrman described it—added to this impression.[12] Parker, with her acerbic tongue (later described by Bob as "a stiletto made of sugar"), complained that he was a "Conversation Stopper," and that trying to talk to him was "like riding on the Long Island Railroad—it gets you nowhere in particular."[13] Yet his cavalier style, marked by the straw hat he wore at a slightly tilted angle, intrigued them both. They hoped that in time he would warm up to them, which he did—but largely because his height had gotten him into an awkward predicament. In an often told story, an incident that Bob later said he could not recall, "Mr. Sherwood" purportedly appealed to "Mr. Benchley" and "Mrs. Parker" (as they initially and humorously called one another) to help him out of an embarrassing situation. Each day at noontime, Bob left the *Vanity Fair* offices on West Forty-fourth Street to find a place to have lunch. He inevitably passed by the Hippodrome Theatre, which at the time was featuring a number of midgets, who harassed him by jeering at him, pretending to nibble at his knees, and, as Parker put it, "always sneaking up behind him and asking him how the weather was up there."[14] Frustrated and humiliated, one day Bob waited for his two officemates to leave for lunch and asked them if he could walk between them, using them as a buffer. They happily consented, an episode that resulted in Parker's and Benchley's taking a liking to him. Although Bob remained aloof when asked about his personal life, especially his war experiences, the three became close companions.

The place where Parker, Benchley, and Bob lunched together each workday thereafter was the dining room at the Algonquin Hotel. Located close to their office, the hotel had been founded in 1902 as a temperance establishment called the Puritan, but in 1919 its manager, Frank Case, renamed it the Algonquin in honor of the Native Americans who had originally lived in the area. Unfortunately for Case, the name change did not alter the hotel's temperance history, for in that same year the nation adopted the Eighteenth Amendment to the Constitution, making the production, sale, and transportation of alcoholic beverages illegal in the United States. Initially, the three writers dined alone on hors d'oeuvres or scrambled eggs and coffee, the only items they could afford on their meager *Vanity Fair* salaries. Soon after, however, an event took place at the Algonquin Hotel which changed all their lives, especially Bob's.[15] John Peter Toohey, a theater publicist, and Murdock Pemberton, a press agent, decided to throw a mock "welcome home from the war" celebration for the egotistical, sharp-tongued columnist Alexander Woollcott. The idea was really for theater journalists to roast Woollcott in revenge for his continual self-promotion and his refusal to boost the careers of potential rising stars on Broadway. On the designated day, the Algonquin dining room was festooned with banners. On each table was a program which misspelled Woollcott's name and poked fun at the fact that he and fellow writers Franklin Pierce Adams (F.P.A.) and Harold Ross had sat out the war in Paris as staff members of the army's weekly newspaper, the *Stars and Stripes*, which Bob had read in the trenches. But it is difficult to embarrass someone who thinks well of himself, and Woollcott beamed at all the attention he received.

The guests enjoyed themselves so much that John Toohey suggested they meet again, and so the custom was born that a group of regulars would lunch together every day at the Algonquin Hotel. In addition to Bob, Benchley, Parker, Woollcott, F.P.A, and Ross, others who joined as the weeks passed included the journalist Heywood Broun, the playwriting team of Marc Connelly and George S. Kaufman, the playwright Howard Dietz, and authors Edna Ferber and Alice Duer Miller. Once in a while the writer Ring Lardner or Bob's songwriter hero Irving Berlin would drop by. Aspiring actresses Helen Hayes, Peggy Wood, Tallulah Bankhead, and Ruth Gordon sat in from time to time, as did innumerable young showgirls and chorus boys hoping to latch onto either a rising star or one already in the magic circle of fame on Broadway or in Hollywood. Mary Brandon was one such young woman whose rising star became Bob Sherwood. For Frank Case, the opportunity to cultivate a group of journalists, writers, and actors who might bring more customers to the hotel was a godsend, and he decided to make them a feature of his establishment. After several months of catering to them at a long side table, he moved the group to a central spot at a round table in the Rose Room, where tourists and other diners could stare and pretend to be sharing in the making of cultural history along with the Algonquin Round Table.

Meanwhile Benchley, Parker, and Bob faced worsening conflicts with their superiors at *Vanity Fair*. As Bob later described it, the Condé Nast "organization" was "beset with Prussian efficiency, administered by an executive named Francis Lewis Wurzburg."[16] In order to quiet the threesome's constant rumblings over the low and arbitrary pay scale, in October Wurzburg sent out a memorandum forbidding employees to discuss their salaries, claiming that pay was a confidential issue. Bob, Parker, and Benchley responded with their own memo, declaring that they resented being told what they could and could not talk about. For them this was clearly an issue of freedom of speech. They then made signs with their salaries etched on them and wore them around their necks at the office. Rather than cause any more mayhem with their employees, the powers that be responded with silence. Wurzburg's next attempt at "efficiency" (and retribution) caused a similar outburst. He established a policy stating that if employees were not at their desks by 8:50 a.m. and working by 9:00, they had to fill out forms detailing the reason for the delay. Benchley, eleven minutes late one morning, reported in the tiniest handwriting he could muster that he had been held up in front of the Hippodrome by a mass of escaped elephants and like any responsible citizen had stopped to help round them up. In an explanation that covered the entire page, he described in minute detail every fantastical moment of his fabricated tale. The effort took time . . . and time was really the main issue.

Because Bob was Parker and Benchley's constant accomplice, he should not have been surprised when Frank Crowninshield denied his request for a raise and informed him that another individual was being considered for his low-paying, menial position. Parker also did not receive the raise she had expected. The situation was pretty clear: their futures at *Vanity Fair* were in jeopardy. Bob was the first to go. Next, Dorothy Parker was fired. The reason given was that her scathing critique of actress Billie Burke in the play *Caesar's Wife* had upset Burke's powerful husband, Florenz Ziegfeld, and that other producers had also complained about the tone of her reviews. After Bob and Parker left, Benchley resigned. By May, no further articles written by them, either commissioned or still in the production line, appeared in the magazine.

The Algonquin Round Table, however, remained a constant for them. It reflected the frenetic side of Bob's life, the place where he could be entertained and entertaining—where he would not have to be alone to think too much. It also reflected his desire to be with creative people who not only made sharp and critical comments about the U.S. government and society but also made their views public through articles, plays, music, and film. Dorothy Parker later described the Round Table as "just a lot of people telling jokes and telling each other how good they were." Since the 1920s was "the terrible day of the wisecracks," she added, "there didn't have to be any truth, you know." Parker admitted that the "whole point" of what was sometimes known as the "Vicious Circle" was "to have fun, to be clever, to know where the best bartenders were, to be knowledgeable about the city, to know all the latest catchwords, to be aware of the latest fads and fashions, to go to all the first nights, to be satirical and blasé and to do as little work as possible." [17] It also meant being in the "in" crowd, something that Bob liked very much indeed.

While the lunches featured intellectual banter and snide remarks, they also provided a venue for a great deal of networking. Before long, the group expanded its time together to include long afternoons and late evenings. The studio and salon of magazine illustrator and artist Neysa McMein on the corner of Sixth Avenue and Fifty-seventh Street became a gathering place for the cohort to consume bathtub gin, sing popular tunes, or play word games. Bob was known for his rendition of "When the Red Red Robin Comes Bob Bob Bobbin' Along," a song he used for entertainment from his childhood into distinguished middle age, with his signature tilted hat and cane (and at times in vaudevillian blackface). People never seemed to tire of it.

Among the games played at the get-togethers were Murder, Twenty Questions, anagrams, guessing games involving famous people or scenes from famous plays, and the favorite, called "I-Can-Give-You-A-Sentence," which required that each member take a multisyllabic word and turn it into a pun within ten seconds. Bob, the slowest talker, was apparently not noted for his success at this exercise, but Dorothy Parker reigned as queen. For the word "horticulture" she quickly came up with, "You can lead a whore to culture, but you can't make her think." [18] For "penis" she quipped, "The penis mightier than the sword." "The Irish Song" became "Irish I was in Dixie," and "The Spanish national anthem" was "José, can you see?" [19] One of Bob's favorite Round Table activities was playing poker. On many occasions, especially after his marriage in 1922, he invited the gang to his apartment for all-night games until John Toohey formed the Thanatopsis Literary and Inside Straight Club, which Frank Case happily housed free of charge in a suite on the second floor of the hotel. (He also happily sold the players bootleg liquor.) The Thanatopsis poker game, which did not preclude playing games on other evenings, became a regular Saturday night event with supper served at midnight and the final round of cards not dealt until around two or three in the morning.

The theater was another one of the focal points of the Algonquin Round Table community. In addition to attending every opening night on Broadway (and being accused of "logrolling," or writing favorable reviews for friends), members of the group also participated in productions—whether as playwrights, composers, or actors. The 1920s in general was a period when the nature of live theater changed drastically in the United States, as melodramas gave way to more realistic and issue-oriented plays.[20] American playwrights were greatly influenced by European dramatists such as Henrik Ibsen, August Strindberg, Anton Chekhov, and perhaps the most admired of all, George Bernard Shaw. To prepare a new generation of theater professionals, some college professors developed courses to train them. Best known was George Pierce Baker, whose 47 Workshop at Harvard educated such 1920s luminaries as S. N. Behrman, Philip Barry, Sidney Howard, George Abbot, and Eugene O'Neill (though not Robert Sherwood) in playwriting, directing, acting, set design, and lighting.

Professionals in the theater also worked hard to change the tenor of the art form. In an effort to end the iron-handed control which a group of theater owners known as "The Theatrical Syndicate" held over productions, repertory companies such as the New Theatre (1909) and the Washington Square Players (1915) formed independent entities which presented modern plays without the pressure of having to earn large profits. Several members of the Washington Square Players, which disintegrated during World War I, went on to create the Theatre Guild in 1918. Whether writers wished simply to amuse, to offer social commentary, to foster new expressions of melodrama, or to critique the human condition and present a serious ideological viewpoint, the post–World War I theater scene was open to them.

The 1920s offered such variety in the theater—with old-fashioned vaudeville existing side by side with new, modern plays—that it seemed an appropriate time for Bob's unproduced Hasty Pudding show *Barnum Was Right* to see the light of day. After leaving *Vanity Fair*, Bob returned to Cambridge specifically to work on the play. While there, he accepted a position at the *Boston Post,* which lasted a mere two days, as *Barnum Was Right* took top priority for him. Produced by the Hasty Pudding Club, it toured Cambridge, Stratford, Philadelphia, New York, and Boston between April 14 and May 1, 1920. The plot revolved around two deities, Jupiter and Ganymede, who are approached by the Spirit of the Movies, who demands a place on Mount Olympus. In order for him to earn that revered position, however, Jupiter requires that the Spirit prove his case by showing him Hollywood. Upon their arrival, the Spirit tells him: "The greatest philosopher in history was P. T. Barnum. And why? He propounded the immortal theory that half the world are squirrels and the other half are nuts. . . . The movies have taken up that great work where Barnum left off." [21] The rest of the script follows Jupiter's transformation into a movie personality and the Spirit's move to Mount Olympus.

Bob's main theme in *Barnum Was Right* was that film, like the circus, made its profits by fooling its audiences: "Abraham Lincoln said: 'You can't fool all the people all the time'; but Barnum answered: 'You can fool enough of the people enough of the time to keep the wolf away from the main entrance.'" [22] According to Bob, what film relied on was "hokum," theatrical tricks used to mesmerize an audience, such as ham acting, tear-jerking scenes, blatantly melodramatic plots, and sight gags, and Bob used each and every one of these devices in *Barnum Was Right*. Indeed, even though, throughout his career, he forever criticized and commented on hokum, he consistently relied on it, feeling that it was a necessary instrument for both providing entertainment and moving the story along.

Hence, when on April 30, 1922, the Algonquin Round Tablers produced their own one-night vaudeville review, *No Siree!* (subtitled "An Anonymous Entertainment by the Vicious Circle of the Hotel Algonquin"), Bob was a primary deliverer of good old-fashioned hokum. Held in the 49th Street Theatre, the show consisted of an assortment of original song, dance, and comedy routines written and performed by the group for the benefit of themselves and their friends. It was here that Robert Benchley first performed his wildly popular monologue "The Treasurer's Report," which Irving Berlin, the creator and producer of the Music Box Revues, then paid him $500 a week to perform and which also became the basis of Benchley's first film. Bob himself performed a musical number in the skit "He Who Gets Flapped." With a contingent of short chorus girls, including June Walker, Tallulah Bankhead, Helen Hayes, and Mary Brandon, he sang Dorothy Parker's lyrics to "The Everlastin' Ingenue Blues," which satirized flappers, those 1920s tomboys who were notorious for wearing their skirts above their knees, dancing, visiting speakeasies, smoking, and flirting with men, and perhaps, though not necessarily, believing in free love. Bob also played the governor of New York in George S. Kaufman and Marc Connelly's three-act mini-play "Big Casino Is Little Casino." Accompanying *No Siree!* Irving Berlin stroked the keyboard in the orchestra pit, and it was most likely at this time that Bob spontaneously played for him his own song "I'm Going Back, Back to Akron, Ohio," for which the great songwriter offered no exciting words of encouragement. As a result, it was the last song that Bob ever wrote.

The following November, the Round Tablers expanded *No Siree!* into a newly titled show, *The 49ers,* with additional skits by both "insiders" and "outsiders." Hoping for a long, profitable run, they were disappointed when the revue closed after a mere fifteen performances. So ended Round Table theatrical productions, except for those of a smaller, more experimental variety. Ring Lardner, who did not particularly enjoy the Algonquin lunches, nevertheless could not pass up a good poker game with the Thanatopsis Society. Through that connection, he invited Bob and other members of the Round Table to participate in what he called his "nonsense plays" or "Dutch Treat Club" shows, sometimes referred to as "Dada plays." In 1927 Bob, Benchley, and Kaufman, among others, performed Lardner's *Dinner Bridge.* As Lardner reported: "The idea is simple: some laborers are being served dinner out of their lunch pails on the Fifty-ninth Street bridge, which is always being torn up for repairs. The principals speak 'correct Crowninshield dinner English,' except when they lapse into outrageous dialogue."[23]

As much as Bob would have liked to spend all his time with his Algonquin friends, he needed to earn his own livelihood. Posie and Arthur were in no position to support him, and his Canadian military separation pay had long since run out. Fascinated by films, he attempted to get a job writing movie titles for D. W. Griffith at his studio in Mamaroneck, not far from the city, but that did not pan out. Then, after working on *Barnum Was Right,* he inquired at *Life* magazine (another periodical with ties to his family), which had first expressed interest in him while he was at Harvard and then had published a couple of his World War I letters. The editor, Edward Stanford Martin, had been a member of the Harvard class of 1877 and, along with Bob's father, Arthur, a founding editor of the *Harvard Lampoon* in 1876. Founded by James Ames Mitchell in 1883, *Life,* under the presidency of Charles Dana Gibson, was at the time a satirical magazine much in the spirit of the *Lampoon.* In fact, it was a perfect place for Bob to end up, and his work there taught him skills he would use throughout his professional life: not simply writing essays, criticism, and stories, as well as silent film scenarios and titles, but all aspects of the business—from hiring staff to enlisting well-known artists to contribute essays, poems, stories, and illustrations, and from organizing an office to supervising the entire enterprise. The one skill *Life* did not prepare him for was playwriting. That he had been learning since childhood.

In the spring of 1920, when Bob started his career as assistant editor at *Life,* its circulation was a healthy 238,813. A magazine that would make fun of just about anything, it emphasized politics and culture, two topics that interested Bob no end. Annual special issues on themes ranging from "Sunday," "Wives," "Husbands," "Armistice," "Christmas," and "Easter" to

"Burlesque," "Movies," and "Theater" were interspersed with regular issues which were more eclectic. In his new position, Bob had the opportunity to hire Robert Benchley as the magazine's drama critic and Dorothy Parker as a freelance poet. At first he himself wrote tongue-in-cheek pieces, as he had at *Vanity Fair*, but in January of the next year he was made the magazine's film reviewer. He thus became one of the first film critics in the country, and within a short time he was acknowledged as the first to take film seriously. *Photoplay, Movie Weekly*, and *McCall's* all published his syndicated columns, and from 1922 to 1924 he also served as film editor for the *New York Herald Tribune*. It was there that columnist Richard Watts poked fun at him for his unenthusiastic review of the now classic Russian film *The Battleship Potemkin*. Watts referred to Bob as "the dean of motion picture criticism," to which he added, "and . . . like most deans, [he] was suffering from hardening of the critical arteries."[24] Although this was written in jest, later authors turned the "dean" label into a compliment. For Bob, viewing a multitude of films each week from 1921 through 1928 was both entertaining and necessary. There was nothing like sitting in a dark movie theater watching other people's problems and foibles unfold to help him repress unpleasant memories.

In 1923 Bob claimed that he saw every film that was released, "about two hundred feature films a year, and a great many shorter pictures, such as comedies, scenics, educational films and news weeklies . . . something like twenty-five hundred reels, which," he figured "when resolved into terms of linear measure, amounts to two million, five hundred thousand feet, or over four hundred miles."[25] This was probably true when he began writing the column, but as the number of films produced increased, he most likely was not able to view them all. On average, during his tenure at *Life*, he screened from four to eight films a week, which added up to anywhere from four to twelve hours in a darkened theater. He also continuously wrote humorous fictional pieces, short essays and anecdotes, a few poems, and even a couple of book reviews. Very quickly Martin promoted Bob to associate editor and then, in 1924, to editor as he cut back on his own responsibilities. In 1926 Bob took advantage of his position to persuade his older brother Arthur to return from Oregon, where he had relocated, to join him at *Life*. Arthur held an editorial position through 1928, leaving the magazine when his brother did.

At the time Bob became a film critic, the world of silent film was blossoming.[26] The motion picture made its official debut on April 14, 1894, when Thomas A. Edison introduced his crank-operated peephole kinetoscope to the public. Two years later, Louis and Auguste Lumière, two French brothers, improved upon the kinetoscope by inventing a projection device. Edison quickly adapted that technology into the vitascope, and on April 13, 1896, just nine days after Bob was born, the inventor began to project motion pictures for paying audiences. From its inception, people loved film. In 1905, when John P. Harris and Harry Davis opened their ninety-two-seat Nickelodeon theater, audiences happily handed over their five cents admission fee to see *The Great Train Robbery*, originally filmed in 1903 as a ten-minute single-reel film consisting of fourteen scenes. Within four years there were eight thousand nickelodeons in the United States. By the time D. W. Griffith produced his smash hit *The Birth of a Nation* in 1915, movies had won a permanent place in American culture. Although it was highly controversial and faced censorship, the film earned $18 million by 1929. The same year it premiered, Carl Laemmle moved his Universal Film Manufacturing Company, a group of independent producers, from midtown Manhattan to Los Angeles, to establish Universal City. It joined the American Studio in Santa Barbara and Vitagraph, also in Los Angeles.

Bob's weekly column, which first appeared on January 27, 1921, was titled "The Silent Drama." In each segment he reviewed three or four films—every so often dedicating the entire space to one special work. He followed each column with a synopsis of new and previously reviewed films in a "Recent Developments" listing. In general, the reviews echoed *Life*'s mocking tone unless the films concerned issues of war or social justice. In those cases, even if he employed humor, Bob's message was deadly serious. The first entry, titled "The Tenth Muse," introduced the young critic's view of this burgeoning art form. Film, he said, was the "tenth art . . . allied to other arts in various degrees and greater in its appeal than all of them." [27] Bob immediately saw film, with its moving and realistic visuals, as having the potential for global outreach. Since people could easily understand the action, the most important purpose for the "subtitles" to serve was to explain gaps in time in the story being told. For Bob, the people most indispensable to producing a film were the director (his favorite being Rex Ingram) and the cameraman (his favorite being Karl Brown). The actors, such as Jackie Coogan, Douglas Fairbanks, and Mary Pickford (with whom he was infatuated), were important, but to him, the star system was a gross exaggeration of actors' talents.

"I like the movies," Bob confessed to his readers in November 1922. "I should go to the movies even if I were not paid to do so." But he had a hierarchy of favorites. He admitted to liking comedies the best, especially if they featured Charlie Chaplin, in his opinion "the greatest genius that the cinema has developed—possibly the only real genius." Harold Lloyd and Buster Keaton, he felt, were "not far behind" Chaplin but could never reach him. At the other extreme, he hated what he called "society dramas," especially Cecil B. DeMille's big, lavish productions, and also "mother-love dramas," which he found maudlin and patronizing.[28] What most annoyed him was the low common denominator of the storylines, for which he blamed the movie companies' placing profit above art. What the film industry needed, he felt, was a system like that of the Theatre Guild, which valued quality over quantity.

According to Bob, even by 1928 there were "few mental giants in Hollywood."[29] Therefore, early on, part of the role he laid out for himself was to educate the public about good movies—those that had realism, beauty, and "vivid drama."[30] In an effort to enlighten viewers, he tried to cover a variety of high-quality films, including documentaries such as *Nanook of the North* (1922), the classic story of Eskimo life, and *Down to the Sea in Ships* (1923), about New Bedford, Massachusetts, whale hunters. For Bob, the film's scene of whale hunting was "one of the most realistically thrilling episodes" he had ever witnessed on the screen.[31] Portraying the world as it really existed rather than as pure fantasy was of great importance to Bob. He had first expressed this belief in February 1920, when his satirical article "The Higher Education on the Screen" appeared in *Vanity Fair*. The premise of the piece was that movies were rapidly replacing schools as the place where children became educated. "In fact," wrote Bob, "the day is actually at hand when the silver screen will supplant the blackboard." The article went on to describe what children would actually learn from the screen. For example, without ever opening a Rand-McNally atlas, they would learn important facts such as "A forest is something which catches fire in Reel 4" or "The Grand Canyon is that ditch which Douglas Fairbanks jumps across." Silent film subtitles would "provide ample reading matter for the young," and classic literature would only need to be presented in condensed form.[32]

But when it came to war, Bob always put satire aside. His anger over the politics of the war which had caused him and others such great suffering was not open to jokes or hokum. He was adamant that the war—in fact, all war—must not be romanticized in film. Although he was not among the most outspoken antiwar voices at this time, he did not hesitate to express his opinions when he felt that others were acting irresponsibly. "The Higher Education on the Screen" is highly revealing of Bob's concern for future generations' perception of the war he had experienced. World War I, he noted, was "the first great historical event to be chronicled by means of the motion picture camera"; indeed, miles of documentary footage still exist to illustrate what the war was like. What fictionalized motion pictures showed, however, was something very different from reality. Their stories generally featured a mythical soldier who "(1) captured a village, practically single-handed, just in time to save an exquisite French girl from an unspeakable fate. (2) lay wounded in the heart of No-Man's-Land until rescued by the Red Cross dog.

(3) received the Légion d'Honneur and a kiss from Marshall Foch . . . [and] (4) returned home to find that he had been given up for lost by everyone except *her*—who had never wavered for so much as an instant."[33] The war which had touched his soul so deeply had been reduced to the lowest form of cheap entertainment.

Bob's annoyance with filmmakers' interpretations of war continued to provide fodder for his columns in *Life*. On March 24, 1921, for example, he reviewed Rex Ingram's movie *The Four Horsemen of the Apocalypse,* which starred newcomer Rudolph Valentino. Representing World War I accurately was essential, Bob said, because within a hundred years there would no longer be any survivors who could relate their stories firsthand. "It is quite important, therefore," he wrote, "that we get the record straight, and make sure that nothing goes down to posterity which will mislead future generations into believing that this age of ours was anything to brag about." He recommended that viewers refer to the writings of Philip Gibbs, Henri Barbusse, Rupert Brooke, Alan Seeger, and John MacRae to hear the true voices of the participants in the war. "And if," he continued, speaking of someone living in the future, "after reading these, he is still doubtful of the fact that war is essentially a false, hideous mistake," then he should view *The Four Horsemen of the Apocalypse.* Bob doubted that the film would be a big hit in the United States because of the rampant patriotism and anti-radical sentiment of the 1920s, but he thought that the French, who had suffered so horribly during the war, would embrace it with heartfelt enthusiasm. He considered the film one that deserved "more than any other picture play that the war inspired—to be handed down to generations yet unborn, that they may see the horror and the futility of the whole bloody mess."[34]

Another film he admired was *J'Accuse,* which he reviewed in June 1921. A love story about an elderly man, a young wife, and a pacifist poet caught in the throes of World War I, the film ended with the German-captured wife returning home from a prisoner of war camp with a baby, and the poet dying of dementia caused by shellshock. Bob praised the filmmaker Abel Gance for omitting Germans per se because the film was really an "accusation of war" and not of any particular group of people. "As such," he noted, "it will be of great interest to everyone who has paid any attention to the lessons of the last seven years."[35]

Bob could make an exception for Charlie Chaplin's light touch in *Shoulder Arms* (1918), "the greatest comedy in movie history," because Chaplin showed the humor of life in the dugouts in contrast to the "unutterably tragic" scene of "the delivery of the mail in the front line when everybody gets a letter but Charlie."[36] He also could acknowledge that *What Price Glory?,* the 1926 film version of the stage play by Maxwell Anderson and Laurence Stallings, had "some tremendously effective war scenes." Director Raoul Walsh was not afraid "to picture the unmitigated brutality" of war.[37] But pervading every scene and every performance in the 1925 film *The New Commandment*, yet another story of romance between a U.S. soldier and a Frenchwoman, was "the pungent and mildly offensive odor of ham."[38] He also could not excuse Chaplin's comedic competitor Buster Keaton's depiction of men being killed in battle in his 1927 film *The General*. He found some of the scenes not just humorless but in "such gruesomely bad taste that the sympathetic spectator is inclined to look the other way."[39] That same year *Lost at the Front* was so bad that it could only draw this comment from its reviewer: "Nearly nine years have passed since the Armistice was signed, but we are still suffering from the horrors of the war in the form of this comedy."[40]

For Bob, the most authentic depiction of the battlefront appeared in the 1925 film *The Big Parade*, with a book by Laurence Stallings, directed by King Vidor, and starring John Gilbert and Renée Adoree, all of whom he admired greatly. Bob could not detect a single flaw, "not one error of taste or of authenticity," even though he watched carefully for defects. He credited Vidor with creating such realistic war scenes that he could personally identify with them. "When [Vidor] advances a raw company of infantry through a forest which is raked by machine gun fire," Bob wrote in an unusual reflection on his own experiences, "he makes his soldiers look scared, sick at their stomachs, with no heart for the ghastly business that is ahead." More important, Vidor created an atmosphere in which those who had not witnessed the bloodbath of World War I could wonder, "Why in God's name did they have to do that?"—a question Bob obviously kept asking himself even seven years after he had been on the front lines. Vidor's army was almost too "recognizable and real," especially the portrait of a particular U.S. soldier who was suddenly seized with the desire to kill and who kept trying to jab his bayonet into the neck of a dying German sniper. Vidor filmed a close-up of the actor's face showing the character's utter revulsion at this heinous act he was committing. "I doubt that there is a single irregular soldier, volunteer or conscripted," Bob recalled, "who did not experience that awful feeling during his career in France—who did not recognize the impulse to withdraw the bayonet and offer the dying Heine a cigarette."[41] *The Big Parade* was a model war film for Bob, a film which recognized that there was "no place for heroic hokum in pictures of a conflict that was, above all things, depressingly real."[42]

Bob's concern about war went beyond the depictions of battle scenes or of life in the trenches, but these other issues inspired a more cynical tone. Overblown jingoism irked him no end. D. W. Griffith's 1924 *America*, a depiction of the War of Independence, for example, gave the viewer "an exalted thrill of patriotism." But unfortunately, according to Bob, Griffith's high-flown love of country made people "forget" such modern problems as "political corruption . . . and the violence of the Ku Klux Klan." The main problem with Griffith's perspective on the American Revolution was that he painted the British as committing gross atrocities and playing dirty tricks on the colonists, thereby carrying on the "ancient tradition" which dictated "that a man really can't love his own country without hating every other nation on earth."[43] Another example of misrepresenting history in the name of patriotism was director Victor Fleming's 1927 heroic biographical film *The Rough Riders*. Bob complained that in the interests of flag waving, the filmmaker exaggerated the U.S. military's performance in the "regrettably unheroic" Spanish-American War of 1898, in which the United States had so clearly overpowered the militarily "weak" Spain as to appear bullying.[44]

As far as Bob and many others at the time were concerned, capitalist greed had led to World War I, as industrialists exploited the public's patriotism to convince them that going to war was a good idea. When in May 1924 he reviewed a documentary titled *The World Struggle for Oil*, Bob forcefully attacked the use of the cinema as propaganda for large corporations. This particular venture was produced jointly by the Sinclair Oil Company and the U.S. Department of the Interior, the "same team," he asserted, "which sponsored the famous Teapot Dome scandal" the previous winter. In that debacle, Secretary of the Interior Albert Fall was fined $100,000 and given a one-year prison sentence for accepting bribes from private oil companies to lease them oil-rich government property. Bob accused the filmmakers of hiding behind a supposedly simple history of the oil business to achieve their deceitful ends. "But when the inspired authors start to prospect in the future," he angrily pointed out, "they drag in their star player, Propaganda," the result being that "one hears in the faint distance the Call to Arms, the menacing tread of marching ultimatums, the shouts of 'Give Till It Hurts' and the irresistible strains of 'Over There.'" The selling point came in the form of a question to the audience: "Under which flag will [oil products] be developed and made profitable?" Here, as the camera panned over "a stirring view of our grand old Navy going into action," Bob's postwar cynicism cut to the quick: "Well, if there must be another war, we might as well face the crisis now. But can't we find any one besides Harry Sinclair to fight for?"[45]

Bob's comments reflected his familiarity with postwar efforts to achieve world peace, which were well publicized and easily understood by the general public. Most were based on the belief that the United States, which had achieved world power status during the war, had a responsibility to be a leader in efforts for international cooperation but at the same time needed to protect itself from being dragged into another nation's battles. Far from being isolationist, the president and Congress took a stance of independent decision making and action within the global community, following the path that seemed best for U.S. trade and economic growth. For example, although Congress never ratified the Versailles Treaty ending the war, and hence the United States never became an official member of the League of Nations, it still participated in most League meetings, committees, and conferences and consulted with other nations on major world crises. The government also fostered several international agreements, including the Five Power and Nine Power naval treaties, which limited the development of battleships, and the 1928 Kellogg-Briand Pact, in which sixty-two nations agreed to attempt negotiations before declaring war.

In reaction to World War I, peace activism was at an all-time high in the 1920s. Hundreds of organizations were formed. Some supported any and all treaties and efforts the U.S. government proposed. Others lobbied for legislation on both the domestic and international levels which would literally make war illegal by prohibiting the manufacture and sale of weapons, much as Prohibition was doing with alcohol. Pacifist groups claimed that all war was immoral and that people should simply refuse to have anything to do with it. Bob's articles addressed the programs of a multitude of peace groups, such as the World Peace Association, the National Council for Prevention of War, the Fellowship of Reconciliation, and the Women's International League for Peace and Freedom. In 1924 *Life* ran a "War Prize Contest" that poked fun at the Bok Peace Prize competition, which itself displayed little imagination. In 1923 Edward Bok, a Philadelphia publisher, offered $100,000 to the person who developed "the best practicable plan by which the United States may cooperate with other nations to achieve and preserve the peace of the world."[46] Over 22,000 entries were received, but the successful proposal was disappointing to most peace activists. The winner, Charles H. Levermore, favored the familiar official efforts of the time: U.S. entry into the World Court, cooperation but not full membership in the League of Nations, and adherence to the Monroe Doctrine, which dictated U.S. hegemony in the Americas.

The theme of *Life*'s contest was "We Want Bigger and Better Wars." First prize, $250, went to the suggestion "Don't let peace become too interesting. Keep it on the usual humdrum level." This approach was sure to bring on another war. Second prize of $125 went to the idea that the next U.S. war be aimed at Japan and should begin with rumors started in California that six little orphan girls had been found in the woods with their throats cut or six little orphan boys discovered with their ears cut off, a direct reference to the baseless reports of German abuses in Belgium during the Great War. In addition, this contestant suggested that if George M. Cohan wrote a racist song called "Let's slap the Jap off the map," war would instantly break out. Third prize went to a man who proposed the familiar World War I domino effect: "Let a demented peasant in the Balkans assassinate an obscure Austrian archduke in a bizarre city with an improbable name," etc. Then "the United States although at first too proud to fight will soon find war becoming so popular a pastime that she will be compelled to come in to save her own share of democracy." [47] In the following number the editors issued a special award to the U.S. Congress "in recognition of their services for the promotion of Bigger and Better Wars." [48] In the same vein, the magazine held a "Question Contest" in which readers sent in the answers to a specific question and the editors chose the best one. In February 1925 the question was, "What is the worst law in the United States?" The winner: "Congress shall have the power to declare war." [49] In March the question was, "Shall we Cancel the French War Debt?" The winner submitted this reply: "Exact it, not because it is France's debt, but because it is a salutary thing to make war unpopular. War costs blood and tears and money, and the payment of money is the part which irks men most." [50]

Besides using *Life* to criticize war and its causes, Bob utilized his columns to educate people about the connection between war and social justice, often forgoing the humorous tone expected in his pieces. In all this he clearly echoed the times in which he was living. In the 1920s, world peace was just one of the urgent issues activists were addressing. There were also considerable efforts being made by women who wanted to exercise their newly won vote to create a more equal society. They lobbied in Washington, D.C., for a variety of reforms, including child labor laws, birth control, prenatal and children's health services, and the still elusive Equal Rights Amendment. African American and white leaders lobbied for anti-lynching measures and racial equality, especially in the South and Midwest, where the Ku Klux Klan launched a new, more lethal offensive against any group it despised—whether blacks, Jews, Italians, Mexicans, Asians, or political radicals. Bob's barbs would have resonated with the many *Life* readers who wanted to see the nation live up to its claims that World War I had been a struggle for true global democracy.

Racism was a very serious issue for Robert Sherwood. Although he continued to admire the work of Buster Keaton, there were times when Keaton's choice of topics bothered him. This was true of *The General*'s depiction of battle scenes. It was also true of Keaton's 1925 film *Seven Chances*. Although he found it full of funny segments, the film made what Bob considered "one bad mistake." He told his readers, "You have viewed many scenes wherein a young [white] man starts out after a shapely young woman, with flirtatious intent, only to find, on catching up with her, that she is 100% African in complexion." Bob had seen the gag many times in the theater and films, but he considered it "an illegitimate one." Because of this and other racial carica- tures, the film reeked of dishonest laughter "tinctured with a certain amount of shame on the part of the audience."[51] He was less upset, however, when Jews were portrayed in *Ben-Hur* (1926) and *King of Kings* (1927) as screaming mobs calling for Jesus to be crucified. When Jewish organizations protested such depictions of their people, Bob complained that to remove the "mob element" would be "to misrepresent history" and "to rob this story of its eternal significance."[52] For whatever reason, in the 1920s he could not make the leap from recognizing racism toward African Americans to recognizing racism toward Jews.

Another issue that irked Bob a great deal was the question of censorship, and he took every opportunity to comment on the undemocratic nature of the practice. Ever since the Puritans landed in Massachusetts in the seven- teenth century, censorship has been no stranger to American culture. Yet to his great dismay, it had become stronger than ever in the late nineteenth century and the early decades of the twentieth century. Some Progressive Era reformers felt that part of their mission was to restore the nation's morality. For them, there was too much partying, drinking, and sex. Many people agreed with them—hence the successful passage of the prohibition amend- ment, the establishment of local vice commissions, and the formation of cen- sorship advisory boards to control the theater and, ultimately, film. Battle lines were drawn over the basic issues of free speech and artistic expression. Before Bob came on the scene as an anti-censorship voice, several cases had been fought before various state boards.[53] The most publicized one involved D. W. Griffith's 1915 film *The Birth of a Nation,* which was censored in Ohio because of its racist depictions of African Americans and interracial relation- ships, its pro–Ku Klux Klan stance, and its endorsement of slavery. The National Association for the Advancement of Colored People (NAACP), an interracial organization founded in 1910, led the campaign, which resulted in the banning of the film in eight states, including Ohio. The case, *Mutual Film Corporation v. Ohio Industrial Commission*, reached the Supreme Court, whose decision became the basis for film censorship into the 1950s. Basically, the Court upheld censorship on the grounds that while movies were profit- making business ventures, they also had the capability of fostering evil intent because of the power of their presentations. As a result of the ruling, state censorship persisted, and internal censorship grew as well, with studio heads cutting scripts and filmed sequences that they felt might cause the film to be banned once it was released, resulting in a loss of profits.

By 1921 the industry was drowning in a sea of state, local, and internal censorship rules. With pressure mounting on Congress to pass federal censorship laws, industry leaders decided to take action first. On January 11, 1922, a group of film company producers and distributors announced that Will Hays, postmaster general under President Warren Harding, was leaving Washington in order to lead the so-called clean up of Hollywood. The Motion Picture Producers and Distributors of America (MPPDA) became Hays's vehicle for censoring films. Industry leaders accepted his guidelines, which forced changes in any films that:

1. dealt with sex in an improper manner
2. were based on white slavery
3. made vice attractive
4. exhibited nakedness
5. had prolonged passionate love scenes
6. were predominantly concerned with the underworld
7. made gambling and drunkenness attractive
8. might instruct the weak in methods of committing crime
9. ridiculed public officials
10. offended religious beliefs
11. emphasized violence
12. portrayed vulgar postures and gestures
13. used salacious subtitles or advertising[54]

Robert Sherwood could not tolerate censorship in any form, even if he abhorred certain film content. For him it was a question of democracy and human rights, as well as artistic expression. Censorship gave power to a small group of people, allowing them to cut off access to knowledge, culture, and entertainment to the many. Within a few months of starting to write the "Silent Drama" column, Bob took a shot at the censors. He did this in a humorous way through a poem he included in his series, titled "The Cinema Primer," a riff on various staples of the film industry, including "The Villain," "The Vampire," "The Scenario Writer," "The Badman," "The Ingenue," "The Press Agent," "The Fans," and so on. In August 1921 he took on "The Censors":

> Ob-serve this Group of right-eous Fos-sils,
> The Self-Anoin-ted Twelve A-pos-tles,
> Who tell the Com-mon Peo-ple what

Is good for them, and what is Not.
They care-ful-ly pro-hib-it Views
Of Po-ker Chips and Ba-by Shoes-
Be-cause these Sights cor-rupt, for-sooth,
The Mor-als of our ten-der Youth.
I am not one to Preach or Prate
But should I ven-ture to re-late
How I re-gard these Gloom Dis-pen-sers,
I'd be . . . (De-le-ted by the Censors).[55]

Bob protested the industry's collusion with Will Hays to "make the movies clean from a morality standpoint." He declared belligerently, "We don't need censors to cleanse the movies. Most pictures are too blatantly wholesome as it is." Censorship made films dull, uniform, and just plain "stupid." What the viewers needed were leaders who would "promote the standard of intelligence on the screen," which Hays seemed to him eminently unqualified to do.[56] Hays's naiveté was clearly illustrated in Bob's report of the censor's visit to Europe in November 1923. After his return to Hollywood, Hays declared that the ultimate benefit of films was that they were "destined to promote greater understanding among the nations, and thereby prevent war." Bob's rage over this perceived idiocy was palpable. Since 90 percent of the world's films were made in the United States, Hays's statement meant that the United States, and Hollywood in particular, would act "as the clearing house for all the understanding." And if Hollywood "were destined to be the hope of the world," what an unreal world that would be![57] To date, Bob claimed, Hollywood's images had been less than truthful or peace seeking. Evil versus good, poor versus rich, crowded cities versus the wide open spaces: these were just a few of the divisive notions perpetrated by films. Everything was black and white with no gray areas. Then, of course, there were all the examples of false information about war (and World War I specifically) which Bob had exposed in previous articles, the racism evident in the industry, the inequalities perpetuated in portraying groups of people. How could Hollywood possibly serve as a conduit for understanding the complexities of the world?

In another example, in 1927 Bob was personally frustrated by the government's censorship of prizefighting films on the grounds that the sport encouraged gambling, depicted partial nudity, and emphasized violence. The censorship came about under the interstate commerce ruling forbidding the transport of prizefight films across state lines. In the particular instance that got Bob's hackles up, it was the Tunney-Dempsey fight that was censored. Jack Dempsey, one of the most popular prizefighters of all time, had contracted to box Gene Tunney, one of his most persistent opponents. The fight took place before a crowd of 104,943 people in Chicago's Soldier Field and brought in over $2.5 million. In an infamous moment in boxing history, Dempsey knocked Tunney down, and the referee, rather than picking up the count from the timekeeper, started from scratch, allowing Tunney an extra four counts to recover. This extended count became highly controversial, especially since Tunney was declared the victor in the final decision. The public wanted to see for themselves what had happened. Bob could not understand why such a history-making event was not to be made available to fans across the country. He complained that the government was acting "in its infinite stupidity" in banning the film. "Motion pictures of two millionaires socking each other are," noted Bob, "presumably, calculated to corrupt public morals and put impure thoughts in the minds of fourteen-year-old adults." Why, he wanted to know, were radio broadcasts, newspapers, and violent films not similarly controlled? Leaving people outside the fight's location unable to view it seemed "a singularly outrageous and unwarranted piece of official interference with personal liberties." Bob could see "no conceivable reason" for the ruling, especially since huge numbers of people were interested in viewing—not just listening to or reading about—the match.[58] Bob himself got to see the fight on film in Michigan, though he claimed to have no idea how the theaters there or in any other place got hold of it.

The question of censorship also led Bob to comment on political campaigns. In 1924 he decided to take on the issues of inside favors and the corruption of electioneering. He charged the censor with stifling documentary footage showing the ugly battles between political opponents, making for a boring campaign and an uninformed and apathetic electorate. Perhaps humor could add interest and spice to that year's presidential race. Bob began his own campaign early in the year through his mythical "Skeptics' Society." He insisted that the society would select its candidates by itself, without following the traditional Democratic and Republican conventions. The candidates would be chosen "irrespective of race, creed, color or previous political affiliations" and would be required to answer questions about their friends and relatives in government, their stand on Prohibition, and their attitude toward "Premier Mussolini . . . the Ku Klux Klan . . . and Will Hays."[59] Bob insisted that the voters should take the opportunity "to select a new administration to govern . . . and to misappropriate their funds." Let the people elect a president who would select men like corrupt oil barons Edward L. Doheny and Harry F. Sinclair to join his cabinet. "Let us send them into the Capitol through the front door, instead of forcing them to sneak in through the rear entrance as they have done in the past," he urged. This way the government would cut out the middle man, and there would be "closer co-operation between the producer and the consumer. . . . If we must be gypped, let us be gypped in a straight-forward and workmanlike manner."[60] This would bring about real honesty in government.

Even more entertaining was Bob's idea to run the humorist, vaudeville performer, and much-loved personality Will Rogers for president during the 1928 campaign, an election that was eventually won by Herbert Hoover. Rogers had begun writing sporadically for *Life* in 1922, and over the years he and Bob became friendly. Hence, when Bob and Fred Cooper, one of the magazine's illustrators, came up with the plan to run Rogers as a commentary on the state of election campaigns, the humorist agreed. In the May 24 issue the main editorial, scripted by Bob and titled "For President: Will Rogers," the humorist announced his intention "to fight Bunk in all its forms" through his Anti-Bunk Party.[61] For $500 a week (an amount Bob later recalled was "a lot of money for *Life* but peanuts to Will"), Rogers agreed to write several hundred words proclaiming his platform and offering mock campaign speeches. In addition, the magazine distributed thousands of campaign buttons displaying Rogers's face and the slogan "He Chews to Run," a pun on Calvin Coolidge's recent statement that he did not choose to run for reelection and his cigar smoking and occasional use of chewing tobacco. One of the local radio stations gave the campaign airtime for weekly broadcasts, and Bob succeeded in getting stars such as Eddie Cantor, Leon Errol, Robert Benchley, and Amelia Earhart to participate in the "fun," although Rogers himself never appeared on the program, largely because of his other commitments.[62]

A number of articles appeared under Will Rogers's name, such as "I Accept the Nomination" and "Prohibition and Farm Relief," which demanded "WINE FOR THE RICH, BEER FOR THE POOR, AND MOONSHINE LIQUOR FOR THE PROHIBITIONISTS."[63] As Bob later recalled, however, Rogers never took much interest in the campaign and was often slow, hesitant, or late in handing in copy. Often what he did write was "very sketchy" and not even sufficient to fill the space, so Bob finished the pieces, imitating Rogers's style as best he could. As a result, the humorist decided that he need not write much at all. In fact, Bob recalled, "I think there were one or two weeks when he did supply nothing and I had to write the whole piece."[64] Rogers liked both Bob and his humor so much that he asked the young editor to write some material for his shows, which he did for weeks for no pay. In the end, *Life* announced that Rogers had won the "Silent Vote" and would keep his campaign promise that if elected, he would resign.[65] Bob recalled being told that there was a large write-in vote for Rogers all over the country, but it was impossible for *Life* to check the figures.

Very early in his career at *Life*, it occurred to Bob that he might have a future in films himself, but to achieve that goal, he needed to go to Hollywood to make personal contact with industry professionals. In early 1922, on the excuse of bringing the place to life for his readers, he arranged for himself, Robert Benchley, Marc Connelly, and *Life* writer Ralph Barton to make "a pilgrimage to Hollywood."[66] They left New York on February 16 aboard the *S.S. Ruth Alexander*, sailing to California via Cuba and the Panama Canal on a trip that took over a month. After several days in the movie capital, Bob admitted to his readers that he had nothing of great interest to tell them because all he had seen were cafeterias. After a couple of weeks he declared that Hollywood was "vastly overrated." Contrary to what his readers might expect, he had "attended no orgies . . . seen no murders . . . been offered no cocaine, hasheesh or bhang." To him, Hollywood looked just like "a quiet college town," with the studios resembling university buildings, "picture people" playing the role of students, and stores catering to a single clientele. Overall, the people labored hard on the job and then relaxed and did not seem "to take themselves or their work very seriously."[67]

While in Tinseltown, Bob met some of his favorite personalities. Seven-year-old Jackie Coogan entertained him at his home, reciting poetry, telling riddles, and doing impersonations. Bob was enthralled by how bright and "unspoiled" his favorite child actor was. Harold Lloyd took him on location and was "as comic" as he appeared on film. Douglas Fairbanks struck up a friendship with him, showed him the sets for his new Robin Hood film, and then "gave a remarkable exhibition of archery." He also persuaded Bob to sit on a "trick sofa" which was electrically wired, giving the young columnist "a terrific shock" and a "hearty laugh."[68] Thomas H. Ince took him on a tour of his studio in Culver City, where Bob was given the opportunity to try operating a camera, and Rex Ingram, Bob's ideal director, met with him and, like Fairbanks, became a friendly acquaintance. While at Ince's studio, Bob made his own short film, *Through Darkest Hollywood with Gun and Camera*, which he sometimes used when requested to present a lecture. Bob left Hollywood with a romanticized notion that there was "little personal vanity among the actors and actresses and little jealousy."[69]

Before going to work at *Life* and becoming so deeply involved in the world of film, Bob had envisioned himself becoming a playwright. But in 1922, after drafting *The Dawn Man*, which he considered an extremely poor play, he changed his dream to that of becoming a film writer, a path which seemed less challenging and far more lucrative. While at *Life*, he was successful in making a few inroads in that direction, but they were not the breakthroughs he had hoped for. In 1924 he was asked to rewrite the subtitles for *The Hunchback of Notre Dame* for $2,500, one-fourth his annual salary at *Life*. In 1926 *Oh, What a Nurse*, a seven-reel Warner Brothers product, credited as a source the short story of the same name by Bob and a colleague at *Life*, Bertram Bloch. The film adaptation, however, was done by a young screenwriter, Darryl Francis Zanuck. The plot revolved around a cub reporter who uses all sorts of techniques to save the woman he loves from a forced marriage in order to marry her himself. In his column Bob stated that, in spite of the difficulty of remaining impartial in reviewing the film, he would still have to say that it was "pretty funny."[70] *The Lucky Lady*, also produced in 1926, a six-reel Famous Players–Lasky production distributed by Paramount Pictures, had a similar plot, involving a young woman in a mythical European monarchy who is supposed to marry one man but through inventive plot twists is able to marry the man she loves.[71] Bloch was credited with the story and Bob and James T. O'Donohoe with the scenario. Although neither of these early films became wildly popular, they did launch Bob in the film industry, where over the years he would do much work, some of it relatively obscure and some of it greatly respected.

Bob lived and breathed film for most of the period from early 1921 to the end of 1928. Even in the summer, the "torrid season" for watching movies in hot theaters before the days of air conditioning, he still sat through every film he could squeeze into his schedule. In 1923 he complained that feature films were becoming so long that there was "scarcely any room left on the average program for spice and snap," and yet he kept going. Even when he found the subjects "dull, hackneyed and stupid to start with," he kept at it.[72] He poked fun at the art form, using his column to create a long-running gag about his own mythical "Great American Movie," whose plot twists mimicked the most melodramatic aspects of the films being produced at the time. Over the years he continued to build on his "movie" until, by June 1925, it reached a length of 380 reels. When he closed out his column on December 28, 1928, the "Great American Movie" was an astonishing two thousand reels long, but, he told his readers, it could never be shown because it was silent, and by now talkies had become all the rage.

Indeed, the advent of "talking pictures" was something Bob found fascinating and most promising. He tried to keep his readers up to date on the developments in the technology of creating sound on film. In 1924 he personally witnessed the results of Lee DeForest's 1920 invention, Phonofilm, which brought the synchronization of voice and picture into "near perfect form," at least to Bob's ears, by adding a synchronized optical soundtrack to film. "The voice follows the action on the screen exactly, giving an effect that is startling, uncanny and just the least bit terrifying," he reported. Yet the effect was far from convincing, because Phonofilm was so unsuccessful in reproducing the quality of the human voice that the actor sounded "rasping, harsh, excessively loud," and atonal.[73] Two years later he was introduced to Warner Brothers' Vitaphone system, which used a device invented by Rube Goldberg which consisted of a record player turntable connected to a film projector. The sound was recorded on a vinyl disk like those used for recording music. The demonstration that Bob viewed included speeches, songs, and instrumental numbers which synchronized both "shadow and sound," but still the effect was not perfect.[74] Inventors were moving so quickly, though, that Bob took a "private guess" that by 1936, all films would be in color and "be accompanied by conversation."[75] When Vitaphone made possible the 1927 film *The Jazz Singer*, Bob "suddenly realized that the end of the silent drama is in sight."[76] He would "shed no tears" over the "passing of the noiseless films," for he felt that their time had come and gone.[77] In fact, in his renamed column, "The Movies," he announced that he himself intended to add "a big talking sequence, with movietone attachment," to his "Great American Movie," a scene in which two Indians carried on a lengthy conversation in sign language.[78]

One day in 1925 Bob received a letter from one of his loyal "Silent Drama" readers who especially appreciated the "Recent Developments" listings because they summarized the longer reviews the reader could not always remember. Bob responded in a self-mocking tone, "This statement is none too welcome to one who likes to feel that he is achieving immortality through the words that he sets down on paper."[79] Indeed, Bob often gave an unadulterated critique of the role of the critic, laments that showed how badly the young writer wanted to create his own film scripts, dramas, or novels rather than remain in the role of "a parasitic creature who gains sustenance from the life blood of his more creative fellows." As early as 1923 he stated, "Show me a critic and I, in my turn, will show you a man who is constantly persuading himself that some day he is going to write something worth while." Bob further commented that if he knew more about the teachings of the eminent psychoanalyst Sigmund Freud, he would venture to say that the critic suffers from a complex, "and that his criticism of others provides him with an elm-lined avenue of escape. He derives an unholy delight from the spectacle of someone else failing to do the thing at which he himself has failed."[80]

Bob's career at *Life* concluded at the end of 1928, leaving him free to become a writer who, in turn, would become the victim of critics like himself.

In January 1929 he was replaced as film critic by Harry Evans and as editor by Norman Anthony. According to Bob, he was fired from the magazine largely as a result of the political barbs he had penned throughout the "Will Rogers for President" campaign. This may have been an exaggeration. The magazine itself had gone through various changes over the eight years he was there. Since April 1925, E. S. Martin had drifted into the background while Bob, Benchley, and other younger writers played larger roles. But in May 1928, in an effort to garner more readers, the magazine underwent a facelift and shifted its emphasis to covering world events, politics, and culture without the sharp satirical edge Bob had fostered. Martin retired the next month, and Elmer Davis, a former reporter on the *New York Times* and the *New York Herald Tribune,* took his place. Most of those who worked with Bob were also let go. In 1936 the publication was sold to Time Inc. and became the *Life* magazine familiar to later readers. Bob may have lost his $10,000-a-year job, but he was feeling neither depressed nor hopeless. As he wrote to his friend Sidney Howard: "I can't tell you what a feeling of relief I've been enjoying lately. The luxury of freedom is one that I haven't known or even suspected for several years." He knew that he should look for work, especially since he now had a wife and child to support, but he loved his "vacation from routine."[81]

Over the years at *Life,* Bob had made several attempts to do some writing on his own besides the stories and subtitles for *The Hunchback of Notre Dame, Oh, What a Nurse,* and *The Lucky Lady* and an edition of his reprinted reviews, *The Best Moving Pictures of 1922–23,* the first of a proposed series which never resulted in more than the one volume. His family firmly supported any effort he made, and in later years Bob noted that his sister Cynthia had been "particularly kind" to him when he was "struggling" to get started as a writer.[82] Although he confessed in 1926 that fiction, especially short fiction, was "a medium in which I am extremely ill at ease because of utter unfamiliarity with the technique, whatever it is," and that plot ideas simply would not come to him, his first two efforts at the genre were quite successful.[83] His story "The Moon of Matanzas" caused one editor to judge on the basis of Bob's "tricks . . . natural feeling for dramatic romance and a first class style," that he had a promising career ahead of him.[84]

A second story, "Extra! Extra!" published in *Scribner's Magazine* that same year, not only was a success at the time he wrote it in 1926 but also became a classic example of a well-written short story.[85] The plot was simple. A married couple, Mr. and Mrs. Whidden, hear a newspaper boy shouting, "Extra! Extra!" outside their apartment building. Mrs. Whidden, tending to their son, wants the paper; Mr. Whidden, tired from his day's work at a job he dislikes, does not want to make the trip downstairs to get it. After a tense back-and-forth, Mr. Whidden goes down to buy the paper and never returns. The story then flashes forward to a day twelve years later when Conrad, the Whiddens' son, is sent outside to play by his mother, now Mrs. Burchall, who complains that he reads too much. While he is playing, his long-lost father shows up and chats with his former wife. It seems that he has become a sailor and written a book (indeed, the same book their son is now reading). His former wife asks what that "Extra" was about twelve years ago, the headline she had so wanted to read about. Oh, he responds, it was the news that the Red Sox had won the World Series (a joke on the part of the author, who was a diehard Yankees fan). The story was selected to appear in *The Best Short Stories of 1926*, received the O. Henry Memorial Award, and was republished in the *Golden Book* in 1930. In 1950 it was reprinted in *Ellery Queen's Magazine*, after which Bob received requests for the Danish, Swedish, and English rights to publish it.

For nearly ten years after he returned from World War I, Robert Sherwood's life was filled with such constant activity that it prevented him from asking hard questions about war. He spent countless hours working at *Vanity Fair* and then *Life*. Every day at lunch through at least 1925 he reported to the Algonquin Hotel, where he laughed and joked with his colleagues for an hour or two before returning to the office. After work, he either attended soirees, a movie screening, or the theater, or else had a long dinner with friends and colleagues. Late at night he could often be found at a Round Table poker game or some other get-together where there was plenty of alcohol. Eventually he would stumble home, at first to Posie's and then later to the apartment he shared with his wife, Mary. Weekends were generally filled with socializing, either in New York City or at the home of various Round Table comrades and followers on Long Island or in Westchester County, or at Alexander Woollcott's vacation home on Neshobe Island on Vermont's Lake Bomoseen.

Although he managed to write a couple of short stories and sketch out a few ideas for films, his involvement in creative writing was fairly slim. It took Edna Ferber, the author of the 1924 Pulitzer Prize–winning best-seller *So Big*, and then *Show Boat* (1926), to wake him up. A supportive friend to many talented writers, Ferber often advised those who were "blocking" and wasting their time socializing rather than writing.[86] In the summer of 1925, when they, along with other Round Tablers, were visiting the home of Margaret and Herbert Bayard Swope on Long Island, she took Bob aside for a serious conversation. As he later recalled, there were crap games to the left of them, "chemin-de-fer games to the right . . . Irving Berlin in front of us," and the usual gleeful laughter and shouting all around. Ferber told him:

"The best thing that could happen to you would be to have you snatched out of the Hotel Algonquin and exiled to Kansas City for two years. At the end of that time, you'd come back with some fine work."[87] Bob took Ferber's advice. Although he did not go to Kansas City, he did distance himself from the Algonquin Round Table and began writing, largely at night after a long day at *Life*. In doing so, he came face-to-face with the issue of war. Because it consumed him so, there was no avoiding it. It was time for him to take a stand and to represent war in a way that he believed reflected reality, just as he claimed films should do. Whether writing comedies or dramas, he made the conscious decision to air his opinion that war was not a romantic, thrilling escapade but rather a mindless, nonsensical element of human behavior which brought nothing but suffering to all those who experienced it.

5

Writing Plays for Peace

IN 1925, WHEN Robert Sherwood decided to take Edna Ferber's advice and become serious about his writing, he knew that he wanted to spread an antiwar message. By then, he had spent almost five years commenting on the way filmmakers handled the subject of war—giving high praise to a very few and damning the many. It was his time to make it right, but not on the screen. He had decided that for this cause he needed to use words, not images, to make his point. The "silent drama" was not the place for him, but the theater was.

Bob was full of personal anger about the war, an emotion he shared with a great many others who he felt would value his critique. There was no end to the blame that constituents placed on the president and Congress for having taken the country to war. Americans saw no reason why their husbands, sons, brothers, or even strangers they had never met had been sent to Europe to fight Germany for some purpose that was never made clear. Certainly, President Woodrow Wilson had stressed the importance of keeping the world safe for democracy, and yes, they knew that it had become dangerous to cross the Atlantic because of German U-boat activity; but by 1925 they still could see no *real* rationale for U.S. involvement other than for some industrialists to earn a profit. Even Henry Ford, the great voice of peace in 1915, had taken up the war cry when he realized that there was a great deal of money to be made in producing tanks rather than pleasure cars. People were angry not only about the loss of life but also about the physical and emotional toll the war was still taking eight or ten years later. Men suffering psychological trauma or living with missing or damaged limbs had become burdens, whereas they previously had been contributing members of their families, and the government was not as helpful in providing veterans' benefits as it would be after World War II.

The world of the 1920s in which Bob started his peace campaign was quite different from what it had been before the war, when he was a starry-eyed patriot. The Treaty of Versailles had literally redrawn the map of Europe. The Austro-Hungarian Empire was broken up into several autonomous nations, including Austria, Hungary, Czechoslovakia, and Yugoslavia. The German Empire was somewhat reconfigured, the most noticeable change being the return of the Alsace-Lorraine region to France. The Russian Empire, which in 1917 became, at least in part, socialist Russia, was also divided into Russia, Poland, Lithuania, Latvia, Estonia, and Finland. Within these nations were factions that were unhappy with what often seemed an arbitrary formation of nation-states, and so there existed in many places an undercurrent of political and ethnic tensions, which frequently made the headlines in the newspapers Bob read religiously. Perhaps for him, one of the most unsettling changes was the rise of the fascist Benito Mussolini in Italy in 1922.

Within the United States, Robert Sherwood was one of the first clear post–World War I antiwar voices to be heard on stage. Before his 1927 debut on Broadway with *The Road to Rome*, Maxwell Anderson and Laurence Stallings's 1924 *What Price Glory?* had broken new ground as the first play to declare that war was a waste. Although the characters in the drama joked with one another in portraying the reality of a professional army, the portrait was not romanticized or even particularly heroic as such depictions had been in the past. Less successful attempts to dramatize antiwar sentiment included Edna St. Vincent Millay's 1919 blank-verse morality play *Aria da Capo* and the unsuccessful 1927 version of the musical satire *Strike Up the Band* by George and Ira Gershwin, which would have more luck in a 1930 revival with a somewhat watered-down book. Throughout the 1920s, Broadway was booming. During the 1920–21 season a total of 157 new productions reached the Great White Way. This number continued to rise until it reached a peak of 268 new plays during the 1927–28 season. *The Road to Rome* shared the Broadway audience with a wide variety of plays and musicals including Paul Dunning and George Abbott's *Broadway*, Jerome Kern and Edna Ferber's *Show Boat*, Maxwell Anderson's *Saturday's Children*, Anita Loos and John Emerson's *Gentlemen Prefer Blondes*, Patrick Kearney's *An American Tragedy* (adapted from Theodore Dreiser's novel), P. G. Wodehouse's adaptation of Ferenc Molnar's *The Play's the Thing*, Sigmund Romberg's operetta *The Desert Song*, and Richard Rodgers and Lorenz Hart's *Peggy-Ann*.

Bob felt able to venture into political waters because audiences of the 1920s believed that serious plays on and off Broadway, works that showed the reality of American life and questioned society's social, religious, and moral principles, were worthwhile viewing. Eugene O'Neill brought a psychological seriousness to the stage with *Anna Christie* (1921), *The Hairy Ape* (1922), *Desire Under the Elms* (1924), and *Strange Interlude* (1928). Elmer Rice adopted European expressionism for his 1923 play *The Adding Machine* and exposed urban poverty in his 1929 *Street Scene*. Sidney Howard painted a picture of immigration and rural life in *They Knew What They Wanted* (1924), and several writers addressed racism and tried to raise the public's consciousness with such works as DuBose and Dorothy Heyward's *Porgy* (1926) and Paul Green's *In Abraham's Bosom* (1926). African American playwrights per se received little support for their work, although musical revues such as Eubie Blake and Noble Sissle's 1921 *Shuffle Along* inspired other similar ventures; success in drama for any but white writers would have to wait until the 1930s. Feminist playwrights also made their mark with Rachel Crothers's *He and She* (1920), Zona Gale's *Miss Lulu Bett* (1920)—which was the first play by a woman to win the Pulitzer Prize—and a number of works by Edna Ferber, who, besides seeing her novel *Show Boat* adapted for the 1927 musical, also collaborated with George S. Kaufman on several plays, including *The Royal Family* (1927).

It was in this open and seemingly friendly intellectual environment that Robert Sherwood started creating his plays. He was a facile writer, one who could draft a play in a few days or weeks. Early on he developed a flexible lifestyle that accommodated his writing. As he told a group of young students, "I write when I feel like it, unless I have to meet a deadline." If he came up with an idea at three in the morning, he got up and allowed his mind to pursue it. If he did not have any creative thoughts for weeks at a time, he simply got on with his other work, leaving ideas to incubate at their own speed. "A writer can never really get away from it all," he said. "He cannot stop that constant flow of raw materials into his mind and soul and heart." [1] He also understood the essence of writing plays, its combination of reality and fantasy. "To be able to write a play," he noted, "a man must be sensitive, imaginative, naive, gullible, passionate: he must be something of an imbecile, something of a poet, something of a liar, something of a damn fool. . . . He must be prepared to make a public spectacle of himself. He must be independent and brave." [2] So when he chose his first topic, he made a concentrated effort to mix fact and fiction and to be the imaginative, independent, and brave man he perceived a playwright to be.

Creating *The Road to Rome* was both a desire and a necessity. At the time he wrote it, although he was employed at *Life* and making freelance money with other work, Bob's lifestyle had driven him into debt to the tune of $14,000. In a bit of questionable lore, a cartoon in the January 16, 1939, *Boston Post* showed Bob writing on the subway. Its caption read that he created *The Road to Rome* while "curled up in the corner of a New York subway train" and suggested that he liked to do most of his writing there. [3] S. N. Behrman claimed that Bob plotted the play out in taxicabs as he traveled between movie theaters while a critic at *Life*. Actually, although he may have scribbled notes here and there, Bob wrote most effectively at home or in an office with a desk. It took him only three weeks to complete the first draft, which was essentially the final one. A lover of history, he felt comfortable incorporating the many mysteries and intriguing characters of the past into his satirical, romantic historical comedies. In this case he credited his interest in the Punic Wars, the setting for *The Road to Rome,* to his Milton Academy teacher Albert W. Hunt. As he wrote in the introduction to the published version of the play, he had an "unashamedly juvenile hero-worship for Hannibal," but he also had come to realize the significance of history as "the biography of mankind." [4]

The Road to Rome tells the story of Hannibal's passion to conquer Rome during the Second Punic War. Before the play's action begins, Hannibal, along with his men and elephants, have fought their way from Spain to Gaul and over the Alps to the outskirts of Rome. There they set up a massive camp and wait to attack. Meanwhile, inside Rome, the newly elected dictator Fabius Maximus is faced with the prospect of having to fight off Hannibal and his Carthaginian troops with a small army weakened by war and absences from the city. After several days Hannibal orders his troops to withdraw, and they leave Rome untouched. Bob's idea was to explore why the real Hannibal retreated just when he was on the verge of his lifelong goal of conquering Rome. To answer his own query, in *The Road to Rome* Bob created the character of Amytis, Fabius Maximus' fictional wife, a woman of mixed Athenian and Roman heritage and with absolutely no interest in politics. Confused by the prospect of war and conquest, she decides to slip out of Rome and confront Hannibal herself. Captured and brought before him, she persuades the handsome Carthaginian to listen to her rather than instantly executing her as a spy. During their conversation, Amytis puts forward hard questions about war and Hannibal's feelings about it. One thing leads to another, and the two spend the night together, the audience understanding that they make love. The next day Hannibal, a changed man, abandons Rome—and war—for good. Bob explains Hannibal's decision as the result of "the human equation," that intimate contact with another human being which makes the suffering of war too awful to contemplate, and therefore will prevent it.

Bob chose Hannibal's dilemma because the Punic Wars were far enough removed from the modern era to allow him to create witty dialogue without offending the sensibilities of his audience. In addition, ancient Rome was a popular setting in movies and plays because there was a romantic aura about it. People were used to reading of its gory battles, torrid love scenes, bold heroes, and vindictive gods and goddesses. *The Road to Rome,* however, while urbane, humorous, and gentle enough to appeal to audiences, contained an angry antiwar message directed at warmongering politicians and at industrialists who had earned huge profits on the backs of ordinary soldiers. Amytis, Bob's spokesperson for peace, attacks her husband's devotion to Roman nationalism and capitalism long before she meets Hannibal. When Fabius lectures her on the superiority of Rome, she shoots back that the empire consists of nothing but "a narrow-minded, hypocritical morality . . . nothing but worldliness, of the most selfish, material kind."[5] Later, Amytis accuses Hannibal and Carthage of similar greed. The shopkeepers of Carthage fear that Rome will interfere with their trade, she says. That is the real reason for his sitting on the outskirts of her city, just as it is Fabius' reason for believing that Rome, like any state, needs a strong military "and a policy of progressive conquest."[6] Those in the audience who applauded this message identified with critics of rampant U.S. capitalism and colonialism, which began in the nineteenth century under the umbrella of "progressive" internationalism.

Hannibal himself represented the professional military man who is all about hate and killing. It is he and his ilk who force the volunteers and drafted soldiers to live in tents (and trenches), fight for reasons they cannot understand, and suffer the damage caused by being on the front lines in the midst of battle while the leaders watch from a safe distance. Hence, when Hannibal says that he has an "undying hatred" of Rome because of an oath he took when he was nine years old, the audience could see the ridiculousness of that oath, as does Carthalo, an elderly warrior in Hannibal's army, who responds dubiously, "That's the proper spirit, sir. It's much easier to kill a man if you hate him."[7] In addition, Hannibal measures his success by meaningless results. As he tells Amytis, his job is not to think about how much blood is spilt and why but "to content myself with a soldier's rewards . . . medals, testimonial documents . . . state banquets."[8] The almost robotic nature of his reasoning resonated with an audience disillusioned by World War I.

The Road to Rome not only addressed the question of why government and military leaders cause men to kill and be killed. It also touched, in an inappropriately humorous way, on the effects of war on civilian populations, especially through looting and rape. Fabius, in an effort to get Amytis to understand why the Romans need to prepare for battle, points out the destruction that Hannibal's army sows wherever it goes. It has "burned homes, destroyed crops, butchered men, and despoiled women." The previous winter when Hannibal's troops were quartered in Cisalpine Gaul, he says, there was "a veritable epidemic of pregnancy."[9] Hannibal's younger brother Mago, in near ecstasy over the impending invasion, imagines that "first, we'll slaughter the men. When we've got them out of the way, we'll start plundering and see what we can pick up in the way of loot. After that, we'll set fire to the houses. . . . And then . . . we'll turn to the women."[10] Even Amytis fantasizes about "what it would be like to be despoiled."[11] At the end of her long conversation with Hannibal, he considers having Amytis executed. "But you ought not to kill me at once, without—without—," she hints. After he presses, she continues, "There's a certain—a certain ceremony to be gone through, isn't there," adding, "But no soldier ever kills a woman until he . . . and especially if she happens to be attractive." [12]

In contradiction to her desire to be sexually conquered, Amytis portrays the voice of reason and sanity when it comes to war. Before running away from Rome and seeking out Hannibal, she suggests that her husband "go out, under a flag of truce, meet Hannibal and talk the thing over in a civilized manner." [13] Talking, not fighting, was very much in the air in the 1920s. The League of Nations provided a place where representatives of member countries could discuss all sorts of international issues, not only conflicts but also disarmament, labor concerns, health, economics, the international white slavery market. Each nation's representatives had one vote in the League's Assembly, giving the semblance of equality among nations which, it was hoped, would foster understanding, negotiation, and an end to war. In 1928, the year after *The Road to Rome* opened, the United States joined sixty-one other nations in signing the Kellogg-Briand Pact, which pledged to "condemn recourse to war for the solution of international controversies and renounce it as an instrument of national policy." [14] Mediation, not instant war, was the goal of those who adopted the pact.

Bob, like many citizens of the United States, valued the ideals behind the creation of the League of Nations, the Kellogg-Briand Pact, and the international disarmament conferences of 1922 and 1927, but he was skeptical about their potential for success. He much preferred more immediate local negotiations which would not involve a large number of possibly contentious diplomats. In *The Road to Rome*, Fabius does indeed take a small delegation to meet Hannibal in the hopes of warding off the invasion of the city. Having taken to heart Amytis' advice, he appeals to Hannibal: "What will be gained by a long, arduous, painful siege . . . but acute suffering on both sides. We will sacrifice the lives of many gallant young soldiers. . . . [A]t the same time, there are the innocent victims . . . the women, and the little children. . . . This is not their war. . . . Why must they be made to pay the terrible price?" [15] In the end, violence is avoided because Fabius speaks out and Hannibal withdraws. In the final diplomatic meeting Amytis is silent, leaving the decision making to the men in power.

Bob was fortunate in that Jane Cowl, a fan favorite at the time, and Philip Merivale, a handsome leading man, were cast as Amytis and Hannibal. Cowl fell in love with the play immediately and shared her script with Edward Sheldon, a beloved and wealthy bedridden playwright. He in turn sent Bob a telegram effusively praising his writing. "I want to tell you," he wrote, "how full of wisdom and humanity I found it . . . shining all through like sunlight on late summer afternoons." [16] After a period of rehearsal, the play had its first out-of-town opening at the Belasco Theatre in Washington, D.C., on January 17, 1927. The Washington preview went extremely well. Cowl's and Merivale's reputations ensured a good advance sale, in fact, unusually large for a novice playwright. After the performance Bob remained backstage, while Cynthia ran "breathless with excitement," as Lydia later put it, to call Posie about its "vociferous success." Bob had accomplished "something creative" and felt pleased that he had done "good work." [17] For an instant, he even claimed that having the play admired and respected was more important than making lots of money from it.

After a short preview at the Broad Street Theatre in Newark, New Jersey, *The Road to Rome* opened at the Playhouse in New York on January 31. Practically all of Bob's family was in the audience, where Posie, Arthur Sr., and Lydia were seeing the play for the first time. When the final curtain fell, there were many repeated curtain calls and shouts of "Author! Author!" Jane Cowl looked around for Bob, telling the audience, "That Sherwood is in there somewhere," but when she went backstage to fetch him, she returned authorless. Shaking her head, she tried again to bring him out from the wings but finally had to tell the audience, "He simply won't come." [18] This became his pattern. A bit shy about facing the opening night crowds, he usually remained backstage or even left the theater momentarily while the audience cheered for him.

The New York critics were generally kind, some remarking on Bob's antiwar message. Charles Brackett of the *New Yorker* praised it as "a hymn of hate against militarism—disguised, ever so gaily, as a love song." [19] Percy Hammond of the *New York Herald Tribune* acknowledged the politics but said that although Bob was trying to preach "a sermon for pacifism," the play remained "a funny and an elaborate cartoon," enjoyable and "canny" but not necessarily an important work. [20] In what could have been perceived as a bit of logrolling, Alexander Woollcott wrote in the *New York World* that the play was "wise and lofty and searching and good." He went on, "It is definitely a play written in the aftermath of the war" and "belongs side by side with another piece written for the theatre under much the same inspiration," namely, *What Price Glory?* [21] An unsigned review in the *New Republic* also recognized the message, citing the play as "one of the most interesting ventures of the season . . . touched by the hint of the glory and exaltation of life that persist in the theme." [22] Brooks Atkinson of the *New York Times*, however, reported that *The Road to Rome*, though a political satire in the vein of George Bernard Shaw, seemed "mechanical and obvious . . . seldom edged with the reproving double meaning of brilliant irony."[23] Nowhere in his review did he mention the issues of war and peace that were so important to Bob. Finally, there was the review written by Robert Benchley for *Life*, titled "Our Mr. Sherwood . . ." How objective could Benchley be expected to be when reviewing his friend and boss? "Lest we should be accused of log-rolling," he plainly stated, he nevertheless found the play charming, adding with relief, "Thank God!"[24]

Ticket sales for *The Road to Rome* were excellent, so good in fact that for months it was hard to get a seat. Although it was to run for 392 performances, talks began instantly about sending it out on tour, as was the custom at the time, and staging it in England the following year. At the conclusion of the 1926–27 Broadway season, Burns Mantle put together the new edition of his *Best Plays* series, a compendium of information about productions on Broadway and on tour which thousands of theater lovers and professionals looked forward to each year. For this season Mantle decided to add variety to his selection of the best plays. He sent a list of 24 productions out of a total of 163 to ten of the leading drama critics, of whom nine responded. The only unanimous choices for inclusion in his new volume were George Abbott's *Broadway* and Maxwell Anderson's *Saturday's Children*. *The Road to Rome* received six out of the nine votes. Mantle, in his evaluation of the play, appeared lukewarm, calling it "lightly tucked with satire" and a "quasi-historical romance."[25] Years later, in 1949, John Gassner published *Twenty-Five Best Plays of the Modern American Theatre: Early Series,* in which he also included *The Road to Rome*. In Gassner's opinion, the play represented the "effervescent" theater of the 1920s "by virtue of its irreverence toward histori-cal reputations" and its "anti-heroic outlook."[26]

Bob himself apparently suffered some sense of guilt about the "quasi-historical" nature of the play, so in its published version he included a thirty-eight-page introduction describing the historical events that served as the background for the script. He traced Hannibal's lineage and life history, quoting from the classical writings of Livy and Juvenal as well as Sir James Frazer's *The Golden Bough*, H. G. Wells's *The Outline of History,* and the writings of the classicist Theodor Mommsen. Still, he could not refrain from inserting comments about current politics. For example, in discussing the first conflict between Rome and Carthage over Sicily in 240 B.C., Bob hinted at commonalities with the supposed World War I mission of making the world safe for democracy. He wrote, "The Roman excuse was that Sicily should be delivered from the Carthaginian yoke, but that was an old one, even then."[27] He wanted to make clear to his readers that in this respect Carthage and Rome were no different from the nations of their own day.

Even Carthage, which had a weak "peace party," could not put its desire for conquest aside, as the government encouraged Hannibal "to go on with the costly but potentially profitable work of eliminating Rome as a competitive power. In this," Bob noted, "it can hardly be said that the Carthaginians were actuated by any motives of altruistic patriotism (if, indeed, there is such a thing); they wanted to make the world safe for oligarchy."[28]

On the Roman side, Fabius Maximus was proclaimed dictator because of the extreme situation which had arisen. This too was similar to the present time, Bob claimed, for Fabius was "like so many politicians, before and since . . . a harmonious and convenient combination of shrewdness and stupidity."[29] Perhaps as a warning, Bob related the end of the true story. In later years Carthage became a tributary state to Rome, paying reparations that were so enormous that the Romans were convinced their enemies would never be able to recover. Bob's implication was that the World War I allies had done the same to Germany, planting the seeds of future vengeance, a warning that peace activists were shouting out loud and clear. Carthage, however, did not just recover. For a time it thrived, causing a fearful Rome to send the army and navy to blockade the land and starve it into submission, perhaps a reminder to Bob's readers that food shipments to Germany had also been blockaded after World War I ended. Carthage fell in 146 B.C., and Rome ruled the world— for a while. As for Hannibal, hounded and hunted for years, in 183 B.C. he poisoned himself. Wanting to make his point absolutely clear, Bob wrote: "The representation of Rome itself, as it existed under the Republic, is not unjustifiable, for the spirit of Fabius Maximus and his brother boosters has become the spirit of America to-day. History is full of deadly and disturbing parallels and this, it seems to me, is one of the most obvious parallels of all."[30]

In the spring of 1928, as his father Arthur lay dying, *The Road to Rome* opened in London. The opening-night audience seemed ecstatic, giving the cast fifteen curtain calls, but the London critics were less than enthusiastic. Posie lamented to Jane that the British did not seem open to embracing an unknown American author, while Bob felt that if they had known about his World War I experience with the Canadian army, they would have been more tolerant of him.[31] Nothing could help to keep the play going, however. Arthur died in early June, and so did *The Road to Rome* after a mere two-and-a-half-week run. Although Bob joked about the play's closing to Posie, she could tell that its failure had been a severe blow. By August, even though the road company was still doing good business in California, she felt that "it is really over."[32] With Jane Cowl moving on to another project, the play seemed down to its last gasp, though it continued on the road with another actress into 1929. That spring two other European productions of the play went into rehearsal. Bob went to Vienna to see the version there, called *Hannibal ante Portas,* which greatly disappointed him. It was done as a "very low farce," he reported. Amytis was "a little blonde, fluffy cutie, terribly flip; Hannibal, a mad-wag . . . who roared with laughter on all his lines." Added to this was the portrayal of the entire Carthaginian army as "drunk and disorderly." Still, the audience cheered, and Bob actually agreed to take a solo curtain call, which garnered him eight more. He came to believe that the play went over so well because it was "so rotten."[33] He was unhappy to see this particular production move on to Munich and Berlin.

At approximately the same time, Bob got a taste of what it was like to have a play produced in Fascist Italy. By this time, Benito Mussolini's militaristic hold on the country was solid, and it seemed doubtful that a play such as Bob's would be able to survive either the official or the self-censorship which existed in the country. Nevertheless, in April, Bob received a letter from the Italian translator that the script had passed the censors and was in rehearsal in Milan. At the fourth cast meeting, however, the actor playing the minor role of the second guardsman protested, "as an Italian and a Fascist," the presentation of "our divine Rome." The manager became so frightened, Posie told Jane, that he stopped production of the play. Apparently the actor in question was a *fiduciario,* an internal spy, a rat, of which there were many in "every office, bank, factory, school, &c," whose job it was to "watch and listen & spy & report." The translator felt that if the show had gone on, it "would have been wrecked by the Fascists," and he begged Bob not to take any action, as it might interfere with other plays he hoped to mount.[34] It was best that the incident be suppressed rather than come to the attention of the officials.

Other efforts to keep *The Road to Rome* alive also met with little success. A British film, *The Private Life of Helen of Troy,* produced in 1927, was supposedly based on *The Road to Rome,* but very little of it has survived except for a fragment in the British Film Institute. In 1933 plans for another film were announced but fell through. In 1936 the play was revived for a short run in the Midwest under the Federal Theatre Project as part of the New Deal program to revive the economy during the Great Depression. As late as 1949 *The Road to Rome* was still on someone's mind, that someone being the famous director George Abbott, who wrote to Bob about the possibility of adapting it as a musical comedy. Bob replied that he would "never want to lift a finger" to work on such a project.[35] In fact, he said, he did not even want to have to read it again. As his first play, it brought back unpleasant memories in terms of the writing. He would not object, though, if some other writer wanted to work on it. Abbott, however, backed off. Most humorous of all for Bob was the 1955 film adaptation of the play as an Esther Williams swimming extravaganza, *Jupiter's Darling*, complete with musical numbers, a chariot race in which Hannibal and Amytis escape the Romans, and Esther Williams leading Carthaginian soldiers in an underwater chase scene as she eludes their grasp. Needless to say, this version bore little resemblance to the original play.

After the success of *The Road to Rome*, Bob decided to try a romantic comedy that did not attack war but did address the issue of Hollywood censorship, a much bigger problem than the lackadaisical self-censorship then occurring on Broadway. For this effort he approached Ring Lardner to see if he would allow Bob to adapt his short story "The Love Nest" for the stage.[36] Lardner, who was still experimenting with his "Dada" plays, was more than happy to see what Bob could do with his story. The plot of Lardner's tale was simple. Lou Gregg, the president of Modern Pictures, Inc., with offices in New York City, invites a journalist named Bartlett to visit him and his wife at their home in Ardsley-on-Hudson, a wealthy suburb of Manhattan. Lou gives Bartlett the impression that he is going to witness the quintessential "love nest," but instead, the journalist discovers a frustrated young wife who married her husband because she thought he would make her a star. Isolated and unhappy, she turns to alcohol for comfort, and tells Bartlett that she never loved her husband, hates her life, but has no escape because she can cite no cause for divorce, which was almost impossible to get in New York State at that time. Ultimately, the reporter leaves, the wife continues drinking, and the husband carries on with his happy, busy life.

Bob's idea was to transport the location of the story to Hollywood, where director Lou Gregg is filming *Hell's Paradise*.[37] He maintained the basic tale of a successful husband with an unhappy, suffocating wife, but he changed two elements. First, he used the play to poke fun at Hollywood, Will Hays, and his own role as a film critic, and second, he drastically changed the outcome of the plot. Bob initially expressed his feelings about Hollywood in the opening dialogue among crew members who report that Will Hays has spies carefully watching Gregg's every move because he feels that there is "too damned much of this sex stuff in his productions."[38] The crew knows otherwise—that Gregg is very clean-cut, with a wife and three children and a beautiful thirty-eight-room home. Meanwhile, New York critic Maureen Milton, thought to be one of Hays's stoolpigeons, visits the set to watch the filming. Bob describes her much like himself as "a movie fan incarnate, and therefore, the ideal movie critic."[39] Gregg invites Milton, along with the crew, to his "love nest" to disprove Will Hays's opinion of him. There, she meets his wife, Celia, whom she surreptitiously observes getting drunk, and

Forbes, an out-of-work actor turned butler, embracing her. Several scenes are built around the themes of love, divorce, drinking, and blame. In the end, Forbes and Celia, with Gregg's blessing, move to New York with the children, the nanny, and financial assistance, while Gregg enjoys the success of his movie. Bob decided to give his play a happy ending—just another of his inside barbs aimed at Hollywood.

The Love Nest opened at the Comedy Theatre in New York on December 22, 1927, and ran for a mere twenty-three performances. At a time when there were so many productions on Broadway, many never got reviewed at all. *The Love Nest* received only two notices. Brooks Atkinson labeled it "a sprawling play—mechanically comic in the first act, mechanically dramatic in the last." He felt strongly that Lardner's story had lost its "swift, relentless quality."[40] The second reviewer was none other than Robert Benchley, who noted that "our" judgment was complicated by the fact that Bob was "our boss."[41] Indeed, Benchley put off saying anything concrete about the play until mid-January, when he noted that "nature . . . relieved us of the necessity of reviewing . . . bosom friends." The show had closed. "Nothing has to be said."[42] So much for logrolling. Ring Lardner told his and Bob's friend F. Scott Fitzgerald that he had seen a dress rehearsal and thought that Bob had done some "very clever" writing, but he also felt that Bob was too much of a neophyte to be able to adapt a short story into a three-act play.[43] Always modest, Bob later told people that "the Lardner part" of the project was good.[44]

Perhaps because *The Love Nest* was so poorly received, Bob decided to return to his more successful use of an antiwar theme wrapped in the robes of romantic comedy. The result was *The Queen's Husband*, a semi-serious tale of political upheaval in a small, mythical, nameless constitutional monarchy, an island in the North Sea lying somewhere between Denmark and Scotland. King Eric VIII, a benevolent and generally uninterested monarch, allows his wife, Queen Martha, to do the ruling. Princess Anne, their only child, has fallen in love with the king's assistant and has no desire to be part of the nation's royalty at all. For diplomatic reasons, Queen Martha betroths Anne to Prince William of Greck. Meanwhile, all is not well in the kingdom. Anarchist revolutionaries rebel violently against the despotic rule of Premier Northrup, who during the melee claims dictatorial powers. Through calm thought, negotiations, and a rereading of the Constitution, the king retakes control, brings peace to the nation, and gets rid of Northrup. He also helps his daughter escape her arranged nuptials, marry the man she loves, and leave the country.

Although *The Queen's Husband* may sound like just another innocuous romantic comedy, it actually reflected two important political issues before the nation at the time while also reinforcing the idea of peaceful negotiations which Bob had stressed in *The Road to Rome*. The first issue was the Red Scare, which had begun during World War I, the second the growth of dictatorships and fascism in the world. "Red Scares" were not new in the nation's history. Persecution had played a part in politics ever since the Salem witch trials of 1692, when farmers, merchants, and social outsiders were unjustly persecuted in Massachusetts. The Red Scare of the 1920s had a similar witch-hunting character. In this case, the U.S. government established official mechanisms to halt the work of socialists, communists, anarchists, labor leaders, civil rights supporters, birth control advocates, women's rights proponents, peace activists, and other dissenters. During the war itself, the rationale for blacklists, government surveillance, and campaigns against protesters was that these activities harmed the war effort and were therefore potentially seditious or treasonous. After the Russian Revolution of 1917 and the establishment of the world's first communist nation, those who embraced the Bolsheviks were seen as dangerous. After all, the last thing a capitalist nation wanted was for communism to spread throughout the world, turning free, exploitable markets into unobtainable ones.

Echoing the United States' anti-Bolshevik foreign policy was a series of government-sponsored domestic offensives designed to destroy those groups that would supposedly introduce communism into the society and eventually take over the government. A. Mitchell Palmer, Woodrow Wilson's attorney general, appointed J. Edgar Hoover to head the newly established Radical Division of the Department of Justice, which was soon enfolded into the Federal Bureau of Investigation. It was Hoover's idea to draw up lists of "dangerous" individuals and organizations, to have hundreds of people arrested through state and local law enforcement, and in 1920, in an action known as the Palmer Raids, to allow government agents in thirty-three cities to break into offices, homes, and meeting halls without search warrants. As a result of this particular action alone, four thousand people were arrested and denied lawyers, and nearly six hundred were deported, several of them naturalized citizens. Perhaps the most famous episode of the Red Scare was the arrest, trial, and execution of Nicola Sacco and Bartolomeo Vanzetti, two Italian anarchists accused of murder. Although controversy about their trial persists to this day, the consensus is that the government used them as scapegoats to discourage others from being too vociferous in expressing their political opinions.

What is also most relevant for the discussion of *The Queen's Husband* was that in 1919, more than 3,300 labor strikes occurred in the United States, fueling the then nascent Red Scare. One of the leaders of a steel workers' strike that took 350,000 workers off the job was William Z. Foster, a member of the militantly radical International Workers of the World (IWW, or the "Wobblies") and later a famed Communist Party leader. Because of Red Scare persecution, government repression of strikes and union organizing, and the efforts of corporations to buy employees' loyalty by offering them more benefits, labor union membership dropped from 5.1 million in 1920 to 3.6 million in 1929.

In Bob's anonymous little kingdom in *The Queen's Husband*, the people are also protesting over issues of employment. Premier Northrup and his buddy, Foreign Minister Birten, are intent on purging the country of these menaces, their solution being to execute the hundreds of "Anarchists" they have arrested. They have the backing of Queen Martha, who is focused on her upcoming trip to the United States, where she hopes to receive a hefty loan to "make us powerful, to increase our army and navy, to combat the red peril and subdue the terrible threat of revolution."[45] Audiences could easily identify with Bob's use of labels such as "anarchists," "reds," and "socialists." Princess Anne, who has been co-opted by Northrup's conservative rhetoric, describes the protesters as "swarms . . . plotting to get rid of us and set up a republic or a soviet or something." Bob has her warn her kindhearted father, "Remember what happened in Russia."[46] He also introduces the character of Dr. Fellman, a softhearted liberal who is intent on warding off violence between the government and the anarchists, led by his hot-headed compatriot, Laker. To Northrup, Fellman is a "half-baked pink college professor" whom Laker easily manipulates.[47] Laker, however, is actually a forceful leader who wants impartial arbitration to settle the nation's labor dispute but who is willing to use violence if necessary. In the first act of the play, the king is mild-mannered and seemingly oblivious to politics in the eyes of the other characters, but actually he is quietly astute. On receiving the orders for the executions of the radicals which he has to sign, he simply has his assistant lose the paperwork so there can be no killings.

At the end of the first act Queen Martha sails to the United States, leaving the king in charge. Northrup then takes the opportunity to antagonize the liberals in Parliament so they walk out, creating the opening for Birten to put forward a provision making Northrup dictator with absolute authority—not exactly the scenario that had put Mussolini in power in Italy but close enough for people to grasp the similarity. This sets up the juxtaposition of a cruel and despotic elected leader versus a benevolent monarch who functions like a figurehead. The question becomes, where does the real power lie, with the king or the dictator? In effect, who ruled 1920s Italy—King Victor Emmanuel III or Benito Mussolini? The play also raises the issue of arbitration versus dictatorial methods to resolve disputes. Fellman and Laker are both willing to negotiate, but Northrup prefers violence so as not to have to share his authority. "Fellman and the rest of the reds are looking for trouble," he says, "and I'm going to see that they get it!"[48] Of course, violence ensues. The people rise up against the despot, who immediately calls on all his military forces and weapons to put down the revolution, and so also begins the struggle between the king and the despot. When Northrup orders the navy to open fire on the people, the king protests that thousands of women and children will be killed or their homes will be destroyed and orders the navy not to proceed. Northrup tries to overrule him, claiming that he is the dictator "by act of Parliament," to which the king responds that he is the king "by the grace of God."[49]

In *The Queen's Husband* the king becomes the voice of reason, that person who sees the benefits of negotiation. Yet it takes a visit from the equally mild-mannered Dr. Fellman to make the monarch aware of his isolation, his "quiet, detached life" in the palace, where he never comes "in contact with reality."[50] He is benevolent but absent. "And while you have been keeping your place," Fellman reminds him, "your people, whom you are supposed to govern and protect, have been done to death by bureaucrats, demagogues, and politicians in general."[51] Because of Fellman, King Eric comes to understand that temporary cease-fires, like the one he ordered the navy to observe, are not the answer. "The country," Fellman says, "must have permanent peace," to which the king replies, "We can find no way to permanent peace while those fools are shooting at each other."[52] Later the king announces to Northrup, "I'm fed up with you and your army . . . I'm fed up with your oratory, and your bombast, and your flag-waving patriotism."[53] Behind Northrup's and the returning queen's backs, the king opens talks with Fellman and Laker, agrees to negotiate the labor dispute, and then orchestrates the resignation of Northrup, the dissolution of Parliament, and the temporary appointment of Fellman as premier, with the agreement that new elections will be held. Even Northrup can run—*if* he can find any followers. Thus violence is avoided, permanent peace established, and order restored. Benevolence, negotiation, and honesty rule—the perfect formula for Robert Sherwood.

The Queen's Husband, which previewed in Providence on January 16, 1928, and opened at the Playhouse in New York on January 25, received mixed reviews. Percy Hammond thought it "a confused semi-satire" with "outcries of Ibsenesque propaganda."[54] Nowhere in his review did he mention the play's pacifist position. Brooks Atkinson acknowledged that the play was political in nature but felt that Bob was "so fickle in his moods and so bewildering in his transitions" that the average playgoer would have a hard time knowing just what to believe. Although the scene in which the military wagons clatter outside in the courtyard and the bombs whine and crash in the palace lent gravity to the drama, still it all made "for a mixed entertainment in which the various ingredients [did] not blend well." [55] Robert Benchley tried to handle his review diplomatically, claiming that Bob's use of "old-fashioned hokum" was effective, especially in the last act. But, he added cheerfully, "there really was no need for the revolutionists to shoot so much. There are other ways of settling political disputes." [56] Bob must have been pleased that the reviewers were at least unanimous in their praise for actor Roland Young in the role of the king, for he claimed to have written the part specifically for him.

The Queen's Husband ran for 125 performances on Broadway and then went on tour. In 1931 RKO Radio Pictures released a very accurate and popular film version titled *The Royal Bed*. A French version, *Le rois s' ennuie*, directed by Gloria Swanson's husband, the marquis de la Falaise de la Coudraye was also very popular. In an odd twist, considering its great success in England, the film was banned in Australia and Canada because it was deemed disrespectful to monarchy. In 1932, however, the play opened in Toronto, where it received rave reviews and played to full houses. Once again, Bob's satire and political message were compared to the work of George Bernard Shaw, one reviewer claiming that Bob was Shaw's "disciple" who imitated him "most freely—and makes the most out of it by doing so." [57] Perhaps with fascism spreading so quickly in Europe and Hitler in the ascendancy, the play meant more to audiences in 1932 than it had in 1928. An interesting footnote to the play's success throughout Canada was that Bob accepted only a small percentage of the profits, and donated even that $2,000 to agencies helping disabled Canadian World War I veterans.

Bob was obviously not pleased with the tepid reviews his play received when it first opened in 1928. His dissatisfaction with the critics took written form in the published version of the play. In an introduction he attacked those reviewers who forced writers to alter their style and message. Bob argued that U.S. authors were writing simply to please critics, whose praise sold the books and plays to the public. The bottom line was that these reviewers were forcing writers to adopt a form of self-censorship. Critics instructed writers that "Romance is Hokum, Fantasy is Hokum, and Sentiment is the lowliest Hokum of all." [58] For Bob, however, hokum was the "life-blood" of the theater, the very reason for its existence. Without it, theater would simply cease to exist. "The theatre," he wrote, "is and always has been a nursery of the arts, a romping-ground for man's more childish emotions." [59]

Bob felt, or so he said, that the theater was not a place for writers to expose "shams and hypocrisies." [60] It did not bother him when he was called a "knee-pants" dramatist, because he held to his belief that the theater was a place where "a playwright should be just a great, big overgrown boy, reaching for the moon." [61] These were strange words from a man whose works vibrated with criticism of the government and whose messages, though cloaked in hokum, were extremely transparent. In 1949, in an article for the *Saturday Review of Literature* anniversary issue, reflecting on the preface for *The Queen's Husband*, Bob wondered over his ever having written "this strange text," claiming that it was "just plain silly." He recalled the American theater of the 1920s as "a wonderfully exciting place in which to work and to progress. Far from being hemmed in by copy desks or censored by a muse with a green eyeshade, it was as wide open as a virgin continent, and as teeming with chances for adventure and fortune." [62] Yet at the time, he had obviously felt that critics were attempting to put a stop to his proselytizing through their reviews.

After *The Queen's Husband*, Bob drafted a play called *Wooden Wedding*, of which there remains not a trace. He then began work on *Horse-Shoes*, "a sort of old type of show—semi-musical," which also fell through and disappeared—as he commented to his close friend Sidney Howard, "thank heaven (I really mean that)." [63] Then, in just four short days, he wrote *Waterloo Bridge*, a semi-autobiographical play set during World War I. Having railed against war in general and government leaders in particular in his previous work, Bob now felt comfortable enough in his antiwar crusade to tell something of his own story. Therefore, he took elements of his experience and incorporated them into both *Waterloo Bridge* and his novel published soon after, *The Virtuous Knight*. In the play, two personal themes emerged: the loneliness he had experienced as a soldier and the comfort two people could find in each other, and more important, the unique difficulties that World War I specifically (and all war in general) caused for innocent victims, particularly women.

Waterloo Bridge, which takes place over two days in November 1917, tells of Myra, an out-of-work American chorus girl stuck in London during World War I. Unable to raise the money for a ticket home, she is forced to turn to prostitution to survive. Roy, a U.S. citizen serving in the Canadian army, has just been released from an extended hospital stay to recover from battle injuries when he meets Myra. A naive young man, Roy thinks that Myra is simply an unemployed actress. Liking his innocent ways, she decides not to solicit him. Instead, she makes him a cup of tea in her room and then sends him away. The next morning Myra's friend and sister prostitute, Kitty, meets Roy waiting for Myra in her room. She convinces him that Myra needs protection and hints that he should marry her. Forever gullible, Roy proposes to

Myra, believing his army pay will keep her fed and housed. She accepts, but then in a fit of guilt she runs away. Roy returns to active duty, where he signs over part of his pay to her and names her as beneficiary for his life insurance. Myra and Roy meet once more as he is crossing Waterloo Bridge on his way to the train station. There he makes her promise to sign the pay and life insurance papers. After Roy leaves, Myra, alone on the bridge, lights a cigarette, allowing the invading German fighter planes to identify her as a target. The ending of the play remains unclear. Do the Germans fire on the bridge and kill Myra? Does Roy die on the battlefield? Although most literary analysts have interpreted the message of the play as one of hopelessness, assuming that neither Roy nor Myra survives, each viewer was left to answer those questions individually.

Waterloo Bridge clearly had its roots in Bob's actual experiences. In November 1918, while recuperating from his wounds, he had celebrated the end of the war with the British in Trafalgar Square, where he found himself "jammed . . . next to a very short and quite pretty girl in a blue tailored suit." Pinned to her blouse was a small silk U.S. flag, which Bob asked her about. She answered him "in a tone that suggested nothing but Broadway" that she had been in the chorus of C. M. S. McLellan and Ivan Caryll's musical comedy *The Pink Lady*, which had arrived in London several years before and become stuck there because of the war. With no job and no income, she therefore had no way to get home. She invited Bob over to her "nice little flat near Leicester Square," but in the excitement of the celebration, he forgot the address and never saw her again. But, he told his reading audience, "I have written about her and about London in this play, which is sentimental, but justifiably so."[64]

As Myra unfolds her story to Roy, the young soldier comes to understand her unique position as a civilian victim of the war. Not only does she have no job, and therefore no money to buy food, she tells him, but also, to add to the problem, the British are facing severe food shortages. There is hardly any meat, no coffee, eggs only in powdered form, and margarine instead of butter. "Gosh!" innocent Roy responds to this news. "You have to join the army to get anything to eat."[65] In actuality, for some women the solution to the problem was to marry several soldiers of different nationalities whom they met and comforted, and then collect part of their pay and their insurance if they died in action. As Kitty explains to Myra, it is all legal and "holy" and makes the men happy when they are on leave.[66] The soldiers are lonely, and hence easy targets for women trying to survive a predicament they had not caused. Kitty sees this option as an honest way out of a difficult situation. In trying to persuade Myra to marry Roy, she presents a practical explanation:

"All you 'ave to do is go through with the ceremony and then sleep with 'im a few times 'til 'is leave is over." After that, Myra can "sit back and collect 'is assignments and separation allowance and live in luxury."[67] If he dies in battle, Myra will benefit from his insurance. There is no end to the war in sight, says Kitty, so why should Myra not benefit from the opportunity which has fallen into her lap?

As Myra and Kitty are well aware, women are in a particularly vulnerable position in a nation at war. When the First World War began, the Victorian era in England had scarcely ended, and the ideal there (and in other countries) was still that married women, especially those with small children, did not work for wages outside the home. Single working-class women often took jobs in factories, as domestics, or in shops, but most earned lower wages than working-class men. When war took a majority of men to the front, the burden of support rested on the women's shoulders. Married women often looked for work but could not find any. Others, with no one to watch their children, could not enter the workforce. Even if men sent part of their wages home, it was often not enough to support their loved ones. If they died, their families lost their wages permanently. There was also danger at home from air attacks, which caused immediate death and destruction. As Myra puts it to Kitty, the high number of deaths has created a pall over London. "I noticed the people in the station, and in the streets," she says. "They looked as if they was all hurrying to a funeral or something." Kitty responds: "That's just what they are doing. I give you my word, London's dead."[68]

It has not been uncommon throughout history for women in desperate economic straits to resort to prostitution, either temporarily or permanently, in order to survive. Other members of their society did not always see their actions as reprobate but understood them as the last-ditch measures they were. In *Waterloo Bridge*, Bob utilized the small role of a military policeman to underscore the sympathy some people feel for such women, even, in this case, making it possible for them to solicit soldiers, while a different man, a sergeant, self-righteously judges the situation as "shameful," seeing the growth of prostitution as a plague, an infestation.[69] Roy himself neither condemns nor laments Kitty's or Myra's status as prostitutes. He simply accepts it as a part of their reality.

Mrs. Hobley, Myra's landlady, enters the profession because the Germans have taken her husband prisoner of war, thereby drastically reducing even the small share of his wages she previously received. Her solution is to rent rooms in her house to women who have taken up prostitution, becoming in effect a madam. Yet she complains angrily about her tenants' immorality and her own misery for sinking so low as to have to house them. She hates herself, the young women, and the war which has destroyed her life. Bob describes her character as "a flagrantly good woman" who had been "compelled by force of wartime circumstance to subsist on the profits of prostitution. . . . At present, her one aim in life is self-justification."[70] Hers is a constant effort to balance her moral beliefs with her current neediness, so when she learns that Roy is flush with cash, she is eager to see that Myra exploits him so she can pay her back rent.

When Mrs. Hobley realizes that Roy has fallen in love with Myra, however, her Christian duty takes the upper hand. She reveals to him that Myra is a common prostitute and warns that "traffic with 'arlots leads only to sin, and sin leads to suffering. And a soldier like you . . . 'as enough of suffering in this awful war without 'aving to be contaminated and robbed by loose women of the streets."[71] But soldiers were thankful for prostitutes, and Roy is willing to overlook his preconceptions on the matter. Military men were alone in a strange land, spending most of their time in the company of other men. They often found themselves in nearly intolerable situations—dirty, hungry, tired, and vulnerable to attack. The idea of having a woman to talk to, to spend time with, to eat with, and ultimately to feel protective toward provided for many the motivation for getting through another day in the trenches.

Robert Sherwood never revealed any of his own experiences with women during his war years, so there is no telling just how autobiographical *Waterloo Bridge* is. Parts of his own story, however, were certainly reflected in Roy's words. Roy is a young American who, after attending "summer camp," stops off to visit "war crazy" Toronto. He tells Myra: "I was trying to elbow my way through the crowd when a military band came down the street. They were playing 'It's A Long Way To Tipperary.' The next thing I knew I was hot-footing it up a gang-plank." It was "just boyish enthusiasm" that landed him and thousands of other Americans in the war, an enthusiasm, he claims, that did not last very long.[72] In the fighting Roy suffers wounds in the shoulder and legs and has to have shrapnel removed, a plight similar to Bob's claims about his own war wounds. Roy, like Bob, spends months in the hospital. Meeting Myra and hearing her American accent reminds him of his home in upstate New York, and in his loneliness it becomes easy for him to believe that he has fallen in love with her. This situation is exacerbated by his belief that he will soon be called to report back to Bramshott (Bob's training camp) to get ready to be returned to the front, a fear that Bob lived with each day he was in the hospital. For Roy, loving Myra means that the war and the military no longer own him. He belongs to her; he has realized Robert Sherwood's "human equation," that experience which makes war an object of derision. Human life, not death, is sacred.

Waterloo Bridge previewed at the Tremont Theatre in Boston on November 21, 1929, continued on to Philadelphia, and then had its official New York opening at the Fulton Theatre on January 6, 1930. Although former Algonquin friend and now popular actress June Walker starred as Myra, the New York reviews were less than good. Eleven years had passed since the end of World War I, and even if the antiwar spirit in the nation was still running high, the critics, as in the past, hardly mentioned the war's influence on the play or the playwright. Brooks Atkinson, for example, felt that although Bob had captured the "basic facts of modern life—the war and the women," the play for him had been nothing more than "a tedious journey . . . lacking in event and structure," a "rather sophomoric" story about a "bad girl with a tender heart."[73] Arthur Ruhl of the *Herald Tribune* agreed that while the plot was "interesting meat of the time," the play as a whole suffered from a "lack of depth and imagination in the lines."[74] But as Bob told Sidney Howard, "There's no use crying over spilt vitriol."[75] In 1941 Bob himself admitted that *Waterloo Bridge* was "almost good . . . but . . . incoherent," an interesting bit of self-criticism.[76] The play ran on Broadway for a disappointing sixty-four performances and then went on tour.

The play's theme of love and loneliness in war was extremely appealing to filmmakers although the actual plot that Bob had written was not. The script was adapted a number of times for film and even television, though Myra's involvement in prostitution was changed. In 1930 Bob sold the rights to Universal Pictures for what he called "a diminutive sum," but he felt that the studio made "a good and faithful picture of it."[77] In that version, directed by James Whale and released in 1931, Roy was given an English (not American) family with a country estate, and the ending was altered: Myra and Roy agree to marry, but after his troop transport takes him away, a German zeppelin drops an artillery shell on her as she stands on Waterloo Bridge. Within a few years, as Hollywood producers under Will Hays's influence began enforcing their own Production Code, the film was suppressed. It was not re-released until late 2006, when it appeared in a DVD collection titled "Forbidden Hollywood, Collection Volume One."

In 1939 Universal sold the story rights to David O. Selznick, who then resold them to Metro-Goldwyn-Mayer for a huge profit. The end product, released in 1940, angered Bob, for "virtually every word was then rewritten and the characters completely changed." The result, he felt, was "somewhat less than excellent."[78] The screenplay by his close friend S. N. Behrman and Hans Rameau made Myra into a dancer in an all-female ballet company with a strict manager. During a London air raid she meets Roy, a wealthy, upper-class British army officer, and they fall in love. They attempt to get married before he leaves for the front but are unsuccessful. She is then kicked out of the dance troupe for being out at night, and her friend Kitty leaves with her. Roy's mother comes to meet Myra, now unemployed, but during their luncheon Myra sees Roy's name listed in a newspaper as missing in action. Upset, she runs away and ends up following Kitty into what is implied to be prostitution. Roy returns, but Myra knows she cannot tell him of her new livelihood, so she throws herself in front of a military truck crossing Waterloo Bridge. To this day, this version of the film remains popular with television and DVD audiences as a classic starring Vivien Leigh and Robert Taylor. The script remained on producers' minds even after Robert Sherwood's death. In 1956 MGM produced another version of *Waterloo Bridge,* titled *Gaby,* which presented Myra (now Gaby) as an innocent young woman played by Leslie Caron. After she and Roy are deterred from getting married and he returns to the front and is reported dead, she turns to having sex with young soldiers as a means of assuaging her guilt over not having slept with Roy before his departure. Her actions are presented as misguided generosity in a Hollywood far from the 1930s. In 1958 and again in 1967 two versions titled *A ponte de Waterloo* were presented as condensed television plays.

After the disappointment of *Waterloo Bridge,* Bob again tried a romantic comedy. This time, he wrote within the context of the early days of the Great Depression, when the unemployment rate was rising and the future seemed very bleak. *This Is New York* was a humorous homage to the corrupt razzle-dazzle city that Bob loved so much, the place where bootleg liquor, drugs, and political chicanery all thrived. The play pitted New York City against the rest of the country, as represented by Senator and Mrs. Krull of South Dakota, the senator having arrived in the city to give a campaign speech. He and his wife actually despise New York and everything "un-American" it stands for, claiming that it should be expelled from the Union and given to Europe, where it belongs. With the Krulls is their twenty-year-old daughter, Emma, who finds New York fascinating. Much to their chagrin, they discover that Emma has become engaged to a wealthy young easterner, Joseph Gresham Jr., a man with a reputation for being somewhat wild. In fact, Joe is being blackmailed by his former mistress, Phyllis Adrian, to the tune of $100,000. Emma visits Phyllis, but before she can persuade her to leave Joe alone, the police arrive to investigate the suicide of Phyllis's neighbor. Emma, one of only two witnesses who can attest that the neighbor's bootleg-supplier lover did not murder her, becomes embroiled with the police and reporters. Everything works out in the end, as the Krulls evade scandal and return to South Dakota, Emma and Joe marry, and New York City remains its happily decadent self.

Bob claimed in the preface to the published version of the play that he wrote it because he was tired of those "aggressive Americans of the West" who were constantly saying that "New York is not America," a phenomenon he connected with Herbert Hoover's 1928 run for president against Governor Alfred E. Smith of New York.[79] Among those who took up the anti–New York cause were Henry Ford; Big Bill Thompson of the America First Committee; the Anti-Saloon League; the Methodist Board of Temperance, Prohibition and Public Morals; the Woman's Christian Temperance Union; and the Ku Klux Klan. Bob wrote the play to flaunt New York's free and progressive way of life and to point out how many young people, like his character Emma Krull, ran away from the deadly, closed-minded areas of the nation to cities like New York, where they could find cultural and political stimulation, liberal attitudes towards race, gender, and sexuality, and lots of theater, music, dance, and alcohol, and even a world-famous amusement park. To Senator Krull's cry that "New York is not America," Bob could only respond that in actuality, New York was America through and through.[80]

This Is New York previewed in Providence on November 17, 1930, and opened at the Plymouth Theatre in New York on November 28. Posie wrote to Jane that opening night on Broadway was a big success and that the play seemed to be "a great hit both with the public and the critics." Bob said that Lois Moran, the actress who played Emma, was so beautiful and appealing that the reviewers would not be able to find it in their hearts to criticize her, whereas he, with his "long dolorous face," was an easy target.[81] In fact, the critics were more kind than they had been to his other plays after *The Road to Rome*. Brooks Atkinson called *This Is New York* "a genial piece of entertainment," Bob's "best comedy so far," even though it "meander[ed]" and seemed to get "dull" at the end.[82] Percy Hammond agreed that it was Bob's "best work," much better than *The Road to Rome*. This play was a "humorous and active comedy."[83] By December 10, however, Posie noted to Jane that even though the play was going well, it was not going "brilliantly." That year nothing was a "smash hit" on Broadway except for *Grand Hotel*, a translation of Vicki Baum's German play.[84] The depression was definitely having its effect on Broadway's box offices.

Hollywood, however, was booming. Bob sold the movie rights of *This Is New York* to Paramount Pictures for a huge $50,000, of which he received $22,500, the same amount going to Miriam Hopkins, the actress who played Emma, and another $5,000 to Bob's agent, Harold Freedman, head of drama at the Brandt and Brandt literary agency. The film, renamed *Two Kinds of Women*, changed Joe Gresham into an unhappily married man whose chorus girl wife is willing to divorce him for a great deal of money. Before this can be done, the wife falls to her death from a skyscraper, creating a scandal for Senator Krull, who persuades Gresham to leave New York and resettle in South Dakota with Emma. Directed by William C. DeMille, the film was in some ways more risqué than the play, which does not suggest that Emma would consider committing adultery. It also subtly criticized New York's strict divorce laws, which keep Joe in a marriage from which he cannot easily extricate himself through legal means. Like the *Waterloo Bridge* of 1931, *Two Kinds of Women* also fell victim to Hollywood producers' self-censorship and quickly disappeared into obscurity.

After *This Is New York*, Bob was again drawn to his antiwar sentiments. In the preface to *The Queen's Husband*, he told his fans to watch for his next play, *Marching as to War*, which he worked on throughout 1928 before setting it aside to write his 1931 novel *The Virtuous Knight*, a close match to the unfinished play. Both were antiwar statements set during the crusades of the Middle Ages which reflected Bob's own war experiences. "I didn't enjoy the war very much," he said in a radio speech on November 5, 1934, "but I never doubted that it would be followed by an unlimited period of peace and prosperity. I was full of optimism then, and a sense of superiority. It was good to be young. I was one of 'our gallant heroes.' It was good to be American. For me, in the war, were so conspicuously altruistic, idealistic— unselfish crusaders for the cause of Right against Might." [85] Unfortunately for Bob, the book received virtually no attention. As he later complained to S. N. Behrman, it was reviewed under the heading "Other Books," "and that was that." [86] Even though sales were apparently very slow, the British publisher Heinemann put out its edition, renamed *Unending Crusade,* the following year, when it received a notice in the *Sunday Times* of London. The reviewer, Ralph Straus, felt that the book brought "those very old days almost startlingly near." While at first the story did not seem very interesting, as he read on Straus became more involved in "the building of a philosophy which would not be out of date even in these enlightened days of our own." [87]

The main characters in the play *Marching as to War* are Stephen, his cousin Geoffrey, and Lady Elinor, the woman both men love, although she is betrothed to Stephen. Stephen has volunteered for the crusade, giving much of his land and wealth to the king to fund the venture. Geoffrey, however, wants nothing to do with it. He plans to leave England for Normandy, where he can avoid the war. But instead, in order to protect Elinor's inheritance if Stephen should die, he accepts responsibility for Stephen's castle, servants, men-at-arms, and all of his possessions. Elinor is pleased to see Stephen go off to be "a great hero" and, as the bishop claims, "to destroy the infidel." [88] Geoffrey, however, believes that in the Holy Land the soldiers will find "nothing but sand, and heat, and hunger." [89] He expresses his anger at the greed of the emperor of Constantinople and the corruption of the church, just as Bob had in his writings about the U.S. government and the world's industrialists.

When the women of the nobility reflect on the return of their men, they give voice to the feelings which Bob's friends believed he was repressing in his profound silence after World War I. The countess says to Elinor: "They'll have memories of this Crusade that they won't care to discuss with their wives. They always go to war, animated by the loftiest ideals, and they come back with strange gleams in their eyes. . . . Ideals are grand and inspiriting while they last—but we can't keep them. They sour on us and we have to throw them out." [90] Meanwhile, Geoffrey is arrested and put in prison until he agrees to make a confession of faith and support the crusade. Soon Stephen returns home to claim that Geoffrey is right; the premise behind the crusade is a lie, and the journey has ended in "disillusionment and defeat." [91] The troops turned away from the Holy Land because they realized that their crusade was the opposite of its stated holy, lofty intention. Stephen and Elinor persuade Geoffrey to sign the confession so he can be released, and the three return to their pre-crusade lives.

Unlike *Marching as to War*, *The Virtuous Knight* was not a traditional love story. Set during the reign of Richard I—that is, Richard the Lion Hearted—it was more of a road story. In the novel, Bob had more space to develop his plot and to describe the hypocrisy and horrors of war. In this case the hero, Martin, an orphan, inherits his grandfather's land. His wise tutor Old Gervas trains him in all the ways to be a good landowner and then a knight. Martin learns to respect others, so when he finds that Jews are being slaughtered during the celebration of Richard's coronation, he defends them. Also caught up in the melee is young Hugh, whom Martin rescues and makes his manservant. Martin signs up for Richard's crusade, selling his land and livestock to the church to raise funds. He then experiences one adventure after another. In France, Richard assigns him to act as a spy against the archbishop of Canterbury, who he believes is plotting against him. In Sicily he meets Angela, who wishes to consort with him, but he remains virtuous. There Richard decides to hang him for being a poor spy, but Martin and Hugh escape and set sail for Acre and the Holy Land.

It is in Acre that Martin experiences a war which is reminiscent of Bob's time in the trenches. Here the novel describes the ugliness and senselessness of war, painting the ridiculousness of complicated secret plans which seem all too obvious to the enemy. The soldiers suffer daily from boredom and heat; they bury the dead, tend the wounded, and observe the prolonged agony of those who wish only to die. Finally, Bob depicts the battle between the crusaders and the Saracens, each believing that God is on their side. Martin, though more an observer than a participant, learns that he fears war and does not have the stomach for it, especially when he witnesses the "liquid fire" the Saracens deploy, "squirt[ing] streams of it through the blow pipes in the prows of their galleys." Like the poison gases and liquid fire of Bob's war, it causes horrible burns, sickness, and death.[92] The Saracens burn out Hugh's eyes with their liquid fire, and in a reflection of Bob's own injuries after he fell into the German booby trap, Martin's legs are crushed by a falling tower that he is standing on:

> Martin had no memory of just how he fell, whether he went with the tower or plunged ahead. At the end of the fall, he was under it, lying on his stomach, his legs pinned down by the timbers. One of his legs was crumpled up and hurting intolerably. He could hear the hissing splutter of liquid fire as the glass bombs burst on the framework of the tower above him. He could not move.
>
> They were drenching liquid fire down from the walls above, and the tower was beginning to burn, the hides smelling evilly. The pain in his leg was awful, and the fumes of the foul smoke were choking him. He called again to Hugh, frantically, and then he lost consciousness.[93]

When it is all over, Martin goes into recuperation, as Bob had, "from the phantasms of the protracted nightmare into a state of unrelieved boredom." He can barely tolerate the "hot, steaming days" followed by "chill, damp nights." He has "nothing to do, nothing to say, nothing that he cares to think about."[94] He can walk with a limp but cannot go far. Martin is Bobby Sherwood, in the war once again.

Like *The Road to Rome* and *Waterloo Bridge*, *The Virtuous Knight* reflects on the effects of war on civilian populations—the inflation, the scarcity of supplies, and the selfishness of those with access to food and other goods who make huge profits from selling them. Martin sees how even dead horses become items of value, as Christian soldiers bid for every part that can be eaten. There is also wine, "which the men consumed in vast quantities in lieu of food," and which then makes them behave badly, desecrating mosques and mistreating women.[95] Bob notes that the Christian soldiers lose heart and are "no longer fighting for ideals but for existence."[96] In the end, Martin abandons the crusade and heads for Haifa and the trip home. But as luck would have it, he is captured by the Saracens, whose leader, Kahtan, is the son of the sultan. The ruler sentences Martin to life (as opposed to execution) as a prisoner of war, with full freedom of movement within the village in exchange for helping Kahtan build an army. During his stay, Martin learns about Islam and rethinks his position on violence and war. In the end he escapes, taking with him an enslaved European woman, and returns to England to embrace Christian pacifism, just as Bob had on his return to the United States.

After purging himself once again of his emotional response to his war experience, Bob turned to a comedy, one that he intended to provide some escape from the cynical disillusionment of the world and the new political alternatives of violent and repressive fascism, on the one hand, and, on the other, the bleak conformity of communism as seen in the Soviet Union. This was *Reunion in Vienna*, a play he had first thought of writing in 1929, when he was in Austria to attend a performance of *The Road to Rome*. While there, he was taken to the famous Sacher's restaurant, whose proprietress showed him a special upstairs room which she used to entertain former aristocrats. Bob peeked in on one such event, which hopelessly re-created the good old days of royalty. The image incubated in his mind while he worked on other projects. Finally, he wrote the romantic romp *Reunion in Vienna*, a work whose despairing preface contradicts the humor of the play.

Indeed, Bob's despair could easily be understood within the context of global affairs in the early 1930s. These were years when the Great Depression engulfed the entire world. It was impossible for impoverished Germany to pay the war reparations imposed on it by the Treaty of Versailles. Without money from that nation filtering into France, Belgium, and England, it in turn became difficult for those countries to continue to pay off their loans to the United States. In an effort to boost world trade, President Herbert Hoover's administration suggested a one-year moratorium on Germany's debts; but the bankruptcy of the German Danatbank led to the closure of all German banks and an end to the flow of money. This and the general instability in Germany caused many to turn to the Nazi Party, which promised to relieve the people's suffering and promoted strong ethnic nationalism. In the 1932 elections, the Nazi Party won 230 seats in the Reichstag, or parliament, as opposed to 133 for the socialists and 97 for the conservatives. By 1933 Nazi leader Adolf Hitler had become chancellor. At the same time, reports were coming out of the Soviet Union of oppressive governmental control and the legislating of economic conformity through the Five-Year Plans.

Bob's hatred of autocracy and his disappointment over the unfulfilled promise of postwar democracy surfaced in the preface to the published edition of *Reunion in Vienna*. It was a message that he later claimed "came closer" than he had ever before "to a statement of what I was trying to think and write." He saw his generation caught in a "limbo-like interlude" between one era and another. In depressing terms, he described the predicament of the postwar mind set: "Before him is black doubt, punctured by brief flashes of ominous light, whose revelations are not comforting. Behind him is nothing but the ghastly wreckage of burned bridges."[97] In this frame of mind, he was beginning to think that the fight for "democracy" had been in vain and that a "spirit of moral defeatism" had taken over.[98] As he looked around him, he saw both personal and political isolation.

Bob felt that people in the United States were turning a blind eye to what World War I had wrought, preferring to let Europe sink into fascist or communist states. In that case, would apathy create the same fate for the United States? Even the deaths of "twelve million soldiers," he was sorry to say, had not prevented every American mother from being "glad to trade her remaining American liberties for the knowledge that she could put her baby in its crib to-night and find it there safe to-morrow morning." Whereas humankind had been so full of hope after the war had ended, that hope had disappeared, and a certain selfishness had taken its place. "Democracy—liberty, equality, fraternity, and the pursuit of happiness!" he exclaimed, "Peace and prosperity! Emancipation by enlightenment! All the distillations of man's maturing intelligence have gone sour."[99] Idealism had given way to scientific rationalism. Marxism, boasting its foundations in historical and dialectical materialism, was the best example. Under communism, humans would no longer have the "right to be out of step as [they] march with all the others into that ideal state in which there is no flaw in the gigantic rhythm of technology, no stalk of wheat too few or too many, no destructive passion, no waste, no fear, no provocation to revolt—the ultimate ant-hill."[100]

Though still a pacifist, Bob, like many others, questioned the effectiveness of the postwar peace efforts. The League of Nations, the World Court, treaties, trade—nothing seemed to be working, at least not as quickly as the war generation would have liked. In fact, all of humanity's efforts to improve the world seemed only to have resulted in stifling individualism and free-spiritedness. Bob saw nothing ahead but doom, and so he wrote *Reunion in Vienna*, a play designed as pure escapism but also as a commentary on some Europeans' misplaced hopes that a return to the past system of empires and all their accouterments would rescue them from their current misery. "It is relieving, if not morally profitable," he wrote, "for an American writer to contemplate people who can recreate the semblance of gaiety in the face of lamentably inappropriate circumstances."[101]

The play takes place in post–World War I Vienna, a city where the police watch every step one makes and where deposed royalty are most unwelcome. Anton Krug, a former revolutionary and noted psychiatrist with a sharp scientific and analytical mind, is married to Elena, former mistress of Archduke Rudolf Maximillian, who is in exile in Nice, where he drives a taxi in order to survive. Anton, who comes from the working class, is sent to the front during World War I as a punishment for opposing the monarchy. In his role as a military physician, he dismisses every soldier who is sent to him as being too damaged to continue serving in the war. He returns home a hero, meets and marries Elena, and helps her to accept the new regime through the use of psychoanalysis, which the audience is meant to perceive as a form of brainwashing. As Elena tells Anton's young interns, "When you have been fully inoculated with the germ of scientific culture you will realize that all the world is your laboratory—and all the men and women in it merely guinea-pigs." [102] Science makes people malleable, and Elena is a clear example of its success.

On the one hundredth anniversary of the birth of the late emperor Franz Joseph I, the small Viennese community of his followers decides to hold a celebration, one that the police watch with an eagle eye, especially to see if the former archduke Rudolf Maximillian appears, which indeed he does, complete with all of the royal egotism he took with him when he left the country. Anton encourages a reluctant Elena to attend the celebration so she can appreciate how much she has changed. Unbeknownst to her and Anton, Rudolph awaits her arrival, hoping to rekindle their love affair. He, of course, assumes that she will immediately fall into his arms and is surprised when she rejects him. Unable to accept the idea that Elena loves her non-royal husband, Rudolf follows her to their home, where he and Anton discuss the matter. As Rudolf tells Elena, "Your husband represents the sublimity of the intellectual, and I the quintessence of the emotion." [103] Elena urges Anton to use his influence to help Rudolf get out of the country safely. But while he is out making the arrangements, she and Rudolph make love, and she remembers what giddy happiness feels like. Nevertheless, after Rudolf makes a safe exit, she returns to her husband and their not so frivolous (or happy) life.

The 1931 *Reunion in Vienna* was designed for the popular acting team of Alfred Lunt and Lynn Fontanne, one of the greatest husband-wife couples ever to work together on the stage. [104] Bob met them for the first time in the winter of 1920, but his aunt Jane and uncle Wilfrid de Glehn had a long history with Fontanne, who in her teens had served as the artist's model for several of their paintings. Jane's painting *The Blue Coat* and Wilfrid's *The Spanish Mantilla* both hung in the Royal Academy of England, and Jane's portrait of Fontanne still hangs in the Lunts' Genesee Depot, Wisconsin, home, now a historical landmark and museum. The Lunts disliked attending large parties made up of strangers, but they often frequented the small teas, dinners, and get-togethers at Posie's and Lyd's homes, where Bob was introduced to them. At one point while he was at *Vanity Fair*, the pair asked him to bring Dorothy Parker to tea. The two writers sat and chatted with the Lunts. but, as Bob remembered it, "nothing much happened." He left with the impression that the Lunts were "gifted Grotesques, sure to shine in the sideshow but doomed never to achieve prominence in the Main Tent." [105] He could not have been more wrong.

The Lunts had met as struggling young actors in New York, fallen in love, married, and then, in 1924, become stars as an acting team in the Theatre Guild's production of *The Guardsman* by Ferenc Molnár. They then negotiated a contract with the Guild which stipulated that they always perform together, and so they did, building up such a strong following on Broadway and on tour that almost any play starring them was bound to sell out. When Bob was thinking of actors who could bring *The Road to Rome* to life in early 1927, he had hoped that the Lunts would do it, but they were committed to the Theatre Guild, which was not interested in producing the play. By 1931, however, he and the Lunts had become important figures in the theater world (they more than he), and both the Guild and the Lunts were enthusiastic about mounting *Reunion in Vienna*. The Lunts actually turned down an invitation to star in Eugene O'Neill's *Mourning Becomes Electra* in favor of Bob's play, largely because they had just completed a long run of Maxwell Anderson's *Elizabeth the Queen* and preferred to take on a comedy for a change.

Rehearsals for *Reunion in Vienna* went well for the actors, including Bob's sister Cynthia in the small role of Gisella, an impoverished Austrian countess. The Lunts themselves had devised an acting style unique in the theater at the time, in which they spoke over each other's lines, much the way conversation is carried on in normal society. One would begin speaking before the other had completed his or her line, but they modulated the level of their voices so that the audience would hear whichever line was the more important. They believed firmly that their main responsibility as actors was to do their best to bring the author's words to life. When they suggested changes to scripts or to stage directions, it was in order to improve the play, not to embellish their own stardom. As Lunt wrote to Bob, "My only reason for being in the theater either as an actor or as a director of acting is to project the author—not obscure or use him for my own purpose but to clarify & heighten whatever *he* wishes to say." [106]

Bob found working with the Lunts a pleasure. They obviously enjoyed collaborating, and therefore the work was fun for him. At the time the three became involved in the play, the Lunts were in Hollywood making what would be their only film, *The Guardsman*, while Bob was there working on a few films, including Howard Hughes's *Age for Love*, which earned him

$15,000 for two weeks' work writing dialogue; the documentary *Around the World in 80 Minutes*, in partnership with Douglas Fairbanks; and then another Hughes film, *Cock of the Air*, released in 1932. These all helped to keep him and his family in a luxurious lifestyle, but in actuality Bob hated Hollywood. Unlike many other New York writers, he never kept a home in California or remained there any longer than he needed to. On this trip, however, he stayed to observe some of the shooting of *Waterloo Bridge* and to discuss *This Is New York/Two Kinds of Women* and the film version of *The Road to Rome*, which never materialized. Bob and the Lunts met several times, and they gave him suggestions about rewrites and casting. He, meanwhile, was entranced by their unassuming demeanor, their enthusiasm, and their obvious pleasure at throwing themselves into the roles of Elena and the archduke.

But when the trio returned to New York for rehearsals, Bob found the Theatre Guild problematic. Whereas he had always praised the organization in the past, using it as an example of quality in the theater and as a model for how film producers should run their businesses, the reality of working with the organization was a rude awakening for him. The Guild followed a system that called for constant meetings, discussions, and input from its board of managers to the writer, director, and actors of any given play. There were usually six members of the board, which at this time consisted of Lawrence Langner, Theresa Helburn, Lee Simonson, Helen Westley, Philip Moeller, and Maurice Wertheim. Their intention was one of collaboration, for they believed that a play could only be improved by constant input from those most interested in its success. The so-called managers' rehearsals were usually held two weeks before opening night, then one week before, and then often at the final dress rehearsal, each followed by copious notes. In addition, throughout the rehearsal period, members of the Theatre Guild board were welcome to give advice to the creative team.

Beyond the annoyance of constant surveillance by the Guild board, Bob had particular trouble with Lee Simonson, who was not enthusiastic about the play from the start. Simonson, the set designer for the production, felt that it lacked real substance. In particular, he saw Bob as being totally ignorant about Freudian psychoanalysis, whereas he considered himself to be something of an expert. By contrast, Lawrence Langner believed Bob to be "one of the most idealistic" of the Guild's playwrights, a man intent on making the world "a better place to live." He felt that Bob's previous career as a film critic helped him write well-structured plays. "Indeed," he later recalled, "with the exception of Eugene O'Neill, I know of no other playwright who produces a manuscript which on first reading, is so ready for production."

In the case of *Reunion in Vienna*, Simonson picked what Langner called "an acrimonious argument" with Bob about whether the character of Anton Krug was "really orthodox or not" in terms of psychoanalytic theory.[107] Langner tried to intercede, but Simonson would not relinquish his sense of ownership about psychoanalysis even after the play had opened. Whether or not the fine points of psychoanalytic theory, about which Bob admitted to not knowing very much, were of great importance to the success of the play is questionable, but the result of Simonson's constant tirades was to antagonize Bob, director Worthington Miner, and the Lunts. Bob began to question whether he would ever want the Theater Guild to produce another of his plays. A few years later he recalled that "the whole experience was just one long quarrel. . . . Because of the never-ending wrangling and jangling I came out of it so shot that rather than go through it again, I would prefer to go to work for Zanuck or Goldwyn or Selznick or the Cohn brothers—or anybody."[108] For Bob even to suggest that working in Hollywood was preferable to Broadway was indeed an expression of frustration and discontent.

The out-of-town reactions to *Reunion in Vienna* were uneven. In Pittsburgh and Baltimore audiences responded quite poorly, better in Buffalo, and in Washington they loved it. The play opened in New York at the Martin Beck Theater on November 16, 1931, to eleven curtain calls. The New York reviews were generally very good. Richard Lockridge called the play "light and frisky," and Gilbert W. Gabriel said that the Lunts played their roles "to the hilt."[109] Brooks Atkinson felt that the writing was not "brilliant," and the play wavered "unsteadily between burlesque and satire," but on the whole the evening was "a lively holiday," with Bob's sense of humor "uppermost."[110] By contrast, Arthur Ruhl found Bob's "course" to be "torturous and foggy . . . thin and dry and rattling when it should have been suave, sensuous and persuasive." For this reviewer, the play fell "flat and futile when it should have snapped with the bite of intellectual farce."[111] In spite of this one negative review, Bob was as happy as any playwright could be. Though hung over from drinking too much beer at his opening night party, he found himself coherent enough the next morning to call the Lunts, who, despite denying that they ever read reviews, knew them all by heart. At the end of the 1931–32 theater season, Burns Mantle recorded that commercially, this had been the worst year in recent Broadway history. Yet among the hits was *Reunion in Vienna*, which he felt met "the Continental dramatists on their own ground and likewise improves upon its model."[112] The show joined the company of other major successes, such as *Of Thee I Sing* by George S. Kaufman, Morrie Ryskind, and George and Ira Gershwin, which won the Pulitzer Prize; Eugene O'Neill's *Mourning Becomes Electra*; Elmer Rice's *Counsellor-at-Law*; and *Abie's Irish Rose,* still running at an unprecedented 2,532 performances.

Indeed, *Reunion in Vienna* was one of the few plays making a profit on Broadway in the spring of 1932, when the depression kept people away from the theater in droves. In June, Alfred Lunt reported to Bob that although business had slacked off a bit, they were "still ahead" of many other shows, and at one matinee performance there had been "seventeen standees." An editorial writer from the *Herald Tribune* who had seen the play five times had returned the night before. Lunt told Bob that the cast could "hardly articulate for the sweat & swelter" of the late June heat, but the writer had said that he was "not aware of the thermometer & enjoyed the play more than ever before."[113] Since there was no air conditioning and little ventilation in the Guild Theatre, the Lunts followed their usual pattern of leaving New York to spend the summer at Genesee Depot. They had played 284 performances, a great success for its time. In the fall they took the show on tour, closing in Philadelphia in November in order to appear with their old friend Noël Coward in his production of *Design for Living.*

Then on January 3, 1934, the Lunts again opened the play out of town, this time in London, where the reviewers scoffed at its down-at-the-heels portrayal of aristocrats. Lunt himself restaged the entire production, consulting with an expert on Viennese manners and royal behavior so that the characterizations were as accurate as they could be. Still, Bob was disappointed when the show closed after 196 performances, a respectable run in any case. Lunt told him that if he and Fontanne had "failed" him in any way, Bob should "then sock me baby & let's call it a day."[114] Bob assured Lunt that they were playing the roles just as they should be. Indeed, for a playwright, Lunt's attitude was a godsend, and his and Fontanne's dedication to constantly tweaking plays and staying with them for long runs was instrumental in keeping at least three of Bob's plays alive longer than they might otherwise have lasted.

Bob was ecstatic to find *Reunion in Vienna* numbered among "the top ten Favorite Plays of all Time" in a poll taken in 1935 by the *Evening Sun*. He wrote to Lunt and Fontanne, "What you two did in, and for, and to that play was enough to make the career of the undersigned playwright worthwhile— and I'm grateful, and shall remain so."[115] Bob sold the film rights to *Reunion in Vienna* for $85,000, and held out hope that the Lunts would star, but they were not interested in working in Hollywood. They found the stop-and-start pace of filming and the interruption of the flow of the acting almost intolerable. Even when Carl Laemmle of Universal Pictures offered them $250,000 for one film, and Irving Thalberg offered $990,000 for a three-year contract, they refused, sending Laemmle a telegram saying, "We can be bought, my dear Mr. Laemmle, but can't be bored."[116]

What was most peculiar about the version of *Reunion in Vienna* published in 1932 was the great divergence in tone between the preface and the play. The preface was full of cynicism and despair, while the script was comic and lighthearted. Bob was known for being humorous, cheerful, and energetic in his work and his social life, but his private thoughts were taking him into more desolate territory. In 1932 he wrote two plays that went nowhere. The first, *The Oxford Accent*, an unfinished piece about a love triangle, contained one notable comment on war. In the 1920s university students at Oxford had promised never to support another war. This "Oxford Oath" spread to the United States, where opponents called it the "Slackers' Oath." Bob, an enthusiastic supporter of the pledge, began his play with a conversation between two Oxford women lamenting the First World War. One says that she cannot help feeling "a certain sense of—of wastage, I suppose you'd call it."[117] Perhaps this play would eventually have pursued the issue had Bob not given up on it. Instead, he attempted a more disturbing play called *Afterglow*, which never left his desk. It is the story of Paul, a chemist who, in order to assuage his guilt over having produced lethal gases during World War I, develops a theory to produce a chemical that will bring about world peace and put an end to people's violence toward one another. Near the end of the script Bob wrote a totally unworkable eight-page theatrical monologue on the weaknesses of the League of Nations. It was full of vitriol and political accusations which audiences would have found off-putting.

According to Paul, the League of Nations has failed simply because it is not a "League of Men" but rather a league of powerful, selfish national leaders who are "incapable of justice and honour in their dealings with their fellow men." Humans are "imprisoned within feudal state anachronisms in an age of supposed enlightenment" because leaders cannot see further than their tightly guarded borders. Therefore, the human race has become "a group of bigoted cliques, trained to hate each other because they fear each other." Members of the League of Nations have become the "agents of this mediaeval tyranny," fostering "the meanest parochialism until it has expanded into the murderous form of delusional insanity which you call patriotism," setting "race against race, class against class, neighbor against neighbor" in the effort to keep the world "in the chaotic state which is most profitable to [them]."[118] Sadly, the leaders have done nothing to ensure that the world evolves into something decent. Bob himself no longer saw any value in the League's efforts to enhance human rights through its many decisions in the International Labor Organization, its efforts to prohibit white slavery, or its addressing the loss of civil liberties in various European and Asian nations. Rather, for him, the results were negligible. Mussolini reigned supreme and Hitler was gaining more power by the day. The blame had to rest with the ties among world leaders, militarists, and industrialists who turned their backs on humanity in the interest of making huge profits.

After attacking the League in general, Paul then singles out individual nations. England is criticized for having "gorged" itself on "land, power and pride"; it must wake up, he says, to the fact that its colonies do not need or want its protection.[119] France is accused of suffering from selfishness, of being too intent on its own interests rather than those of humanity in general. Furthermore, France suffers from fear of Germany, a nation seeking vengeance for the stipulations of the Treaty of Versailles, which have resulted in the starvation of its economy and its people. As a result, France cannot reach out a hand to Germany, and Germany cannot feel any sort of warmth toward France. The United States is accused of thievery and dishonesty, of using any kind of salesmanship to acquire what it wants, no matter what the method. Selfishness is the key to all sins. Paul charges: "France has exalted nationalistic selfishness. Britain has exalted appetite. Germany in her time has exalted imperialistic ambitiousness," and Japan (which invaded Manchuria in 1931) is now "imitating her—though God knows why, under the circumstances."[120] Finally comes Russia, with its great goals of establishing "the perfect state of liberty, equality, and fraternity, the brotherhood of man." But the means of achieving this utopia are neither modern nor enlightened. Rather, they are "prehistoric" and will lead right "back into the jungle."[121] Relying on "coercion, on the suppression of freedom of conscience, of association, of speech, on the arbitrary, inhuman enforcement of uniformity," Russia is bound to fail.[122] Paul is just about ready to reveal his formula for solving all these weaknesses when the subjects of his tirade cut him off and carry in his coffin. Back in his room, Paul has shot himself, the tirade having been his pre-suicide fantasy. Like Bob, Paul has no magic formula. All he has are words.

In 1933, the same year that he co-wrote with George S. Kaufman the screenplay for the silly Eddie Cantor film *Roman Scandals*, Bob read Adolf Hitler's hateful book *Mein Kampf*, in which the Nazi laid out his racist beliefs and touted Aryan superiority. The book upset him so that in response Bob wrote *Acropolis* "to show the imposition of totalitarianism on a free-thinking society."[123] One of his favorite plays, *Acropolis* turned out to be another frustrating failure. The action of this historical drama takes place during the last years of Pericles in the fifth century B.C. The Parthenon, in its early stages of construction, is the scene for a rally before the workers. Hyperbolus, an army general, lectures the crowd about the great Athenian democracy which allows the voters to decide whether expensive monuments dedicated to the likes of the egotistical Pericles should be built or not. Hyperbolus and the next speaker, Cleon, oppose the structure. Cleon, a statesman, claims that the money is being wasted by "effeminate aesthetes" such as the sculptor "Pheidias," instead of being used to prepare the nation for a possible assault from Sparta.[124] He also openly despises the "house of recreation" run by Aspasia and regularly attended by artists, writers, and philosophers such as Pheidias, Polygnotus, Aristophanes, Alcibiades, and Socrates. He claims that while the Persians and Spartans are closing in on Athens, the Athenians concern themselves only with frivolous conversations about art, beauty, and religion. Cleon then confronts Pericles, accusing him of relying on the misinformed guidance of his elderly adviser Anaxagoras, who uses superstitious astronomy to "devitalize an entire state, to kill patriotism and ambition."[125] Cleon claims that Pericles is misappropriating funds and says that he will prove it and destroy his power.

When Aspasia, who loves Pericles, visits him out of concern that Pheidias might be harmed by those wishing to stop the construction, Pericles expounds his great belief in Athenian democracy. He desperately wants the monument to be built but feels equally committed to the will of the people. Aspasia then persuades Pericles to send Cleon and Hyperbolus off to a small, harmless war on Samos to get them out of the way so that the Parthenon can be completed. Unexpectedly, the troops are butchered, and once back in Athens, Cleon and Hyperbolus promise "to work vengeance on the betrayers, the thinkers, the talkers, the builders of hypocrisy."[126] With the Spartans rapidly approaching, Pericles persists in the building of the Parthenon, but Cleon arrests Pheidias on the false grounds of misappropriation of funds, thereby stopping the work. At the hearings before the senate assembly in Athens, Pheidias proclaims his innocence and his great belief that with his architecture he is creating art in order to defeat demoralization and despair. With Cleon and the war party in control of the senate, the assembly votes to spare Pericles for his past service, to exile Anaxagoras, and to put Pheidias to death. Aristophanes, Socrates, and Polygnitus are to do military service in the war against Sparta. The young artist Alcibiades tearfully tells the accused, "I know that when you are gone, I'll still be able to hear you talking, talking, reasoning, preaching, tearing up faith by the roots, sowing the seeds of eternal dissatisfaction and bewilderment and despair," which, as Aristophanes adds, "forms the best possible nourishment for those who know how to digest it."[127]

Finally, before going off to war, the artists and philosophers meet Pericles at the Acropolis. Pericles feels death waiting for him, for without democracy he can no longer exist, and war cannot cease until it has burned itself out.

The cycle is never done. After all the Athenians and Spartans are dead and their structures destroyed, new Athenians and Spartans will rebuild, divide politically, fight wars, and die, on into eternity. In effect, this speech reflected Bob's perception of the chaos of the 1920s and early 1930s as he had experienced it—first, a war to end all wars, then rebuilding and the creation of monuments, then the endless debates over how to end war, then nationalistic divisions followed by the repression of dissent, and then, as seemed likely, another war. Yet there would always be people who would struggle to keep freedom of expression alive, whether by building Parthenons or writing plays. Bob considered *Acropolis* "the most positive affirmation of my own faith" and the best play he had written to date, a reaction against the despair he had felt while writing *Reunion in Vienna* and a "rebellion" he would carry on after that.[128] Athens may have succumbed to Sparta's power (as modern-day Italy was espousing fascism and Germany becoming more authoritarian each day), but no matter how successful these governments were, they would never control people's souls. The history of freedom and democracy in Athens would live on and give hope to other people at other times.

In December 1932 the Theatre Guild expressed its interest in producing *Acopolis*, but nothing came of it. Meanwhile, Bob kept working on the script, trying to improve its story line and characterizations. The play finally opened on November 23, 1933, not on Broadway but at the Lyric Theatre in London, where the critics were diplomatic but not effusive in their praise. W. A. Darling wrote in the *Daily Telegraph* that it was "an attempt at a very fine play" and that it commanded "both interest and respect." "Sadly," though, he predicted that it would be "an honourable failure."[129] The problem, he felt, was that while Bob had made clear his theme, the choice between war and civilization, it was not apparent what, exactly, he had set out to say about it. The critic in the *Morning Post* claimed that while it was not "rubbish," the play was far from perfect. Yet *Acropolis* was "full of fine suggestion, and with some moments in which beauty of thought and scene are blended in a way that seldom happens nowadays."[130] M. Willson Disher in the *Daily Mail* thought that Bob should be praised "for his courage" in trying to dramatize such an "immense" topic, while the critic in the *Daily Sketch* found that though it was at times "a clever, amusing . . . and very beautiful play," it had a tendency to be talky. Still, he had never once lost interest, and considered the dialogue "brilliant, vigorous and stimulating."[131]

Acropolis had a brief London run of only twelve performances. Bob's aunt Jane saw it on opening night and wrote to tell Lydia how moved she was by it: "I think it is noble & Beautiful. Subtle & witty too. Not a human Drama but a drama of humanity." But although the press was favorable, she found the audience "a little puzzled" by it.[132] Indeed, for many, the ideas were too intellectual, the characters too abstract, the plot too undramatic. Bob, however, never stopped working on *Acropolis*, and small, experimentally minded theater companies did perform it. In April 1934 Edward Sheldon saw one such performance and wrote to Bob that he perceived the play "as a group of certain highly gifted people arguing brilliantly and absorbingly about certain highly important ideas." This was, however, "something quite different from a good actable play and never the twain shall meet."[133] In December of the next year, the set designer Jo Mielziner saw a version of *Acropolis* at the Amateur Comedy Club of New York, a seemingly inappropriate venue for such a serious piece, and had found it "thrillingly beautiful."[134] There seemed to be no middle ground; either people loved it or were totally baffled by it. Even as late as 1939, Lawrence Langner of the Theatre Guild asked Bob to make changes in the script for a possible production which Bob wanted to stage for the Lunts. Langner was pleased, as he considered the play's theme an important one. As he later wrote, *Acropolis* "presents the collapse of Athenian democracy; and this was a timely subject while Nazism was continuing to extinguish freedom in Europe. The play also shows, through the immortal story of Pericles and Aspasia, that art endures while time obliterates most of the other efforts of man."[135] Bob had every intention of doing the rewrites, but he felt more compelled at the time to work on another play, *There Shall Be No Night*.

Bob's playwriting career up to this point was like a roller-coaster ride. He hit it big with *The Road to Rome*, *The Queen's Husband*, and *Reunion in Vienna*, especially in light of the movie adaptations and the theatrical pull of Alfred Lunt and Lynn Fontanne. But he also had several failures and near misses, including *The Love Nest*, *Waterloo Bridge*, *This Is New York*, *Acropolis*, and his novel *The Virtuous Knight*. Both his work in Hollywood on the film versions of some of his own plays and the payments he received for their use gave him financial success, especially in the case of *The Royal Bed*, *Waterloo Bridge*, *Two Kinds of Women*, and *Reunion in Vienna*. His screenwriting work for *The Age for Love*, *Cock of the Air*, and his uncredited *Rasputin and the Empress* proved to be so lucrative that he was able to turn down offers he felt were "punk and I couldn't have written dialogue for them even for love."[136] (In 2005 figures, his income over this period topped $1.5 million.)[137] Only *Roman Scandals* proved a financial failure for Bob, as MGM withheld some of his $25,000 fee and profits because he and co-writer George S. Kaufman refused to make revisions which Eddie Cantor demanded. After a long legal battle, the two received $20,000, but most of it went toward paying their legal fees.

On the personal side, Bob's life at this time was equally rocky. World War I continued to haunt him so that he could not write simply for entertainment. Rather, he tried to use his writing to work out the traumatic memories that continued to haunt him; in this he was not always successful. His home life also proved problematic, reflecting an inner turmoil experienced by veterans throughout the ages.

Rosina Emmet Sherwood (Posie) as a young woman. Courtesy of the Emmet Family Papers, 1792–1989. Archives of American Art, Smithsonian Institution.

Bobby Sherwood, the theatrical child, at age six, 1902. Houghton.

Sherwood and the Black Watch band in Montreal, 1917. Houghton.

Sherwood's drawings done in an École normale notebook while in the hospital in France recovering from war wounds, 1918. Houghton.

Robert, Little Mary, and Mary Brandon Sherwood in happier times. Stockbridge, Mass., 1925. Houghton.

Humphrey Bogart (as Duke Mantee) and Leslie Howard (as Alan Squier) in a friendly pose advertising *The Petrified Forest*, 1935. Vandamm Studio. NYPL.

Robert and Madeline Sherwood. Houghton.

The Playwrights
at a rehearsal.
From left to right
are Sherwood,
S. N. Behrman,
Sidney Howard,
Elmer Rice, and
Maxwell Anderson,
1938. Vandamm
Studio. NYPL

Achille Weber
gives Irene
(Lynn Fontanne)
her useless League
of Nations passport
in *Idiot's Delight*,
1936. Vandamm
Studio. NYPL.

Raymond Massey (sitting) as an emotionally torn Abraham Lincoln in *Abe Lincoln in Illinois*, 1938. Vandamm Studio. NYPL.

Sherwood, Alfred Lunt, and Lynn Fontanne consult about the script for *There Shall Be No Night*, March 1940. Vandamm Studio. NYPL.

STOP HITLER NOW!

WE AMERICANS have naturally wished to keep out of this war —to take no steps which might lead us in. But—

We now know that every step the French and British fall back brings war and world revolution closer to US—our country, our institutions, our homes, our hopes for peace.

Hitler is striking with all the terrible force at his command. His is a desperate gamble, and the stakes are nothing less than domination of the whole human race.

If Hitler wins in Europe—if the strength of the British and French armies and navies is forever broken—the United States will find itself alone in a barbaric world—a world ruled by Nazis, with "spheres of influence" assigned to their totalitarian allies. However

different the dictatorships may be, racially, they all agree on one primary objective: *"Democracy must be wiped from the face of the earth."*

The world will be placed on a permanent war footing. Our country will have to pile armaments upon armaments to maintain even the illusion of security. We shall have no other business, no other aim in life, but primitive self-defense. We shall exist only under martial law—or the law of the jungle. Our economic structure will have to be adjusted to that of our gangster competitors. We shall have to change ourselves from easy-going individuals into a "dynamic race."

"Government of the people, by the people, for the people"—if Hitler wins, this will be the discarded ideal of a decayed civilization.

Is this "Alarmism"? Then so is the challenging scream of an air-raid siren, warning civilians that death is coming from the skies. We have ample cause for deepest alarm. It should impel us, not to hysteria, but to resolute action.

It is obvious that there is no immediate danger of direct invasion of the United States. Hitler doesn't strike directly when he doesn't have to. He edges up on his major victims, approaching through the territory of small and defenseless neighbors.

We have twenty-one neighbors in this hemisphere, in addition to the colonial possessions of Britain, France, Holland and Denmark. We must not forget that however wide the Atlantic and Pacific oceans may be, the Canadian and Mexican borders are no barriers to invasion.

The Monroe Doctrine is not an automatic safety catch, securing the entrance to our hemisphere from all intruders. We have to enforce it—all the way from Greenland and Alaska to Cape Horn. Furthermore, we have to guard eight and day against the manifold enemies from within. We can not ignore the fact that Trojan horses are grazing in all the fertile fields of North and South America. The Western Hemisphere contains the richest territory for exploitation on earth today. And the international gangsters want it. They have already started the process of taking it. For many years the agents of the Nazis have been effectively at work in

Latin America, gaining ground by persuasion, bribery, intimidation. They have been fighting a trade war and a political war; and what we have lately seen in Norway and Holland and Belgium proves to us that these agents are ready to fight a military war when the orders come through from home.

"Divide—and conquer!" has been the Nazi watchword in the insidious invasion of all countries. The preliminary work of division has been carried on here with devastating success.

We can and should and will devote ourselves to a vast program of defense. But we must not try to fool ourselves into thinking that security can be bought. It will be achieved only by unity of purpose among ourselves, by the spirit of sacrifice that we can summon from our own hearts and minds. Overwhelming destiny will not be stopped "with the help of God and a few Marines."

This is a job for *all* of us! It will take years for us to build the necessary machines and to train the men who will run them. Will the Nazis considerately wait until we are ready to fight them?

Anyone who argues that they will wait is either an imbecile or a traitor.

How long will we wait before making it known to Hitler and the masters of all the slave states that we are vitally concerned in the outcome of this war—that we would

consider a victory for them an unmitigated calamity for civilization?

Whatever our feelings about the tragic mistakes of statesmanship in England and France we know now that the free people of those nations are willing to fight with inspiring heroism to defend their freedom. We know now that such men will die rather than surrender. But the stoutest hearts can not survive forever in the face of superior numbers and infinitely superior weapons.

There is nothing shameful in our desire to stay out of war, to save our youth from the dive bombers and the flame throwing tanks in the unutterable hell of modern warfare.

But is there not an evidence of suicidal insanity in our failure to help those who now stand between us and the creators of this hell?

WE CAN HELP—IF WE WILL ACT NOW

—before it is forever too late.

We can help by sending planes, guns, munitions, food. We can help to end the fear that American boys will fight and die in another Flanders, closer to home.

The members of our government are your servants. In an emergency as serious as this, they require the expression of your will. They must know that the American people are not afraid to cast off the hypocritical mask of neutrality, which deceives no one, including ourselves.

Send a postcard, a letter, or a telegram, at once—to the President of the United States, to your Senators and your Congressmen—urging that the *real* defense of our country must begin NOW—with aid to the Allies!

The United States of America is still the most powerful nation on earth—and the United States of America is YOU!

COMMITTEE TO DEFEND AMERICA BY AIDING THE ALLIES

(Composed of representative Americans from all sections. Sub-committees are already in existence in eighty-five cities and towns.)

National Chairman—WILLIAM ALLEN WHITE, *Editor, The Emporia (Kansas) Gazette*

NEW YORK OFFICE: 8 WEST 40TH STREET

THIS ADVERTISEMENT, appearing in newspapers from coast to coast, has been paid for with funds contributed by a number of patriotic American citizens who believe in all seriousness and sincerity that the safety of our country, the whole future of our national faith, is gravely threatened by the world revolution of Hitlerism. The names and addresses of all those who contributed to the publication of this advertisement are being filed with the State Department, Washington, D. C.

IN A DICTATORSHIP, THE GOVERNMENT TELLS THE PEOPLE WHAT TO DO. BUT—THIS IS A DEMOCRACY—
WE CAN TELL THE GOVERNMENT WHAT TO DO. EXERCISE YOUR RIGHT AS A FREE CITIZEN.
TELL YOUR PRESIDENT—YOUR SENATORS—YOUR CONGRESSMEN—THAT YOU WANT THEM TO HELP THE ALLIES TO STOP HITLER NOW!

Sherwood the interventionist. The Stop Hitler Now! ad, originally measuring 16¾" x 23", June 10, 1940. Houghton.

Sherwood in the Philippines, 1945. NYPL.

A frustrated Spencer Tracy, a concerned Garson Kanin, and a haggard Sherwood discussing
The Rugged Path, 1945. Photo courtesy of Eileen Darby Images, Inc., and NYPL.

Interlude

6

Marriage, Divorce, and
The Petrified Forest

ALTHOUGH World War I remained the defining moment of Robert Sherwood's life until the day he died, the experience most affected him over the years from 1919 to 1934. His eleven-year marriage to Mary Brandon illustrates the impact the war had on his psyche and his behavior. His emotional ups and downs and his frenetic restlessness juxtaposed with periods of silence characterized their early years together. But as time passed and the scars of war more or less healed, his lifestyle also changed. He became more dedicated to his work, which meant fewer parties and late nights of gambling. Although he would never be anything resembling a hermit, he delighted now in being at home with his daughter and in the company of his extended Sherwood family, as he had before 1917. As he changed, however, Mary, a Broadway gadabout, did not. The distance between them grew, eventually leading to divorce.

In the years when Bob was scurrying between the Algonquin Round Table and *Life* magazine, viewing films, attending plays, and socializing, he was searching for some meaningful and creative path. Despite the constant support he received from his family, he craved the love and companionship of someone to run around with him, to keep him from being alone with his memories, someone who was more vulnerable than himself. For him, that someone was Mary Judah Brandon, the daughter of divorced parents, Helen Armstrong Malone and Henry Judah Brandon of Indianapolis. Mary was a short, pretty, and somewhat flighty nineteen-year-old aspiring actress when Bob met her through the Algonquin circle, one of the young women who attached themselves to that group of shining stars. Mary attended innumerable social events where she and Bob enjoyed each other's company, and then performed with him in the Algonquin's *No Siree!* Her acting career never went very far, however. From December 1919 to September 1920 she had a small role in Aaron Hoffman's comedy *Welcome Stranger* in Chicago, traveling with it to New York, where it ran from September 1920 to June 1921. Hopeful after such a long run, she was devastated when her next two shows, *Up the Ladder* and *Nature's Nobleman*, flopped. In addition, Mary appeared in one

1921 silent film, *The Bashful Suitor*, but then no other offers came her way. In any event, she may have seen a better opportunity in becoming Mrs. Robert Sherwood than in continuing to audition for Broadway plays.

It is not easy to paint a truly accurate picture of Bob and Mary's relationship because almost all the documentation left behind depicts Mary solely from Bob's point of view. Posie, Lydia, Rosamund, Arthur, Marc Connelly, Dorothy Parker, and even Bob himself all told stories about Mary's apparent obnoxious behavior and chronic hysteria. Her concern for herself, her short temper, and her public outbursts were constant grist for the New York gossip mill. Bob's first biographer, John Mason Brown, portrays Mary as a bundle of contradictions: "She appeared soft and was tough, seemed yielding and was demanding. She was self-absorbed to the point of egomania, self-deluding to the verge of pathos, and bantam in everything except her faults."[1] The same type of uncomplimentary portrait is repeated in numerous other sources. Neither Mary's family and friends nor even Mary herself left anything but a few tales behind. Therefore, her version of what it was like to be Robert Sherwood's wife has always been missing, and even a careful reading of the letters and reminiscences combined with some thoughtful analysis is bound to be fraught with broad supposition. By the end of this telling, Mary's story will still be veiled in mystery.

What is obvious from the start is that no matter how annoying Mary seemed to Bob's friends, for most of their time together he was enthralled by her. She was as energetic as he, enamored of the theater and films, and available at all hours of the day and night to accompany him to dinner, shows, salons, and trips to Long Island or Vermont to spend time with the Algonquin regulars. Always eager for a new adventure, she was, however, very impatient if she was not receiving the attention she demanded. Marc Connelly describes one vivid example of Mary's desire to be the main attraction. One evening in the early 1920s Bob was hosting the Hollywood director Rex Ingram; his wife, the movie star Alice Terry; and some friends at a lavish dinner in a private room at Delmonico's, one of New York's most expensive and elegant restaurants. At the time, Bob, although a burgeoning movie critic, was intent on pursuing a career as a film writer. According to Connelly, he had three objectives in planning this dinner: first, to convince Ingram that he had an exciting script which he was not likely to sell cheaply, as he was supposedly a wealthy man; second, to impress Mary; and third, to give a few of his friends an entertaining night out. The group he chose to treat included the actress Margalo Gillmore, Dorothy Parker, Robert Benchley, and Marc Connelly, all of whom Bob persuaded to wear formal attire, put on sophisticated, upper-class airs, and praise him to the limit.

Apparently, the dinner party was doomed from the start. Alice Terry arrived tipsy from a day at cocktail parties and spent the entire evening making trips to the women's room. Dorothy Parker, who found it entertaining to continually ply the actress with spiked espressos, accompanied her. Ingram, also happy on alcohol, was eager to chat about other things besides ideas for new films. In fact, he told the group, his studio contract had just expired, and he and Terry were on their way to the Riviera, where he planned to spend his days painting and enjoying life. Throughout the evening he waltzed around the table, showing off his new tweed suit to each guest. Mary, meanwhile, grew impatient with what she considered boring talk about men's fashions. Unable to suffer in silence, she became "a bit of a trial" to the others, constantly expostulating in a loud voice about Bob's "inadequacy in organizing dinner parties."[2] Margalo Gillmore became so upset by Mary's disparaging remarks that she left the table on the pretext of searching for Dorothy Parker and Alice Terry. Meanwhile, Ingram fell asleep, and Connelly and Benchley left so that Bob could mollify Mary in private.

In spite of his friends' negative feelings toward her, Bob pursued Mary as tenaciously as she did him. Believing they had a love that would last, the couple wed on October 29, 1922, in an affair that was featured in the *New York Times* under the headings "Stage Folk Attend Marriage of Editor-Reviewer and Movie Actress" and "Douglas Fairbanks Ushers."[3] It was a star-studded event, one that bolstered Bob's own vision of himself as a talent worthy of public recognition. Posie took on the job of writing out close to a hundred invitations for the ceremony, which took place at the Church of the Transfiguration, commonly known as the Little Church Around the Corner—as Posie put it, "so dear to actors"—and was officiated by the Reverend Dr. Cameron. For the Sherwoods, more than the Brandons, it was a family affair. Bob's brother Philip served as best man, and Cynthia's young daughters, Elizabeth and Julia Townsend, were flower girls. Mary had two attendants: her friend Roberta Arnold and Bob's friend Margalo Gillmore, who was maid of honor. Ushers were plentiful and appealing to the news photographers. They included Douglas Fairbanks, Marc Connelly, Robert Benchley, Alexander Woollcott, Sidney Howard, and Frank Case (of the Algonquin Hotel), among others. The guest list was impressive, with Mary's distant relation Booth Tarkington; Fairbanks's wife, Mary Pickford; Rex Ingram; and F. Scott and Zelda Fitzgerald all adding glitz and glamour to the occasion. Posie described the wedding to Jane as "really nice and touching and at the same time gay."[4] After a reception given at the home of film writers John Emerson and Anita Loos, the couple departed for a brief honeymoon in Washington, D.C.

Back in New York, Bob and Mary moved into a small apartment at 71 West Twelfth Street in Greenwich Village. The place was so crowded with newly bought furniture and wedding gifts that they could hardly turn around, but they were happy nonetheless. Bob continued his busy life of editing, going to movie screenings, and socializing, and Mary joined in. Perhaps as a favor, Sidney Howard cast her that December as a duchess in his play *Sancho Panza*, an effort that met with complete failure. In any event, Mary's career was soon put on hold as she became pregnant. Almost immediately, her condition was a point of discussion among family and friends, apparently because the young woman could talk about nothing else and enjoyed exaggerating her physical changes. At times she purposely made comments designed to evoke sympathy and commiseration. Lydia told Jane of one such incident when Bob, Mary, and friends were having lunch in a restaurant. Mary was in her ninth month, looking "like a fat rosy dimpled child who had been playing in a meadow all summer," belly protruding far out from her slight figure. "I hope I'm not going to die or anything like that," she said jokingly, whereupon her doting husband, according to his aunt, "turned green & fainted."[5] Mary's comments grew tedious for some of Bob's friends. Alexander Woollcott later remembered that the baby's arrival seemed to take forever. "For months," he wrote, "the whole town had been kept uneasily aware of her approach. For months the little mother had filled the public eye with a kind of aggressive fragility."[6] When the baby, named Mary, was born on October 26, 1923, Dorothy Parker sent the proud mother a cable that read, "Dear Mary, We all knew you had it in you."[7] Mother and daughter became known as Mary and Little Mary.[8]

At first, Bob's family acted very favorably toward Mary. Lydia, in particular, took to her quickly, thinking her very well suited to Bob. She loved the young woman's pretty face, talkative nature, and easy laugh. Mary, in turn, reciprocated Lyd's great affection for her. She felt immense gratitude, too, for the consistent financial help Lyd supplied until Bob achieved a livable wage. As she wrote her aunt-in-law in a touching, though theatrical, letter: "You are as much a part of my life as my child or my husband—No woman could say more to another woman." It was Lyd who provided a "net" under them, making Mary feel that "if we should fall we couldn't be really hurt."[9] Posie, meanwhile, played a less active role in the young couple's life. Financially strapped, she traveled around the country a good deal, painting commissioned portraits. During her time away, Lydia substituted as the doting mother-in-law and surrogate mother, as Mary had no family nearby except her emotionally distant father, who had moved to Long Island in 1923.

From the start, Bob and Mary enjoyed living the high life and took little care to save money. By late 1925 they had their own home on the Upper East Side of Manhattan, a lease on a summer place, and the expenses of the social life appropriate to an Algonquinite, a film reviewer, and a theater fan. Perhaps the steady flow of money running as if through a sieve was the inspiration for Bob's short story "Brother Preble Catches the Spirit," which tells of a family man who loses all his money and then some in a poker game.[10] Bob's family was quite worried about the couple's spending. During the rehearsals for *The Road to Rome*, Lydia complained to Jane that the pair had "no notion of good management" and were "hard pressed for money."[11] Within a couple of months she had altered her perception somewhat. Bob, who was earning a hefty profit from the play, would never save a penny, she claimed, if it were not for Mary, who was "going to salt down just as much" as she could lay her hands on.[12] Lyd felt that Mary's greatest fear was that she could not stash the money away quickly enough to prevent Bob from spending it.

But Mary herself could not resist using the money Bob earned. She loved giving and attending parties. She coveted expensive furniture and fine objects for her home and, according to John Mason Brown, badgered Bob to buy them for her even when he considered them too extravagant. He gave in just to gain some "peace."[13] Of course, it was not her fault that her husband needed a custom-made bed to accommodate his length, with sheets and blankets to match. The couple spent a good deal on a trained nurse and then governesses, private schools, and lessons for Little Mary, as well as two maids and a cook for their home. Bob preferred to have a car and chauffeur rather than having to rely on taxis, use public transportation, or drive himself. Mary bought fashionable clothes and jewelry, and Bob required handmade shirts, suits, shoes, and socks. The only items he could buy off the rack were hats and neckties. For all these possessions, the couple carried "about ten times" more insurance than they needed, according to Bob.[14] In the spring of 1929 they added another expense by renting a house in Surrey, England, for summers abroad and for longer stays when Bob had a play running in London or a film script to write.

Although Bob earned large commissions when he traveled to Los Angeles to work on films, his expenses were high there as well. In fact, Bob's Hollywood expenses were particularly large because Mary hated going there, and so he had to make sure that her trips west were both enjoyable and luxurious. In 1928 she adamantly refused to move to California, leaving Bob wondering if he could request that his scripts be written in New York. The following year, fearing that the talkies would "kill the theatre," he told Sidney Howard that he would "just simply have to go into some other racket; either that, or get another wife." When he made up a story about being offered $5,000 a week for ten weeks to work in Hollywood, Mary told him "not to consider the offer at any price."[15] Eventually, of course, Mary had to give in to his need to write scripts in Hollywood because the money was simply too good to pass up. But when she and Little Mary went along with Bob, so did the governess and chauffeur. Servants were hired in Los Angeles while others remained in New York. On one such cross-country trip in May 1931, the small family made several stops to visit Mary's family and friends. At each stop there was so much socializing and spending that Posie began to worry. "They are so extravagant & generous," she wrote Jane, "that I tremble for the future."[16]

In their world of constant activity and creativity, Little Mary remained the apple of her father's eye, making unexpectedly funny comments to and about him. After the successful opening of *The Road to Rome*, Mary told the little tyke what a great man her father was. The smart and sophisticated four-year-old responded: "How lovely. Daddy's simply marvyellis!"[17] By the age of eight, Little Mary had become part of the uppermost social circles of New York society, being great friends with the daughters of Kermit Roosevelt, Theodore's son. When Bob asked her if she knew that her friends' grandfather was "one of the greatest & best men this country . . . ever produced," his daughter responded, horrified, "Am I on the verge of thinking that my daddy is not as important as I thought he was?"[18] By the spring of 1932, when Bob, Mary, and nine-year old Little Mary headed for London with a pleasure stop in Paris, the little girl could speak fluent French. She told her grandmother that she could not wait to wear her new spring clothes in Paris: "When I walk in the street all the Frenchmen will say, 'voilà Marie Sherwood elle est chic n'est-ce pas'?"[19] Bob was Little Mary's idol, and Little Mary was his true sweetheart. He basked in the glow of her adoration, especially as his and Mary's relationship grew tense and distant.

Early in 1932 Lydia's feeling toward Mary took a turn, an indication that she may have been observing conflicts between Bob and Mary in which she naturally sympathized with her nephew. Her criticism grew out of her perception that the pair were so self-involved and Mary so demanding of Bob's attention that they ignored her and the other Sherwoods. Another early complaint of Lyd's was that Bob and Mary continued to squander their cash instead of offering to help the family out during the difficult years of the depression. Arthur Jr. and Posie were struggling to make ends meet, and Lyd herself, though still a productive artist, feared that as she aged, fewer people would commission her to paint their portraits. What was she to do then, especially since she had generously helped the less financially successful Posie? Bob, the one person in the family who by that time was earning a considerable income, "has never offered to help with one cent." In order to make ends meet and save for her uncertain future, Lyd had to give up her apartment in New York and move more permanently to her house in Stockbridge, Massachusetts. When in New York, she stayed with Posie and Rosamund. "I don't care so long as I can just keep our heads above water," she wrote Jane, but it was disappointing that the couple she had helped so much when they were first married were not returning the favor.[20]

Not wanting to believe that Bob would be ungenerous to his family, Lydia decided that the source of the problem had to be Mary. Although she enjoyed her company and could not make herself dislike her niece-in-law, Lyd came to feel that Mary was "too utterly grasping & selfish," a quality she connected with her being Jewish. Mary's religious and ethnic roots had not been an issue before now, and Mary herself seemed totally disconnected from them. Lydia (and Posie, too), however, had given vent to racial stereotypes in the past, referring to Jews as "Yiddish" and "sheenies" and to African Americans as "niggers" and "apes."[21] It is not possible to tell if their language reflected their beliefs or simply reflected the casually racist language of the time, but in Mary's case it does seem that as the years went by, her ethnicity became the rationale for placing blame on her so that in their eyes Bob came out of the marriage a victim.

Greed was an easy racial stereotype to pin on Mary, for Jews had often been portrayed in literature and popular culture as misers and money-grubbers, the most obvious example being Shakespeare's Shylock in *The Merchant of Venice*. For people uneducated in the history of the racist repression of the Jewish people, it was easy to accept this anti-Semitic ideology. The Sherwoods, as educated and worldly as they were, seem to have fallen into that trap. Unlike in the early years of their marriage, when Mary's preventing Bob from squandering his earnings was seen as a virtue, it now became a fault. Lydia told Jane that Mary refused "to part with anything" and had control over "the purse strings." Bob was the innocent, the man who did not know exactly how much surplus money he had, so of course he could not aid his family. Lyd's complaint, however, was that the couple's selfishness went beyond money. They were ungiving of their time and luxuries as well. She told Jane that Bob and Mary never gave her "anything, not even drives in their car," which she could see from her apartment window parked at the curb, "standing there for hours."[22] Posie at first disagreed with Lydia's judgment, claiming, "If it were not for Mary, Bob would never have kept a cent." Instead, he would have "given it away & thrown it away."[23] In one instance he had given $3,000 to Canadian war veterans and $1,000 to New York's unemployed. Yet when he would not offer to help one of his cousins pay for college expenses, Posie blamed Mary, not Bob, for being too stingy and secretive about how much the couple had in the bank. Bob, it seemed, was simply careless, whereas Mary was made out to be a deliberate shylock.

After ten years in the Sherwood family, it appeared that Mary had chosen to distance herself from her husband's mother and aunt. Perhaps the trouble was not all her fault. After all, Mary was surrounded by Sherwoods; Ros, Cynthia, Arthur, Lyd, and Posie all lived within blocks of one another. While initially she was content with the situation, as time passed and the novelty wore off, she began to feel that they were spying on her, constantly hinting that she and Bob ought to be more generous with their time and money than Mary felt was appropriate. In any case, one rainy day Rosamund phoned Mary to ask if her chauffeur could drive Posie, who was now fragile and nearly deaf, to Cynthia's place, a mere two blocks away. Mary told her that she was sorry but it was impossible. Ros then called a taxi for Posie, who upon her arrival at her daughter's discovered the chauffeur and car outside and Mary inside visiting Cynthia herself. Lydia told Jane that she found this incident "almost too awful to write." She wanted to believe that Mary's slight was unintentional, but she could not. Rather, she came to feel not only that Mary was cruel and uncaring but also that she was withholding information from Bob. Lyd simply could not believe that Bob, who was "so sweet" and had "such a lovely refined nature," would in "his wildest dreams" ignore the family's financial problems or Mary's insults if he were truly aware of them.[24] But how much of a fog could Bob have been in? How much of Mary's mistreatment of his family was real and how much imagined?

At the time that Lydia wrote these thoughts in 1932, Bob was in the middle of the run of *Reunion in Vienna,* working on several films—the most recent being *Cock of the Air* and *Rasputin and the Empress*—and was receiving income from the touring companies and/or the films of *The Road to Rome, The Queen's Husband,* and *Waterloo Bridge.* A playwright's and screenwriter's life was somewhat precarious, and Mary, if she was indeed the member of the pair most responsible about money, might have been reluctant to give away too much. If she wished to pad her bank accounts while continuing to enjoy a luxurious life, she could not spare money for others. In spite of her unaired tensions with the Sherwoods, Mary continued to play her role at family gatherings. When Bob's thirty-sixth birthday arrived, Lyd invited everyone to her place for a party, for which Mary brought all the food and drinks. It was at that get-together that the guests performed a parody of *Reunion in Vienna* with Little Mary playing Lynn Fontanne's role, complete with an English accent, a performance Bob and the Lunts enjoyed no end.

In spite of the Great Depression, Bob and Mary continued to spend most of his earnings. During the summer of 1932, when they were in England, they saw a large estate in Surrey which he wanted to purchase. Called Great Enton, it consisted of a beautiful stone house (a mansion in U.S. terms) with several acres of land. Bob immediately entered negotiations for its purchase, which he quickly concluded, paying $21,428 (the equivalent of over $260,000 in 2005). When he and Mary returned to England the next year, they did some remodeling of the place and furnished it. From then on Great Enton became "home" in England, a place where Bob spent every summer until World War II and some months during the rest of the year if his work took him to Europe. For example, in 1934, when he checked in on the London run of *Reunion in Vienna*, worked with producer Alexander Korda on the film *The Scarlet Pimpernel*, and adapted Jacques Deval's French play *Tovaritch* into English, he spent much of his time at Great Enton writing, reading, playing croquet with friends, and betting on the horses. It seemed as if the only effect the Great Depression had on him was a dip in ticket sales on Broadway.

A more serious situation, which Bob kept locked away deep inside his heart, had its roots in the couple's 1932 stay in Europe. That summer he and Mary spent generous amounts of time with Marc and Madeline Connelly in both London and Paris, and Bob found himself falling in love with his best friend's wife. Madeline, born on December 12, 1899, was a native of Federalsburg, Maryland. Like Mary Brandon, she was a short, perky former actress, but one who had had considerable success. After acting stints in Philadelphia and New York, Madeline was discovered by Mack Sennett, the king of Hollywood silent comedy, and became one of his "girls." From 1923 to 1928 she was featured in no fewer than fifty-four silent films, not leaving the industry until talkies exploded on the screen, bringing with them a new cast of supporting actresses and actors. After a very brief, unhappy marriage, she moved to New York, met Marc Connelly, and married him two years later on October 4, 1930. Little is known about their life together except for a relayed comment from Posie to Bob in 1934 or 1935 that "Mrs. Laddie Sanford told someone who told Arthur that Marc Connelly had always treated her unkindly, and that his Mother had been horrible to her."[25] Indeed, the crux of the Connellys' immediate marital problems may well have been Marc's mother, who lived with the couple from the start of their marriage. Connelly himself did not write about his marriage or divorce in his autobiography, *Voices Offstage*, and information does not appear about either in his biography.

At first the Sherwoods and Connellys were great friends, often socializing together. Marc and Madeline were present at some of the Sherwoods' most intimate family celebrations, including Bob's, Mary's, and Little Mary's birthday parties and the fete marking the Sherwoods' tenth wedding anniversary. The trip to France and England in the summer of 1932, followed by

Connelly's involvement in Bob's play *Acropolis* the following year, however, threw Bob and Madeline into almost constant contact. Bob spent a considerable amount of time in the Connellys' apartment in Paris reading the play aloud to the pair, and Marc eagerly agreed to direct its London production. At the time, both couples were experiencing difficulties in their marriages, and Bob and Madeline found solace in each other. Neither Marc nor Mary seems to have had an inkling about their growing attachment. In addition, by the early spring of 1933, problems between Mary and the rest of the Sherwood family had become more serious. Feeling that the Sherwoods interfered too much in her and Bob's business, Mary often shut her door to them. Bob seems to have been oblivious, but Posie complained that she saw him only when it "suits Mary's convenience to have me."[26]

At the heart of the matter remained money and the couple's lifestyle. Lydia and Posie both continued to believe that Bob and Mary were living "on the brink of a precipice," spending money as if there was no end to it. In the summer of 1933, however, Bob finally acknowledged the severity of his family's problems and agreed to underwrite some of his brother's family expenses and his life insurance premiums, on the condition that Arthur be told nothing about it. He also consented to help various young Sherwood cousins with their education and travel expenses. This alleviated some of the stress between Lydia and Posie and Mary but may very well have resulted in more tension between Mary and Bob. Meanwhile, the Sherwoods' dislike for Mary had grown. Lydia simply could not understand her nephew, for, from her perspective, although his wife "goads him to madness at times, Bob adores her as much as ever." Ros felt that Bob had an "ideal" of Mary that he would not let go of even though she teased him about her attractiveness to other men."[27] To his family, Bob was just a blind puppy, the innocent they loved to believe him to be. They gave no thought to the possibility that Mary's caustic comments might have been a defense against problems in the marriage which they kept to themselves.

Bob received a blow with the failure of *Acropolis* in London, but he was about to receive a bigger blow upon his return to New York in late 1933. While the rest of his family had correctly perceived that Mary was distancing herself from them and from him, he had not noticed the change until, while he was in England, Mary broke off contact with him. He told his mother that he could not understand why he had not heard a word from his wife for over three weeks. When he arrived home, their relationship appeared so strained that Posie suggested perhaps she should visit her recalcitrant daughter-in-law to try to find out why she had been ignoring her absent husband. In a moment of self-deception she wrote, "We have always got on well together as you know, as all I asked of her was that she should make you happy."[28] For a while things returned to normal. Christmas went as usual, with the traditional Sherwood dinner, party, breakfast, and stuffed stockings. But in mid-January 1934, Bob and Mary's marriage shattered.

Lydia wrote to Jane that "Bobby . . . has borne all he can," and the rest of the family felt "grateful" that he had come to his senses. They would all soon be rid of Mary, who had been "too abominable" since her husband's return from England, "drinking fearfully & consorting with awful cheap fast people & circulating the most abominable lies about Bobby's brutality to her."[29] Bob suspected that she might be having an affair, but he had no proof. In any case, immediately after this first break, Mary became frightened about her future and extremely contrite about her behavior. Bob, however, took the opportunity to push for a divorce so he could pursue a life with Madeline, telling Mary that he also wanted full custody of Little Mary. Of course, he did not tell Mary that he had fallen in love with another woman, one who was still married to his friend Marc Connelly and undecided about whether to leave him or not. Instead, Bob simply allowed Mary to become the focus of the ensuing turmoil while he kept his contact with Madeline to a minimum.

And Mary did not disappoint. At first, she fluctuated between demanding a divorce and than begging for a reconciliation. Bob wanted her to move out of their home, but she refused, and he realized that he had no legal grounds to force the issue. Indeed, the house and a good amount of their savings were in her name, and she also shared ownership of Great Enton. The couple seemed at an impasse until Mary blundered. After a few too many drinks one day, she whispered to June Walker that she was having an affair with a wealthy man. It was just a tryst, she said; neither one was in love with the other. Walker, calling Mary "the most awful little bitch that ever lived," turned around and told Posie.[30] Once Bob learned about Mary's adultery, he hired private detectives to produce the evidence that would entitle him to go to court and request custody on the grounds that Mary was an unfit mother.

Throughout their struggle, Mary took on the role of the misunderstood and ill-treated wife. She told anyone within earshot that Bob had been abusive to her, and although there is no concrete evidence that he was a violent husband, it is easy to see from various episodes how she could raise the issue. John Mason Brown, for instance, relates an account he heard from some of Bob's friends about the opening night of *The Road to Rome*. Mary was excessively loud and Bob somewhat drunk. She, adorned in "a cluster of orchids," sat confidently in the second or third row while he, too nervous to watch the performance, left the theater for a "nearby speakeasy." After the curtain was rung down, he returned to escort her backstage. "You're drunk," she reportedly screamed, yelling at him all the way to Jane Cowl's dressing room, where Bob, "mortified and angered," pulled Mary's orchids off her dress and gave them to Cowl. "As he bowed his apologies" to Cowl, Brown relates, "he made a wide gesture with his windmill arms," knocking Mary to the floor. At the party later that evening, in response to Mary's comment, "Bob, I always knew it would succeed," he reportedly snarled, "Don't be such a god-damned liar!" and then struck her. Brown claims that although Bob told him a decade later that this drunken episode had been "a disgraceful performance, especially by me," his friends (and Brown) felt that he was justified.[31]

Brown also mentions that in another instance, when Bob wanted to leave a party but Mary refused to go, he physically lifted his wife, packed her under his arm, and carried her "kicking and screaming" out the door.[32] This must have been extremely humiliating for her. Even as late as 1949, a columnist for the *Boston Herald* recollected that at the Washington, D.C., opening of *The Road to Rome*, Mary "read the rave notices on this, his first success, and jumped up and down so ecstatically that she fell and broke her leg."[33] Although no explanation accompanied this quip, the public displays of violence and the harsh words between the two point to marital discord otherwise kept hidden from and by friends and family. In all recollections left behind, these were seen as humorous episodes caused by Bob's efforts to control Mary's embarrassing behavior.

Their friends' reactions reflect the casual ease with which plays and films of the time portrayed violence against women, including Bob's own works. In *The Road to Rome*, Amytis gleefully looks forward to being sexually overpowered by Hannibal, and the Carthaginian soldiers speak humorously about raping women. In *This Is New York*, one character makes a supposedly funny comment about Harry Glassman going upstairs to punch his mistress in order to discipline and control her. In *Reunion in Vienna*, Archduke Rudolf threatens to strike Elena as part of his ploy to get her into bed. In all of this banter, the tone is entirely nonchalant. Such dialogue brought laughs, though not, or at least not willingly, from battered women sitting in the audience. In the general atmosphere of the times, and because existing accounts all sympathize with Bob, it is not possible to know if there were moments when Bob was privately violent with Mary or not. She claimed that he had ill-treated her, "often knocked her down & given her black eyes," and in their last emotionally fraught moments together had gone after her with a knife.[34] Yet in all fairness to Bob, no remaining documents mention any bruises or cuts on Mary's face or body.

It was not violence or adultery but custody of Little Mary that became the central issue in the divorce struggle. Lydia claimed that Mary did not love her daughter, that she had neither shown her great affection nor physically taken good care of her. That was why Bob, the attentive and loving father, wanted his daughter with him. He was willing to pay a large amount of alimony, but in exchange he wanted sole custody. His lawyer, Thomas Finletter, advised him to take the child and hide her. Concurring, one day when Mary was not at home, Bob simply walked out the door with Little Mary and her governess, taking only the clothes they wore, and disappeared to a quiet hotel. He told no one except his friend Geoffrey Kerr where they were staying, and he hired a private detective to keep watch over Little Mary. Mary, of course, was frantic. She called all the Sherwoods, trying to locate Bob and her daughter, but Lydia claimed that to none of them did she express any feeling for either her husband or her child. Instead, she told everyone a different story, "adopting a different role sometimes pathetic, sometimes abusive, that Bobby is crazy."[35] After some hours Bob called Mary, phoning from a drugstore so she could not trace the call, to say that he had acted on his lawyer's advice and that he was absolutely inflexible about his decision. He wanted sole custody. That was his bottom line.

For several days Bob chose to communicate with his wife through letters so that there would be no personal conversation. He showed these notes to his mother, who then reported them to Lydia. His aunt described them as "the last word in dignity & character, chivalry & generosity & moderation," not at all reflecting the trauma that Mary was putting him through. To the family, Bob was a hero and a martyr. His sister Ros saw him as the most faithful and devoted husband to put up with a wife who was trouble from day one. His cousin Ev claimed that there were only three men "who could show the forbearance & patience he has: Jesus Christ, Abraham Lincoln, & Bobby."[36] To that comment he replied that he felt more like Casper Milquetoast, the H. T. Webster cartoon character in the popular newspaper series "The Timid Soul," a pushover who never had the confidence to stand up to his bossy, henpecking wife.

Little Mary could not help but be affected by the one-sided comments she heard. She was sequestered from Mary and often cared for by Sherwood relatives. To make matters worse, just before Bob absconded with his daughter, Mary had had a juvenile temper tantrum in front of her child and told the little girl she had never been wanted. So when asked by someone if she was going home to her mother, she quickly replied: "Oh my mother does not care anything for me. She did not want me but I just came." Apparently no one in the Sherwood family chose to contradict her. Rather, they simply praised her father, causing Little Mary to comment, "My Daddy says he will never ever leave me."[37] It did not help Mary's case that she fluctuated between claiming that she would rather not see her daughter at all if her visits were to be few and far between and asking to make arrangements to see her as often as possible. These changes of mind simply confused Little Mary, who asked her father to keep her away from the home whose environment had become so painfully intense.

Once Bob had absolute proof that Mary had had an extramarital affair, she was given the choice of signing over custody of Little Mary to her husband or facing embarrassing court proceedings in which her private indiscretions would become fodder for the gossip columnists—not the kind of attention she craved. Once the custody papers were finalized, Bob pressured Mary to sign consent forms so he could take up residency in Reno, Nevada, in order to receive a quick legal divorce. Toward the end of January 1934 Bob left for Hollywood to write the dialogue for a film about Marie Antoinette, a project that never reached fruition for him. Lonely and depressed, he hoped to go immediately from there to Reno to obtain the divorce so he could return to New York and present himself to Madeline as a free man. Mary, however, decided not to cooperate, and without her written consent, there would be no easy divorce. To pressure her, protect Little Mary while he was away, and gain some peace of mind, he sent his daughter to live with his brother Phil's family in Dedham, Massachusetts.

Mary's stance was that she and Bob still loved each other and that they would surely get back together. She used her acting skills to try to convince him as well. Posie, Lydia, and Ros were terrified that he would give in, as from their point of view, he had always been under Mary's spell. Lyd believed that Bob saw Mary as "deserted by every one," and that being chivalrous, he pitied her. But, she added to Jane, "if he condones what she has done he has lost his one chance to be rid of her & will be doomed for life to her miserable atmosphere." [38] The day Bob left for Hollywood, Mary had gotten up early to see him off, and they had kissed each other. That one kiss made Posie almost frantic with worry. "I can't think, no matter what sacrifice he might make of himself," she wrote Jane, "that he would ever take Little Mary back to that home." Arthur concurred, but he felt that his brother was "the most monogamous man he ever saw and very home loving," and that he had been happy with Mary for most of his time with her. Arthur felt that the marriage had soured because Bob had "spoil[ed]" Mary, "giving her everything and letting her have her own way." [39] By early February, even the Lunts were in on the discussion. With Mary "not so easy" about the divorce, friends worried, what was going to happen to Bob? [40]

March arrived, and still Mary refused to sign the papers enabling him to go to Reno. As a result, he could not make plans to go to Great Enton, either, because he wanted to be ready to leave for Nevada at a minute's notice. In mid-March, Lyd reported that Mary was "going around acting as if this whole thing will blow over." At one party she was heard to say in a voice loud enough so everyone could hear, "It won't be long now before Bob & I go to England." She also took it upon herself to visit Bob's lawyer, telling him that "there is nothing in this whole affair," and that it had been a "misunderstanding . . . invented & fostered by the mischief making" of June Walker and Geoffrey Kerr. Lydia wondered how Bob could deal with "such shifty stuff."[41] Back in New York, Bob apparently could do nothing but wait. He generally avoided large social events because he did not want to hear any comments about his situation or run into Marc and Madeline Connelly. His friends criticized him for continuing to see Mary and, once Little Mary was returned to New York in April to live with him at the Plaza Hotel, for allowing Mary to see her twice a week. His being nice to Mary, in their opinion, merely aided in her denial that their marriage was at an end.

Mary, meanwhile, continued to act erratically, confusing everyone, especially Little Mary. In one instance, she promised the child that she would buy her a watch she had wanted for some time, but she used the watch as an instrument of torture. "Tell me truthfully," she asked her daughter one day. "Which do you like best to be with, me or your Daddy?" Little Mary answered coyly, "Well, Mommy, it is a hard thing to answer truthfully but I have to say I like best to be with my Father." Mary flew into a rage at the answer she had not expected and shot back: "Very well. You shan't have the watch then." Lydia related this story to Jane as an example of the damaging atmosphere the "sensitive intelligent child" was subjected to.[42] Lydia's and Posie's impression was that Bob did nothing to curtail such episodes.

In April, Bob invited Mary to lunch. There he proposed an alimony of $6,000 a year, but Mary told June Walker that she could not possibly get along on such a measly sum. She needed at least twice that much and not a penny less. Evidently she also had no intention of giving up her rights to Great Enton, telling Walker that she expected to spend part of each year there. Twelve thousand dollars a year was much more than Bob wanted to pay, and he would never consider sharing Great Enton with her, so the two remained deadlocked. Then in early May, Bob pulled a switch on Mary. He proposed that she buy out his share of Great Enton, an offer he knew she could not afford. During their seemingly amicable chat, he made a breakthrough in getting her to understand their financial situation, and as a result she finally consented to the divorce, along with alimony, a trust fund (which eventually added up to $100,000), the car, half the securities bought from his savings, and half the future royalties on his plays up to the time of the divorce. Great Enton and full rights to his future work went to him—and so did Little Mary. Before she could change her mind again, Bob made travel arrangements, packed his bags, and said his good-byes. For the next six weeks he would be in Reno, hoping that Mary would not go back on the arrangement. In the meantime, he allowed Mary to live in his suite at the Plaza with Little Mary and the governess. Bob asked Posie, Lydia, and Ros to keep an eye on them.

It was during this time that Lydia had a revealing visit with Mary which convinced her that the family would never see the last of her. To the artist Lyd, Mary had grown "thickened and harder," giving "a sort of impalpable wooden effect of consistency." The woman who had once seemed the perfect match for their "Bobby" was now an "albatross" to the family, a lonely and dependent creature who would "always hang round Bobby & us." Arthur reminded Lyd of the time when Bob had broken a coccyx bone in a fall while playing tennis, and Mary had proven to be a very poor nursemaid and wife. In fact, Bob complained that whenever he suffered one of his chronic and painful sinus attacks (later diagnosed as *tic douloureux*), Mary behaved as if he got sick just to annoy her. Because of this cold attitude, Jane Cowl had scolded her: "You will lose everything, your husband & child's love. I can't say you will lose your friends because you haven't got any, but you will lose everything you have." Lydia felt both pity and abhorrence for this poor soul who had "nothing but us to tie to." The Sherwood family was her "best asset," and since Mary herself had "no pride, no sensitiveness," she feared that they would always be saddled with her in one way or another.[43]

At last, at 2:15 A.M. on May 3, Bob left for Reno from Newark Airport aboard a Boeing monoplane with "two motors, two pilots, a stewardess, and 10 passengers." A real puddle-jumper, it stopped in Cleveland, Toledo, Chicago, Moline, Council Bluffs, Des Moines, Omaha, Cheyenne, Salt Lake City, and, finally, Reno, "a mad, thrilling dash to nowhere." The plane flew at 175 miles per hour about two to three miles above the earth. For Bob, crossing the Rockies was the most frightening part of the trip, as the plane rocked and bumped. Looking down, he noted: "I can see no soft spot on which to land. Any trouble here, and my near and dear ones will never know whether or not I died game." Also unpleasant was the segment from Salt Lake City to Reno, "about as dismal looking as bare, gaunt and un-chummy as terrain can be." The ride was turbulent indeed, and the Boeing bounced "like a ping-pong ball." After eighteen hours of being crushed in a small space, and at the very point when he was "really scared that the engines just won't make it," the wheels touched the landing field, and out of relief, Bob burst out laughing.[44]

For the next forty-three days Bob resided at the Hotel Riverside, a "recognized resident" of Washoe, Nevada. While his lawyer Lester D. Summerfield worked on getting him what Bob termed a "diploma" from the "Nevada School of Disillusionment," the happy and relieved playwright got to know Reno.[45] He thought it "about the oddest, most interesting and I can even go so far as to say one of the most fascinating spots" he had ever visited. For a town of only 22,000 residents, there were "enough bars, night clubs and gambling houses to satisfy a population of five million." And yet he found "nothing that is vicious and very little that is sordid about all this hilarity." The only sour note was the extreme commercialization of divorce, the "one really unpleasant and unwholesome element here." Yet, coming from the highly conservative legal environment of New York, which recognized very few grounds for divorce (only adultery with a co-respondent, extreme brutality, or presumed death after five years' absence), Bob was impressed by the "extreme liberality" of the system in Nevada. A local judge had recently recognized "mental cruelty" as a legitimate claim, an idea Bob called "a masterpiece of judicial wisdom."[46]

One of Bob's favorite places in Reno was the Ship and Bottle, a bar where many "lonesome and pleading and depressed" people hung out from one o'clock in the morning until dawn.[47] Bob, however, was not one of those depressed people who lined up to phone home, begging for forgiveness and reconciliation. Instead, he was understandably happy in Reno, for he was soon to be rid of Mary and on his way to Madeline. Whereas in New York his effort to write a comedy, *Milk and Honey*, had come to naught because of his inability to concentrate, in Reno he felt more than ready to write almost from the minute he arrived. Within a week he rented a furnished office for twenty-five dollars a month and went to work on a play, *The Petrified Forest*, which was inspired by his surroundings. As he wrote to his friend Geoffrey Kerr, "With the zest for work, the cheerfulness of the surroundings and this remarkably healthy atmosphere, I don't feel lonely or depressed."[48] He wrote, played tennis, went fishing with his lawyer, and was generally full of energy.

Meanwhile, back in New York, things were not as placid. Posie, Lydia, and Ros kept a careful watch on Mary and Little Mary as they had promised to do. But this forced them into almost constant contact with Mary, who was making outlandish plans of her own, talking "wildly" about going with Bob to Great Enton, claiming that as soon as he returned, they would be re-wed.[49] Lydia thought this fantasy the most "idiotically stupid" thing she had ever heard.[50] Mary also spoke of plans to take Little Mary out of New York's early summer heat to cool Great Enton, but this idea raised questions. If Bob allowed it, a judge could rule that he considered Mary a fit mother, and then he might lose custody of Little Mary, but if he forbade her to go, Mary might instantly stop the divorce proceedings, which under Nevada law she had every right to do within the six-week waiting period before the decree became final. After consulting long-distance with his lawyer, Bob wrote Mary that he had just received "a very lucrative offer" from Hollywood and might have to be there for the entire summer.[51] He figured correctly that in his soon-to-be ex-wife's state of denial, she would give up the Great Enton idea, thinking that she would join him in Hollywood instead. The Sherwood women, meanwhile, made every effort to mollify Mary. Bob had left strict instructions that if there was any threat at all to his daughter, he was to be alerted and would return home at once. Not wanting to disrupt the divorce process, Posie and Lyd kept quiet about their fears that Little Mary was fretful about her future or their concern when Mary reiterated her accusations about Bob's alleged abuses.

Finally, on June 17, Bob and Mary became officially divorced. He immediately returned home to take Little Mary to Great Enton, where the effects of his entire ordeal crashed down upon him. For three weeks he succumbed to accumulated exhaustion and remained in bed, losing twenty-five pounds in the process. Posie's and Ros's company helped somewhat—and Madeline's even more. Conveniently in England at the same time to take a break from her own marital problems, she made several visits to Great Enton. Mary also sailed for England but surprised the family by staying clear of them. To Posie's dismay, she did, however, still claim to be "Mrs. Bobby Sherwood," since Bob had told her that she could continue to use his name as long as she liked or until either of them married again.[52] Posie remained uncomfortable with Bob's gracious behavior toward Mary. As she wrote to her son Phil, "I think Bobby makes a mistake in treating her as he does." In her view, he saw Mary too frequently and called her "my dear," which Posie felt merely encouraged her. To his mother, Bob explained that while Mary "bothered him dreadfully," he had to consider what was best for his daughter.[53]

During the time between the divorce in 1934 and Bob's departure for an extended stay in England in 1935, the drama he wrote in Reno, *The Petrified Forest*, was mounted. It is a cynical work reflecting the state of the world, as in the introduction to *Reunion in Vienna*, and on marriage as well. It is sprinkled with Bob's famous wit, but it is also deadly serious. *The Petrified Forest* features two men of opposing natures: Alan Squier and Duke Mantee. Squier is a thin, pale, gentle intellectual who is down and out. A self-confessed gigolo whose wealthy European wife recently kicked him out, he is hitchhiking across the United States with the idea that he might drown himself in the Pacific Ocean. Duke Mantee, meanwhile, is a strong, virile criminal who is trying to escape to Mexico after having killed six people in Oklahoma. The two come face-to-face at the isolated, rundown Black Mesa Filling Station and Bar-B-Q in the desert of eastern Arizona on the outskirts of the Petrified Forest, a desolate place where dead trees have turned into a substance as hard as stone. The other main character is Gabby Maple, a beautiful young woman dreaming of a way out of her deadly boring life as the waitress at this desolate establishment owned by her grandfather and run by her equally unhappy father. The action revolves around Gabby's infatuation with Squier and his romantic desire to help her out of her situation. The climax, in a plot device reminiscent of *Waterloo Bridge*, involves Squier's naming Gabby (without her knowledge) as beneficiary of his life insurance policy and then begging Mantee to kill him as he is leaving for Mexico.

Writing *The Petrified Forest* helped Bob pass the time quickly in Reno. As S. N. Behrman later related, the play was inspired by Bob's talks with Lester Summerfield about the contradictions between the natural desolation of the Nevada valley and the "thick sedimentary stream of decadent urban society" that passed through it.[54] The story itself is set in Arizona, not Nevada, an arbitrary choice. As Bob told Ward Morehouse, he picked the location by looking at a road map he obtained at a local gas station. "In the First Act," he noted, "I came to the point where the girl says to the man, 'Where do you go from here?' I thereupon looked at the road map to see where it did lead, and found some little criss-crosses on the map and the words, 'The Petrified Forest.'"[55] For the four weeks it took him to write the play, Bob lived in the world of Alan Squier, Duke Mantee, and Gabby Maple, creating a tense story of rugged individualism versus intellectualism—or civilization, as many literary critics have suggested. Yet he also lived in a world where he could look on with amusement at his own life and attitudes.

Unlike in his other plays, the published version of *The Petrified Forest* had no introduction or editorial comment, but in the 1940 introduction to *There Shall Be No Night*, Bob remarked that *The Petrified Forest* was his first attempt to write about the contemporary United States. He identified a specific section of dialogue as containing the "essence" of the work. In it, Squier asks Gabby if she realizes what it is that is causing "world chaos." In response to her "no," he explains: "Well, I'm probably the only living person who can tell you. . . . It's Nature hitting back. Not with the old weapons—floods, plagues, holocausts. We can neutralize them. She's fighting back with strange instruments called neuroses. She's deliberately affecting mankind with the jitters. Nature is proving that she can't be beaten—not by the likes of us. She is taking the world away from the intellectuals and giving it back to the apes."[56] For Bob, "Nature" meant something like God, fate, natural instincts.

In other words, humankind's basic animal instincts, instead of their common sense, was making a comeback. In *The Petrified Forest*, the basic instinct is criminal brutality. In the larger world, it was fascism and communism, greed and uninhibited national expansion, and the vast desire for power harbored in the hearts of all—whether power over another individual or power over millions. Each was causing uneasiness among people who could not go about the business of living their lives in an atmosphere of peace and plenty.

In that vein, Bob opens the play with dialogue between Gramp Maple, the feisty patriarch of the Bar-B-Q, and two telegraph linemen who have stopped there for lunch. Bob conceived one of the linemen to represent that "jitteriness" he felt people were experiencing in the United States of the 1930s. Working hard to lay telegraph lines in the desert, the man expresses unhappiness with his life and extols the Russian communists who have brought revolution and equality to their nation. In direct opposition, his partner compares communism to slavery. Boze, a young man working for the Maples, chimes in against the "cock-eyed system" in Russia, where people are not able to call their souls their own. To this the first lineman responds that he has no idea what "soul" refers to, but if he has one, he supposes it is "locked up in the safe at the Postal Telegraph Company, along with the rest of their doubtful assets."[57] For this man, Russia is more desirable because the system works for the collective whole, not for "rugged individualism! Every man for himself!"[58] Yet, as all the other characters argue, whether capitalist or communist, a system that curtails the freedom and prosperity of its ordinary citizens is as corrupt as fascism.

For Bob, the issue is that the majority of those at the Bar-B-Q (and in the nation) believe in the ideal whereby everyone can reach for the stars, go from rags to riches, obtain all the money and material possessions a person can grab. Such people have no interest in collectivity, for it threatens the traditional American dream. As Gabby's super-patriotic but milquetoast American Legion father, Jason, warns the lineman, "Belittling our system of government, preaching revolution and destruction, and red propaganda—well, it isn't a very healthy occupation."[59] Soon after, he politely orders the lineman to leave the premises, but then announces to Gramp that he will make "inquiries" about the man and attempt to get "that Bolshevik" fired.[60] Gramp, the representative of the pioneering past, prefers the era of individuality and savors stories of the Old West, remembering the likes of Billy the Kid and practically idolizing Duke Mantee. Though settled in a godforsaken desert where he makes but a few dollars a day, this spirited and humorous old man prefers the Bar-B-Q to anyplace else. Here he believes that he is free to be his own man and, though Prohibition had ended in 1933, free to sell moonshine to all those who will pay his price. He is not, however, the free individual he thinks he is. Rather, he is forbidden more than one drink a day, a family law imposed by his son and enforced by his granddaughter.

Once Alan Squier enters the scene, the discussion becomes more personal and abstract. Squier is the epitome of the intellectual. Physically, he does not look like anyone else at the Bar-B-Q. He wears a brown felt hat, a brown tweed coat, and gray flannel trousers, and, as Bob describes him, is "diffident in manner, ultra-polite and soft spoken," his accent "that of an Anglicized American," actually, that of a New Englander. Squier perceives himself as belonging to a "vanishing race," the intellectuals. He sarcastically terms himself a "Homo Semi-Americanus—a specimen of the in-between age."[61] Squier intends to commit suicide, just as civilization is voluntarily killing itself. Perhaps the world is getting what it deserves for not taking care of humanity. As Bob himself put it, Alan Squier "questioned whether it was worth while living on in a morally petrified world."[62] For Bob, Squier is one of a dying breed, whereas Boze, the former college football player, is truly caught in the middle between being civilized and being bestial. Boze recognizes that gun-toting criminals like Duke Mantee understand only weapons and violence "instead of . . . *principles*."[63] It is Boze who knows the civilized way to behave but who experiences the force of human nature when he violently seizes Mantee's gun, only to have the tables turned on him as he is shot in the arm.

Duke Mantee serves as the prime example of man reverting to his animal instincts. Mantee is an unrepentant criminal, a man who can rob and kill without remorse. When Squier, in a state of growing inebriation, tries to get Mantee to agree to kill him, the man answers in the most casual manner, "I'll be glad to."[64] At the end of the play, when Mantee is leaving the Bar-B-Q without having carried out the deed and Squier reminds him of his promise, Mantee shoots him without looking back. Duke Mantee has no conscience. He lives for the robbery, for the kill, and waits for no man. He does, however, make the mistake of waiting for a woman, who, with the other half of the gang, is to meet him at the Bar-B-Q. Caught before she can arrive there, she informs the police of his whereabouts. Women cannot be trusted. "They always snitch," proclaims Jackie, a member of Mantee's gang.[65] In the film version of the play, her betrayal leads to Mantee's capture; in the play, his end is left uncertain. Although they are opposites, Squier identifies a commonality between himself and Mantee. They are both passé. "You'd better come with me, Duke," he tells Mantee. "I'm planning to be buried in the Petrified Forest. . . . It's the graveyard of the civilization that's been shot from under us. It's the world of outmoded ideas. Platonism—patriotism—Christianity— Romance—the economics of Adam Smith—they're all so many dead stumps in the desert. That's where I belong—and so do you, Duke. For you're the last apostle of rugged individualism."[66]

Although in later interviews and writings Robert Sherwood contended that the play was about the breakdown of civilization, there are several moments in which he reflects humorously on himself and his marriage. After all, it is a play that finds its characters stuck in a desert and features a man giving up his money to a woman. Even in his isolated, unpressured situation in Reno, Bob could not help incorporating his feelings about Mary and himself in the play. A bit of each of them is encapsulated in four of its characters. Squier, for example, purports to be an intellectual, but in the span of his thirty-five or so years (Bob himself was thirty-eight), he has not accomplished much. Squier's one achievement has been the writing of a novel, which, like Bob's own novel *The Virtuous Knight,* was a failure, selling slightly over six hundred copies. And though not a veteran of World War I, he is, like Bob, "looking for something to believe in . . . something that's worth living for—and dying for."[67] Squier finds that something in Gabby, with her youthful spirit and enthusiasm for life.

Gabby is, in a way, like Mary Brandon. She is young, a bit resentful of her position, a budding intellectual with great curiosity about the world, and pretty, with big eyes that make men melt. She wants to study painting, although her dubious talent is evident in Squier's ambivalent response to her work. A lovely, untalented dreamer, she is looking for a way out of her deadly life. The answer to her prayers, she thinks, is Alan Squier, a writer headed west who just might take her along with him. Within minutes of meeting him, she decides that she is in love with him. He is her ticket out. The scenario is reminiscent of the moment when Mary Brandon, the aspiring young actress with the big eyes, latched onto Robert Sherwood, the man she perceived as her ticket out of a life of beating the pavements of New York, looking for any kind of acting role. He had the connections she needed to make her a star, and if that did not work, he could be the star who would support her in luxury and bring her into the society she so wanted to belong to. "That wife of yours must have been terrible," Gabby tells Squier. "She's talked all the heart out of you."[68] The loquacious Mary Brandon had taken much of the heart out of Robert Sherwood, but she was also exiting the marriage with a large chunk of his possessions and his income. Gabby, though unwittingly, does much the same. She has hoodwinked Squier with her innocence. He is all too eager to take care of her in the only way he knows how—by leaving her an inheritance of five thousand dollars. "There ain't a woman alive or ever did live that's *worth* five thousand dollars," Gramp insists. But to Alan Squier, "any woman" is worth "everything that any man has to give—anguish, ecstasy, faith, jealousy, love, hatred, life or death."[69] Woman was the reason for living—even a woman like Mary Brandon . . . or Madeline Hurlock Connelly.

Bob wrote into *The Petrified Forest* an older married couple, the Chisholms, who become trapped as hostages at the Bar-B-Q when Mantee holes up there. Mrs. Chisholm is obviously unhappy in her marriage. As she tells Gabby, she once dreamed of becoming a great actress. Her family prevented her from doing so, however, and she ended up being married to a banker. "He took my soul and had it stencilled on a card, and filed," she laments. She tells her husband that he has not the "remotest conception" of what is inside her. To Gabby she says that she knows what it is to "repress" herself and "starve" herself "through what you conceive to be your duty to others."[70] Through all this, she says, she has never complained. Instead, she gave her husband her self-respect and her individuality. Mr. Chisholm soon explodes, insisting that he has given his wife everything that she ever asked for. He has never asked for anything in return, and yet she has often stormed into his office and created a scene. Bob saw himself in both these people—the repressed wife and the exploited husband. For him, obtaining his freedom felt a bit like suicide. So much of what he had worked for was to go to Mary. But men, he felt, had to take care of women financially, not the other way around. When Mr. Chisholm tells his wife to seek out his lawyer if he should die, she responds dismissively. Of course he will see that she is taken care of. That is his job. Like Mary, both Mrs. Chisholm and Gabby take it for granted that a man will come along and provide for them. Then they will live a parasitic life, make him miserable, and end up with a sizable portion of his worldly goods. If he is killed or commits suicide, so what? As Squier assures Mantee: "You'd have a hard time finding a more suitable candidate for extermination. I'll be mourned by no one. In fact, my passing will evoke sighs of relief in certain quarters."[71]

The Petrified Forest went into rehearsals in November 1934. Bob had pursued the English actor Leslie Howard for the role of Alan Squier. Besides being a superb performer, Howard shared the same World War I experience that had so affected Bob. In 1917, when Howard was diagnosed with shellshock, his physician suggested that he take up acting as therapy. In this he found a successful career. Bob and Howard had recently worked together on the 1934 film version of *The Scarlet Pimpernel,* and the popular star eagerly accepted the role in *The Petrified Forest,* where he was teamed with a young Humphrey Bogart as Duke Mantee. The play previewed in Hartford, Connecticut, on December 10 and in Boston on December 24, and finally opened at the Broadhurst Theatre in New York on January 7, 1935.

In general, the critics loved *The Petrified Forest*, and in a season that saw other successful plays and musicals including Lillian Hellman's *The Children's Hour*, Cole Porter's *Anything Goes*, and Clifford Odets's *Awake and Sing*, it did a rousing business. Brooks Atkinson called it "good gutsy excitement," referring to Bob as a "mentally restless" man with an "earnest idealism." For him, this "literate melodrama" captured the American spirit of the time. He particularly appreciated Bob's story of the "roaring" West mixed in with his wry comments on the American Legion, intellectuals, and "desperadoes."[72] Richard Watts of the *New York Herald Tribune* saw the play as "patriotic," and Gilbert Gabriel of the *New York American* considered it Bob's best play—clever, hard, and "significant."[73] Burns Mantle found it an "effective melodrama with an interesting philosophic content uncommon in dramas of so patent a theatrical base." He added that just having Leslie Howard in the cast added "glamor" to the production.[74] Bob's harshest critic was Mary Brandon. Whether because she recognized herself in Bob's barbs or because she would no longer profit from his hits, she was quick to tell anyone who would listen that it would never be successful. In fact, she surprised the family by staying away from the opening night festivities, a relief for the playwright.

At least two literary and theater analysts of the time also addressed *The Petrified Forest*. Eleanor Flexner, in her contemporary study *American Playwrights: 1918–1938*, took a potshot at it as "one of the most amoral hodgepodges of philosophy that ever rejoiced the hearts of our dramatic critics and fashionable audiences."[75] For her, Bob's portrayal of the death of the age of individualism was, as he might have put it, just one big display of hokum. The playwright and theorist John Howard Lawson, writing at approximately the same time, had a distinctly different opinion of the play, seeing it as "among the most distinguished products of the English-speaking stage." Still, he did not consider the work to be perfect. Rather, he felt that Bob followed "the time-worn circle: the philosophy of blood and nerves leads to pessimism; the denial of reason leads to acceptance of violence." There could be only one conclusion: death. No change could occur in Gabby and Squier's relationship because the characters could only accept as "man's fate" that "cruelty and violence" are necessary parts "in Nature's scheme—the life-force operates through love and violence, sentiment and cruelty, sacrifice and sadism."[76] Bob himself had some criticism for the play, especially with regard to the ending, which he considered weak. He told Lucius Beebe of the *Herald Tribune* that, as in his previous work, he had started "with a big message" and ended up "with nothing but good entertainment," but that was what the public wanted. In Gabby especially, he felt that he had "lost control of the idea" and not effectively presented her as "the renewal of courage and vitality and fresh ideas."[77]

The Petrified Forest ran on Broadway for 194 performances and had a successful tour. It was Bob's greatest critical success up to that time, with nary a derisive word to break his happy spirit. In fact, it was so popular that he was able to sell the rights to Hollywood for the huge sum of $110,000. With Will Hays in mind, the 1936 film adaptation by Charles Kenyon and Delmer Daves cleansed some of the references to Bolshevik Russia, but it was otherwise true to the play. Leslie Howard and Humphrey Bogart reprised their roles, but the popular movie star Bette Davis replaced Peggy Conklin as Gabby. The role of Duke Mantee set Bogart on the path toward huge success in tough-guy roles, whether gangsters or appealing private detectives. He had Leslie Howard to thank for that, for Howard insisted that the film role go to him. For Bob, the film was perhaps "too exact" a copy of the play; he felt that it lost some of its flair, which did not effectively translate into the film medium.[78]

Soon after *The Petrified Forest* opened on Broadway, Bob left for an extended stay in Europe, taking Little Mary with him. The eleven-year-old continued to have difficulty adjusting to her parents' divorce, especially since her father was now socializing with people she did not know, and some of whom she did not trust. His busy life left her feeling alone and lonely, especially since leaving New York also meant leaving her friends and extended family. Posie encouraged Jane to see as much of Little Mary as she could. "She is pretty young to stand all she has been called upon to put up with," she told her sister. "You can talk to her on almost any subject and she is very easy to make friends with."[79] Jane promised to do all she could to fill in the family gap. Meanwhile, Bob's work on the Alexander Korda film *The Ghost Goes West*, a light romantic comedy about a pacifist ghost, took up a considerable amount of his time in England, as did mounting the adaptation of Jacques Deval's comedy *Tovaritch*, the story of two deposed Russian royals who find work in Paris as domestic servants while protecting four billion Russian rubles put in their trust by the now deceased czar. This was the only play by another playwright which Bob ever adapted. In fact, it may have been this experience that deterred any later adaptation efforts, as Deval was quite unhappy with the liberties he felt Bob had taken with his script—all actually minor changes. The play, now spelled *Tovarich*, however, became extremely successful in London after its opening on April 24, and on October 15, 1936, it opened for another successful run of 356 performances in New York.

Meanwhile, Bob was busy pressuring Madeline to leave Marc Connelly. Her 1934 solo trip to England had awakened Connelly to the fact that he might lose her. Trying to make amends, he ordered flowers to be delivered to her on board the *Île de France* every day during the week's voyage between England and New York, but the romantic gesture was to no avail. The Connellys' tax returns indicate that the couple separated that November, when Marc and his mother moved from the couple's home on West Fifty-seventh Street to the nearby Hotel Gotham.[80] By early 1935, Madeline was attending Sherwood family get-togethers where Marc Connelly was conspicuously absent. Yet no one seemed to notice that she and Bob had become quite serious. Soon after Bob and Little Mary arrived in England, however, so did Madeline. She became such a constant presence in their rented house in Regency Park, London, that Little Mary revealed to her grandmother that her father was "so much in love" that he was not spending much time alone with her.[81] The preadolescent girl instantly took to Madeline, who provided her with a sense of stability while she was away from her New York home.

After Madeline obtained a quick divorce in Riga, Latvia (the Reno of Europe), the couple announced their engagement, a hard blow to Bob's friendship with Connelly, which Connelly never totally recovered from. Little Mary, however, was overjoyed. Her mother reacted, as usual, in an outrageous manner. When she found out about the engagement and visited her daughter in London in the hope of prejudicing her against Madeline, Little Mary told her to keep quiet. On that same brief visit to England, Mary had the audacity to ask Bob if, when he gave Madeline a ring, he would give her one as well. The Sherwood family, meanwhile, expressed concern about the new woman in Bob's life. It seemed to them too soon after his divorce to commit to another partner, and although they had met Madeline many times, it had been in her role as Marc Connelly's wife. They really knew very little about her. Nevertheless, after visiting her in London, Wilfrid and Jane claimed that they liked Madeline a great deal and were "very hopeful" about the relationship.[82] Longtime friend Geoffrey Kerr agreed, stating that Bob's happiness with her was "assured" and would be lasting, for unlike Mary, Madeline was "honest to a fault."[83] Posie, Lydia claimed to Jane, "with her happy faculty of seeing what she wants to & leaving the rest," had accepted Madeline "without reservation."[84] Lydia just hoped that her sister's instincts were correct.

The courtship between Bob and Madeline was not an easy one. He himself described it as "turbulent and often unbearably harrowing," admitting to Alexander Woollcott that whereas he knew he was hurting his friend Marc "sorely" and that to many of their friends and colleagues he would "inevitably appear a prime shit," he could not help himself. "I love her very much indeed," he confessed, "and want to make her happy." All he could hope was that time would heal Connelly's wounds and that eventually he would forgive his friend for stealing his wife. "But time will have to do some mighty drastic therapy." [85] So embarrassed was Bob about the situation that he hesitated to tell many of his friends. But he did feel compelled to write the Lunts, covering up his personal sense of humiliation by assuring them that he would "not take anyone to wife who does not feel as reverential as I do" about them. [86] It was important to Bob for key people in his life to get used to the idea that he had a new mate, someone they would have to get to know.

Still in Europe in May 1935, the couple traveled to Budapest, the only place on the continent where they could obtain a license to wed without going through complicated, time-consuming diplomatic red tape. Standing in their way, however, was the acceptability of his Reno divorce, not her Riga one. After about two weeks at the Duna Palota Hotel, they had almost given up hope when a prominent Hungarian author and editor, Lajos Zilahy, personally visited the prime minister and gave an exaggerated account of Bob's importance. It would be seen as an insult to the United States, he declared, if Bob and Madeline were denied a license. His ploy was successful; a license was granted on June 14, and on the following day at 12:30 P.M., they were wed. Bob described the ceremony to Posie as "simple and dignified," which he considered a "relief after all the opera bouffe nonsense" they had been through. Immediately after a brief champagne reception, the two left for a three-day honeymoon in Paris, then returned to London, where Little Mary greeted them at the station. At first pale and nervous, she soon brightened up, realizing that this marriage was a good thing, not the unpleasant change she had feared. She suddenly burst out, "My father has gone back to being what he used to be—and I thought I'd lost him." As Bob told Posie, "She could see that I had at last been relieved of the burden of uncertainty that has oppressed us all in the last bad years." [87]

By the end of the year, when the newly reconstituted Sherwood family was back in New York, everyone who met Madeline came to believe that Bob had made an excellent choice. The Lunts, who had been introduced to Madeline in April, were most impressed with her. Fontanne had her "sized up exactly," Lyd told Jane. "She thinks she is rather a remarkable little creature for dignity & character & extreme intelligence combined with a child like quality which is very . . . appealing." Fontanne also appreciated her witty and "brilliant" comments and her ability to be the "life of the party," which made Bob "very proud & delighted." The actress apparently grilled Madeline, discovering her roots in "extreme poverty & Obscurity: sort of poor white trash," as Lydia characterized it. Now, she was "a lady," a complete break from her past. [88] If there was any leftover doubt, the annual Sherwood Christmas celebration put it to rest. Mary Brandon always loved Christmas, but as Posie attested, she never did any work to help produce the huge family gathering. Madeline, by contrast, "expects to do everything herself & is making infinite plans." Of course Posie and Ros insisted on helping her. "She is sweet and unselfish and makes that house blissfully happy and comfortable for Bobby and Little Mary," Posie reported.[89]

Mary, however, still proved a sore spot. For Christmas she gave her daughter a radio, which Bob had to pick up and pay for. In addition, she treated Little Mary and some of her friends to a theater party, and again Bob had to pay for it. She even invited him and Madeline to a cocktail party in their honor, which they attended, thinking it was a joke, though it was not. Bob continued to pacify his former wife. He filled the traditional Sherwood Christmas stockings, adding one for Mary, and, as Posie put it, "one for her gigolo as well." Posie found this "not only ridiculous but totally mistaken," but she could not help "loving the spirit that prompts it. It is so the essence of Bobby."[90] The next month Mary started making a fuss if she could not visit her daughter whenever she pleased. Although Bob insisted that she abide by his rules, he remained friendly and flexible so that Little Mary would not be exposed to any more upsetting discord.

The greatest gift Bob received that Christmas day was from his daughter. When Lydia asked Little Mary what she called her new stepmother, the twelve-year-old answered: "Stepmother! She's my best friend—I call her Madeline."[91] For Bob as well, Madeline brought happiness. She teased that she had married him because he was "so quiet & unobtrusive" but now he never stopped talking. "Well," he noted in his private diary, "she makes me feel good & confident, instead of harassed & diffident as I was before."[92] With Madeline and the success of his work, Bob had, in many ways, finally found some resolution to his feelings about the war and his actions after it. His divorce from Mary marked the end of that period. His tension and depression lifted, giving him a clearer view of the world around him. He did not run around as much as he had before in search of something he could not find. His work also became more serious and more directed. As he later claimed, *The Petrified Forest* "pointed me in a new direction, and that proved to be the way I really wanted to go."[93]

Bob knew that he believed in two things: "true Democracy & true Christianity." He wrote in his diary early in 1936: "I hope to God neither of them dies before I do. Certainly, nothing can kill them but brutal stupidity . . . in its most malignant form . . . in the high priests of capitalism. . . . All I want to do with my life is go on and on attacking such betrayers of the human race and expounding the simple doctrines in the Sermon on the Mount."[94] These thoughts were consistent with those he had expressed previously. The world's peoples deserved to be free and to live in equal, just, and peaceful societies. Capitalism was good when not excessive, and communism had potential but not if applied autocratically. He, as a playwright, would continue to spread this message. This period of marriage, divorce, and the writing of *The Petrified Forest* was a turning point for Robert Sherwood, and although the direction he took as he confronted the growth of fascism and Nazism in Europe might seem inconsistent with his post–World War I pacifist stand, it was in fact a sincere and logical development.

Act Two

7

From Pacifist to Soldier

On January 18, 1938, Robert Sherwood wrote in his diary: "Made up my mind today that I'm interested (in writing) in nothing less than reforming the world. The other day I said to Alex Korda, 'I'm sick of world affairs, war, etc. I wish I could write a plain drawing room comedy.' He laughed and said it was impossible. 'You can't even keep world affairs out of the drawing room.'"[1] The British film producer had hit the nail on the head. Bob's life was consumed by world affairs. World War I remained the key experience in shaping his responses to an international scene that turned uglier with each passing day during the latter half of the 1930s. In his extant diaries dating from 1936, he tracked events around the world and the U.S. government's reactions to them. He then used those events to write plays that would entertain, inform, and inspire people to think and act. His particular mission was to investigate the causes of war and their effects on personal lives and civil liberties. If critics accused him of writing propaganda, so be it.

By the mid-1930s many playgoers saw Bob as the most important antiwar voice in the American theater. Granted, there were other playwrights who addressed the issue, but none were as consistently prolific or successful, especially on Broadway. The Federal Theatre Project, begun in 1935 as part of Franklin Roosevelt's New Deal legislation to put people to work and end the economic depression, circulated a list of plays and pageants with antiwar themes, but none of them were commercially viable for the Broadway stage. They included *David Whitlock* and *Salesmen of Death*, both of which dealt with the family dynamics between armaments makers and salesmen versus pacifists; *Wooden Soldiers*, which dramatized the harmful results of allowing children to play with war toys; and the symbolic *War on Trial* and *The Way of Peace*, about the tragedy and futility of war.[2] The commercial theater saw a small number of antiwar plays produced between 1932 and 1937, none of which, except Bob's *Idiot's Delight*, had a truly significant run on Broadway, on tour, or as a film.[3] Largely issuing warnings about the tragedy of war or the imminence of another conflict, they included Reginald Lawrence and S. K. Lauren's 1932 *Men Must Fight*; George Sklar and Albert Maltz's 1933 *Peace on Earth*; John Haynes Holmes and Reginald Lawrence's 1935 *If This Be Treason*; the 1936 productions of Irwin Shaw's *Bury the Dead* and Paul Green and Kurt

167

Weill's musical *Johnny Johnson*; and Sidney Howard's 1937 *The Ghost of Yankee Doodle*.

The lack of successful antiwar productions reflected both depression economics and changes in the political climate. In terms of economics, whereas there had been 239 productions during the 1929–30 Broadway season, there were only 100 in 1938–39. The intervening years saw a steady decline in ticket sales and available money for investment. While disappointment in the international peace process and fear of war created an audience that preferred other topics for entertainment, the tone of the antiwar movement grew both urgent and frustrated. With Mussolini's tight control on Italy and his roaming eyes turning to Ethiopia and Albania, and Hitler's rise to dictatorial power putting people at risk within and outside Germany, residents of the United States began to fear that their nightmare of Europe dragging the nation into another war would become a reality. Although Asia was less of a focal point for the general public, Japan's hold on Manchuria since 1931 and its subsequent aggression against China added to this concern. The position that most staunch antiwar organizations and individuals took throughout much of the 1930s was one of cautious neutrality. If the United States could remain out of conflicts and instead, in a calm and resolute manner, persuade world leaders to make treaties, stay within their borders, and honor the ever-weakening League of Nations and World Court, perhaps another world war could be averted. Although some voices in the nation expressed concern for those peoples who were being harassed and imprisoned, or who were fleeing fascist countries, the U.S. government itself took no forceful position on such injustices. For most senators, representatives, and their constituencies, as long as the United States was safe, at peace, and making some headway resuscitating economic prosperity, life was fine.

Through much of the 1930s, Robert Sherwood's viewpoint was largely the same as the general public's. Although like many he remained cynical about the munitions industry, he supported the idea that neutrality ensured safety. As the decade neared its end, however, again like many others, he became frightened by the seemingly unquenchable desire for power on the part of the fascists, and his feelings changed. Three Robert Sherwood plays stand out as his contribution to the debates around the question of war versus peace in the 1930s: *Idiot's Delight* (1936), *Abe Lincoln in Illinois* (1938), and *There Shall Be No Night* (1940). In each he made his viewpoint clear and in a serious but entertaining manner attempted to sway audiences to his way of thinking. Like *The Petrified Forest*, these three plays confirmed Bob's reputation as a serious playwright rather than a creator only of sophisticated urban comedies with gently humorous political messages.

In 1955 Bob told the drama critic Walter Kerr that *Idiot's Delight* was "about the outbreak of a second world war." In it, he "meant to express the conviction that the responsibility for such a potential tragedy was shared by everybody who was complacent about the upsurge of tyranny."[4] He claimed that the seeds of the plot had been planted as early as November 1933, when his friend Harry Carr of the *Los Angeles Times* told him about "the supreme hotspot" he had visited in Harbin, Manchuria. The hotel in question featured a "dramatic mixture of nationalities," including one permanent fixture, "some beautiful phony, White Russian girl, who was formerly a Grand Duchess." In addition, Carr noted that "all" the people in Manchuria seemed to be "continually looking up into the skies for the bombers that would herald the start of the Second World War," which they assumed would erupt over the competition between the Soviet Union and Japan for land in the northeastern-most regions of Asia. Inspired by this tale, Bob decided to write a play, but somehow the ideas did not fall into place until 1935, when in Budapest he stopped in at the Club Arizona and saw "battered-looking American chorus girls doing an act." When he asked about them, the proprietor replied, "Oh, they have been touring the Balkans for years." Bob immediately saw that the women could provide "the line on which the whole play could be strung."[5]

Also inspiring Bob was the fact that Alfred Lunt and Lynn Fontanne wanted very much to perform in another Sherwood play. They had found the experience of *Reunion in Vienna* both exciting and pleasurable and appreciated that Bob was open to Lunt's participation in the direction and the duo's constructive suggestions about plot and dialogue. Bob, in turn, wanted to put the Lunts in another play, not just because their names meant almost guaranteed commercial success, but because he likewise valued their talent, their working style, and their friendship. Soon after Bob wrote to inform them of his marriage to Madeline, Lunt responded that they were ready for him to write for them: "You could put us in Budapest this time—say a Chicago man on his way to Bucharest to put in those slot machines or a former 'barker' now managing a troupe of midgets—who meets the elegant Hungarian . . . between a couple of hot violins and a zimbalum! Easy! Bobby you could do it on your ear."[6] That summer Bob eagerly concurred, writing what was to become one of his best known and most respected plays, *Idiot's Delight*, a contemporary antiwar drama sparkling with witty dialogue.

Idiot's Delight has a similar structure to *The Petrified Forest*, as the plot revolves around a group of people being held hostage in an inn. In *The Petrified Forest* the controlling force is an outlaw—a thug. In *Idiot's Delight* it is Italian fascism—an abstract thug. The play tells the story of a group of people caught on the border between Switzerland and an area of Italy that belonged to Austria until the end of World War I. Because another world war threat-ens, Italy has forbidden anyone to cross the border; hence the characters are stranded in the Hotel Monte Gabriele, which sits next to a brand new Italian airbase from which warplanes regularly take off and land. Among those at the inn are the Italian owner Pittaluga, the Austrian (now Italian) worker Dumptsy, and the U.S. social director Donald Navadel. The "guests" con-stitute a sampler of the Western nations and factions that had been involved in World War I. England is represented by a young honeymooning couple, the Cherrys; France by a socialist-pacifist, Quillery; Germany by the scientist Dr. Waldersee; industry by the independent munitions dealer Achille Weber; refugees by the stateless, supposed former Russian noblewoman Irene; and the United States by hoofer Harry Van and his six chorus girls, Les Blondes. Soldiers and hotel workers filter in and out, often speaking in Italian. Bob most likely chose Italy as a setting because of that nation's invasion of Ethio-pia in October 1935.

Idiot's Delight takes place over a twenty-four-hour period during which the characters have various interactions, largely with Harry Van. The conversa-tions present a range of antiwar opinions, most designed either to highlight how war affects civilians or to comment on the political and economic chi-canery that allows wars to occur. Wrapped around Bob's political messages is an unusual love story involving Harry Van and the White Russian émigré, Irene. Harry, upon meeting Irene, realizes that she is the same young Russian woman he met in vaudeville several years before and with whom he spent a night in an Omaha, Nebraska, hotel. Until the end of the play, she denies that she knows him, sticking to her story that she is of noble birth, dislodged from Russia by the Bolsheviks. It is only when she is left desperately alone that Irene confesses to being the woman Harry cannot forget, as she has never forgotten him.

Achille Weber, Irene's lover, is the most evil character in *Idiot's Delight*. Weber is a munitions merchant who is not identified with any one nation. As Irene tells Harry, Weber is "a true man of the world. He is above petty nationalism; he can be a Frenchman in France—a German in Germany—a Greek—a Turk—whatever the occasion demands." [7] Only interested in making money, Weber rationalizes that he is simply giving people what they want, which is "the illusion of power." He explains, "That is what they vote for in their frightened governments—what they cheer for on their national holidays—what they glorify in their anthems, and their monuments, and their waving flags." [8] People want power, and they act only out of self-interest and greed. Weber and his kind simply profit from these desires. His belief that when nations have an excessive supply of weapons, they will counterbalance one another's desire for war echoed Bob's own cynical view of munitions manufacturers' claims that they did not cause war. In this he foresaw the concept that Cold War leaders later termed "mutually assured destruction" (MAD), which supposedly resulted in "deterrence." So relevant did Sherwood's idea remain that in 1983, at a moment when nuclear war seemed a real possibility, Alan Jay Lerner and Charles Strouse wrote the musical *Dance a Little Closer,* based on *Idiot's Delight.* Unfortunately, this Cold War version of the play ran on Broadway for several previews and then closed after the official opening night performance.

Bob's attack on the munitions industry came at a time when peace activists were forcing the U.S. government to look into its reasons for having taken the nation into World War I. On February 8, 1934, Senator Gerald Nye, an isolationist Republican from North Dakota, introduced a bill calling for an investigation. After nearly two years of research, the Senate Special Committee investigating the munitions industry declared that President Wilson and Congress had been swayed by industrialists seeking war profits. Indeed, many businesses had made tremendous amounts of money from World War I and continued to do so in the 1920s and 1930s, especially in the global marketplace. Companies such as Standard Oil had contracts with Italian companies during the Ethiopian conflict, and DuPont and Union Carbide, as well as Standard Oil, had contracts with German companies. What the tycoons did not want was for this information to become public. In reaction to Bob's use of the Dupont name in the play, the company at first threatened to sue him, but after considering the publicity such an action might create, they quietly withdrew the complaint.

While writing the play, Bob wondered if he should make Weber more sympathetic but decided against it. "I believe that such people are the arch villains of mortal creation," he wrote in his diary. "What has clinched my determination," he continued, "is reading in *Time* a quotation from Sir Herbert Laurence of Vickers, 'The sanctity of human life has been exaggerated.' Such men are sons of bitches & should be so represented."[9] In fact, Bob's selection of the name Weber for the character might be explained by references in a letter from his aunt Lydia to her sister Jane during the rehearsal process. "Bobby was talking of this web of . . . fiends which rule the destinies of mankind," she wrote, "the secret web which entangles men in war. He says one force [from the Comité des Forges] alone operates under an English name in England & under French & German names in those countries. That he was the chief factor in bringing Hitler to the front, financed & pushed him on the silly German people, meanwhile in France inflaming them. . . . Servants of the devil."[10]

To emphasize his point about the evil of the munitions industry, Bob made Weber the most powerful character in the play. Irene understands that Weber has such tremendous influence that only he can orchestrate their exit from the hotel and across the border. In spite of this, she cannot suppress her contempt for his source of income. Adopting a sarcastic tone, she offers him her congratulations for all the "great, wonderful death and destruction" that he promotes. Weber responds that he is simply "the humble instrument of His divine will." "Yes," she agrees. People should do more honor to God, for that "poor, lonely old soul. Sitting up in heaven, with nothing to do, but play solitaire . . . Idiot's Delight. The game that never means anything, and never ends." [11] Indeed, "Idiot's Delight" (or "Aces Up"), which Bob apparently had spent many hours playing, was such a difficult and frustrating game that the chances of winning were approximately one in twenty. [12] Irene's outburst causes Weber to respond that he has a problem when those nearest and dearest to him, such as his former wife and Irene, complain that he has crossed some moral line which they have drawn. Although she is the beneficiary of his great wealth and therefore complicit in its origins, his former wife cannot tolerate his involvement in the sale of poison gas. "Revolvers and rifles and bullets she didn't mind," he tells Irene, "because they are also used by sportsmen. Battleships too are permissible; they look so splendid in the news films. But she couldn't stomach poison gas." [13] She has left him, but only to marry a flighty duke, who, along with her, lives off Weber's fortune. Underlying his speech is a threat: Irene should be careful of what she says.

Weber's most outspoken opponent in the Hotel Monte Gabriele is Quillery, the radical French socialist on his way home from an international Labor Congress. Quillery is a farmer turned factory worker in the lucrative post–World War I production of artificial limbs, a job that takes him into the world of international socialism. Late in the play, when news arrives at the hotel that Italy has bombed Paris, this outspoken opponent of war blames Weber for the coming global conflagration. "He can give you all the war news," Quillery tells the Cherrys, "Because he *made* it." Weber has been organizing the weapons industry: "To kill French babies. And English babies. France and Italy are at war. England joins France. Germany joins Italy. And that will drag in the Soviet Union and the Japanese Empire and the United States. In every part of the world, the good desire of men for peace and decency is undermined by the dynamite of jingoism. And it needs only one spark, set off anywhere by one egomaniac, to send it all up in one final, fatal explosion." Weber, Quillery claims, belongs to the international munitions makers' league—the "one *real* League of Nations—The League of Schneider-Creusot, and Krupp, and Skoda, and Vickers and Dupont. The League of

Death!"[14] Quillery's antiwar outburst to Weber and his antifascist tirade in front of the Italian soldiers lead to his arrest and immediate execution. Bob designed Quillery's fate to show dramatically that the advent of war spells the immediate and acute curtailment of free speech.

The other arch-villain in *Idiot's Delight* is Italian fascism. In the play, the Italian government is an arbitrary and oppressive force which is unseen except through the army captain and a few soldiers who carry out its orders. Yet within a few moments of the curtain's going up, it is indicted for being mindless. When Dr. Waldersee queries the captain about the airplanes and the airfield, the army official explains that Italy has to be prepared for any "visits" from enemies. "And who is that?" asks Waldersee, only to be told, "I don't quite know, yet. The map of Europe supplies us with a wide choice of opponents. I suppose, in due time, our government will announce its selection—and we shall know just whom we are to shoot at."[15] When Irene later challenges the captain, insisting that he has a mind of his own and can refuse to fight, he simply ignores her comment and heads to the bar to get himself a drink. Not only are the Fascists arbitrary; they are also heartless, not concerned in the least with the well-being of the nation's people. They want to project the image of the superhuman, much as Nazi Germany was doing at the same time. The bellboy Dumptsy explains to Harry that the hotel was formerly a sanatorium for victims of tuberculosis and other respiratory ailments. "But the Fascisti," he adds, "they don't like to admit that any one can be sick."[16]

Dr. Waldersee and the Cherrys embody Bob's criticism of unquestioned nationalism. Dr. Waldersee brags about his great experimentations in a cure for cancer, a discovery that may save millions of human lives. He is afraid that being stuck at the Swiss border will harm the rats he is taking to Zurich to further his research, something he can no longer carry on in Germany, where the Nazi government's "chauvinistic nationalism" emphasizes the development of poison gases, not the cure for disease.[17] As "a servant of the whole damn stupid human race," he wants to be on his way.[18] Once the war begins, however, Waldersee changes his plans in order to go back to his homeland and help his government. He is not an international humanitarian but rather a nationalist who, above all, wants Germany to be free from anyone who would wish to harm it. "I have heard too many Hymns of Hate," he angrily asserts. "To be a German is to be used to insults, and injuries."[19]

Like Dr. Waldersee, the Cherrys also suffer from an overblown nationalistic spirit, but Bob paints their nationalism as youthful, innocent, and gullible. They are stereotypically British—formal, polite, provincial, inanely optimistic, and full of a sense of superiority. For them, England is the center of the universe, a nation that epitomizes democracy. Without England, the world cannot function; not even war can take place. "No matter how stupid and blundering our government may be," Mr. Cherry declares to his wife, "our people simply won't stand" for war; therefore, it is not to be.[20] Quillery, echoing the sentiments that Bob had voiced in the never produced *Afterglow*, counters with the portrait of an England that is the voice of hypocrisy, the "grabber—the exploiter—the immaculate butcher!" It is England, he claims, that has "forced" this new war because "miserable little Italy dared to drag its black shirt across your trail of Empire."[21] This insult to his nation pushes Cherry to challenge Quillery physically, but his wife coaxes him to retreat.

Meanwhile, in a dreamlike reverie, Irene foresees what a war will really mean for the Cherrys. She envisions him in the army, "shooting a little pistol at a huge tank" that will run him down, leaving "a mass of mashed flesh and bones—a smear of purple blood—like a stepped-on snail." At the moment of death, his thoughts will turn toward his wife and their unborn child. "But I know where she is," Irene conjectures. "She is lying in a cellar that has been wrecked by an air raid, and her firm young breasts are all mixed up with the bowels of a dismembered policeman, and the embryo from her womb is splattered against the face of a dead bishop."[22] As soon as they are able, of course, the Cherrys hurry home. "England is coming into the business. We have to stand by France, of course," Mr. Cherry states, and his wife concurs that "Jimmy" has to "do his bit, manning the guns, for civilization."[23] Although England and Italy are declared enemies, the Cherrys are allowed to leave because of a technicality: the declaration of war occurred seventeen minutes after their release papers were signed. The Cherrys and the Italian captain part, each apologizing to the other that the war and its results are not their fault; they are only doing their duty, obeying orders from above. For Bob, extreme nationalism and patriotism meant obeying orders without question, no matter how cruel the methods or the outcome.

The theme of displacement is also important in *Idiot's Delight*, especially the homelessness caused by shifting national boundaries and changes of sovereignty. Both Dumptsy and Irene are victims of these changes. Dumptsy, the gentle forty-year-old bellboy, was born in the area when the territory belonged to Austria. He was raised to live, speak, and think in German, but as he tells Harry, the Treaty of Versailles dictated that this section of the mountains be given to Italy, "and I became a foreigner." Dumptsy's children learn Italian in school and cannot understand their parents when they speak German. In addition, the name of the mountain was changed, as was the name of the hotel. He adds: "Even my old father—he's dead—but all the writing on the gravestones was in German, so they rubbed it out and translated it. So now he's Italian, too." In effect a stranger in his own homeland, Dumptsy is most pragmatic. "It doesn't make much difference who your masters are," he says. "When you get used to them, they're all the same." [24] By the end of the play, Dumptsy finds himself in an Italian army uniform, drafted for the second time in his life, and hoping that he may be taken prisoner of war as quickly as possible so as to avoid the fighting.

Irene is the other homeless character. Without a country, an income, or family, Irene is forced to live off her wits, which she apparently does quite well by pretending to be a deposed Romanoff. In the background story to *Idiot's Delight*, she was actually a vaudeville performer with a Russian troupe, a young woman who, Harry claims, was "the God-damnedest liar I ever saw." [25] In recent years she has apparently lived in luxury as Achille Weber's mistress. But she is also at his mercy, for Irene is stateless. In order for her to travel, Weber obtains a vague letter from the League of Nations which acts as a passport, but by the end of the play her so-called passport is worthless, and Irene is stranded.

Harry Van is the unchallenged focal point of *Idiot's Delight* and a symbol of U.S. neutrality. The 1935 Neutrality Act, aimed specifically at Italy after its invasion of Ethiopia, stated that there was to be an arms embargo against all belligerents once the president had officially recognized that a war was in progress. In the case of Italy and Ethiopia, Franklin Roosevelt suggested that U.S. businesses also withhold sales of nonmilitary products. Oil, in particular, was necessary for use in ships leaving Italy for Ethiopia. The oil companies simply ignored the request for a "moral" embargo, the result being that Ethiopia had no chance against the more powerful, wealthier Italy. Robert Sherwood, though an opponent of fascism, supported neutrality because it kept the United States out of war. This would become a serious dilemma for him.

Just like Bob, Harry is part optimist, part wit, part cynic. As Edward Sheldon told him, Bob should say, "Harry Van . . . is I." [26] Bob uses Harry to reflect the voice of the U.S. government and business interests. When Irene asks him if he is one of those "noble souls" who do not approve of the munitions industry, Harry is diplomatic. "Your friend is just another salesman," he replies. "And I make it a point never to criticize anybody else's racket." [27] The same thinking engulfs Harry when it comes to war. As he says to the captain, "Weber—and a million like him—they can't take the credit for *all* of this!" [28] But perhaps the most puzzling expression of Harry's neutrality is his ordering the band to play the Italian Fascist anthem when several military officials enter the hotel. It is difficult to believe that Bob himself would have made such a diplomatic gesture, but it rings true as a comment on the U.S. government's behavior toward the Italian Fascist government at the time.

Harry hides his blind neutrality behind a veil of optimism. Bob points out in the preface to *There Shall Be No Night* that the passage in *Idiot's Delight* that most represented his own point of view was Harry's speech to Dr. Waldersee:

> I've remained an optimist because I'm essentially a student of human na-
> ture. You dissect corpses and rats and similar unpleasant things. Well,—it
> has been my job to dissect suckers! I've probed into the souls of some of the
> God-damnedest specimens. And what have I found? Now, don't sneer at me,
> Doctor—but above everything else I've found Faith. Faith in peace on earth
> and good will to men—and faith that "Muma," "Muma" the three-legged girl,
> really has got three legs. All my life, Doctor, I've been selling phoney goods to
> people of meagre intelligence and great faith. You'd think that would make me
> contemptuous of the human race, wouldn't you? But—on the contrary—it has
> given *me* Faith. It has made me sure that no matter how much the meek may
> be bulldozed or gypped they *will* eventually inherit the earth.[29]

Harry is an "ingenuous, sentimental idealist," as Irene calls him. He agrees with this assessment, saying that he has known millions of people "intimately" and never found more than one out of a hundred that he did not like.[30]

Bob claimed that *Idiot's Delight* was "completely American in that it represented a compound of blank pessimism and desperate optimism of chaos and jazz."[31] Hence the ending, when Harry and Irene sit by the piano singing "Onward Christian Soldiers," is appropriate to Bob's attitude at the time— optimistic but cynical. He maintained his hope that war could be avoided, writing in the postscript to the published version of the play that he felt the world was still populated largely by "decent people" who did not want war. The only reason good people agreed to fight was that they were "deluded by their exploiters," who were "members of the indecent minority." War would come only if people continued to be "intoxicated by the synthetic spirit of patriotism, pumped into them by megalomaniac leaders," and maintained faith in the "security" they felt in those "lethal weapons sold to them by the armaments industry." In that case, war would be "inevitable," and the world would succumb to the power of the minority.[32]

Bob did not believe that this would happen. The legacy of World War I, in particular, would prohibit it. People in the United States, however, had to stand up to the same militarists who had fueled that war and face the growing fascist powers with "calmness, courage, and ridicule." The United States, the Soviet Union, England, and France could defeat fascism in Germany, Italy, and Japan if they used these three qualities rather than force. Under their sway, fascism would crumble. Bob concluded, "By refusing to imitate the Fascists in their policies of heavily fortified isolation, their hysterical self-worship and psychopathic hatred of others, we may achieve the enjoyment of peaceful life on earth, rather than degraded death in the cellar." [33] *Idiot's Delight* was certainly Bob's strongest antiwar statement to date.

The process of writing *Idiot's Delight* was inspired. Bob sat down to begin on November 25, 1935, and by December 19 the Lunts had read it and agreed to purchase it as one of the first shows for their own Transatlantic Productions company. The three offered to share the production with the Theatre Guild, which accepted, and of course the Lunts signed on to perform in it. Alfred Lunt told Posie that he thought it Bob's best play to date and that he was "so excited he could hardly breathe." [34] Bob himself felt that it was "the best drama I've ever had to discharge ideas that have been long boiling in my mind & heart. In fact, this play is like a 100% orgasm." [35] To Sidney Howard he described it as "a chance for speaking out on subjects that we all feel pretty rabid about—Fascism, jingoism, mad-dog desperation, etc." [36]

Wanting to be as authentic a Harry Van as possible, Lunt spent hours attending cabaret performances to study how a song-and-dance man performed, and he sought out the great singer-comedienne Sophie Tucker and the up-and-coming comic Milton Berle for tips. He then took tap-dancing lessons from Morgan (Buddy) Lewis, who was brought on as the dance director for the production. Fontanne hired a young Russian salesgirl (who purported to be of royal descent, of course) to teach her a Russian accent. Bob recruited Irving Berlin to supply Harry Van's big number. The two decided to use Berlin's 1929 hit "Puttin' On the Ritz," and during rehearsals, Berlin came in to coach Lunt in performing the number. Throughout the rehearsal process, which began in January 1936, and out-of-town tryouts, the Lunts suggested changes, even rewriting small sections of *Idiot's Delight*. Their ideas were invaluable, but comments from the Theatre Guild managers were not. Lee Simonson, the set designer who had been at the center of Bob's feuds with the Guild during the creation of *Reunion in Vienna*, again objected to the play. He and Lawrence Langner told Bob that having a "declaration of war" for the "background" would "kill the comedy." "How they under-rate me!" Bob exclaimed in his diary." [37] The Guild insisted on continuing its endless meetings which Bob so hated. During one session Lunt walked past the meeting room, heard the melee going on inside, and stormed away cursing. Eventually the Guild board backed off, leaving Bob "in an absolute stew of excitement. . . . The cast is perfect, the whole feel of the thing is perfect." [38]

On the train to Washington, D.C., for the initial preview, Bob read the news that Hitler had ordered the German army to invade the Rhineland, a distinct violation of the Treaty of Versailles and the Locarno Treaty of 1925. Because the events in *Idiot's Delight* were becoming all too true and therefore could make the play outdated before it even opened, Bob felt some trepidation about the previews. What if his wit failed because the headlines were so authentically tragic? On opening night the audience responded enthusiastically, but the reviews were lukewarm. Bob immediately set about rewriting as the cast and crew moved on to Pittsburgh. It was there, amidst extensive flooding from constant rain and melting snow, that the Lunts confirmed their true dedication to the theater, their audiences, and the adage "The show must go on."

Bob reported in his diary that the waters overflowing the banks of the Ohio, Allegheny, and Monongahela rivers which traversed the city had reached forty-eight feet, "filling streets to within a few blocks of hotel and theater." [39] When he went to the hotel to say good-bye to the cast before returning to New York, he found two of the orchestra members waiting for a boat to rescue them from a second-floor window. Despite the flood, the company honored its performance schedule even when the March 19 matinee proved almost impossible. With no water, no light (except for that provided by the theater's own generator), and rising waters, the curtain was still rung up for the few people who had managed to arrive by rowboat. The Lunts began the play, all the while hearing water rushing into the cellar beneath them. When the flood knocked out the generators, Lunt and Les Blondes kept on singing and dancing in the dark. Lunt lit his cigarette lighter, and stagehands gave the performers candles and flashlights. At last the emergency generator kicked in. In spite of everything, the Lunts were determined to continue, though Bob begged them to leave Pittsburgh when typhoid was reported in the city. The Lunts were unwilling to stop even then, but the Pittsburgh authorities made the decision for them, ordering the show closed. The cast and crew, carrying costumes and anything else they could manage, crowded into a car of a special train taking people away from Pittsburgh, and twenty-four hours later they arrived in New York. Miraculously, the set arrived, having followed on a separate train.

On March 24 *Idiot's Delight* opened in New York. Bob was extremely nervous and did not arrive at the theater until the middle of act two. The audience's reception, however, quelled any lingering fears that the play would not work. After nineteen curtain calls and "vociferous cheers," he could relax. [40] The New York reviews, though not all raves, were quite thoughtful. Bob reacted, however, as if they had all been pans. Tickets sold like mad, and in fact the play lasted for three hundred performances, closing largely because Bob's agent Harold Freedman persuaded the Lunts to take it on tour. This led to another twenty-two sold-out weeks, in which they updated the political references, changing Ethiopia to Spain and then later to Czechoslovakia. Still, the New York reviews were frustrating to Bob because he thought they underestimated the seriousness of the message and the imminence of another world war. "God damn it—why do they deliberately close their ears to everything of importance that is said in a comedy?" Bob lamented. "You'd think it was a crime to state unpleasant truths in an entertaining way." [41] Perhaps the problem was that Bob heard so much laughter that he believed the critics had missed the forewarnings of the playwright.

Brooks Atkinson wrote that Bob's "love of a good time and his anxiety about world affairs result[ed] in one of his most likable entertainments," but the play could not stand up to the realism and seriousness of Irwin Shaw's *Bury the Dead*, an abstract work in which soldiers' corpses refused to be buried so they could walk among the living to speak out against war. He thought that *Idiot's Delight*, though not as fine as *The Petrified Forest*, was "interesting," as it illustrated "that grotesque distinction between the personal, casual lives people want to live and the roar and thunder that crack-brained governments foment." [42] Percy Hammond thought it "excellent," noting that "for a play that disapproves the stern and foolish arbitrament of arms, *Idiot's Delight* is peaceful." [43] Thoughtful praise also came from John Anderson of the *New York Evening Journal,* who claimed: "Some of us had just seen a momentous play and were feeling a little unsteady; some of us had just seen the most peaceful warrior among our playwrights deliver, with shattering impact and unfaltering aim, a blow against the stupidity of war. . . . Take it as you please, it is heady and exciting stuff." Gilbert Gabriel appreciated Bob's humor and "hectic melodrama" in an era when such antiwar plays as *Bury the Dead* were almost too grim to bear. Richard Lockridge called it Bob's "best . . . a play of flashing moods, racing and shining like quicksilver from comedy to stinging protest," and John Mason Brown of the *New York Post* thought it showed "once again Bob's uncommon ability to combine entertainment of a fleet and satisfying sort with an allegory which reaches for a larger meaning." Finally, Robert Garland of the *New York Telegram* stated that Bob, "with bitterness in his heart, with mockery in his pen," had "turned out as bizarre a theater piece as you have seen. You could not pigeonhole it, even if you tried. But whatever manner of make-believe it may or may not be, it causes you to shake with laughter and with fear, to remain around and cry out 'Bravo!' at the end." [44]

While in England in May, Bob received a telegram informing him that *Idiot's Delight* had been awarded the Pulitzer Prize. The prize had been

established in 1917 "to be given annually for the best original play to be performed in New York, which shall best represent the educational value and
the power of the stage in raising the standard of good morals, good taste, and
good manners."[45] The decision, a unanimous one, was particularly meaningful because the committee had changed its ruling stating that an author who
had won before could not be considered. Because the competition was now
open to all, Bob felt it was especially gratifying. He was also most pleased
with the bronze plaque he received from the Drama Study Club naming the
play the best of the year.

Whereas censorship was not a problem when the staged production of
Idiot's Delight traveled to England for a very successful run (but without
the Lunts), it proved to be a major challenge in the film version, which was
produced by Metro-Goldwyn-Mayer and starred Clark Gable and Norma
Shearer. Because of Bob's reputation as a gifted playwright and a superb
screenwriter, he was able to sell the rights to *Idiot's Delight* for $125,000. In
addition, after the 1936 release of *The Petrified Forest*, which was met with
great praise, he was asked to co-write the screenplay for *Thunder in the City*,
a romantic comedy about a young American capitalist who made it big by
saving a British family's fortune. He also adapted *Tovarich* for film and wrote
the screenplay for Samuel Goldwyn's *The Adventures of Marco Polo*, a light-
hearted historical comedy about the Venetian-born nobleman's initial trading expedition to the Far East, which included gentle commentary about
freedom of speech and equal rights and decried violence and the surveillance
of populations. In 1937 Frances Marion, a prominent woman screenwriter of
the time, chose the screenplay of *The Adventures of Marco Polo* as "the best
example of scenario form and content" for her book *How to Write and Sell
Film Stories*. To her, the writing "succeeded in making this almost mythical
adventurer a very real character, gallant, courageous and wise."[46]

With such an excellent reputation within the film industry, Bob began the
venture of turning *Idiot's Delight* into a screenplay with great confidence. Although he had experienced censorship over sex, language, and minor political
references in *Waterloo Bridge, Two Kinds of Women, Tovarich, The Petrified
Forest*, and *The Adventures of Marco Polo*, he did not expect the kinds of problems he faced because of *Idiot's Delight's* portrayal of Italy. Bob's old nemesis
Will Hays was still the man primarily in charge of Hollywood censorship. As
president of the industry-created organization the Motion Picture Producers
and Distributors of America, he wielded tremendous power over the final
content of films. In 1934, however, in order to mollify the Catholic Church,
which had organized its constituency around the issue of immorality in film,
Hays established the Production Code Administration, which had complete

control over approval of film content. Once the PCA was established, every film had to have its seal of approval before being shown in a major movie theater. Hays placed Joseph I. Breen in the position of director of the Production Code Administration, and Breen was a man who took his job very seriously.

Idiot's Delight was an unusual case because the film script caught the PCA's attention before it was even produced. Apparently, several studios were interested in filming the play, but all were concerned about its "numerous diatribes against militarism, fascism, [and] the munitions ring" and so consulted Breen about it.[47] The PCA office decided that the script was not just antiwar; it was also anti-Italian. Interestingly, the implied sexual liaison between Harry Van and Irene was not of major concern for the studios, the feeling being that this could easily be altered. The greater dread was that the film would be banned in some countries and end up a financial disaster. Because it was such an expensive property to acquire and necessitated the costs of star power as well, film companies were reluctant to take it on until MGM decided to produce it. Not one month later, the Italian embassy caught wind of the news and took action. This was not the first time the Fascists had come into conflict with the Hollywood film industry. Previously, the Mussolini government had demanded that three-fourths of all revenues from box office sales in Italy and its colonies go into its coffers. It took a U.S. film company boycott and a personal visit from Will Hays to negotiate a settlement. Still, the Italians banned twenty Hollywood films between 1935 and the spring of 1937 because of unacceptable moral content and the stereotyping of Italian characters.

In spite of the fear of a foreign boycott, MGM proceeded with its plans. As a result, in January 1937 the embassy demanded that Hays use his influence to stop production. Joseph Breen was then instructed to tell MGM that if the film turned out to be a duplicate of the play, all the studio's subsequent movies would be "banned in Italy and France, and there will be trouble all over the rest of the world."[48] The Italian vice consul Robert Caracciolo made it clear to Breen that the film would pass the censors only if it bore no resemblance to the original play, if it contained nothing that the Italian government would find offensive to itself, if he was allowed to approve the final script, and, most stinging of all, if the name Robert Sherwood was eliminated from any version distributed in Italy. Because his name was "poison" there, the Fascists also wanted it removed from all copies of *The Adventures of Marco Polo*.[49] In order to placate the Italians, Hays ordered Breen to make Caracciolo a technical adviser on the film.

Bob and Madeline, who at the time were vacationing in Italy and Greece, had no idea of this controversy over the film. They would not have been surprised to learn of it, however, given their experiences in Italy. Soon after they boarded ship, an Italian traveler introduced himself to them and told Bob he had read *Idiot's Delight* and then gone to the theater to see it. He also mentioned that he would destroy his copy before he reached Italy. If this was not upsetting enough, once in the country, Bob and Madeline witnessed "a troop of little boys marching along in naval uniforms with a Fascist officer barking at them." [50] Then, on their way to Greece, they spent nine hours on a local train, where they occupied a compartment with three Italian army officers. When they parted, the men gave them the Fascist salute. As Bob noted to his mother, the two had the unpleasant feeling that they were "on the road with the company of *Idiot's Delight*." [51]

In the meantime, MGM told Breen that it had no intention of dropping the project or changing the title as the Italians had requested. *Idiot's Delight*, with its Pulitzer Prize and its $125,000 price tag, was too "valuable" a name to alter, especially since the screenplay would "have little left" of the play. [52] The studio would, however, consider removing Bob's name from copies distributed in Italy. MGM also assured the Italians that the film would concentrate on the love story between Harry Van and Irene, filling in a great deal of the back story of their brief, supposedly (in the Hollywood censors' minds) asexual encounter in Omaha. Although all anti-Fascist statements and references to Italy would be expunged, the basic antiwar message would be retained. MGM producer Hunt Stromberg informed Breen, "We will delete . . . any speeches or ideas that incriminate or needlessly ridicule any nation or character representing a nation," and the antiwar argument "will be expressed by private individuals with no Governmental connections whatsoever and by characters of American and English nationality, definitely not Italian." [53] The studio then offered Bob an additional $135,000 to make the changes. Besides accentuating Harry and Irene's relationship, he moved the setting to an unnamed country in central Europe, where the film industry was not a major moneymaker, changed all the Italian dialogue to Esperanto, and fictionalized the place-names by spelling them backwards.

Breen kept Caracciolo abreast of all the changes, which the Italian generally approved. But he remained so adamant that audiences might still pinpoint Italy as the guilty nation that Bob created a new character early in the film who enters, states that he needs to get back to his homeland, Italy, and then remains in the background. This seemed to satisfy Caracciolo. The delays in the film's production lasted until May 1938, when Breen sent the final revisions to the Italian consulate in Los Angeles. Caracciolo, however, was in Naples, and although another official was substituting for him, no action seemed forthcoming. Since Breen was traveling to Italy "on a jaunt," he hand-delivered the script to Caracciolo himself. At the end of July, after much back-and-forth, Breen returned to Los Angeles, where a month later word reached him that the Italians were "very much opposed" to the film and "would not approve of any such picture." [54] Again there were more meetings. By the end of August, MGM took the risk of going into production.

Idiot's Delight was finally released in February 1939, almost two years after MGM and Breen had first begun discussions. In general, the critics panned it for its ridiculous use of Esperanto and its turn away from specifying anything Italian. For them, it had lost its antiwar zing and its political meaning, and had become, basically, a betrayal of Americans' freedom of speech. In the United States, the thousands of people who had seen or read the play in its original form preferred to experience the Lunts performing it faithfully rather than view the fraudulent movie version. Hence, the touring company consistently filled its theaters. The film industry's intention of protecting its foreign markets also failed. In Italy, stricter rules resulted in early 1939 in the creation of the Ente Nazionale Industria Cinematografica, the government office with total control over film distribution. That agency banned *Idiot's Delight,* as did the governments of Spain, France, Switzerland, and Estonia. Interestingly, a representative of the Motion Picture Producers and Distributors Association traveling in Italy in 1939 discovered quite by accident that the film was being shown in many second-run and rural theaters. He had no idea how it had been obtained.[55]

Bob and Madeline considered the film "tiresome." Bob wrote the Lunts: "So much has been cut that whole scenes seem utterly pointless—for one instance, it is never established that Dr. Waldersee has rats until he is leaving. No one can make out who or what the hell Quillery is. . . . The final air raid was a big disappointment—not nearly as exciting or convincing as it was on the stage." [56] The story had become a garbled mess. Added to this was Bob's own evolution. In 1938, when his pacifism was waning, he regretted the extent to which the play "hammered in the anti-war argument, from the mouths of all characters, over and over again," and so felt somewhat relieved that most of those references had been cut from the movie.[57] As he later told Walter Kerr: "I suppose I over emphasized the importance of the munitions makers. I certainly would not have written this play after the Second World War started in 1939." [58]

Bob's stable and happy home life with Madeline was making it possible for him to pay close attention to politics. From time to time, however, he ended up sleeping on the sofa, reprimanding himself for his unacceptable behavior which he never described in any specific way. At a high moment, he reported "previous troubles departing like sewage in the sea," and at a low point: "I wish to God I did better in fulfillment of my obligations to the one I love the most. When I left her this morning she was crying over my behavior of last night."[59] Indeed, whatever these mysterious incidents were, they made life so unpleasant that Madeline angrily called him "Connelly."[60] Still, these episodes were minor compared to his previous problems with Mary. "I feel quite sure that there's no one on earth who has such a happy life as I have," he wrote in November 1937. "There are certainly many lives fuller of accomplishment & excitement, but none that I can conceive of so full of days contentment [sic], and admiration and love for my sweet companion."[61] His one lasting disappointment was that his friendship with Marc Connelly was over. When Bob and Madeline attended the opening night party for George S. Kaufman's *I'd Rather Be Right*, Connelly spotted them and, as Bob related, "sped like a mechanical rabbit." He lamented this "absurd behavior. A man of wisdom, rare humor, and no grace."[62] Bob's betrayal of their friendship had so hurt Connelly, that it took more than fifteen years before he could even begin to meet Bob for an occasional lunch.

Although the troubles with Mary Brandon also never totally disappeared, it was Little Mary, not Bob, who continued to suffer the aftereffects of their divorce. Mary actively competed with Madeline for her daughter's attention, which caused the girl constant confusion. Mary also took up with a man Little Mary did not get along with, creating another layer of unhappiness. Being an adolescent, Little Mary expressed her dismay in two of the only ways within her control. First, she ate. Second, she performed poorly in school. Bob reacted strongly to both situations, lecturing and shouting at his daughter. When Little Mary, as short as her mother, weighed in at 155 pounds, he forced her onto a diet, as he viewed overweight women as unattractive, unlikely to appeal to men, and inevitable objects of derision. But his efforts were uniformly unsuccessful, especially his ploy of making his daughter watch him eat fattening foods in fancy restaurants. When she reached 185 pounds, he constantly harangued her. In later years Little Mary's weight fluctuated with her emotional state, but this remained her area to control, not Bob's.

The same was true of Little Mary's schooling. At the exclusive Chapin School in Manhattan, her grades deteriorated with each term, so that in the long run she failed almost every course. Even her teacher at the Mann School of Music commented on her lack of interest and refusal to work hard. Bob lectured her about this, all the while feeling hypocritical because of his own shoddy performance as a student. Eventually his answer to Little Mary's educational problem was to send her to St. Timothy's boarding school in Baltimore, where little by little she improved, eventually graduating with honors. Throughout her difficult teen years, Bob tried to be a loving father. He surprised her with gifts, wrote poems on her birthday, and took her to the theater and films; but he was a busy man who traveled a great deal and spent endless hours in the theater or writing in his studio. Little Mary needed much more from him than he could give either emotionally or in terms of time.

The most troubling aspect of Bob's personal life was his continuing headaches. He remembered first experiencing their sharp pain, similar to electric shocks, soon after returning from World War I, so he believed that the chronic condition might be caused by his having been gassed. As the years passed, the pain worsened, until in September 1939 doctors diagnosed the cause as trigeminal neuralgia (then more commonly known by its French name, *tic douloureux*).[63] The disorder is caused by the pressure of a blood vessel on the fifth cranial nerve ganglion in the head, resulting in intense, stabbing pain in various areas of the face. Most commonly affected are the lips, eyes, nose, scalp, forehead, and the upper and lower jaws. As the condition worsens, as it did for Bob over the years, the painful episodes become more frequent and are often connected by periods of dull ache. Many nights, Bob's nose plugged up and he was in such pain that he kept his eyes covered or paced the floor because he could not sleep. Sometimes the pain was concentrated over the right side of his face so that his right eye refused to open. Other times it was on the left. Sadly, the doctors told him, the condition had no known cure.

Tic douloureux certainly affected Bob's ability to write. Edna Ferber, who suffered a similar malady later in life, commented after his death: "I now know, and, too late, can be empathetic to what Bob suffered then. Poor, poor fellow. That he could get past the AB in Abe to write a masterly play is astonishing."[64] In 1938, when he experienced pain for eight and a half weeks straight, he found it almost impossible to complete revisions on what he thought would be productions of *Acropolis* in Colorado and New York. Yet he tried to put a humorous spin on his suffering. That April he wrote in his diary that he was starting to associate the pain with the boring task of working and reworking the screenplay for *Northwest Passage* (for which he received no screen credit) "or maybe any picture. God thinks I'm making too much money too easily."[65] The mystery about Bob's condition is that it usually does not begin until around the age of fifty, but for him, it started by the time he was twenty.

Another problem that affected Bob was his "jitters"—feelings of restlessness, boredom, and impatience. This state could have been caused by fatigue or by the fact that he sometimes lacked confidence in his artistic abilities. For a time after the completion of *Idiot's Delight,* for example, he went through a period of feeling "insanely critical & insanely uncertain" of himself.[66] He thought that perhaps he was burned out from his emotional trauma during the years between 1922 and 1934, when he had worked nonstop and then had his bad time with Mary Brandon. But in spite of his physical ailment and psychological doubts, the late 1930s were also productive. After the opening of *Idiot's Delight*, Bob had the idea of writing a historical drama about one of his all-time heroes, Abraham Lincoln. Unlike in the past, however, the script did not develop within a few days or even weeks. Rather, it evolved over a year's time. For one thing, Bob had to keep postponing the writing in order to work on several films, the income from which he needed for his immediate family expenses and Mary Brandon's upkeep as well. Movie work was steady, even those jobs in which he either doctored a script or failed to please the studio with his own work but was paid nonetheless. As soon as *The Adventures of Marco Polo* was done in early 1937, he began making changes on *Idiot's Delight*, but then rewrites were needed on the former when Douglas Fairbanks withdrew from the leading role and Gary Cooper was cast. A few months later he wrote the script for *Over the Moon* and began fixing other writers' work on *The Divorce of Lady X,* for which his contribution went uncredited on screen, and the already mentioned *Northwest Passage.*

Another reason for Bob's slow work in writing a play about Abraham Lincoln was his wish to do historical research. In fact, with this project Bob acted much like a biographer in that he read extensively about Lincoln and other historical figures such as Stephen A. Douglas, Joshua Speed, William Herndon, and Mary Todd Lincoln. As he stated in the sixty-one-page essay "The Substance of *Abe Lincoln in Illinois*," published with the play, his most important sources included Carl Sandburg's *The Prairie Years*, William Baringer's *Lincoln's Rise to Power*, John G. Nicolay and John Hay's *Complete Works of Lincoln*, Emanuel Hertz's *The Hidden Lincoln*, and William Herndon's letters and early biography of Lincoln. Being historically accurate became so important to him that the essay included a comparison of Lincoln's real life to the playwright's imaginings so that readers could see which parts of the play dramatized actual highlights of Lincoln's life. In fact, at one point Bob worried that he had done "too damned much reading" and had therefore created a historical document "instead of what it should be—a play by me." [67] As he admitted to his readers: "The playwright's chief stock in trade is feelings, not facts. When he writes of a subject out of history, or out of today's news, he cannot be a scholarly recorder or a good reporter; he is, at best, an interpreter, with a certain facility for translating all that he has heard in a manner sufficiently dramatic to attract a crowd." [68]

According to Bob's diary, he began intensive reading on Lincoln sometime in 1936 and came up with a possible "scheme" for the play in January 1937. [69] His interest in Lincoln, however, dated back to 1909, when as a thirteen-year-old he took part in a nationwide essay contest in celebration of the one hundredth anniversary of Lincoln's birth. Bob submitted an entry because he had fallen in love with the winners' medals then on display in a Fifth Avenue jeweler's window. As he told *World Telegram* reporter Edd Johnson in 1938, "I certainly was surprised when the awards were announced and I didn't even get an honorable mention."[70] The experience, though, turned him into a Lincoln enthusiast. He came to think of his idol as "the embodiment of all that was noble and courageous and heroic." In fact, Lincoln seemed scarcely human "but rather a statue symbolizing perfection and greatness." Besides that, he later joked, "I think every tall person, particularly when he is an awkward, overgrown, self-conscious boy, develops a Lincoln complex."[71] Later, when he was reviewing films for *Life,* he paid particular attention to George Billings's biographical portrait *The Dramatic Life of Abraham Lincoln,* which presented the story "as it should be told, with dignity, with human sympathy and with humility." The movie reminded him of the "readily forgettable fact that [Lincoln] was a man."[72] Bob obviously recalled this film when he made up his mind "not to have a line of hokum in the play. I love hoke in the theater. But this time I decided that while they might say the play was dull, they couldn't say it was 'theater.'"[73] Elsewhere he remarked that hokum "seemed a violation of the essentials of Lincoln's character. Therefore, I religiously avoided it."[74]

In May 1937, when Bob and Madeline visited Greece, Bob saw the Acropolis for the first time. Standing at this site of the roots of democracy, he wrote his mother, he felt that "this is what I was born of, for and by—which is what leads me directly from a play about the Acropolis into one about Abraham Lincoln."[75] For months he researched and wrote, all the time wondering whether he or any actor would ever really be able to do justice to his subject. Then he saw Raymond Massey in the film *Ethan Frome,* and from then on he knew he had a Lincoln for the stage and was inspired to journey on with the project. As he later recalled, "One evening I was sitting in my apartment in New York reading *The Adventures of Marco Polo* when without any warning to myself, I put the book down and went across the desk and wrote the outline for the twelve scenes of a play about Abraham Lincoln."[76] But the writing took him on an emotional rollercoaster ride. Finished with the first draft on November 20, Bob reflected that after two years of being nearly idle as a playwright, he had finally written a good play. Two weeks later, the play had him depressed. He thought it dull and fell into despair over it. Madeline read it and declared it "perfectly wonderful." With that important vote of confidence, he once again felt elated: "All the years of work on *Acropolis* are justified, for *The Petrified Forest, Idiot's Delight. . . .* Mine eyes have seen the glory of the coming of the Lord. Horray for self-satisfaction."[77] So enthralled was he with the play and so invested in the subject that on December 30 he recorded in his diary that he had had "many dreams lately in which A. Lincoln has appeared to tell me I did a good job. Is this the wish fulfillment mechanism in operation?"[78]

The final reason for the long period of germination was that Bob was going through a sea change in terms of his pacifism. In the year or so it took to complete the script, several ominous events had taken place, and as he noted them in his diary, he also noted his changing political positions. At first, while working on *Idiot's Delight*, he simply recorded each aggressive action with sorrow or disdain. In 1936 these included the war between Italy and Ethiopia, which the African nation quickly lost; the murder by fascist Japanese army officers of several members of the cabinet in their effort to gain power; Hitler's ordering German troops into the Rhineland; and the bishop of London's renunciation of his pacifism "as contrary to the will of God."[79] In addition, war broke out in Spain between the legitimately elected Republican government and fascist insurgents headed by Francisco Franco.

In 1937 Bob's diary entries became more emotional and ranting. He followed the demise of democracy in Spain, noting several disturbing episodes in that war, including the armed assistance to the fascists provided by Italy and Germany. "They rightly call it 'The Little World War,'" he wrote. "But there are amazing numbers of people here (rich) whose sympathies are emphatically with Fascism."[80] Most disturbing was his brother Phil's statement that "we can learn a lot from Hitler and Mussolini," which caused Posie an emotionally draining sleepless night.[81] For Bob, the Nazis were "pathological," the most "fantastic" case of extreme government he had ever heard of, indeed a "supreme tragedy" in the making.[82] How could his own brother see any good in such evil? All this talk of war also brought on a bout of World War I–like nightmares. One "curious dream" took Bob back to 1918 Europe: "I joined with some veterans of the A.E.F. in retracing an advance they had made in the world war. We came through a barn and ran smack up against a trench full of . . . French soldiers, who were alarmed at our sudden appearance and opened up on us with blank cartridges. I shouted to the others to duck." The dream brought back a memory of an incident when "the service ammunition got mixed with the blanks & a man near me was killed."[83] To think that this could happen again was unbearably frightening.

In October 1937 the U.S. State Department turned its eyes to Asia, issuing a statement condemning Japan's aggression toward China. About this Bob commented that his "pacifism wavers every day." He was astonished at the rapid change going on within himself: "I'm ready to cheer newsreels of the U.S. Navy streaming out of Pearl Harbor to go & trounce the Japs! I who used to be sickened by the sight of a battle-ship. . . . The Hitlers, Mussolinis, Jap war lords have outraged and insulted every standard of decency so steadily that it's impossible not to cheer when someone strong stands up & indicates an intention to kick the living shit out of them. How much there is to kick!"[84] Soon after, when Mussolini offered a hand of friendship and assistance to Japan in any war it might fight with China, Bob quipped, "The murderers' league is tightening up its unity." When Mussolini invited Hitler for a chat, he noted: "A fine pair of megalomaniacs. . . . What a spot for a well directed bomb! But there was no one over there to heave it."[85] Bob was disturbed that as Japanese troops murdered, raped, and abused the Chinese citizens of Shanghai, the U.S. government took no action. The only responses he witnessed were the changing of the name of "The Japanese Gift Shop" in Washington, D.C., to "The Chinese Bazaar" by the owners Mr. Cohen and Mr. Goldberg, and the transformation of Chinese villains on a radio melodrama into Japanese villains. In December 1938, when the Japanese invaded Nanking and committed horrible atrocities, Bob was appalled.

Events in Europe earlier in 1938 had him equally upset. In March, almost two years to the day after the Washington, D.C., opening of *Idiot's Delight*, Bob's tone grew panicky as he noted the "calamity" of Germany's march into Austria and the *Anschluss*, the union of the two nations under the Nazi flag. "Two years," he wrote, "and that play still seems to have been written yesterday. A sorry comment."[86] After carefully looking at a map, he foresaw the Nazi march into Czechoslovakia and on toward the Black Sea. Again, his pacifism wavered: "Austria has disappeared into the Nazi state. Jews & workers are being flogged into submission. Oh God—how I hope to live to see the day when those unspeakable barbaric bastards get their punishment."[87] Bob kept a close watch as Germany, Italy, and Japan carried on with their aggressions without any other nations attempting to stop them. "The entire world . . . is being wiped out with hardly a sign of resistance from the supposed victors" of World War I, he lamented. Although he had remained optimistic over the years, at this moment Bob felt that another war, a "far more terrible" one "than anyone could imagine," was on its way, "and I suppose the sooner it comes, the better."[88]

Pacifism, especially his own, had been wrong, he decided, and all those who had believed in the Versailles Treaty, the Kellogg-Briand Pact, and the other efforts to promote peace and equality were "now confronted with the disgusting fact that enlightenment has got us into this mess."[89] He felt dejected and perhaps confused. "I do not believe that democracy is dead (or doomed)," he wrote at the end of the month. "If the day comes when I have to choose between communism and fascism, then I choose death."[90] In this,

Bob practically echoed Lincoln's sentiments ten days before his first inauguration as quoted in his essay on the play: "If this country cannot be saved without giving up that principle [liberty], I would rather be assassinated on this spot than surrender it."[91]

In September 1938 the infamous Munich Agreement was reached between the British, French, Italian, and German governments, in which the four nations agreed never to make war against one another. It also handed over the Sudetenland of Czechoslovakia to Germany (without consulting the Czechs) on Hitler's promise that he would have no further need to expand Germany's empire. England and France came under great criticism for their appeasement of Nazi aggression. Bob, too, was extremely upset by this news, for while it might avert a world war for the moment, in yielding to Hitler's desire to seize other nations' lands, the French and English guaranteed nothing but "a record of triumphs for . . . brute force."[92] For him, the Munich Conference brought an end to his strict pacifism. "I feel that I must start to battle for one thing: The end of our isolation," he wrote in his diary. "There is no hope for humanity unless we participate vigorously in the concern of the world and assume our proper place of leadership with all the grave responsibilities that go with it."[93] The Nazi horror and fear for the peoples left in free Europe were much on his mind. What about his aunt Jane and uncle Wilfrid? What about Raymond Massey, who had already taken the precaution of sending his children out of England for safety's sake? What about Great Enton and his own future?

In this atmosphere of fear, uncertainty, and the questioning of his own pacifist beliefs, Bob needed a contemporary hero. He hoped to find one in Abraham Lincoln, combing through his works to see if the former president could offer any words of comfort, but he quickly found that Lincoln could not address the problems of twentieth-century global conflicts; but the current president, Franklin Delano Roosevelt, could. Unlike his staunchly Republican immediate family, Bob had not opposed Roosevelt's run for president in 1932. In fact, he wrote a poem celebrating Roosevelt's inaugural parade, which was published in the *Saturday Review* on March 3, 1933. What Bob initially liked about Roosevelt were his New Deal policies, the so-called alphabet soup legislation designed to put people back to work during the depression. Beginning in 1932, Bob applauded as various pieces were put into place, including the Banking Act and the establishment of the Federal Deposit Insurance Corporation to protect people's money. He also approved of the many agencies created to provide work such as the Civilian Conservation Corps, the Tennessee Valley Authority, the National Industrial Recovery Act and later the Emergency Relief Appropriation Act, the Works Progress

Administration, and the National Labor Relations Act. Certainly the Federal Theatre Project and the Federal Writers Project endeared Roosevelt to him on the most personal as well as professional levels. As he told Sidney Howard in 1936, he was "a typical Roosevelt . . . liberal-democrat-bloodless revolution boy."[94]

Bob also generally supported Roosevelt's foreign policy positions. In 1933 he expressed approval of the president's officially recognizing the Soviet Union in the interests of opening up trade. He also praised the Good Neighbor policy, which promised a peaceful and friendly relationship with Caribbean and Latin American countries, where U.S. foreign policy had traditionally interfered in national decisions and relied on the intervention of the U.S. military. In 1934, when Roosevelt ordered U.S. troops out of Haiti, where they had been stationed since 1915, Bob thought that he recognized a man who was dedicated to ending colonial militarism. When Italy invaded Ethiopia in 1935 and Congress instituted the first of Roosevelt's Neutrality Acts, Bob agreed with the move. He also supported the second Neutrality Act, which was declared in reaction to the Spanish Civil War in 1936, and which forbade loans to belligerents, whether international or domestic. In the case of the conflict in Spain, no arms shipments, loans, or even humanitarian aid could be sent to either side. Once Germany and Italy sent armed support to the fascists, some Americans criticized the act, but Roosevelt held strong, believing that involvement would drag the United States into a wider war. Though disgusted by the threat of fascism to Spain, Bob agreed with Roosevelt's neutral stance.

Starting with his diaries in 1936, Bob was even more explicit about his support of Roosevelt. Early on he backed the reelection campaign of this "good" president and expressed confidence in having Roosevelt as the country's spokesman in "the international crises that may be ahead."[95] He could even support his unsuccessful attempt to add justices to the Supreme Court, stating, "If, at some future time, a dictator arrives in this country . . . he won't bother to pack the Supreme Court by devious means: will simply shoot the boys on the bench." Bob decided that the president should have power to put through his policies: "Let him go ahead. He has provided leadership for democracy all over the world and a rallying point for the forces opposed to fascism & Communism. Let him continue to lead. If he goes in the wrong direction he can be howled down & voted out."[96] Bob's support for Roosevelt continued to grow, to the point where it seemed to him that his family had "gone so far to the Right" that they regarded him "as a Communist."[97] As far as Bob was concerned, Roosevelt understood democracy, and because of him there was not a chance that fascism would take hold of the government. The president was "a phenomenon—a statesman who is both overwhelmingly popular and right."[98]

Bob, like others who wanted to keep the country out of any impending wars, believed it would be a good thing for the United States to join other governments in blockading or quarantining any nation that broke international law or committed human rights violations. Therefore, he was overjoyed when in October 1937 the president made a forceful speech stating his support for this type of nonviolent interventionist action. Outside of direct war, Bob wished for the U.S. government to extend some sort of aid to the nations threatened by Nazism, Italian fascism, and Japanese imperialism. "The United States is now, and by far, the sanest, most enlightened, most civilized of nations," he wrote in his diary, "and the sooner we Americans realize this important fact, and assume and assert our leadership of the human race, the better it will be for the world at large."[99]

In 1938, the year that *Abe Lincoln in Illinois* was completed and performed, Bob took particularly close notice of Roosevelt's activities. His hope for a relatively peaceful year was offset by his belief that it would also be "an awfully ticklish year, internally & internationally."[100] Roosevelt needed to remain strong to ensure his place in history and to maintain what Bob saw as the legacy of the nation. "If the world should end tomorrow," he wrote, "the world of men as we know it, and a new breed of men appear on earth, with access to all the history, they would find the story of the American people the one that most nearly indicates the human race to date. Here has been focused the triumph over nature, the establishment of a decent society, the cultivation of self-respect, the realization of the Christian ideal, by *all* races."[101] "That man," as Bob's family referred to the president, pleased Bob that summer when he delivered two speeches in Canada in which he came as close as he could legally to announcing that if another war came, the United States would hold true to its lifelong commitments to the British Empire.[102] Bob had found his hero.

Abe Lincoln in Illinois is a play about soul-searching, or as Bob later put it, "the story of a man of peace who had to face the issue of appeasement or war."[103] It was written about three men—Abraham Lincoln, Franklin D. Roosevelt, and Robert E. Sherwood—and their search for an answer to their moral aversion to war in a world in which horrific deeds were being committed. Granted, the play was biographical, painting both a historical and dramatic version of Lincoln's life, from his beginnings as a shopkeeper in New Salem, Illinois, to the day in 1861 when he left that state to take his oath as president of the United States. It portrays many of Lincoln's traits which modern theatergoers recognized—his seriousness, his loneliness, his need for more assertiveness (to which he was urged by friends and an ambitious wife, Mary Todd Lincoln), his humor, his intellect, his sense of humanity, and of course his honesty. But the essence of the script is Lincoln's transformation from a man desirous of keeping to himself to one who accepts his role in leading his nation in a time of potential civil war (which actually comes about after the period treated by the play). It is the story of personal and political neutrality or appeasement versus intervention and entanglement. In a letter to his aunt Lyd, Bob wrote that he was not so concerned about Lincoln's position in history, as that was well known. What he was interested in was Lincoln's "remarkable character." To him, the former president embodied "all the contrasted qualities of the human race—the hopes and fears, the doubts and convictions, the mortal frailty and superhuman endurance, the prescience and the neuroses, the desire to escape from reality, and the fundamental unshakeable nobility. . . . He was a living American and in his living words are the answers . . . to all the questions that distract the world today." [104]

The theme of neutrality and appeasement (and, hence, an avoidance of responsibility) emerges at the beginning of the play when Ninian Edwards, Lincoln's supporter and later brother-in-law, asks him what his political leanings are. "They're all about staying out," he responds. [105] Lincoln is a loner, happy to remain out of the public life and to take no political positions. Although seeing slaves in shackles shocks him, he is willing to turn a blind eye. Lincoln is a moderate. Say nothing. Do nothing. For him, opposing slavery is the step before going to war, and as Lincoln tells his friend Judge Bowling Green, although in spirit he opposes slavery, he is "even more opposed to going to war." [106] When Green and Joshua Speed pressure him to run for Congress, Lincoln balks because he might find himself in the position of having to vote "on the terrible issue of war or peace." Whether it be war with Mexico over Texas or war with England over Oregon or "even war with our own people across the Ohio River," this is something he does not want to do. "To go to war, for a tract of land, or a moral principle? Or to avoid war at all costs? No, sir." [107] Congress is not the place for him. As he later tells Green and Edwards, he often feels divided within himself about many issues including war, peace, love, and marriage. It is as if both sides have equal weight and at some point he will find himself split in two and parting company with himself.

Bob utilized the character of William Herndon, Lincoln's law assistant and future partner, to express the antislavery voice. It is he who spills out facts on slavery and expresses the opinion that Southerners would rather destroy the Union than give up their "property rights in the flesh and blood of those slaves." It is he who stresses that slavery is spreading, and that each new territory and state entering the Union will face the struggle which at present the slavery proponents are winning. To all this Lincoln responds: "I'm minding my own business—that's what I'm doing. And there'd be no threat to the Union if others would do the same." And as for slavery, he adds, "property rights are guaranteed by the Constitution, the law of the land." [108] Nothing that Herndon says can change Lincoln's mind, so Bob created a scene on the prairie to serve that purpose. Lincoln's old friend Seth Gale and his family and handyman Gobey (a free African American) are heading west via the northern route because the Fugitive Slave Law places Gobey in danger of being claimed by a Southerner as his property. If the Oregon territory, where they plan to settle, threatens to become a slave state, then Seth promises he will fight to cut the area loose to join free Canada. The thought that a territory can leave the Union, that slavery can be imposed upon it, or that slavery is spreading to the far west are ideas that serve as motivation for Lincoln's changes in the play.

Bob included in the play a brief reenactment of the famous Lincoln-Douglas debates, which take place after Lincoln's transformation on the prairie. In the actual debates regarding the expansion of slavery, Douglas stressed his desire for each state to mind its own business "and leave its neighbors alone," whereas Lincoln spoke of equality under the law through the principles of the Declaration of Independence and the ideals of the nation's founders. In the play, Bob quotes almost verbatim from the debates. With some poetic license to make the play relevant to his audiences, he has his Lincoln proclaim, "If *we* accept this doctrine of race or class discrimination, what is to stop us from decreeing in the future that 'All men are created equal except Negroes, foreigners, Catholics, Jews, or—just poor people?" [109] Going further, Lincoln says that the concept of neutrality or minding one's own business is "the complacent policy of indifference to evil, and that policy I cannot but hate. I hate it because of the monstrous injustice of slavery itself. I hate it because it deprives our republic of its just influence in the world; enables the enemies of free institutions everywhere to taunt us as hypocrites; causes the real friends of freedom to doubt our sincerity; and especially because it forces so many good men among ourselves into an open war with the very fundamental of civil liberty . . . and insisting that there is no right principle of action but *self-interest*." [110]

Once Lincoln is elected to the presidency, his view broadens. Although he is a Christian, his belief expresses itself in the broader terms of democracy and human rights. As he prepares to take his place in the White House, the president ponders the status of democracy in his time. "We gained democracy," he claims, "and now there is the question whether it is fit to survive." If it should end, Lincoln cannot see how it can ever come into existence again in the pure form created in the United States. "Let us live to prove that we can cultivate the natural world that is about us, and the intellectual and moral world that is within us, so that we may secure an individual, social and political prosperity, whose course shall be forward, and which, while the earth endures, shall not pass away." [111] With these words, Lincoln's train leaves for Washington. He has no idea at that moment that the nation will be split by the Civil War, and at the moment of the play's production, no one knew that the United States would soon be involved in another world war.

Roosevelt, like Lincoln, however, was moving away from neutrality and appeasement. The same month that *Abe Lincoln in Illinois* opened, he asked Congress to allocate $300 million for national defense and appealed to congressional leaders to repeal the arms embargo law so that in case of a war, England and France could purchase weapons. The next month he spoke out vehemently about Hitler's persecution of the Jews and recalled the U.S. ambassador to Germany. He also began a program which included the construction of more than 100,000 warplanes which the French government could covertly buy, thereby sidestepping Congress. The parallels were clear. Lincoln and Roosevelt swam in the same murky waters, and Bob paddled along right beside them.

The production of *Abe Lincoln in Illinois* came about at the same time as the development of a new and democratic theatrical institution, the Playwrights Producing Company (or the Playwrights' Company, as it was most commonly called). Bob was the instigator of the project, for when it came time to think about producing the play, he did not want to risk being victimized once again by the Theatre Guild, and the property was not suitable for the Lunts. As the playwright, the one who had created the characters and story, Bob wanted to retain control over what happened to his script once it left his typewriter. Playwrights' control over their creative property was not a new concept. In 1926 the Dramatists Guild had established its Minimum Basic Agreement between Authors and Managers, which guaranteed playwrights permanent ownership of their work and what was then considered a fair share of any profits derived from their production. Producers could no longer change scripts at their whim, sell movie rights, or choose the directors and casts without the writer's approval. Since the writers refused to work with any producer who would not sign the agreement, management was forced to give in. Bob was a staunch member of the Guild, serving as secretary from 1935 to 1937 and then as president from late 1937 to 1939.

The idea of the Playwrights' Company had germinated in Bob's mind for some time, but it became urgent to him in December 1937, directly after a particularly trying Dramatists Guild meeting. Elmer Rice remembered that the discussion during this "griping session" led Bob and Maxwell Anderson to speak out "vehemently of their disenchantment with Broadway producers, particularly the Theatre Guild, which had presented many of their plays. They were harassed by disagreements about casting, revisions, and the disposition of subsidiary rights."[112] They were also tired of the constant interference. After the meeting, Bob invited Rice and Anderson to have a drink at the nearby Whaler's Bar on Madison Avenue and Thirty-eighth Street. There the conversation turned to the idea of producing their own plays. The three knew that efforts had been made in the earlier part of the decade to establish just such an enterprise; in fact, Bob and Anderson had participated in one advisory group organized by producer Arthur Hopkins. The Dramatists' Theater and the New Playwrights had also been established, but none of the attempts had succeeded. This time, however, they were sure that things would be different.

Bob, Anderson, and Rice decided to invite two other playwrights into their scheme. The first was Bob's good friend Sidney Howard, who in turn approached S. N. Behrman, who at first was "bowled" over by it. "I was flabbergasted," he later wrote, by the thought of leaving the Theatre Guild, its security, and all the friends he had there. "I just didn't know what to say." Still, Behrman made an appointment to meet with Bob. "I was overwhelmed by the intensity of his feeling about it. It was as if it mattered to him more than anything else in the world," he wrote. Bob was "voluble and bitter" in describing his relationship with the Theatre Guild, grievances that seemed minor to Behrman, "trivialities that tear people apart for a few hours during rehearsals and are forgotten the next day." He realized that there was something else operating in Bob's desire to form the Playwrights Producing Company, some "fundamental impulse for self-assertion." With much encouragement, Behrman signed on, later recalling, "Who was I to resist a man so eminent and lovable as Bob Sherwood?"[113]

Sam Behrman may have extolled Bob's importance in his memoir, but in fact each of the five writers who formed the Playwrights' Company was distinguished in his career. Each had been actively creating since the mid-1920s (or earlier in Rice's case) and had written either an antiwar or antifascist play, giving them common political ground. As Bob wrote to Behrman in the early stages of the company's planning: "What impresses me most about the association is that, while our five methods of writing plays are widely different (and with no obligation on any of us to give undue approval to any other's method,) the basic points of view of all of us toward the headaches, heartaches and bewilderments of current life seem to me to be exactly the same. It's the genuinely liberal attitude which is the world's sole hope. I think one would have difficulty finding five other writers of whom this is true."[114] The Playwrights' Company, he hoped, would be more of a brotherhood than a business.

Sidney Howard, a journalist turned playwright, wrote his first drama, *Swords*, in 1921. Although he scripted other plays, his first major success was the 1924 *They Knew What They Wanted*, which won the Pulitzer Prize. Howard was quite prolific in the 1920s, scripting the play *Ned McCobb's Daughter* in 1926, which was Alfred Lunt's first Theatre Guild success. Howard became a respected playwright, whose 1937 play *The Ghost of Yankee Doodle* was one of the first to address the moral question of neutrality. He eagerly joined the Playwrights' Company experiment and was a valued member until his shocking death on August 23, 1939, in an accident on his farm in Tyringham, Massachusetts, when his tractor, in gear, crushed him against the wall of his barn.

Maxwell Anderson, whom Bob considered the most distinguished playwright of the time, was equally busy in the years before the Playwrights' Company came into existence. In 1923 his first play, *The White Desert*, appeared to a lukewarm reception, but when he teamed up with Laurence Stallings the next year to write the first successful antiwar play based on World War I, *What Price Glory?*, the two received critical acclaim. He subsequently scripted several plays, including *Elizabeth the Queen* (1930), *Mary of Scotland* (1933), and *Winterset* (1935); the last, written in blank verse form, was the first play to receive the New York Drama Critics Circle Award. Anderson was also known for his political messages. Besides the antiwar *What Price Glory?* he dramatized the Sacco and Vanzetti case in *Gods of the Lightning* (1928), Spanish resistance to U.S. advances in early-nineteenth-century New Mexico in *Night Over Taos* (1932), and a story of a doomed interracial marriage in *Wingless Victory* (1936).

A lawyer before becoming a playwright, Elmer Rice was equally, if not more, political. His first play, *On Trial*, appeared in 1914, followed by *For the Defense* (1919) and *It Is the Law* (1922). Theater enthusiasts today know him largely for his expressionistic work *The Adding Machine* (1923). *Street Scene*, his 1929 dramatization of life in a New York tenement, won a Pulitzer Prize. In the early 1930s Rice wrote plays addressing the issues of free speech and civil liberties, especially his 1934 *Judgment Day*, which dealt with the destruction of these rights in an unnamed fascist nation, presumably Italy or Germany.

Finally, there was S. N. Behrman, who was especially successful with sophisticated urban comedies that belied his roots in a Jewish working-class neighborhood in Worcester, Massachusetts. Behrman had become popular for plays such as *The Second Man* (1927), *Biography* (1932), *End of Summer* (1936), and the adaptation of Jean Giraudoux's *Amphitryon 38* (1937), with Alfred Lunt and Lynn Fontanne. Less well known was his 1934 play *Rain from Heaven*, a drawing room drama with an underlying theme of anti-Semitism and fascism.

These five men, all major players in the world of Broadway, invited three others into their venture: John Wharton, a lawyer who became an essential part of their operation; Victor Samrock, their general manager; and William Fields, their press representative. On April 12, 1938, the five playwrights signed an agreement which stated their intention to produce their own plays and those of other playwrights as well. Since they wished to have full control over the organization, each agreed to raise $10,000 for a starting capital of $50,000. All investors would share 50 percent of the profit; Wharton would receive 10 percent, and the rest would go to the corporation. A board of directors of no fewer than six nor more than nine members was to guide the organization. It was assumed that the five playwrights and Wharton would compose the basic six.

The most important part of the agreement involved the production of plays. It stated that "the corporation shall be obligated to accept for production any play written hereafter and during the term of this agreement by any of the playwrights" as long as its production budget did not exceed $25,000 and it presented a reasonable weekly operating budget including union costs. The author would receive 10 percent of the weekly gross box office receipts; if a play was sold to a movie company, to radio or television, or for foreign presentation, the corporation's interest would be 40 percent. Complete control of all matters dealing with the artistic side of any Playwrights' Company production, "such as determination of choice of cast, director, designer, selection of properties, sets, size of theatre, and other like matters," belonged to the playwright.[115]

The board of directors was to make all other decisions, including road tours, the closing date of the play, the terms of any British production, the price of tickets, decisions as to prior out-of-town runs, and publicity and advertising; but since the five playwrights made up most of the board, these decisions actually rested in their hands. The agreement stipulated that each of the five playwrights had the right to direct his own plays and for that would receive an extra $2,000, and they could also vote to admit another playwright to membership as long as all of the others agreed in writing. The Playwrights' Company worked as a collective. Each member agreed to be in New York as much as possible from August 1 through February 15 of each year and to share in the work of the company. When away from the city, each constantly wrote letters to the others. All, including Wharton, Samrock, and Fields, commented on play manuscripts and productions, but the atmosphere was not stifling or punitive as it had been at the Theatre Guild, at least for Bob.

When news reached the New York theater community that the Playwrights Producing Company had been formed, there was a minor uproar. The Theatre Guild was rightfully angry that it had lost four of its major playwrights, Elmer Rice having had only one of his early plays (*The Adding Machine*) produced by them. Bob refused to acknowledge publicly that the company had been formed because of his grievances against the Theatre Guild, telling Lucius Beebe of the *Herald Tribune* that the whole idea of the Playwrights' Company being a rebellion was "pretty silly." Rather, the company would offer a new "boon" to the theater, creating more jobs for actors, a demand for more theaters, and, he added jokingly, "so many more traffic congestions in Times Square."[116] Bob's hope, he told Ward Morehouse in October 1938, was that the company would become "so permanent that it will outlive not only the usefulness but the actual lives of its members." As for himself, the company had been nothing but "fun" from its inception. He wished that its profits would keep him out of Hollywood, as his "job's the theater. I'm now in the theater—heart and body and soul and mind." The only role he could not see himself taking on was that of directing: "I haven't the gift. Never have and never will."[117]

The first two plays produced by the Playwrights' Company were *Abe Lincoln in Illinois* and Maxwell Anderson and Kurt Weill's *Knickerbocker Holiday,* which opened four days apart, the former on October 15 and the latter on October 19, 1938. Anderson and Weill's production was a musical with an unexpectedly high budget, but the company agreed to produce it anyway. In December, Rice's *American Landscape* opened, followed in April by Behrman's *No Time For Comedy*. This was a promising first year. The only play that did not do well was Rice's, which closed after only forty-three performances. The other three had respectable runs of 168 performances for *Knickerbocker Holiday* and 185 for *No Time for Comedy* followed by tours and the filming of *Knickerbocker Holiday*, but the outstanding smash hit was *Abe*

Lincoln in Illinois, with 472 performances on Broadway followed by a tour, runs in several European countries, and a film.

Abe Lincoln in Illinois previewed at the National Theatre in Washington, D.C., on October 3, 1938. After good success there, it moved to the Plymouth Theatre in New York. The official word, which Bob, Madeline, and its director, Elmer Rice, read at midnight under a streetlamp in Times Square, was that once again, Bob had written a major work. Several reviews noted both its brilliant portrayal of Lincoln and its relevance to current affairs. Brooks Atkinson stated that "through the life and spoken thoughts of Lincoln, Mr. Sherwood has been able to express his own high-minded convictions with a deeper emotional force than ever before." Bob had crafted a play that was not an "idyll or song of devotion" but a realistic view of the president. "He has looked down with compassion into the lonely blackness of Lincoln's heart and seen some of the fateful things that lived there."[118] Sidney B. Whipple of the *New York World Telegram* reported that the play could "be described only in superlatives." For this critic, it was "the most searching, the most human, the most compelling stage picture of the Great Emancipator of our time." For Burns Mantle of the *Daily News,* it was a "magnificently humanized study of Abraham Lincoln," and for Heywood Broun of the *New York World Telegram,* it was "the finest piece of propaganda ever to come into our theater." In its message that neutrality is not always the moral high road, Broun joked that the play would earn Bob a call to appear before the Dies Committee, the governmental group investigating alleged Nazi and communist propaganda inside the country. "To the satisfied and the smug and the sanctified," he added, "it will seem subversive to its very core. And they will be right. The play is thrilling and heartening, and it is also disturbing. It sounds a trumpet note. It is the very battle cry of freedom."[119] Only John Mason Brown grumbled that Bob used too many of Lincoln's exact words, indicating that in essence, he had had a co-author.[120]

Two critics also took note of the debut of the Playwrights' Company. As Sidney Whipple enthused, this first production of "that glorious company of playwrights . . . who have banded together for the good of the theater and their own spiritual comfort" had been successful indeed. "If this is the criterion of their product, the living theater has indeed been restored to magnificent health." Burns Mantle chimed in: the company was "a quintet of dramatists with high aims, an acknowledged respect for each other and a love of the theatre that begins back stage and works toward the box office, rather than the other way about." For him, the creation of the Playwrights' Company was "of greater theatrical importance than any other that has taken place since the Theatre Guild first became a force in play production."[121]

Its presence signaled the promise of high-quality plays not hindered by the uncontrolled greed of producers.

Bob took home his second Pulitzer Prize for *Abe Lincoln in Illinois*. The play was a huge success on Broadway and on tour, bringing the group a very healthy profit. By the end of its first year, the report to the stockholders proudly declared that the Playwrights' Company was "remarkably sound financially, with every prospect of continuing so." Perceived by the theater community as having "extraordinary prestige," it had impressed the business community and the public with its members' great ability to work together "in harmony, to conduct our business with an efficiency and economy that is rare in the theatre, to be scrupulously fair in our dealings with actors and all other workers in the theatre, and with the public and press as well."[122] Having ownership of the play also gave Bob more leeway in its use. Special benefit performances raised over $7,000 to aid refugees in Europe, and Raymond Massey spoke several times in support of the Theatre Arts Committee's Campaign to Aid Refugees. The film rights were sold to RKO for $225,000, plus 10 percent of the gross over $2 million, an exorbitant amount. Of this, Bob's share was equivalent to about $1.5 million in 2005 dollars.

Audiences flocked to see both the play and the movie. There were personal as well as political reasons for this. For older audiences from Posie and Lyd's generation, Abraham Lincoln was a real person. Posie, born in 1854, not only remembered when Lincoln was alive but also had witnessed his funeral procession. Lydia, born in 1866, had heard about him as a tot. For masses of elderly people, the play was about someone whose life had touched their own. Even for those in Bob's generation, there were stories heard on their parents' and grandparents' laps that made Lincoln live. In other words, even though the play was a historical drama, its subject had not yet entirely passed into national memory.

Abe Lincoln in Illinois also reflected the debates going on all over the country. Should the United States remain neutral or take a stand on fascist aggression? On one side were the interventionists, a minority in 1938, who believed that the U.S. government should take forceful action to stop the German, Italian, and Japanese offenses against other peoples. More pronounced were those on the other side, the isolationists, who could not be described in any one way, except that they all supported neutrality. There were, of course, the diehard pacifists who could not sanction war no matter what the cause. A good example was the War Resisters League, whose members (both male and female) would rather face time in prisons and camps than take another human life. The Fellowship of Reconciliation and the American Friends Service Committee (the organizational wing of the Quaker faith) took equally pacifist stances, as did the Women's Peace Society and the Women's Peace Union.

There were organizations like the 1936 Veterans of Future Wars, formed as a *Lampoon*-like organization at Princeton University, which drew the attention of many antiwar advocates when it demanded that the government issue a $1,000 veterans' bonus to young men *before* they got killed in a war so they could enjoy the money. Also in 1936, the coalition-based Emergency Peace Campaign attempted to nurture international cooperation in an effort to ward off possible world conflict. Under its auspices, Eleanor Roosevelt gave a radio talk after which half a million high school and college students walked out of their classes to voice their desire for peace over war. In its first year of existence, 278 U.S. cities witnessed antiwar activities, and people in twenty-four states enjoyed skits performed by campaign-sponsored theatrical touring companies. Speakers traveled throughout the nation to speak in favor of peace candidates on the November ballots. The Emergency Peace Campaign lasted through most of 1937. By that time, its influence had resulted in the creation of local peace committees in towns and on campuses throughout the country. Another popular effort, which came about in 1939, was the Keep America Out of War Committee, which organized against U.S. involvement in any altercation.

The more sinister America First Committee was founded on September 4, 1940, in direct response to Roosevelt's expressions of support for the English and French struggles against the Germans and his loose monitoring of the Neutrality Acts. America First reached a peak of 800,000 members, largely within three hundred miles of Chicago. It was a fiercely isolationist organization, which claimed Charles Lindbergh as one of its representatives. When the world-renowned pilot made anti-Semitic statements accusing Jews of trying to lead the United States into the war and then expressed favorable impressions of the German Luftwaffe, the committee appeared decidedly pro-Nazi. Communists in the country also entered the debate. Before the autumn of 1939, most supported neutrality because it helped to postpone Nazi aggression against the Soviet Union, but once war was declared, they wished the United States to intervene on the side of the Allies so as to protect and aid the Soviets.

Isolationism was certainly a tricky issue, and as the situation in Europe became more serious, some lifelong pacifists questioned the whole idea of neutrality. Bob, who had dined at the White House in honor of *Abe Lincoln in Illinois*, was certainly cognizant of the fact that Eleanor Roosevelt, who held a lifetime membership in the Women's International League for Peace and Freedom, had expressed both her aversion to war and her sense of global responsibility in her 1938 *This Troubled World,* suggesting that economic sanctions and international tribunals be organized to intervene with the aggressive nations. As a humanist, she asked: "How can we study history, how can we live through the things that we have lived through and complacently go on allowing the same causes over and over again to put us through those same horrible experiences? I cannot believe that we are going to go on being as stupid as that."[123] Another pacifist, Emily Greene Balch, a Quaker and a founder and officer of both the international and domestic organizations of the Women's International League for Peace and Freedom, declared in 1939 that neutrality was "impractical, amoral" and selfish.[124] These were Bob's sentiments exactly. He could not understand how people could interpret *Abe Lincoln in Illinois* as favoring isolationism. As he told Archibald MacLeish, he wrote the play "primarily for the purpose of expressing (in your words), 'the conviction that there are final things for which democracy will fight.'" To Bob, Lincoln was "the supreme non-isolationist in his essential faith." Indeed, the play ends in a suggestion that neutrality is morally reprehensible. "Time and again," however, people wrote him "approvingly," noting that the play "teaches a great lesson in Americanism—that we can sustain our democracy by minding our own business and keeping out of Europe's war." For Bob, "discouraging" was "a faint word for it."[125]

After *Abe Lincoln in Illinois,* Bob was unsure whether he could ever write another play again. Perhaps the Playwrights' Company kept him too busy, or the creation of ANTA (the American National Theater Association), which he helped organize in 1939 to "bring good plays . . . to the greatest number of people in communities large and small throughout the nation," distracted him.[126] His work as president of ANTA from 1939 to 1943 included fund-raising, organizational work, and publicity—no small task. Perhaps it was burnout. In his 1938 diary he reiterated that he lacked "the old nervous endurance—the imperiousness" he used to have before 1934, that trying year which seemed to have damaged him permanently.[127] Two years passed before he produced his next play. But probably the best reason for the delay was that Bob was consumed by world events. If he could not write a play to address the terrible global situation, then he believed he could not write at all. "I wanted to write about that which was uppermost in my own mind and in the minds of most other men who were still free to speak," he wrote in 1940. "But how could any play hope to compete or even keep up with the daily headlines and the shrieks of increasing horror heard over the radio?"[128]

In his 1939 diary Bob noted those particular events which had him so preoccupied that he could not create, and which added to his headaches and drinking. Every day he read "practically every word of foreign news in the papers—columns, editorials—and listen[ed] to news broadcasts as much as I can."[129] The only thing that soothed him throughout the year was Roosevelt's assertive words warning the German and Italian governments that the United States stood strong in its support of freedom and democracy. In February, Britain and France recognized Francisco Franco and his fascist government as the legitimate power in Spain, bringing the world one step closer to global fascism. In March, between Bob's efforts to write a play for the Lunts about Nazism in Austria and his receiving an honorary doctor of letters from Dartmouth College, Germany marched into Prague, Madrid fell to Franco, and war seemed so close that Bob and Madeline discussed the possibility of moving to England for the duration. In addition, Bob continued to suffer from jitteriness, as he noted on April 5, the day after he turned forty-three: "These are horribly nervous days. I buy evening papers all day, listen to news broadcasts while shaving and bathing before dinner—for news may come at any instant that hell is let loose on earth, that London or Paris have been or are being bombed. The moment you stop to think about it, reason recoils. It is like being in The Death House—but you don't know when the sentence is to be executed."[130] Two days later he was stunned to read that Italy had invaded Albania. He pondered, "Is it possible that some of those Italians felt no sense of shame at what they were doing?"[131]

In May, Bob and Madeline took a trip to England, where Bob heard the fear in his aunt Jane and uncle Wilfrid's voices. Living near a power station, they dreaded a German attack which might destroy their home and their life's artistic work. Bob helped them move their paintings, sketches, and some of their furniture to Great Enton for storage in a locked room. By August the couple had temporarily relocated to Grantchester, leaving a neighbor to keep an eye on their house. At the same time, Bob fixed up his barn so that if war came, soldiers could use it as a barracks and a storage place for food and ammunition. Jane impressed her nephew with her concern for her Jewish friends and the hundreds of thousands of homeless refugees traveling through Europe. As she wrote her sister Lydia, "I would far rather die than be under the heel of Fascism, or Nazidom, which I consider is a degradation of the Human & Divine spirit & the negation of everything I love & believe in."[132]

The talk of war in London upset Bob because his pen still lay inactive upon his desk. "I cannot rest easily until I have done what I can to help bring the unspeakable criminals to justice," he wrote. "I have to write that play & it must be good. I think about it all the time, but something is still not quite right," and it would remain so, for the play about Austria that he was experimenting with never came to fruition, and no trace of it exists today.[133] While in England, he felt the presence of war most palpably. A sudden blackout reminded Bob of the horror of clear moonlit nights in 1919, and he shuddered. His jitters mounted when he heard of Japanese soldiers' humiliating English citizens in Tientsin, China, stripping them in public. The rules of civilization were crumbling all around him as the number of insufferable crimes against civilians in Europe and Asia mounted.

Although Bob was working as co-adapter with Joan Harrison on Alfred Hitchcock's film *Rebecca*, and responsibilities for the Playwrights' Company kept him busy upon his return to the United States, nothing took the place of worrying about an impending war and the fact that he could not seem to put his play together. Then on August 23, when Germany and the Soviet Union signed a nonaggression pact, a symbol to Bob of Soviet treachery, he interpreted it as the move he had predicted in *The Petrified Forest* of "nature . . . indeed taking the world away from the intellectuals and giving it back to the apes," thereby opening the way for the "horrors of the Apocalypse."[134] Within a week, the cataclysm had begun. As Bob and Madeline spent an evening out in Hollywood at the Trocadero night club, where producers, directors, and "blonde, false-breasted cuties" danced the conga, a group huddled over a little portable radio heard the news that Germany had bombed Warsaw and had declared war, condemning "millions of decent, helpless people to death."[135] When England and France declared war in return, Bob's nightmare became a reality. He sympathized with Roosevelt's message that the United States would remain neutral in action but not in thought, but predicted that the nation would enter the war within six months and help bring about its conclusion before the end of 1941. He could not have been more wrong.

What should have been more worrisome to Bob was the fact that his jitteriness was contagious. Little Mary was terrified of this war that obsessed her father. The previous winter when Bob talked about Hitler, she ran out of the room and hid in her bed sobbing with a sheet over her head. She thought the Nazis had attacked the United States. Then in the summer, when she was staying with Lydia in Massachusetts, the poor teenager covered her eyes and "wailed in trembling tones" when a morning flight of U.S. fighter planes on a practice run flew over the house in formation. "Are they American?" she cried to her great-aunt.[136] Bob seemed oblivious to her fright. His obsession with world affairs also caused Posie to worry that he would impulsively run off to Canada or some other place and join the military. "I know what I can bear and what is unbearable," she wrote Jane, "& I could not bear to see Bobby go to war again."[137]

Yet Bob needed to do something constructive. Not knowing where to

turn but determined to take action, on October 3, 1939, he received a telegram from the Republican editor of the *Emporia Gazette*, William Allen
White. The cable, sent to several hundred potential supporters, asked Bob
if he would join forces to pressure Congress for a revision of the Neutrality
Acts which would ensure that the United States remained out of the war
but would repeal the arms embargo. The effort, which came to be called the
Non-Partisan Committee for Peace through Revision of the Neutrality Law,
worked under the auspices of the American Union for Concerted Peace Efforts, a group that wanted to see the end of fascism while the United States
remained untouched by war. Bob responded in the affirmative, although this
did not involve much more action than including his name with the others
and corresponding a bit with White.

Then on November 30 Bob heard the "sickening" news that Soviet troops
had invaded Finland. He could not comprehend the bombings of such a
"civilized . . . progressive, enlightened, peaceful" people. "How long can the
conscience of the U.S. remain dormant?" he wondered.[138] To William Allen
White, he expressed his opinion that the United States must "go to war NOW
to defend Scandinavia."[139] Of course, it did not. At 4:15 in the afternoon on
Christmas Day, Bob listened to the radio as White's son, W. L. (Bill) White,
broadcast from Helsinki. The journalist described a setting in the cold, snowy
north of Finland, where a small Christmas tree with wax candles and a few
impromptu decorations stood next to a tiny stove in an army dugout just
a few hundred yards from the Soviet line, facing "the land where there is
no Christmas."[140] This broadcast and some seemingly anti-Semitic remarks
Charles Lindbergh had made in September served as the impetus for Bob's
writing *There Shall Be No Night*. By January 8, 1940, he had formulated the
idea for the play which he shared with no one but William Allen White—not
even with Madeline. It was "the God damndest strangest effort" of his career,
but he felt instinctively that it was going to be good.[141]

With his ear to the news, especially Bill White's reports from Finland, Bob
kept working. Sometimes depressed, sometimes frustrated, he kept going.
Ideas and even words from *Acropolis*, *The Petrified Forest*, *Idiot's Delight*,
and *Abe Lincoln in Illinois* all found their way into the script. Tension with
Madeline that resulted in her taking a trip to Jamaica by herself, a mix of flat-
tery and reservation from his friends at the Playwrights' Company, and the
news of the worsening war all added to his fervor to write this play. Bob's goal
was to finish the script before the Lunts left for a long vacation in Genesee
Depot after an exhausting run in a revival of Shakespeare's *The Taming of the
Shrew*. He had written this new play with them in mind, for Alfred Lunt's
ancestors were from Finland, and as a child he had spent time in that country

with relatives. Since war had broken out there, the Lunts had performed eight benefit performances of *The Taming of the Shrew*, raising close to $25,000 for Finnish relief. For one week Bob wrote nonstop, except for a few short walks. Posie worried when he became so tired that he could not even type. But he met his deadline, delivering the play to the Lunts, who read it on the train the next day and announced that they were "crazy" about it and "wanted to do it at once." Posie, meanwhile, wished for the day when the world would be "so peaceful and pleasant that Bobby may take off his armor and sheethe his sword and feel free to write a play with no motive except entertainment."[142]

Bob was driven. On February 13 he was on his way to Wisconsin to discuss the fine points of the script with the Lunts. Alfred Lunt wanted to direct the effort; Bob approved. Within a few weeks the Lunts were back in New York, the Alvin Theatre was reserved, scenery painted, actors and crew hired, and rehearsals begun. The Theatre Guild agreed to co-produce, which was fine with Bob as long as the Playwrights' Company and the Lunts dominated. During the rehearsal period, Finland signed a peace treaty with the Soviets, and the Nazis invaded Denmark and Norway. Still, the company proceeded, feeling that the slice of resistance depicted in the play and the public support it would engender might serve to boost the confidence of those in other nations, especially England, still fighting the foe.

There Shall Be No Night was Bob's cry for U.S. intervention of some kind in the European war. Even though Finland collapsed before the opening, there were other nations still struggling in Europe and in Asia as well. In the introduction to the published version of the play, Bob explained that he had always been an "internationalist" but not a "warmonger," as the communist *Daily Worker* characterized him.[143] (Actually, its precise words were "the stooge of the imperialist war mongers.")[144] His identification as a pacifist had come about because he was a humanitarian and a lover of peace, democracy, and prosperity. Thus, *There Shall Be No Night* evolved out of his other plays and was more of a "sequel" to *Idiot's Delight* and *Abe Lincoln in Illinois* than a new way of thinking.[145] Bob informed his readers that one of his most "bitter moments" was when he found himself "on the same side as the Big Navy enthusiasts."[146] In addition, as a self-professed liberal who had previously accused the Soviets of crushing democracy, he said it broke his heart to realize that the communist nation could no longer even be considered a "force for world peace," but had become an aggressor and a collaborator with the fascists.[147] Bob was both shocked and disappointed that the United States would do nothing to help the Finns, so he decided to write his play as a protest against "the hysterical escapism, the Pontius Pilate retreat from decision," which seemed to him to dominate U.S. public opinion.[148] The title of the play was derived from the words of Saint John in the Bible: "And they shall see his face, and his name shall be in their foreheads. And there shall be no night there and they need no candle, neither light of the sun; for the Lord giveth them light; and they shall reign forever and ever." For the main character, Kaarlo Volkonen, the words meant that "man" would "find the true name of God in his own forehead, in the mysteries of his own mind. 'And there shall be no night there.'"[149] Human thought would lead to human evolution and then to peace.

There Shall Be No Night is a contemporary drama about the Valkonen family. Kaarlo, a medical doctor turned researcher, has just won the Nobel Prize in medicine for his work on the causes of insanity. His wife, Miranda, is a transplanted New Bedford, Massachusetts, housewife. Their son Erik and his girlfriend, Kaatri, are training with the Finnish military to resist an anticipated Russian invasion. Uncle Waldemar, an elderly Finn, lives with them. The gist of the plot is that Kaarlo and Miranda, both pacifists, believe that war will not come, but if it does, they should resist it by nonviolent means. But then the Russians invade, and Erik leaves to help the resistance. Kaatri, pregnant, cannot participate and is soon sent to the United States to live with Miranda's aunt. Toward the end of the play, Kaarlo becomes involved in the conflict, first as a medic and finally as a combatant. He and Erik die in action; Miranda and Uncle Waldemar, it is assumed, perish while fighting off the invaders outside their home. In spite of its sad ending, Bob felt that the play expressed his optimistic belief that humans could reach a level of consciousness in which they might "find the means of . . . redemption," that out of the tragedy of this and past wars, people could learn to value humanity and nonviolence.[150]

Bob set forth his political messages in several ways. The play begins as Kaarlo is being interviewed by Dave Corween, who, much like Bill White, is a correspondent for a U.S. radio network. In his interview Kaarlo speaks about the psychological deterioration of the world, a situation that threatens to leave more insane people on the streets than sane. Although he names no specific individuals, the audience knew that Kaarlo was speaking about Hitler and Mussolini. People, Kaarlo says, seem happy to give up their "moral sense" to follow "the leadership of a megalomaniac who belongs in a psychopathic ward rather than a chancellery." This fascist seeks "to create a race of moral cretins whom science has rendered strong and germless in their bodies, but feeble and servile in their minds."[151] At the time he speaks these words, Kaarlo does not consider the Soviets to be duplicates of the Nazis. He has studied and worked in the Soviet Union and knows its people and government to have an aversion to war and an interest in humanitarian experiments. Soon his opinion will change. Meanwhile, in words resembling those in *The Petrified Forest*, Kaarlo expresses his fear that humans will not learn to know themselves well enough to save themselves "before the process of man's degeneration has been completed and he is again a witless ape, groping his way back into the jungle."[152] Dave Corween agrees with Kaarlo. He has traveled the world and seen this disintegration into insanity in Europe, Asia, and Africa. Uncle Waldemar, who has not traveled much beyond Finland, also agrees. As he explains to Erik, Kaarlo's feeling that men might return to the apes has already come to pass: "The lights are out in Berlin, Paris, London. And in Warsaw, they crawl through the ruins like rats."[153] The world has turned into a dystopian nightmare.

The Valkonens' neighbor Dr. Ziemssen represents the voice of fascism, especially Nazism. Ziemssen informs Kaarlo that the Soviets are simply stooges in the Nazi plan to take over the world. "Communism," he says, "is a good laxative to loosen the constricted bowels of democracy. When it has served that purpose, it will disappear down the sewer with the excrement that must be purged."[154] The Soviet experiment is simply a diversion from fascism, which creeps in through the capitalist system and is therefore not initially perceived as a threat. The Nazis, Ziemssen feels, are not weak like the Russians. Their aim is clear—to ensure that every nation they conquer never reappears in its same form. Whether through occupation, the displacement of people, or genocide, nationalities such as the Poles will weaken while the Germans simply grow stronger. At this point Bob was attacking what seemed to him the harmful U.S. policy of neutrality, for as Ziemssen informs Kaarlo, as long as the United States minds its own "shrinking business," it will remain secure.[155]

Bob's message of the insanity of war was the same one that he had delivered in his plays since *The Road to Rome*. Perhaps the argument had become more abstract, but the meaning was the same. He now felt, however, that the world had reached such a bad state that he also needed to rationalize interventionism. The character of Miranda represents the United States. Her nationality sets her apart from the other people in her family. Kaatri, from a nationalistic Finnish family, feels that Miranda can afford to be against war because she has the exaggerated sense of security of an American who feels protected by the two great oceans on the country's coasts. Miranda has never had to fight for her land or her freedom and so does not understand the need her son Erik feels to put his life on the line for the nation he calls home. Kaarlo, Kaatri claims, is an internationalist and so also lacks the commitment to Finland. Erik, however, sees his father in a different way. For him, Kaarlo is a man with faith in humankind and in God who, like Bob, embraces Christ's vision in the Sermon on the Mount of brotherhood, love, kindness, and humanitarianism. Therefore, war is unthinkable, but nonviolent action is not.

Bob's answer to the terror in Finland or anyplace else in the world was international intervention of some kind. In *There Shall Be No Night*, he created an assortment of men who come to help out in Finland from various places, for various reasons, and to accomplish different jobs. They include the above-mentioned Dave Corween, who is there to report what he sees. There is the American, Joe Burnett, who flies planes for the Finns to observe Soviet movement, carry messages, and deliver people from one place to another. Joe has spent two years in a Spanish prison for aiding the Republicans in their struggle against the fascists. There is Major Rutowski, a Polish officer whose regiment has been wiped out by the Nazis. The few survivors have been wandering around northern Europe trying to find a way to link up with the rest of the Polish Legion, and in their search, they have aided in the war against fascism. Bob also wrote in two American ambulance drivers for the Red Cross—Frank Olmstead and Ben Gichner. Frank is an exchange student and Ben a former American Express employee. Frank is a pacifist, Ben a lapsed one. The last foreigner in their war is Gosden, an unemployed, bored Englishman who finds his way to the Finnish military. Although neutral and in most ways antiwar, these men represent international intervention in the Finnish-Soviet war, most of it nonviolent. In a small one-room schoolhouse where Kaarlo and all these men, except Dave Corween, are about to take up arms to resist the Russians, Kaarlo insists that as long as people ask questions, there is light in the world, and as long as there is light, there is resistance and hope. Even the pacifists in the play, however, can see that there comes a time when it is morally right and necessary to take up arms.

In the scene in which he parts from Miranda, Kaarlo expresses the true meaning of global responsibility. "I am trying to defeat insanity," he tells her, "degeneration of the human race. . . . And then—a band of pyromaniacs enters the building in which I work. And that building is the world—the whole planet—not just Finland. They set fire to it. What can I do? Until that fire is put out, there can be no peace—no freedom from fear—no hope of progress for mankind." [156] Pacifist Emily Greene Balch expressed a similar sentiment in 1941: "It is *not* enough to sweep before your own door, nor to cultivate your own garden, nor to put out the fire when your own house is burning and 'disinterest yourself,' as the diplomats say, when the frame house next door is in flames and the children calling from its nursery windows to be taken out." [157] The fire analogy held up in Maxwell Anderson's reaction to *There Shall Be No Night*. He was proud of Bob, he said, "for having raised your voice and spoken out like a man at a fire when everybody else (including myself) was still clinging to dubious hopes. It's seldom that anybody is so prophetically accurate and right."[158] It was time for the United States to end its neutrality.

There Shall Be No Night had previews in Providence, Boston, and Washington, D.C., while Bob, Lunt, and Fontanne continued revising the script and the production. Lunt worked closely with the actors, including young Montgomery Clift, who played Erik, to deepen their analysis of war. As the actor William Le Massena remembered: "We sat in his dressing room and we argued . . . about what makes a man go to war. Was it patriotism or a need to show independence? Do men really want to be heroes?"[159] In Washington, the Finnish foreign minister hosted a party for the cast after the performance, but at the opening night in New York on April 29, 1940, the Theatre Arts Committee passed out leaflets headed "Warmongers Capture the Alvin Theatre," calling the play "a weapon pointed straight at the hearts of the American people."[160] Bob responded in the *New York Times* that to him isolationism seemed dangerous to the nation, but he in no way supported U.S. entry into the war. "We should . . . take the view that we are not neutral but that we are also not at war," he stated. A "partisan" view on the part of the U.S. government and an economic blockade might just shorten the European war without any U.S. military intervention.[161] If that did not work, lifting the arms embargo might.

Although Bob agreed that there were weaknesses in the writing caused by his sense of urgency over the political situation, the production received rave reviews for its message and its acting. The Boston critic L. A. Sloper's comment that "his play is a cry that this is not only Finland's war, but everybody's war" must have pleased Bob greatly.[162] Brooks Atkinson claimed that this "practicing liberal . . . in search of some truth that can put a violent world in order and give a man peace with himself" had written a play "of public responsibility."[163] Richard Lockridge, however, felt that Bob was just "whistling in the dark" in terms of his interventionist message.[164] Gilbert Kanour wrote that the play's subject of war's challenge "to the rights and dignity of peace-loving mankind" was never given "such eloquent and discerning treatment."[165] And Richard Watts claimed that this "first play of the second World War" was "a play of stature, dignity, and high emotion, thoughtful, eloquent and heartfelt."[166] At the end of the year Burns Mantle declared it "one of the finer plays of the American theatre record . . . the most stirring event of the theatre season." He hoped that its message of resistance to "the appalling thraldom of ignorance and bestiality expressed through war and the emotions bred by war" would seem dated fifty years hence.[167] On a personal level, Alexander Woollcott marveled at Bob's development as a playwright since his days as the writer of *The Love Nest* and *The Queen's Husband*. As he told Lynn Fontanne, "I look back on that young and extraordinarily gifted crowd that used to mill around the Algonquin at lunchtime. . . . Not one of them has made such good use of the stuff he had in him."[168]

After 181 performances on Broadway, the company headed out for thirty-eight weeks of playing to full houses and standing ovations throughout the United States and Canada. In total, they covered over twelve thousand miles, performing in forty-six cities, nineteen states, and two Canadian provinces with very few rests worked in. In general, audiences were greatly moved by the play. In Boston, a Finnish woman in the audience who had not heard from her son for three months fainted. When Noël Coward saw it, he cried from the moment the curtain went up until it fell. When on tour, runs sold out before the production even reached town. Theatergoers, of course, wanted to see the Lunts, but they also wanted to understand something of the world about which Robert Sherwood wrote so eloquently. Very few people agreed with the Theatre Arts Committee's protests, although in one town a newspaper refused to advertise the play or have it reviewed. In Chicago, the center of America First activity, the editor of the *Tribune*, responding to publisher Robert McCormack's staunch isolationism, issued orders that not one word of the play was to be printed in the paper. As the Lunts wrote to Alexander Woollcott, "It was a silly, futile gesture on his part, as we were sold out for the whole three weeks before we got there."[169]

In Philadelphia, a corps of isolationists picketed the theater, but the demonstration only resulted in increased sales. As Alfred Lunt told a Philadelphia reporter: "Lynn never used to read the papers. Now she reads them all—every word." The entire cast and crew, he said, were "infected" by the play and the audiences' reactions to it. It gave them "a definite sense of taking part in world events. It's something like playing in *Uncle Tom's Cabin* before the Civil War."[170] Once again, Bob had successfully utilized his pen in the cause of educating audiences to his point of view. Even Supreme Court justice Felix Frankfurter acknowledged this when he wrote Bob: "You have again proven that art affords the most powerful access to minds and feelings. . . . It is the artist's function to make his perception contagious, and that you have done superbly in your play. . . . Everyone who cares about the painfully gained achievements of civilization—one ought not to be ashamed to express ultimate beliefs these days—is your debtor."[171]

There Shall Be No Night made a hefty profit for the Playwrights' Company, for the Theatre Guild, and for Bob. In 1940 alone, Bob's royalties for the play equaled $64,889.01. For the same year, his profits for *Abe Lincoln in Illinois* came to $29,939.08. Having added another hundred thousand dollars to his income, he felt able to donate some of it to the interventionist cause. From this money, he sent $1,000 to the Red Cross, $100 to the Committee against Nazi Propaganda, $808.23 to the Canadian Red Cross, $150 to the Emergency Rescue Committee, and $1,920.15 to the Canadian Hurricane Spitfire Fund for the building of fighter planes.[172] The Lunts also donated one week's salary to the Spitfire Fund, and the Playwrights' Company donated one week's profits. The Lunts gave another $900 to the British Ministry of Aircraft Production for the purchase of military planes. It seems as though the entire company was defying the Neutrality Acts on its own. From other moneys, Bob donated $2,750 to the Finnish Relief Fund and $2,250 to the American Red Cross for relief in Poland and Norway.[173]

For this play, Bob received his third Pulitzer Prize and the Gold Medal from the National Institute of Arts and Letters, the latter a particular honor as it was very infrequently given. As critic Sidney B. Whipple noted after the Pulitzer Prize was announced in 1941, *There Shall Be No Night* had "grown in importance since its first production. . . . [I]t has been so prophetic of the results of the totalitarian war enterprise that its profound lessons have been more sharply etched on the public mind with each succeeding month and each succeeding Nazi conquest." He then added that the words spoken by Kaarlo Valkonen were "beautiful . . . hopeful. The world needs them, particularly at this time."[174] Hollywood came calling, but in this case Bob and the Lunts decided not to make the film as the script might be censored and cut to shreds.

Soon after the opening of *There Shall Be No Night*, Bob decided to take his own concrete action against Nazism. In early May he gave an interview to a New York columnist in which he again tried to make his position clear. Audiences, he claimed, "seemed to be entertained" by *Idiot's Delight,* but they "evidently weren't impressed by its argument" that another world war was in the making. In *Abe Lincoln in Illinois* he described "how the greatest American tried to evade his great responsibility, (just as we are trying to hide under the bed until the storm blows over)." Once Lincoln faced up to his duty, he gave his life to preserve the U.S. government, "which is again in violent danger." In *There Shall Be No Night*, Bob concluded, "I am trying to be as direct, as immediate, as I possibly can. I hope that this time the true meaning won't be missed."[175] Soon after the interview, Bob accepted William Allen White's invitation to form a new, more potent organization out of the more or less defunct Nonpartisan Committee for Peace Through Revision of the Neutrality Laws, the new group to be called the Committee to Defend

America by Aiding the Allies. Although it started out with only fifty-three members, by the end of its first month the committee counted approximately three hundred more.

In mid-May the German army invaded France, Belgium, Luxembourg, and the Netherlands, and by the end of the month, Allied troops were being evacuated from France. Frustrated by the passive nature of meetings, Bob came up with a more dramatic idea to capture people's attention about the immediate danger to England. With White's approval, he designed an ad to run in as many newspapers across the country as possible, titled "Stop Hitler Now!" John Wharton was so moved by Bob's passion for the project that he took it upon himself to raise most of the $24,000 needed for advertising costs. Sam Behrman stayed up all night working with Bob on its content, while Maxwell Anderson looked on pensively thinking over his noninterventionist stance, and Elmer Rice, still deeply antiwar, demurred.

The ad appeared on June 10, 1940, the same day Italy declared war on Great Britain and France, and Roosevelt, in the same breath in which he condemned Italy, pledged to England all the material resources the United States could provide.[176] Under the bold black letters stating "Stop Hitler Now!" was a long explanation of the committee's (and Bob's) stance. In an alarmist tone, the text read in part: "If Hitler wins in Europe . . . the United States will find itself alone in a barbaric world—a world ruled by Nazis with 'spheres of influence' assigned to their totalitarian allies. However different the dictatorships may be racially, they all agree on one primary objective: '*Democracy must be wiped off the face of the earth.*'" If this basic message did not frighten people enough, several others followed. The world, Bob wrote, "will be placed on a permanent war footing. Our country will have to pile armaments upon armaments to maintain even the illusion of security." The "only aim in life will be self-defense." And "*Government of the people, by the people, for the people*—if Hitler wins, this will be the discarded ideal of a decayed civilization." To dampen the sense of immediate urgency, in smaller print Bob included a statement that the United States was really in no immediate danger of a direct invasion, but if it did not act quickly, it might be too late.

Next came suggestions for possible action. In a section under a smaller boldface heading saying "WE CAN HELP—IF WE WILL ACT NOW," Bob listed concrete ways the U.S. government could protect its own people. For example, "We can help by sending planes, guns, munitions, food." These were items forbidden under the Neutrality Acts, which enabled the fall of Spain and Finland. If the United States aided in these material ways, no U.S. soldier need enter the war. "We can help to end the fear that American boys will fight and die in another Flanders, closer to home," he wrote. "There is nothing shameful in our desire to stay out of war to save our youth from the dive bombers and the flame throwing tanks in the unutterable hell of modern warfare." In a belligerent tone guaranteed to offend he continued, "Anyone who argues that they will wait is either an imbecile or a traitor."

In a separate small box in the ad, labeled "The Fifth Column," Bob attacked domestic "Nazis . . . Communists and their fellow travellers," who he claimed were "well trained in the dissemination of poisonous propaganda." Here he echoed the government's tactic of linking fascists and communists so that in the future, the nation would be free to take the offensive against the Soviet Union. These traitors' objectives, he wrote, were to "destroy national unity, to keep the United States in a state of confusion over all world issues" so that people would be "weak and helpless" when the time came to attack. Bob warned readers that all people in the United States should be aware of "Nazi-Communist propaganda which attempts to capitalize our desire for peace by opposing all our moves toward national defense." These fellow travelers also sabotaged any attempts to aid the Allies by "preaching" that Hitler had already won "and we must meekly appease him." The ad ended with a narrow horizontal black box running across the bottom which read in white capital letters: "In a dictatorship, the government tells the people what to do. But—this is a democracy—we can tell the government what to do. Exercise your right as a free citizen. Tell your president—your senators—your congressmen—that you want them to help the allies to stop Hitler now!"

The response to the ad was most interesting—and not necessarily positive, especially as to the tone. White immediately let Bob know that he was "bringing my gray hairs in sorrow to the grave." He had received five critical letters to each favorable one and thought that the offensive "imbecile and traitor" line ought to be expunged. He advised Bob to use "milder, more tolerant language" if the ad was to run again.[177] Bob responded that he was "shocked" by the angry responses, as he had received many favorable letters, but perhaps he had acted with "undue temerity" in the limited time he had. Still, he hoped to raise money from it, and whatever the committee members decided to do next, they must "identify ourselves as unwavering upholders of Civil Liberties."[178] Interestingly, the London Evening Standard reported that Franklin Roosevelt praised the ad, finding it "a great piece of work and extremely educational."[179] Rumor had it that Joseph Goebbels, the head of Nazi propaganda, read about it in Berlin and gave it a sneer. The Playwrights' Company loved it, as it gave There Shall Be No Night a great deal of publicity and attracted curious playgoers.

Four days after the ad appeared, the Germans marched into Paris, stunning all Americans. Less than a month later, the famed Battle of Britain began. Bob could hardly stand to hear the news. Two weeks later the Soviet Union annexed Lithuania, Latvia, and Estonia. Where would it end? Bob was frantic. Lynn Fontanne observed that he was working "like a dog" for White's committee.[180] But it was not enough. He also became involved with other interventionist groups, namely, the Century Group, Union Now, and the Council for Democracy, all dedicated to obtaining aid for Great Britain. The Century Group, which had Roosevelt's private approval, pressured Congress to pass the destroyers-for-bases proposal. Congress refused, and so Roosevelt put it through as an executive order allowing the United States to lease eight British military bases in exchange for fifty outdated U.S. destroyers. Union Now lobbied for a U.S.-British alliance on the basis of the nation's Anglo-Saxon heritage, an idea Bob particularly favored. He could not stop himself from saying yes to any group that seemed worthwhile, admitting to Posie that at one point he was on at least ten committees at the same time.

Bob gave speeches and interviews to whoever asked, including periodicals such as *Life*, the *Ladies' Home Journal*, and *Reader's Digest*. The *New York Times Magazine* carried a story on him in which he stood by his claim that he did not wish to see the United States enter the war but simply wanted to give aid to the Allies already in it, especially England. Helping the British for him was the "best insurance against our becoming involved." If aiding them was not enough, then he agreed "with his noted ancestor in Ireland, after whom he was named, that there is not much good in life if it has to be spent in slavery."[181] Next he spoke to the Canadians in a radio broadcast. They had nothing but admiration for Bob because of his World War I experience and his support for them now. In this speech he spoke of "the democratic ideal—the Christian ideal . . . based upon faith in the essential dignity of the individual" as opposed to "Hitlerism . . . based upon the contempt for the individual and denial of every right to the individual." In his most aggressive statement to date, he implored, "We must be prepared, every one of us, to fight . . . to the death."[182] Canadians, one editorial claimed, were "not surprised that in this new war he is again serving the cause of democracy and the Allies, this time with the creative power of his heart and mind."[183] Bob also assailed isolationists Charles Lindbergh and Henry Ford, calling them "two outstanding exponents of what I and many other Americans consider a traitorous point of view."[184] Columnist Walter Winchell loved the playwright's strong criticism of these two, especially Lindbergh, and his "let's crawl to Hitler" oration. Bob, he claimed, was the best speaker he had heard in months in going after those who "go in for swastikow-towing."[185]

Even though the large majority of people in the United States opposed armed intervention, Bob had declared his own war. He gave serious thought to once again going to Canada to enlist, but he was a famous forty-four-year-old celebrity with health problems who would most likely see only a desk job in North America. But somehow, some way, he was going to be a soldier in this war. First, he was going to get others to listen to him and join the antifascist campaign. Then he would find a way to actively help the Allies whether the United States joined in the war effort or not. Finally, he would reach Franklin Roosevelt and offer him his help. Little did he know at the time that Roosevelt's closest aides were already keeping tabs on him. Within a short while, Bob's wish came true as he joined the Roosevelt team which took the United States through the Second World War.

8

Sherwood and Roosevelt

ROBERT SHERWOOD had to play an active role in World War II because, like some interwar pacifists, he believed that his support of self-protective isolationism and neutrality had contributed to its cause. He blamed himself for aiding in the breakdown of what he termed "civilization" and the return to "the apes" by using his role as a playwright and screenwriter to sway public opinion. Therefore, he was guilty of "peace monomania" (a term the dramatist Paul Green coined in his 1936 antiwar play *Johnny Johnson*) and was culpable for the rise of fascism, tyranny, unchecked imperialism, and crimes against humanity.[1] "My attempts at that time to express my pacifism far and wide in my writings," he revealed in 1954 to a group of schoolchildren at his alma mater, Milton Academy, "were naive and futile, as it turned out," and directly resulted in aiding "the rise of Adolf Hitler in Germany, the militaristic caste in Japan, the Fascists in Italy, and Stalin's ruthless mobilization of the Soviet Union." In other words, for Bob, "it turned out that all the pacifist activities had contributed materially to making a Second World War inevitable, and to reducing democracy's chances for survival in such a war."[2]

Bob's disparaging comments about the well-meaning efforts which had resulted in the creation of the League of Nations, the World Court, the Kellogg-Briand Pact, and various treaties illustrate a deep internalization of his sense of powerlessness. His own actions had not helped to stave off war; therefore, he was to blame for the war. To make up for his perceived grave error, he now had to work to undo the damage. Writing plays seemed a good way to disseminate his changing beliefs, but with his productivity curtailed by a combination of physical deterioration, emotional upheaval, and creative burnout, he had to find some other path. As one of the most respected playwrights of the day, he decided to use his reputation and the contacts he had made over the years to reach President Franklin D. Roosevelt in order to persuade him to adopt a more interventionist stance, and to offer his own assistance in this effort.

In September 1938 Bob and Madeline spent a weekend at the Long Island estate of Herbert and Margaret Swope, where he was introduced to Roosevelt's trusted adviser Harry Hopkins. Although Bob got the impression that Hopkins was "profoundly shrewd and faintly ominous," he was attracted by his close relationship to the president.[3] For Roosevelt, Hopkins was an insightful, intelligent, trusted worker—a New Dealer of the highest order and a very good friend. This frail, sickly man, just six years older than Bob, had dedicated his life to public service, working for such New York City agencies as the Association for Improving the Condition of the Poor, the Bureau of Child Welfare, and the New York Tuberculosis Association. He had met Roosevelt in 1928 during the latter's successful run for governor of New York State and joined his administration, heading the first state relief effort in the nation, the Temporary Emergency Relief Administration. After Roosevelt was elected president, he invited Hopkins to join him in Washington, where he supervised the work of the Federal Emergency Relief Administration (FERA), the Civil Works Administration (CWA), and the Works Progress Administration (WPA). He also created the National Youth Administration and supported the creation of both the Federal Writers and Federal Theatre projects. Though never elected to any public office, Hopkins was indeed a key figure in U.S. domestic and then international politics. Bob came to understand and like him for their shared evolution from pacifism and isolationism to support for some type of intervention and their devotion to Roosevelt.

Despite his initial reservations about Hopkins, Bob cultivated a relationship with him. When *Abe Lincoln in Illinois* opened in Washington, D.C., in October 1938, he invited Hopkins to a performance; in return, the president's adviser personally escorted Bob, Madeline, Elmer Rice, and Raymond Massey around the White House, making sure to show them Lincoln's bedroom. Over the next year or so, Bob kept up intermittent contact with Hopkins, inviting him in October 1939 to the Washington opening of *Madam, Will You Walk*, Sidney Howard's posthumously produced play. In December he arranged for the film of *Abe Lincoln in Illinois* to be shown at the White House for Hopkins's viewing and, the next month, for Franklin and Eleanor Roosevelt. The following day, Hopkins asked Bob for his opinion about Roosevelt's almost certain run for a third presidential term. "I answered that I considered it was his duty to run . . . [that] the United States was the only power that could prevent the world from going to hell and Roosevelt was the only man with the personal strength and prestige as well as intelligence to lead the United States in the way it should go," he later recalled.[4] He also volunteered to help in any way he could. The following April, Bob invited Hopkins and others to the Washington opening of *There Shall Be No Night*. Hopkins, too ill at the time to attend, invited Bob to visit him in the White House, where they again discussed Roosevelt's possible reelection.

The month after the appearance of the "Stop Hitler Now!" ad in June 1940, Bob became more assertive. He asked Hopkins for two theater-related favors. The first was to obtain a visa for the French director René Clair to work in the United States, and the second was for an extension of the immigration permit for the English actor Maurice Colbourne so he could continue to perform in *There Shall Be No Night*. Hopkins exerted his influence without any reservations. Bob also told Hopkins in his letter of July 30, 1940, that he was collaborating with a group including Archibald MacLeish, John Steinbeck, and Henry Luce to form a "Bureau of Propaganda for American Democracy, an attempt to appetite the psychological and spiritual mobilization of the people" toward intervention as a form of self-defense.[5] He hoped that Hopkins would be sympathetic to such an effort.

Bob's active courting of Hopkins (and hence Roosevelt) became an issue within the staunchly Republican Sherwood family. Throughout the spring and summer there was constant debate about the upcoming election, in which most family members supported Wendell Willkie, who, as Lyd put it, was willing to give up a huge salary "to take on this stupendous job in a disheartened disgruntled country in a world of tragedy & danger because he feels he has something to give."[6] Posie claimed that she hated Roosevelt and the New Deal because it "paralyzed industry, strangled initiative and prolonged the depression and unemployment."[7] Jane, fearful about England's future, supported Roosevelt's reelection. With Wilfrid, in his seventies, actively serving as quartermaster in the Home Guard and their London home vacant and vulnerable to attack, she felt that the greatest chance of gaining U.S. aid and possible intervention lay with Roosevelt. "We know & we all believe in 'R'," she wrote the ever-sniping Lydia, "& I think that some day when the scales have fallen off your blind eyes & you republicans have at last understood that it is R who leads the USA & not the USA-R, you will acclaim R as . . . the greatest President you have had since Lincoln."[8]

Meanwhile, Bob continued to take small steps toward the possibility of working with Roosevelt in a concrete way. When he met Hopkins in early July, the two had an impassioned discussion about neutrality during which Hopkins was obviously testing Bob's knowledge of political issues. Following this, Bob sent Hopkins a copy of the text of a telegram he had wired Roosevelt, saying that if the Democratic Party platform continued to embrace isolationism, it would spell disaster for both Roosevelt's foreign policy and the New Deal, which would "be as cold as liberty, equality and fraternity are in France."[9] In August he sent another telegram to Roosevelt urging him to take action on the destroyer-for-bases proposal and offering his assistance in the election campaign. True to his word, in September he spoke in support of Roosevelt at the World's Fair in New York; in Hartford, Connecticut; at the *Herald Tribune* annual forum; in Englewood, New Jersey; and on several radio stations. When Posie heard a broadcast lauding Roosevelt and realized after the first three or four sentences that the speaker was none other than her son, she lamented, "My poor boy. My poor boy," and then sent him a scolding telegram demanding, "How dare you call yourself a Republican," which, of course, he certainly did not. On a more playful note, when Arthur asked his brother to bring home a souvenir the next time he visited the White House, Bob replied: "What would you like? His scalp?"[10] Ignoring his family's caustic comments, Bob continued his personal campaign while Madeline raised money through the Fund for the Reelection of President Roosevelt.

Finally, in early October, Bob made an important breakthrough. Like most busy politicians, Roosevelt relied on writers to draft his speeches. During his third presidential campaign this responsibility rested primarily with Samuel I. Rosenman and Harry Hopkins (when time permitted). A World War I veteran and graduate of Columbia University's law school, Rosenman practiced law in New York City until he was elected to a seat in the New York State Assembly, which he held from 1922 to 1926. In 1928 he met Franklin Roosevelt and started a long personal and professional relationship with him. A New York State Supreme Court justice from 1933 to 1943, he left the position to become the first official White House counsel, serving between 1943 and 1946. During the years leading up to and including World War II, Rosenman spent much time in Washington, D.C., writing speeches and advising Roosevelt, but in early October 1940 he informed Hopkins that he alone could not draft the many campaign speeches needed in the next month and suggested that they invite another writer to join them.

As the two men thought about possible candidates, Hopkins suggested Bob. Rosenman agreed to meet him. First, however, Hopkins quizzed Bob about what he thought the president should say about Hitler in his next speech. Bob later claimed that he was "somewhat flabbergasted" by the request but managed to blurt out his views. Before he knew it, he was in Rosenman's apartment. "At first," Bob later wrote, "I did not know why I was there but I soon found out that I had been pressed into service as a 'ghost writer.'"[11] Being recruited onto what became Roosevelt's final speechwriting team was a dream come true. What better way was there to get his own views across than through the mouth of the president of the United States, who shared those views? This was as close as anyone could come to informing world affairs without being a politician himself. As Sam Rosenman put it, presidential speechwriters were "in a peculiarly strategic position to help shape . . . policy."[12]

For the next four and a half years, Hopkins, Rosenman, and Sherwood worked as collaboratively as the five writers of the Playwrights' Company.

Hopkins, who acted as Roosevelt's liaison on many European trips, worked on fewer speeches, Bob and Rosenman on more. It was Hopkins who usually approached Roosevelt initially, the one who lobbied for those words and proposals which the three thought most important; but Bob and Rosenman sat in on many sessions in which Roosevelt pondered world history and current events, discussing, debating, and generally working through the ideas which they then formed into a speech. Sometimes a speech needed to be drafted out in a short period of time; on other occasions the team worked for a week or more, planning, reworking drafts, consulting with Roosevelt, and rewriting again. Bob once remarked that "when working for Franklin D. Roosevelt, his [the ghostwriter's] one purpose was to haunt the White House day and night, until a speech by Franklin D. Roosevelt (and nobody else) had been produced."[13]

The president was acutely aware of his audiences and often met with the three writers to stress the points he wanted to make to a specific group of listeners. They then imitated his style in the drafts they wrote. Roosevelt was happiest when using the vernacular, as Bob recalled, "even the tritest phrases" such as "clear as crystal," "rule of thumb," "neither here nor there," and "simple as ABC."[14] In addition, he "worked so hard and consistently on his speeches himself, made so many corrections and inserted so many paragraphs of his own that by the time it was delivered it was thoroughly impregnated with his own style and personality." Usually the team spent hours creating a speech that was far too long for the amount of time Roosevelt had, whereupon the president read it through and dictated cuts and insertions to his secretary, Grace Tully. "Grace—take a law," he would say.[15] The line was not his own but one borrowed from the George S. Kaufman–Richard Rodgers–Lorenz Hart musical *I'd Rather Be Right,* in which George M. Cohan played the part of Franklin D. Roosevelt. The president never saw the show, but he had heard the line and quickly adopted it.

After a hard day of writing, the team would sit down with Roosevelt in his study to hear his reactions. Because of his damaged legs, he mixed drinks from a tray while sitting at his desk, as by this time he could neither walk nor stand without aid. A limited drinker, he enjoyed these special moments of chatting, sipping bourbon old-fashioneds or martinis, and munching on small snacks of cream cheese or fish paste on toast. Bob sometimes felt sorry for Roosevelt because in their effort to offer the executive healthy foods, the White House chefs inevitably prepared tasteless dishes, and as much power as he held in the world, Roosevelt seemed reluctant to complain about the food or the service. One day, however, he lamented to Rosenman and Bob that even though he loved roasted peanuts, security provisions dictated that every morsel of food given to him had to be inspected. If somebody wanted to send him a package of his beloved peanuts, he told them, "the Secret Service would have to X-ray it and the Department of Agriculture would have to open every shell and test every kernel for poison or high explosives. So, to save trouble, they would just throw the bag away and never tell me about it." [16] So sympathetic were the two men that they went to the corner of Pennsylvania Avenue and Fifteenth Street and bought a large bag of peanuts and sneaked it into the White House. The roasted peanuts also served another purpose. One day Bob and Rosenman sorely needed to meet with Roosevelt, but he was in a rush and had only five minutes to spare. Bob ran out and bought a bag of peanuts. The relaxation of munching on his favorite food drew the meeting out to forty minutes.

After working through dinner, Roosevelt would read a proposed speech aloud to get a sense of its effectiveness, and then as he drifted off for a much-needed rest, the tired writers would move to the Cabinet Room, where they produced yet another draft of the speech to be ready by breakfast. At times, Eleanor Roosevelt, a warm and constant presence in their White House life, noticed the lights on during the wee hours of the morning and called down to order the men to get some rest. As Bob noted, "Of course, the fact was that she herself was sitting up working at that hour." [17] Once Roosevelt approved a speech down to its very punctuation, various facts, figures, and policy statements were then rechecked by the Army and Navy departments, the War Department, or other relevant agencies. Bob and Rosenman also made repeated fact checks, fearful that through some fault of their own the president of the United States might make an error.

By the end of preparing each speech, Bob felt as if he had experienced a true blending of like minds. He later wrote, "The collaboration between the three of us and the President was so close and so constant that we generally ended up unable to say specifically who had been primarily responsible for any given sentence or phrase." [18] Roosevelt himself freely admitted to asking people for assistance. "In preparing a speech," he noted, "I usually take the various office drafts and suggestions which have been submitted to me and also the material which has been accumulated in the speech file on various subjects, read them carefully, lay them aside, and then dictate my own draft. . . . Naturally, the final speech will contain some of the thoughts and even some of the sentences which appeared in some of the drafts or suggestions submitted." [19] In addition, the president never gave up his right to ad lib, which he did with great amusement and pleasure.

The first month of Bob's commitment to speechwriting was the month before election day 1940, and Roosevelt was wildly busy on the campaign trail. Bob learned exactly what that meant at his initial Sunday meeting in New York with Rosenman and Hopkins, when Rosenman announced: "Boys, there comes a time in the history of every speech when it's got to get written—that time for this speech is *now*. So let's get to work." This particular speech was to be a general Columbus Day message of unity among the Americas. Immediately, the three men talked through a draft which had been run by the State Department. Bob stressed that its interventionist subtext was too mild. Encouraged by this comment, Rosenman sent him off to the dining room to sketch out a few paragraphs while he worked on another angle. He later remembered that Bob looked "mystified" when he was told to start writing, as if to say, 'How is that going to do any good in a speech the President is now writing in Washington to be delivered in Dayton?' But instead of saying what I am sure was in his mind, he pulled his six feet six inches out of the chair, picked up a pack of cigarettes, and with a shrug of the shoulders, went in to work." [20]

For several evenings Bob and Rosenman worked on the speech. As they did so, it evolved from being a generic Columbus Day message to one in support of Roosevelt's foreign policy. Three days before it was to be delivered, Rosenman carried the draft to Washington. Bob heard no further word until October 12, when the Rosenmans invited him to their apartment to listen to it on the radio. Bob sat anxiously with a carbon copy in his lap, sure that it would not match up with the words Roosevelt was about to speak. As he compared the written text with the actual address, however, his face lit up. "He was getting his first thrill of hearing some of his words spoken by the President of the United States," Rosenman recalled. "That first thrill was always the deepest for each person who worked on a speech, but no matter how many times the experience was repeated the pleasure was always great." What surprised Bob most was that the lines he had written sounded so different coming from the president's mouth. "Since Sherwood was a playwright," Rosenman said, "he should have been used to hearing his lines spoken by others." [21] But somehow, hearing the president speak his words was just not the same as hearing actors say them. Uncharacteristically, Roosevelt did not change much of this first speech Bob worked on. To the traditional Columbus Day sentiments about peace and prosperity in the Americas, the address added an assertive message of a united defense against fascism, plans to continue to aid the British as much as possible, a claim of the right of freedom of the seas without threat of attack, and a strong no-appeasement policy.

Within a week, Roosevelt announced plans to deliver five campaign speeches between October 23 and November 2, election day being November 5. In addition to countering isolationist attacks on his statements about defense, he spoke of the Selective Service Act, which Congress had passed on September 16, the first peacetime draft in the nation's history. The first day for registration was October 16, and there was much tension surrounding it. The opposition used the issue of conscription to make exaggerated claims that the president was getting ready to plunge the nation into war and that his running for an unprecedented third term indicated his intention to do away with elections and overthrow democracy. Bob, Rosenman, and often Hopkins were immediately wrapped up in fending off these attacks, spending most of every day writing and discussing ideas and strategies. It was immediately clear to Rosenman that Bob was the speechwriter he would most enjoy working with in all his years with Roosevelt. "He never showed any pride of opinion or authorship," he later noted. "He was an excellent judge of the effect of words upon audiences. . . . He was a burning enthusiast for the New Deal and for a strong international policy; if anything, he had to be restrained rather than encouraged." [22]

In his speech in Philadelphia on October 23, Roosevelt put to rest Republican rumors that he had made secret treaties that would drag the country into war. Next, on October 28, he ended a tour of the five boroughs of New York City with a speech in which he took on opposition claims that he was too slow in building up U.S. defenses. Roosevelt ticked off innumerable examples of attempts he had made to get Congress to pass his budget requests to build up the military after it had been shrunk as a result of isolationist thinking. He also underlined his efforts to repeal the embargo on shipping armaments to warring nations through his cash-and-carry proposal, another move that Republican senators and representatives had blocked. Among the opposition leaders he specifically named were Joseph Martin, Hamilton Fish, and Bruce Barton.

Rosenman recalled how, when he and Bob were putting this particular speech together, they "almost simultaneously hit on the more euphonious and rhythmic sequence of Martin, Barton and Fish." [23] They worked the jingle-like sound in twice, first as a humorous nod to the audience: "Yes, the Act was passed by Democratic votes but it was over the opposition of the Republican leaders. And just to name a few . . . now wait, a perfectly beautiful alliteration—Congressmen Martin, Barton and Fish." A brief time later, they used it again: "So, we can well say that Britain and a lot of other nations would never have received one ounce of help from us—if the decision had been left to Martin, Barton and Fish." [24] When they handed the draft to Roosevelt, they did not mention this little inside joke, but, as Rosenman recalled, by the time he finished reading it, "his eyes twinkled; and he grinned from ear to ear. . . . He repeated it several times and indicated by swinging his finger in cadence how effective it would be with his audiences."[25] Roosevelt had great fun with the rhyme, and so did his audiences, who roared with laughter the first time they heard it. The president used it so often, including in radio addresses, that by the time he reached Boston, audiences were chanting the phrase along with him.

Bob and Rosenman worked on the October 30 Boston speech both in Washington and on the campaign train, which stopped in several New England towns for rear-platform rallies. Besides the usual comments on depression economics and the need to build up the nation's defenses, Roosevelt addressed the fear that he believed mothers, in particular, had about the draft. Once again, Rosenman and Bob came up with a catchphrase which caught on, this time in the words "again and again and again." Roosevelt assured parents that their conscripted sons would be well housed and taken care of, adding, "I have said this before, but I shall say it again and again and again: Your boys are not going to be sent into any foreign wars. They are going into training to form a force so strong that, by its very existence, it will keep the threat of war far away from our shores. The purpose of our defense is defense."[26] Years later, Bob recalled that he had felt it was a mistake for the president to make such a "sweeping reassurance" but still encouraged him to do so in order to win the election. "I burn inwardly whenever I think of those words: 'again—and again—and again,'" he wrote.[27]

Cleveland was to be the final major campaign stop where Roosevelt could sum up the issues and send the voters off with enthusiasm to cast their ballots for the Democratic Party. Just seventeen hours before he was to deliver his speech, however, Bob, Hopkins, and Rosenman had not written a word, so they had to rely on material collected primarily from columnist Dorothy Thompson. Bob and Rosenman spent the night drafting the message, and the next morning Roosevelt made his own changes. In the end, Rosenman believed this to be the best of the president's 1940 campaign speeches. His delivery was enthusiastic, the audience warm and welcoming. In general, the Cleveland talk celebrated democracy in the United States, but it also discussed the importance of preserving the values which the nation had been founded upon. Toward the end Roosevelt said: "There is a great storm raging now, a storm that makes things harder for the world. And that storm, which did not start in this land of ours, is the true reason that I would like to stick by these people of ours until we reach the clear, sure footing ahead. . . . We will make it; and the world, we hope, will make it, too. When that term is over there will be another President," at which point the audience shouted back, "No! No!"[28] Rosenman remembered watching Bob with "considerable amusement" as they sat on the speakers' platform, Bob "mouthing every word in unison with the President." After the final words, when the applause was at its peak, Rosenman turned to him and shouted in his ear that he should take a bow as well "because he had just delivered the speech himself, albeit inaudibly." [29]

On election eve Bob joined the Roosevelts and their close friends and supporters at Hyde Park. He later described how the president's mother sat knitting and talking with friends in "the Snuggery," seemingly paying little attention to the frantic activities in the adjoining room. Eleanor Roosevelt was busy taking care of the guests, and the president, in shirtsleeves, sat in the dining room at the head of a table with secretaries, aides, his sons, and "his Uncle Fred Delano." "A news ticker or teletype machine was clattering" while Roosevelt kept score on a huge chart. "When I looked in for a moment," Bob related, "the President introduced me to Uncle Fred, who asked me, 'Are you the author of that play the Lunts are in?' When I said yes, Mr. Delano launched into a long and generous discussion of the play. . . . I was grateful but acutely embarrassed as I felt there were more important topics just then." Bob, Madeline, and Sam Rosenman spent most of the evening upstairs in Harry Hopkins's bedroom listening to the returns on a small radio. What impressed Bob most was the sense he had of "the power of democracy" as the sitting president waited just like any other nervous candidate for election night results. At about midnight everyone was called onto the front porch, where the press and neighbors had gathered. One man carried a sign, "Safe on Third!" [30] Roosevelt had won a third term, carrying 54.8 percent of the popular vote and 449 of the possible 531 electoral votes. Rosenman turned to Bob and said, "It looks as if you and I have four busy years ahead of us." [31]

There was no question that Roosevelt enjoyed working with Bob and would have been very disconcerted if the FBI background check had discovered any reason why he should not continue on the team. Indeed, the agents assigned to interview his associates must have found New Yorkers a bit flippant. Harold Ross, for example, responded: "Investigate Sherwood? You might as well investigate the American flag." [32] Elmer Rice found it amusing that the FBI should approach him about someone else's progressive politics. "I managed to keep a straight face," he later recalled, "but as he was leaving I could not resist saying, 'If you want more information I suggest you try the White House, because Sherwood is living there now, helping the President write his speeches.'" The agent "nodded gravely." [33] Rice was indeed correct.

When Bob was in Washington, he and Sam Rosenman stayed either at the Willard Hotel or in the White House itself, where the widowed Harry Hopkins also lived with his young daughter. Hopkins's suite on the second floor had once served as Abraham Lincoln's study, and was therefore a sacred space to Bob. On the same floor were two small bedrooms, each with a bath, which he and Rosenman were assigned during intensive speechwriting sessions. Missy LeHand, Roosevelt's private secretary until her death in 1941, also had a small suite; her successor, Grace Tully, was the person Bob most identified with Roosevelt's work. Bob loved staying at the White House. The rooms inhabited by the Roosevelt family had the look and feel of their Hyde Park residence and were informal and welcoming. As he later wrote: "In the years of Franklin Roosevelt, the whole place was obviously filled with the fierce loyalty and warm affection that he inspired. If you could prove possession of these sentiments in abundance, you were accepted as a member of the family and treated accordingly."[34]

Working close to Roosevelt and eventually being accepted as a friend was one of the greatest joys in Bob's life. Besides their common bond of hating fascism and loving the New Deal, Roosevelt, as one reporter wrote, "found Mr. Sherwood a congenial and relaxing companion." Bob's quiet nature, his slow speaking style, his "long face" which "masks a salty, pointed, dead-pan humor" were all "irresistible" to the president.[35] Perhaps Bob's sense of humor explains the inscription Roosevelt wrote on a photo of himself in his favorite suit: "Here's the seersucker picture, Bob—with affection from the sucker to the seer."[36] Roosevelt also enjoyed the fact that Bob was a show business personality and could fill him in on the nation's popular culture. Bob recalled how one evening as he described to Roosevelt a movie he had just seen at Radio City Music Hall, the president hesitantly asked him what went on in that great center of entertainment. Did the Music Hall have continuous showings, or did it divide them up into matinees and evening performances? What were "these so-called stage shows?"[37]

It struck Bob that the president, with all his "vast understanding of the American people," had been "completely cut off" from many of the changes that had taken place during his twenty years in politics and as an invalid. "Once I mentioned the term 'juke joint,'" he related, "and he did not have the faintest idea what I meant; he was amazed when I described the co-educational saloons where boys and girls could drink together and dance to mechanical music." Roosevelt had seen such things in films but had no idea of the reality of them. For a man who had appeared on as many movie screens as he had, the president had rarely seen the inside of a movie theater or had a "'lunchette' at a soda fountain."[38] Roosevelt liked to tease Bob for being "a Broadway wisecracker" and sometimes spoke to him, Bob remarked, "as if he were an actor who had been reading my lines." After a speech in

Philadelphia, the president asked Bob if he thought his timing in one spot was good, and Bob responded that it was perfect. Roosevelt then gave him "one of his sly looks and asked, 'Do you think Lunt could have done it any better?' " [39]

For all the pleasure, pride, and prestige Bob got out of his new role, this change in his life had repercussions. Being a soldier at war (which in essence Bob was) meant that the work he would normally have done was curtailed. From October 1940 until April 1945, Bob was in the employ of Franklin Roosevelt and/or the U.S. government. This meant that he was no longer a fulltime theater and film writer as he had previously been. During that period he did not write a single play or film, although he watched over those plays that were in production, especially *There Shall Be No Night,* which was still on tour throughout the United States and would eventually have a dramatic run in Great Britain. He certainly continued to be the major voice in the Playwrights' Company even though he could not often be physically present, especially after the nation entered the war in December 1941.

The company, which maintained a most prestigious reputation, spent the first half of the 1940s struggling economically. In 1941 it mounted only three productions, and had only moderate success, with Elmer Rice's *Flight to the West* running for 136 performances but no tour and Maxwell Anderson's *Candle in the Wind* 95 performances and a twenty-week tour, while S. N. Behrman's *The Talley Method* failed, with only 56 performances. The next year saw only two new plays: Anderson's successful *The Eve of St. Mark* with 306 performances and a tour of twenty-eight weeks and Behrman's *The Pirate,* a Lunt-Fontanne success that ran for 176 performances. The 1943 season saw two productions. Sidney Kingsley's *The Patriot* was the company's first play not written by one of the five original playwrights, but it was a success at 172 performances and a twenty-four-week tour, while Elmer Rice's *A New Life* flopped with only 69 performances. The next year featured only one play, an unsuccessful attempt by Anderson, *Storm Operation,* which ran a paltry 23 performances in January 1944. Until November of the next year, no successful production was mounted, leaving the company in a precarious financial situation.

In addition, since Bob received no salary for writing speeches, the family income took a big dip while his cost of living remained high. In addition, his royalties from the Playwrights' Company decreased, as did his profits from Hollywood films and commissioned articles, which also declined in number. Although he and Madeline were not driven into poverty, they could not afford to live at the level of luxury to which they were accustomed without using

vast amounts from their savings, which they did. Another reason for their rapidly diminishing resources had to do with an unrelated financial catastrophe
which struck them in 1940 just when Bob began working with Roosevelt.
Soon after the success of *The Road to Rome* in 1927, Bob had become a client
of the Wall Street broker Joseph W. Burden, a man known as a reliable and
ultraconservative financial adviser. Because Bob considered Burden to be one
of the most boring men in the world, he avoided him. After all, money was
flowing in, and he was experiencing no financial problems. In fact, Bob felt
so secure that he told Sam Behrman he was "very foolish" to keep his money
in a savings bank. Bob had "entrusted his entire capital," even Little Mary's
savings, to Burden's care and felt that as the depression encircled everyone
else, he was lucky to have Burden, who did "wonderful things" for him. In
fact, he eventually arranged for his entire income to go directly into Burden's
hands while he lived "on an allowance" allotted to him.[40]

Then, in early November 1940, Bob's sister Rosamund sent him a note
relating "some disturbing rumors" about Burden. The office she worked in
handled several parcels of his real estate which had been put up "for immediate sale at any price," and it was said "on good authority" that Burden
would shortly go through bankruptcy.[41] Bob learned the truth only when
his "allowance" stopped arriving. Burden had swindled him out of the entire
$300,000 which the playwright had turned over to him. Instead of investing
the money, he had embezzled it, living a life of luxury, sending his children
to expensive private schools, and building a few country homes, one of which
he actually tried to sell to Bob. To make matters even worse, Bob was in debt
for $100,000, the money that was supposed to have been in a trust fund for
Mary Brandon. In 2005 terms, this $400,000 equaled close to $5.5 million.
Burden's brothers, all wealthy, agreed to restore the trust fund, an offer Bob
accepted after all of Burden's servants and other employees had been paid the
salaries owed them. Still, he and Madeline had to start saving again almost
from scratch.

Bob nevertheless refused to testify at Joseph Burden's trial because he
thought it might result in unpleasant publicity. Sam Behrman joked: "Tom
Dewey was then the District Attorney. Bob would not aggrandize the reputation of a political enemy of Franklin Roosevelt's."[42] In fact, he maintained
his mild response into 1941, when Burden came up for sentencing. The judge
requested that Bob state in a letter what course of action he preferred—severe
punishment or leniency. Bob chose leniency, but Burden ended up serving
time in Sing-Sing. Since Bob was not destitute, Roosevelt found the incident
amusing. When Bob received the 1941 Pulitzer Prize for *There Shall Be No
Night*, the president teased him, saying that he had had Missy LeHand write

the committee to have the prize money sent directly to the White House for safekeeping.

Roosevelt's 1940 reelection did not spell the end of hard work for Bob. He had imagined that he could relax now, but that was not to be, and he was not unhappy about it, especially after hearing on November 13 that Great Enton had been bombed. Although there was no damage to the house except for some falling plaster, Bob was incensed. "It's strange how we personalize everything," he wrote to the Lunts, "but the news of those bombs gave me a feeling of physical rage and revulsion that I have not felt reading all about the horrors. The bastards!"[43] With his ire up, Bob eagerly answered the increasingly frequent summonses to Washington, so much so, in fact, that he and Madeline gave some consideration to moving there for however long he was needed. An offer to stay at the White House made this plan unnecessary—a great relief, since both loved New York, and at times Bob needed to escape from the intensity of his work in the capital. Besides, as Madeline told Posie, once he heard that many houses in the District of Columbia were "full of rats and mice," the decision was made for him.[44] His first important post-election tasks involved writing speeches in support of the Lend-Lease legislation that Roosevelt was trying to get through Congress. The policy would allow the British to lend or lease war supplies from the United States. When they were no longer necessary, they could be returned. Getting the votes he needed and moving the isolationists out of his way became so frustrating for Roosevelt that he decided, as he usually did, to take his case to the people.

Roosevelt wanted to introduce the Lend-Lease concept on his December 29, 1940, fireside chat radio broadcast. His approach was to convince the public that the best way to keep the United States out of the war was to support Great Britain in every way possible, for if the British fell to the aggressors, the United States would certainly be in great danger. Bob later claimed that it was Harry Hopkins who came up with the phrase "the arsenal of democracy," which characterized the speech and the entire effort to get Lend-Lease passed.[45] The morning after the broadcast, the *Chicago Tribune*, that conservative paper which had so hated *There Shall Be No Night*, headlined the talk as having been written "With Assistance from Robert Sherwood" so as to try to discredit Roosevelt, but this only made the president more determined.[46] A few weeks after the broadcast Roosevelt was to deliver his annual message to Congress. Between speeches, Bob hurried to New York to spend New Year's with Madeline and the rest of the family, then quickly returned to Washington. The January 6 message to Congress is best known as the address in which Roosevelt spelled out his "four freedoms," a concept that each of the three writers later credited directly to the president. Freedom of speech and expression, freedom to worship however one pleased, freedom from want, and freedom from fear became the watchwords of the Roosevelt administration.

In addition to writing speeches, Bob agreed to serve as temporary chair of the Committee on Education, Recreation, and Community Service, created by the U.S. Army to evaluate quality-of-life issues on military bases. His specific job was to inspect facilities and give his advice on matters such as living conditions, entertainment, and education. While on a wintry visit to Fort Dix, New Jersey, Bob caught a flu which was still with him when at Carnegie Hall five days later he received a gold medal from the Institute of Arts and Letters and then once again immediately reported to the White House to help the president with his inaugural address. The day before the swearing-in ceremony he was so sick that Roosevelt had a navy physician and a trained nurse sent over to care for him. Too ill to act as master of ceremonies at the inaugural gala, Bob settled for the satisfaction of knowing that his contributions to the event, including the participation of Ethel Barrymore, Irving Berlin, Charlie Chaplin, Raymond Massey, Mickey Rooney, and Nelson Eddy, were well appreciated. At his invitation, Edna Ferber and Alexander Woollcott visited the White House just before the celebrations. Woollcott, who spent ten days there, became a favored guest after that.

The next week, though still under the weather and exhausted, Bob made an emergency visit to the Baltimore tryout of Sam Behrman's *The Talley Method,* which presented unsolvable problems. From there he went home to write a radio drama about the abolitionist martyr Elijah Lovejoy. He was definitely on the mend, having gained five pounds, but he was also absolutely "pooped." [47] Desperately needing a break, he and Madeline headed for the La Osa Ranch, seventy miles south of Tucson, Arizona, the first time since the Nazi march on Europe the previous May that Bob had paused to catch his breath. Even though he was still as weak physically as he had been in July and August 1934 after his divorce trauma, he "thanked God" not to have "the spiritual diseases" which had afflicted him then. [48] He even began thinking about possible plays and books to write, though none of them materialized until 1945. From Arizona, the Sherwoods went to Los Angeles to see the Lunts and to discuss whether they should all agree to the filming of *There Shall Be No Night.* After putting the issue to rest, Bob and Madeline returned to New York, only for him to be summoned immediately to Washington after the March 11 signing of the Lend-Lease bill. Before leaving, he put in a call to the William Morris theatrical agency to request that some of its stars visit the military training camps and entertain the troops.

The address for which the writing team had been pulled together was for the White House Correspondents' Dinner. In it, Roosevelt planned to lash out at those opponents who had given him so much trouble with the Lend-Lease campaign. Indeed, the draft he recited was so scathing as to shock Bob. After Roosevelt went to bed, Bob asked Rosenman and Hopkins about it. They told him not to worry, that it was rare for the president to express such anger, that they would not include it in the speech, and all would be fine. Roosevelt just needed to get his frustration off his chest. The incident, though, moved Bob to compare Roosevelt to Abraham Lincoln—the president he was getting to know personally and the one he knew only intellectually. "I think, as a matter of fact, & or considerable study, that F.D.R. is a lot more honest with the people than Lincoln was," he mused. "I think Lincoln was more of a genius, in his inexplicable combination of political shrewdness & Biblical mysticism (poetry). F.D.R. is a lot less complicated as a character than Lincoln was. But when people picture Lincoln as a forthright, honest, artless character—& F.D.R. as a tricky, devious, artful politician, by contrast—they are talking arrogant nonsense. I don't think F.D.R. would be nearly as interesting a subject for a psychological play as Lincoln—but dramatists of the future may differ. Both Lincoln & F.D.R. can be rated as great show-men." [49]

Bob also felt that Roosevelt used people, and in that he was "a great egotist" and "in a way ruthless." To prove his point, he contemplated his relationship with the president. He was sure that Roosevelt enjoyed his company and was "extremely even over-appreciative of the work that I have done because of my devotion to him & all that he stands for in the history of this country and this world." If he asked the president to invite Madeline and him to stay at the White House while one of his plays was in Washington or even to publicize it in some way, he would. But he was also certain that if he never made another "legitimate" request, Roosevelt "would not give me another thought as long as I live—unless he needed me, for some purpose." [50]

Throughout the several months of traveling between New York and Washington, Bob never revealed the extent of his relationship with Roosevelt to anyone, not even his family. Rumors circulated around the press, and family members plied him with questions, but he remained silent, as he was expected to, explaining that he helped Rosenman and Hopkins with various tasks or stressing his work with the War Department. Of course this was silly, as everyone knew that Bob was writing speeches. When Posie asked him why he was constantly going to Washington and how he came to be living in the White House, her son's response was, "Mother you know why." When she asked, "Was it the President's Saturday night speech?" he simply nodded and changed the subject. [51] Little Mary and Madeline also wanted more information on exactly how closely he was working with Roosevelt, so the two conspired to have a loud conversation about how little they thought of one of Roosevelt's speeches. Finally, Bob could not stand it any longer and blurted out, "Oh! & I sweated blood over it"—which, Posie noted, "was what they wanted to know."[52]

There was no doubt that Bob's political work encroached on his commitment to the Playwrights' Company. John Wharton lamented to Sam Behrman, then in Hollywood, that Bob was spending four days a week in Washington and therefore had only one day for the organization. Wharton and the playwrights' sole wish was that, in spite of his other work, Bob would appear "with a play in his pocket," but at the moment, that did not seem a real possibility.[53] Instead, Bob got caught up in the debate swirling around publisher Henry R. Luce's article in *Life*, "The American Century," which presented the argument for U.S. leadership in the global community. Luce firmly believed that if the world was to enjoy peace, justice, economic prosperity, and political stability, the United States needed to take the leadership role.

Invited to respond to the essay, Bob eagerly set down his interventionist position. If, after the present conflict subsided, the U.S. government returned to its "introverted, neurotic isolationism," there would be no world peace. No longer could the nation avoid its responsibility in the interdependent world as it had by turning its back on the Versailles Treaty. "All attempts to enforce neutrality were bound to fail," Bob wrote, "because they constituted denial of essential features of our American character: we have an incurable sympathy for all those who fight for freedom and independence on any front; we have an irrepressible desire to express that sympathy in something more than words; and we also have an extremely lively sense of our own interests." Besides, the United States symbolized freedom to the rest of the world. Bob concluded with Lincoln's words, spoken in February 1861, before the start of the Civil War, about freedom in 1776: "Americans gave [to the world] that hope. Americans now have the power to fulfill it or to destroy it, forever." This was equally true in 1941.[54]

Throughout the spring of 1941, Bob continued to move between New York and Washington, worrying constantly over the worsening conditions in Europe. The news that his aunt Jane and uncle Wilfrid's house in London had been bombed and totally destroyed brought back the same anger he had felt upon hearing about Great Enton; the de Glehns had lived in the house for thirty-five years. Sometimes, as in April after the Nazi invasion of Greece and Yugoslavia, Bob felt frustrated by his work in Washington. Although he loved the speechwriting, he found the War Department meetings deadly dull. After receiving news of his Pulitzer Prize for *There Shall Be No Night*, he told his mother that he felt he should be writing something "to sway public opinion" on his own terms, not Roosevelt's. But the War Department had ordered him not to write anything more about "public questions," making him feel at times like "just a cheap theatrical agent" rather than a prizewinning playwright.[55] The jitters seemed to be settling in again.

Then in May, when an address to the governing board of the Pan American Union demanded intense concentration, Bob's restlessness subsided. The emergency tenor of the talk resulted from military warnings that the German battleship *Bismarck*, after sinking a British warship, seemed to be on its way to the shipping lanes of the Atlantic Ocean. Bob, Rosenman, and Hopkins utilized Roosevelt's offhand remark that the nation might be facing an unlimited national emergency to frame the speech. The "Unlimited National Emergency" address prepared the public for another move toward war. After once again summarizing the steps the United States had taken to protect democracy and to give aid to those nations which had lost theirs or were under great threat, Roosevelt explained that Nazi warships were moving closer to the Western Hemisphere: "The Battle of the Atlantic now extends from the icy waters of the North Pole to the frozen continent of the Antarctic" with the sinking of merchant ships in "alarming and increasing numbers by Nazi raiders or submarines." The answer to "this peril" must be an increase in the U.S. military shipbuilding program and intensified patrols of both the North and South Atlantic waters. What was needed was active resistance, if necessary, to "every attempt by Hitler to extend his Nazi domination to the Western Hemisphere, or to threaten it," and "every possible assistance to all . . . [who] are resisting Hitlerism or its equivalent with force of arms."[56] Roosevelt then read Proclamation 2487, calling on all citizens of the Americas to come together to cooperate in the defense of the hemispheres.

Lydia told Jane that this speech was the best she had ever heard Roosevelt give. "I suppose," she wrote, "Bobby's fairy touch was in that." Roosevelt obviously needed her nephew, as the president himself was "devoid of originality."[57] Indeed, Bob's gift with words earned him an honorary degree from Yale University and election to the Board of Overseers of Harvard University, the same school which had expelled him, and from which he never graduated. "What a chaotic world!" he mused.[58] He also began talks with Sam Rosenman, Harry Hopkins, and William Donovan about the possibility of working on anti-Nazi propaganda, something for which he felt his dramatic talent made him eminently qualified. Although he would continue to help with Roosevelt's speeches, he needed to have his own outlet. In creating propaganda to combat fascist ideology, he would once again be master of his own words. In fact, propaganda had been on many American leaders' minds for quite some time.[59] They were all too aware that Joseph Goebbels's Ministry for Popular Enlightenment and Propaganda had developed a sophisticated and successful campaign on behalf of Hitler's government, promoting racial pride, ethnic hatred, and terror. He masterfully utilized the press and broadcast media to sell Nazi ideology and trained propaganda specialists to work within Germany and in diplomatic missions around the world. During the 1930s, forces in the United States became fearful that Nazi sympathizers would also use propaganda to sway the U.S. public to look favorably upon fascism. They wrongfully targeted organizations and individuals claiming pacifist, communist, or other liberal viewpoints, while outspoken anti-Semites such as Father Charles Coughlin, Charles Lindbergh, and pro-Nazi organizations openly spewed their venom in public venues, holding parades and giving speeches. Out of a fear that German fascism could easily infiltrate the United States came the realization that the U.S. government and military had to develop its own propaganda.

Numerous individuals tried to convince Roosevelt that it would be in the nation's interest to establish an official agency to produce U.S. propaganda, but the president was reluctant to take such a step. When he was assistant secretary of the navy during World War I, George Creel and his Committee on Public Education had fostered the Red Scare, and he did not want to duplicate that oppressive atmosphere of fear and suspicion. It took the hard work of men such as Archibald MacLeish, Bill Donovan, and Bob to change his mind. At first, Roosevelt approved a few meager efforts, such as the establishment in 1939 of the Office of Government Reports, which acted as a clearinghouse for government materials and information on public opinion; the Division of Information of the Office of Emergency Management, also an information disseminating agency; and the Office of Facts and Figures, which organized national defense materials for authorized agencies to act upon.

In July 1941, however, the president finally recognized the advantage of creating a larger, overarching office to coordinate these information-gathering duties. He named Bill Donovan to head the newly created Office of the Coordinator of Information (COI) to collect, analyze, and make available to Roosevelt all materials related to national security. Bob was very excited about this agency because, in addition to collecting and analyzing intelligence information, it was to create propaganda from the data for consumption outside the United States. His most fervent wish was for the COI to develop the use of shortwave broadcasting as a "peace offensive that will convince the German people that their ruin as a nation is not contemplated."[60] Bob envisioned using multilingual actors speaking Roosevelt's words as a propaganda tool. The president liked the plan, telling Bob: "I think your idea of a hard-boiled little bureau to give Adolph a little electric spark in the same identical spot of his anatomy every two seconds while he encumbers the earth is grand. Do please see Bill Donovan on this."[61]

In Bob's initial communications with Donovan, he emphasized the need for the government to have its own broadcasting system separate from that of commercial networks, an idea at which Roosevelt at first balked because he did not want the business world to accuse the government of interfering in its domain. Nevertheless, Bob's arguments were sound. When speaking with a Boston newsman, he learned that radio station WRUL had been broadcasting messages in Arabic denouncing Great Britain's policy in Palestine, but because nobody at the station understood that language, the announcers had no clue about what they were saying. They simply read the transliterated words placed before them. How could the government entrust such sensitive topics to such insensitive people? Bob suggested that it was "just plain crazy" to leave the important area of psychological warfare "to the tender mercies" of these commercial ventures and urged Donovan to pursue "a big government appropriation" for equipment, linguists, newsmen, psychologists, writers, artists, actors, musicians, and technicians to produce round-the-clock broadcasts to combat the "radio war" the Axis powers had been carrying on for years.[62] Only a dedicated full-time staff with permanent government funding would be able to create such a project.

Bob was also very specific about the objectives of such a program. "The only effective propaganda," he noted, "must follow a definite policy, must have a specific objective, and must stick to accomplishing that objective by continual repetition of the same thing in a thousand different forms of expression." All involved would need to understand the "weak places in the German psychological armor" so as to hit their vulnerabilities. The German people, he claimed, were not "barbarians"; rather they were "for peace and their lack of enthusiasm for all their victories, the intense apathy and weariness and the longing to return to a normal life" were what propagandists should address. Hitler's guilt and the violent nature of "his gang" should be juxtaposed to the peaceful nature of the German people. At the same time, while constantly demonizing Hitler, the broadcasts should "make a peace offensive, not for a negotiated peace, but for an intelligent peace," one of love, not hate.[63] To succeed at their work, the propagandists had to understand the differences among the Germans—the Rhinelanders, Silesians, Bavarians, and Austrians. Dialects, colloquialisms, ways of life, class—all had to be taken into consideration for effective psychological warfare.

Donovan was impressed by Bob's ideas and quickly incorporated him into his organization as the first appointee. Roosevelt approved so wholeheartedly that he created the Foreign Information Service (FIS) as a department of COI specifically for Bob. He could now take his creative genius and apply it to designing materials to inform the rest of the world about U.S. governmental objectives and postwar plans, make other peoples familiar with the American way of life, and send messages using Roosevelt's own words. Bob persuaded Donovan to locate the FIS in New York, a media center, certainly, but also Bob's hometown. With the authority to hire, he immediately brought on people he knew and trusted. First was Joseph Barnes, a former foreign correspondent in Moscow and Berlin and then foreign editor for the *New York Herald Tribune.* Bob asked him to oversee the work of monitoring and analyzing German, Italian, and, later, Japanese propaganda. Since Bob was frequently in Washington, Barnes also quickly assumed the position of deputy director in charge of operations. The next man he hired was James Warburg, a former bank executive and musical comedy writer (under the name Paul James) who had served as one of Roosevelt's New Deal economic advisers. Bob asked him to establish a department of linguists who could design programs in several languages. Percy Winner, foreign correspondent in North Africa and Rome with experience at CBS and NBC, joined the team, as did Edd Johnson, the assistant managing editor of *Collier's* magazine and an experienced shortwave operator for CBS. Together, this New York office created what Bob called the "Voice of America."

Bob's new job resulted in some teasing from his sister Ros, who referred to him as "Goebbels," and Madeline, who claimed that she was going to go to work as a "spy" and call herself "Q 37." Posie was equally intrigued, although for her the best (but also most worrisome) part was that Bob was about to make a trip to England to study that nation's broadcasting system; during his brief but busy stay, he would be able to check in on Jane and Wilfrid.[64] A less enamored and otherwise unidentified correspondent named "Slim" wrote Bob: "You are a playwright, and that makes you an expert on international affairs. I am an engineer, and that makes me an expert on Chinese porcelain."[65] Such teasing and minor criticism did not bother Bob at all. As he wrote for the *Ladies' Home Journal* in August: "Those who shut their eyes to the future are ignoring realities which are horribly visible. . . . The front line in this war is no system of trenches and concrete fortifications; it can be drawn on no map of continents or islands or oceans. The front is in the hearts and minds of all of us, of all races, who are determined to go forward in the ways of freedom and justice."[66] Bob's new responsibilities answered his need to pacify his jitters and to play a more active role in the as yet undeclared war. As he doodled on a sheet of White House stationery in November: "It is far better to die in the courageous pursuit of a chimera, a mirage, than to live stolidly in contemplation of your navel—even though you are rich enough to do the latter or nothing else. . . . For the restless, insatiable attempt to attain that which is impossible and beautiful is of the very essence of life; whereas the placid acceptance of one's lot—whether it be pleasant or unpleasant—is death. . . . Those who wish life must be ready ceaselessly, perhaps, senselessly, to fight for it. Those who prefer to quit the fight, and rest, are already dead."[67]

Bob's trip to England on behalf of the COI took place from September 5 to October 1, 1941. There he established his first contacts with the British propaganda and political warfare agencies and spoke with executives of the BBC and the minister of information about possible broadcasting, leaflet work, and combat propaganda operations, namely, dropping or disseminating leaflets from airplanes into war zones. While the British agreed with him that broadcasting from the United States should have a distinct voice, they also offered to relay those broadcasts through their shortwave networks.

Although Bob had taken an immediate liking to Bill Donovan, from the start there were basic differences between them which eventually caused tremendous problems. As Bob put it, Donovan "was concerned only with the short wave radio or secret, subversive operations, or 'black propaganda.' I saw [FIS] from the very beginning as the organization which it was to become . . . not only the radio but publications, news and features, motion pictures, etc., in fact every possible medium by which the word could be carried throughout the world."[68] Whereas Donovan was interested in the more dangerous, subversive underground uses of propaganda, Bob wanted the FIS to disseminate positive messages about the United States based on Rooseveltian ideals. He told Harry Hopkins: "Ever since I started the job I am now doing, I have gone on the following basis: that all U.S. information to the world should be considered as though it was a continuous speech by the President. That is the real voice of the U.S.A. and that is what the world (including our own people) must steadily hear."[69]

Another difference between the two men had to do with their conceptions of authority. First, Donovan believed that propaganda should be the province of the military while Bob believed it should be under civilian control. Second, Bob insisted on "decentralization." As he later put it, "I did not believe that the organization . . . under the extreme pressure of those times, could be masterminded from Washington." There had to be freedom to improvise and to produce immediate responses to Axis moves without having to deal with a bureaucratic structure that bogged down the work. Bob preferred to delegate tasks to people who would carry out the assignments without constant supervision or the need for official approval. He resented what he called the "cloak and dagger stuff" of the COI.[70] In actuality, the New York FIS headquarters was fairly autonomous, largely because of its distance from Washington, D.C., and the vast scope of Bill Donovan's job there, but also because Bob spent on average only two days a week at the office. So intense were the differences between Donovan's way of running things and Bob's that within three months of its founding, Bob wrote him, "We cannot afford to lose invaluable time through childish bickerings, puny jealousies or backstairs intrigue."[71]

Throughout the summer and fall of 1941, international events continued their terrible trend. Germany attacked the Soviet Union in July and carried on its aggression there, while England signed a mutual assistance agreement with that beleaguered nation. In August, Roosevelt and British prime minister Winston Churchill met for the first of several wartime conferences designed to discuss the ongoing conflict and make plans for the postwar world. This Atlantic Charter Conference took place on the battleship *U.S.S. Augusta* in Placentia Bay, Newfoundland. For four days the two leaders hammered out ideas, in the end authorizing an eight-point statement, including support for collective security, self-determination for nations, freedom of the seas, a denial of any plan for territorial aggrandizement, and a commitment to working together to stabilize and improve their economies. Although Churchill wanted to proclaim support for a newer and better League of Nations, Roosevelt would not go any further than expressing the commitment to the establishment of a system to guarantee general security. The Atlantic Charter meeting, though a symbol of U.S. moral support for England, did not help the situation in Europe. Rather, things simply grew worse.

For the United States, relations with Japan were also deteriorating. During the late 1930s and into the early 1940s, Roosevelt's foreign policy and personal concern centered on Europe. Even after 1937, when Japan aggressively moved deeper into China, the United States did little to interfere. By not invoking the Neutrality Acts, the nation was able to sell arms to China, but the real aim was to continue its lucrative trading with Japan. In 1940 alone, U.S. trade to that nation added up to over $220 million, as opposed to only $78 million in trade to China. A problem arose, however, when the Japanese government's eyes wandered south of China to the European possessions in Southeast Asia which lay unprotected after Germany conquered their colonizers' homelands. Particularly enticing were the petroleum-rich Dutch East Indies and the areas of French Indochina (Laos, Cambodia, and Vietnam) which produced rubber, tin, tungsten, and rice.

On September 27, 1940, Japan, Italy, and Germany signed the Tripartite Agreement of cooperation in case of attack from a nation not currently involved in the war, except for the Soviet Union. This seemed to indicate that the Axis powers were expecting to gang up on the United States. Then in April 1941, when the Japanese signed a separate neutrality treaty with the Soviet Union, the U.S. government understood that it had been issued a warning to stay out of Japan's expansionist plans for Asia. In early July, in response to Japan's move into southern Indochina, Roosevelt ordered all Japanese assets in U.S. institutions frozen and an end to all oil sales. Since Japan required twelve thousand tons of oil each day, this was a serious move indeed. All these factors resulted in Japan's provocation of war through its attack on Pearl Harbor on December 7. That aggression took the United States into war not only with Japan but with Japan's allies Germany and Italy as well.

Very soon after Robert Sherwood heard the news about Pearl Harbor, he also received word from Sam Rosenman that Roosevelt needed them to leave for Washington immediately. By the time they arrived, the president had drafted most of the speech he would deliver to Congress the next day, but he wanted Bob and Rosenman to stand by in case he required some aid in putting together his planned fireside chat. The war message to Congress, which Eleanor Roosevelt invited Bob and Rosenman to hear in person in the Capitol, was very brief. Most people know it as the "Day of Infamy" speech, in which the president lambasted Japan for its sneak attack against a nation at peace. Roosevelt also listed the other places bombed that same day: Malaya, Hong Kong, Guam, the Philippine Islands, Wake Island, and, the next morning, Midway Island. The last four all fell under U.S. protection. Finally, the president asked Congress to declare "that since the unprovoked and dastardly attack by Japan on Sunday, December seventh, 1941, a state of war has existed between the United States and the Japanese Empire."[72] Within thirty-three minutes of hearing the address, the Senate unanimously, and the House by a vote of 388–1, passed a joint war resolution. Representative Jeannette Rankin of Montana, a longtime peace activist, was the only antiwar vote.

Bob had been waiting for this moment for some time. Although he would have preferred that the United States had never had to go to war, since 1939 he had seen no other path. As he and Rosenman left the White House on December 8, the entire city was blacked out in case of attack. Rosenman wondered how long it would be before the lantern over the White House entrance came on again. "I don't know," Bob replied, "but until it does, the lights will stay turned off all over the world. That light has been the only ray of hope to millions of people, and those millions will still look to this house and to that man inside it as their only hope of deliverance."[73] During the next few days, thousands of letters and telegrams reached the White House, and Bob read many of them, happy to see that Roosevelt had great support among the people. As usual, however, Bob's family was split over the announcement. Jane wrote Lydia to say how awful it was that "this horror" had finally come to her, but now she "must be learning . . . to take it."[74] Lydia, after all her snide remarks, was feeling contrite. She was angered by the "beastly & dastardly attack" on Pearl Harbor and felt that she understood the true purpose of this world war, which was "to force all men everywhere to see & choose between Good & Evil."[75] Posie, however, admitted to Jane her great displeasure at the whole affair. It kept her "Bobby" away from home for long periods of time and frightened her. Even though she felt very sad about the damage "those little yellow devils" had done, she still could not get up any "martial enthusiasm" and felt the whole thing "so silly and unnecessary."[76] Ros, meanwhile, as a volunteer air warden, had been out in the streets the entire afternoon because there had been a false alarm that German airplanes were heading for New York.

Bob's life became more complicated after the United States entered the war. There were great demands upon his time from the FIS, the White House, and the Playwrights' Company, though the last saw the least of him. He managed to squeeze in a visit home for Christmas and New Year's, each time running back to Washington to help in preparing the many speeches, press conferences, and fireside chats that took place in the months immediately after war was declared or to engage in work—or internal conflicts—within the COI. Posie, often ill and growing quite feeble in her eighty-seventh year, treasured moments like Christmas Eve, when her son "gave himself up" to the spirit and was "like a happy little good boy" as he sat by her side on the sofa, holding her hand and reading aloud "The Night before Christmas."[77] Posie needed her boy, especially since Cynthia was in and out of the hospital with cancer. "Bobby works so hard that I worry over it," Posie told Jane. "I don't see how anyone can keep it up so steadily at such a pace."[78]

Bob's greatest concentrated effort in 1942 was his work for the Foreign Information Service and the Voice of America, which Roosevelt officially approved soon after the bombing of Pearl Harbor. But his path was riddled with territorial conflicts among various governmental agencies. The Departments of State, War, the Army, and the Navy all had people working on propaganda, and each wanted control over what the others were doing. In February 1942 a congressional investigating committee interviewed Bob about the FIS, asking why progress was so slow in his agency. Bob replied that he was hampered by the fact that there was "no clearly defined mandate in the field of political warfare" and his agency's "precise relationship to the State Department, the Army or the Navy." He suggested that the committee take the initiative in calling for "co-ordination from above" so that "all the infighting because of internal area competition" would come to an end; then things might run more efficiently. Bob strongly believed that propaganda and psychological warfare should be part of "subversive political action integrated with military and diplomatic strategy" and recommended that FIS activity have input from representatives from the COI, the army, the navy, the State Department, and the Board of Economic Warfare Office.[79] The war effort, in other words, should function as a whole rather than as parts not knowing what the whole was; after civilian FIS technicians drew up its plans, a broader military and diplomatic committee should vet them.

Bob was convinced that the various propaganda and military agencies as then constituted were operating in a vacuum and therefore were not helping the war effort. Many meetings were simply "a mess and a waste for all concerned."[80] Until someone of "unquestioned importance and authority and [who] is close to the President" was selected to head these operations, they would never function well. Bob told Hopkins that this person had to be a "real genius of political warfare," by which he meant someone who not only excelled at "verbal propaganda, domestic and foreign," but also was well-informed about every newsworthy item, such as the little-known 1942 "proposal to send that Negro aviation squadron to the Southwest Pacific to refute Japan's propaganda on racial grounds." A good leader would know what actions "make news in the right way at the right moment" to give the "verbal propagandists" the material they needed. "I believe that the information set-up," he concluded, "should have a genuine military point of view, that it should be good and tough, and that on the domestic front it should consider the Father Coughlins . . . as enemies of this nation and sock them as such."[81]

As an example of what was not happening because of poor leadership and coordination, Bob pointed out that among the "greatest propaganda weapons" for the United States were the different foreign-language-speaking groups within the nation, especially "the Nisei in California." But "nobody knows who has authority to develop this weapon." Bob did not mention Roosevelt's order of February 19, 1942, to intern Japanese Americans. The only fact that concerned him was that his own agency did not have the authority to recruit Japanese Americans for use in foreign propaganda. Nevertheless, he told Hopkins, someone should consider the ways in which the foreign-language press could be "a tremendously effective medium—at home and abroad."[82]

At the same time that Bob was making bold suggestions for the reorganization of the propaganda agencies, he also had some doubts as to his own abilities. He knew that he had the creativity to develop propaganda but not necessarily the wherewithal to run an office. Remaining on Roosevelt's speechwriting team while keeping somewhat involved in the Playwrights' Company interfered with his being in the FIS office on a regular schedule. His habit was to show up at irregular hours, and as James Warburg put it, he was "slow . . . and moody."[83] Slowness was one of Bob's general characteristics, but moodiness may have been a result of his tensions with Donovan or his still recurring and persistent bouts of *tic douloureux*. Bob's private secretary at FIS, Lucille Gibbons, later reported that he often neglected piles of correspondence, so she "resorted to the expedient of putting a darning needle through a document to force him to pay attention to it."[84] He was also known to put work in his suit pocket before leaving for home, forget he had it with him, and later discover that it had disappeared to the laundry.

Still, Bob was happy, as each day he was working on spreading democracy to all parts of the world. In an effort to improve FIS operations, early in 1942 he invited the gifted screen and theater director John Houseman to head the department of Overseas Radio Programming. Born in Romania to a British mother and an Alsatian Jewish father and raised in France and England, Houseman was just the sort of multilingual European American whose talents Bob sorely needed. The showman, who had produced the controversial Federal Theatre Project play *The Cradle Will Rock*, had been impressed by Bob's final speech as president of the Dramatists Guild, in which he had said: "We are writers and we are living in an age when communication has achieved fabulous importance. . . . There is a new and decisive force in the human race, more powerful than all the tyrants. It is the force of massed thought—thought which has been provoked by words, strongly spoken. Words which originate with someone in this room may be brought to people of all kinds—people who are hungry for them, who may be stimulated by them to a new faith in the brotherhood of life, who may, for all any of us can tell, be saved by them."[85] So when he received the call to join the Voice of America effort, Houseman eagerly signed on.

At first, Bob, Houseman, Joseph Barnes, Edd Johnson, and James Warburg spent hours trying to figure out exactly what tone they wanted to strike in their first broadcast. Bob insisted on "truth . . . unmistakably sincere."[86] In addition, he felt that the broadcasts "must attempt to spread the distinctively American word throughout the world . . . [and] stick to factual material and avoid improvised propaganda."[87] The initial scripts sounded boring, however, until Houseman came up with a simple dramatic solution. Instead of replicating the single-voice broadcasting approach of the commercial networks and the BBC, he suggested that they use "several voices of different quality and pitch carefully orchestrated to achieve a maximum of variety and energy." [88] One voice would read one paragraph, a second another, and so on. Different voices were used whenever quotations appeared in the script. The style that the Voice of America copied was one used in the *March of Time* radio broadcasts and film newsreels, which involved the use of high-energy voices, often almost singsong in their punctuation of words.

The other approach the Voice of America took was not just to report diplomatic news but to relate traumatic war stories from cities, towns, and villages around the globe where people still remained hopeful because they had beaten the odds. In the case of France in 1942, the Voice of America faced a challenging situation. Because official U.S. policy was to avoid provoking a breach between the nation and Philippe Pétain, the leader of the collaborationist Vichy government, the radio station generally avoided any mention of France. But in March, when the State Department received word that Hitler was pressuring Pétain to turn over the reins to Pierre Laval, a notorious Nazi sympathizer who would kowtow to Hitler even more thoroughly than Pétain did, the Voice of America decided to broadcast to France, calling Laval "a detested gangster—a traitor." [89] As Houseman later recalled, this had no effect on events, as Laval was indeed put in place, but it made the radio staff feel good.

Bob, meanwhile, was constantly distracted by concerns over the internal conflicts within the COI. Finally, on June 13, 1942, Roosevelt took control of the situation, issuing Executive Order 9182, which established the Office of War Information (OWI) within the Office for Emergency Management in the executive office of the president. The proposal had been one which Bob and others had worked on constantly and which he had personally presented to the president, only to see it left lying untouched on his desk for some time. The OWI brought under its nonmilitary umbrella the Office of Facts and Figures, the Office of Government Reports, and the Foreign Information Service. At the same time, the president created the Office of Strategic Services (OSS) under the Joint Chiefs of Staff, an agency responsible for covert operations. The rest of the COI, including Bill Donovan, became part of the OSS. Bob remained with the FIS, which was renamed the Overseas Branch of the OWI, of which he was appointed director.

The executive order gave the OWI the authority to do what the FIS had already been doing. It could collect information about war aims and progress and then use the press, radio, and films to disseminate it. As Roosevelt wrote to Bob on the day the order was signed: "You are, of course, aware of what I am doing in the way of tying all the Information Services together. It means taking you out of C.O.I.—but I strongly feel that your work is essentially information and not espionage or subversive activity among individuals or groups in enemy nations." Roosevelt realized that Donovan did not agree that he and the rest of the COI belonged under the Joint Chiefs of Staff, but the restructuring would put a stop to the immobilizing conflicts. Before signing the order, Roosevelt had invited the journalist and radio personality Elmer Davis to head up the OWI, and Davis had accepted. Bob felt optimistic, as he had worked with Davis at *Life* when, toward the end of his term as editor, Davis had written regularly for the magazine. "I think that Elmer Davis, with his long experience and his genuine popularity in press and radio circles, will be able to tie together the many factors of information in the broadest sense of the term," Roosevelt told Bob. "Very definitely he wants you . . . to continue—and so do I." [90]

Elmer Davis, even more so than Bill Donovan, was willing to allow Bob almost total control of the Overseas Branch of the OWI while he supervised the work of the domestic branch. Although he hired new personnel who were not as closely tied to Roosevelt and New Deal politics, the men in the higher ranks, including James Warburg, Edd Johnson, and Joseph Barnes, retained their philosophy of New Deal liberalism. The FIS/Overseas Branch had grown immensely in the past year. By October 1942, 1,800 people worked in the New York City offices, and there were eighteen overseas outposts. The radio station, the heart of the OWI foreign operations, broadcast in twenty-two languages. Each of the 253 programs broadcast every day lasted fifteen minutes. Radio stations were set up in California in 1942, and in 1943 the agency broke through the "formidable resistance of the Navy" and received authorization "for the installation of further transmitters across the Pacific." [91] Bob told Harry Hopkins how important these stations were. "The words, 'This is the United States of America calling,' have a tremendous effect everywhere," he noted. "In addition to this, the San Francisco short-wave radio has an additional importance in that the men of our armed forces, on land and sea, dispersed all the way from Alaska to New Zealand, depend on it for their news from home." [92] Along with the broadcasts, the office produced innumerable leaflets, news articles, and documentaries about the United States and the war effort. Interestingly, during Bob's years as head of the FIS and then the Overseas Branch of the OWI, he did not rely on any specific psychological theory in his propaganda efforts and called on few experts in the field. As he remarked about his successful work: "When I was a playwright, everybody called me a propagandist. Now that I am a propagandist, everybody refers to me as 'that playwright.' . . . My most valuable weapon is the imaginative use of truth." [93]

The relationship Bob had established with the British Psychological and Political Warfare Agency also grew stronger. In July 1942 he sent James

Warburg to London to collaborate with Sir Robert Bruce Lockhart, Ritchie Calder, and members of General Dwight D. Eisenhower's staff in preparation for the invasion of North Africa, known as the TORCH operation. Members of the civilian OWI team accompanied the military to disseminate anti-Nazi, pro-Allied propaganda. They immediately took over the radio station in Algiers, renamed it Radio Hippo, and began broadcasting to Algeria, Morocco, Tunisia, Spain, southern France, and Italy. Radio Tunis, which the Nazis damaged before fleeing, was repaired and resumed operating two months later. When the North Africa campaign ended that fall, Bob was "jubilant," Posie told Jane, as he had been "in charge of all the propaganda that went to Africa to soften them up for the big invasion."[94] After July 1943, when Mussolini's government fell, the agency took over stations in Palermo and Bari. A bit later it added Radio Luxembourg, the second most powerful station in Europe, and in November, Radio Swindle, also in Algeria, which broadcast to the Balkans. In April 1944 the OWI office in London, the U.S. Army, and the BBC established the American Broadcasting Station in Europe (ABSIE), which reached places that the Voice of America could not. Eventually, the station had outposts in Great Britain, Australia, India, and Iceland.

While the Voice of America and the print propaganda spread news and information about the war, the leaflets were aimed at persuading people to disrespect and even abandon their pro-Axis governments. The "black propaganda" leaflets spread subversive lies and gossip, but the "white propaganda" of Bob's operation used a different approach. One French leaflet carried a translation of a May 1942 speech in which Roosevelt spoke of the bright future facing the French people and France's colonies. It carried a photograph of the president at a microphone with a U.S. flag behind him. Yet another French leaflet featured a picture of the Statue of Liberty with the heading in French, "To you who gave us liberty we will restore liberty." A similar leaflet guaranteed the people of the Philippines their freedom as well.[95]

The areas of France that were not under German occupation also received a four-page weekly newsletter titled *L'Amérique en Guerre* (America at War), much of it filled with information and maps relating the progress of the Allied struggle. Bob relied on a number of professional journalists and writers to supply the articles on a volunteer basis. Each one had to be read by an editorial panel, submitted to military censors, and then delivered to OWI outposts around the world. As Bob described to the mystery writer Rex Stout, chairman of the Writers' War Board in New York City: "A single article from a member of the Writers' War Board may be translated into a dozen languages, published in the press of twenty-five to fifty nations, and used in a variety of languages on OWI short-wave radio around the world. An important article may appear almost simultaneously in the newspapers of Stockholm, Berne, Sydney, Cape Town, Cairo, Bagdad, Bombay, Chungking, London, and Istanbul." He understood how difficult it was for writers to do such work without pay. "But these readers today form an audience which runs into the millions," he assured Stout, "an audience of men, women and children struggling desperately through one of the great turning points in history." [96]

The OWI also dropped leaflets on every major city in Germany, except Berlin, with the following message: "To the citizens of [name of city]: This is to warn you that your city is scheduled for complete devastation. It is to be destroyed as completely as Rostock, Cologne, Luebeck and Essen. Today there is only one safe place in Germany for you—THAT PLACE IS BERLIN. . . . In the interest of humanity we solemnly pledge that *Berlin will not be bombed.* . . . If you wish to save your lives go to Berlin. But go at once—tomorrow may be too late." [97] This message was intended to cause not only widespread panic and despair but also anger that the Nazi capital was not to be harmed. By 1944 the joint OWI-British campaign was dropping 11 million leaflets a day over Europe. Leaflets were also dropped on Japan. Half a million copies of the following message were sent to General Delos C. Emmons and Admiral Chester W. Nimitz in the Pacific for delivery. The leaflet contained a photograph of an air raid and the message:

> The high leaders of the Japanese Army and Navy have bragged that the homeland of Japan would never be violated. This pamphlet which has been dropped from an American heavy bomber . . . is proof to you that they have lied. . . . Your Emperor's great heart has always wished for peace; yet the high leaders of the armed forces have plunged you into the middle of a great war. Why? Under the pretty name of the establishment of the Greater East Asia sphere they have betrayed all Japanese from the lowest to the highest in the realm and they have thought only of making names for themselves and their own personal desires. [98]

Bob's international fame as a playwright and screenwriter made him an easy target for counter-propaganda. Several times when monitoring the Axis's radio airwaves Bob heard his name mentioned, especially by the Japanese. As he later explained, the Japanese propaganda ministry must have possessed a copy of *The Queen's Husband,* from which it usurped some of his words in the introduction. "I was referred to as 'this American propagandist,'" he wrote, "'author of a play called *Idiot's Delight,* who once admitted that he is something of an imbecile, something of a liar, something of a damn fool.' Evidently this went over so well that the Goebbels's office in Berlin picked it up and used it." [99] On another occasion, Bob heard the German radio report that his visit to North Africa was part of a plan "to establish a Jewish State on behalf of my master, Mr. Rosingstein." [100]

Because the OWI and Roosevelt captured so much of Bob's time, there was little left to spend with Madeline or to comfort Cynthia, whose son Jim was killed in a flight training accident. One weekend Bob was able to take Madeline with him to Shangri-la (now known as Camp David), the retreat that Roosevelt had established in the Catoctin Mountains of Maryland, near the Pennsylvania border. Madeline traveled from the White House in the same car with Roosevelt; Harry Hopkins's new wife, Louise; and the president's small dog, Fala. She later told Bob that Roosevelt "chatted and joked all the way in the most lighthearted manner," paying most of his attention to Fala, who scrambled from window to window until the president "admonished him in language that was not too far from baby talk." Bob rode in the next car with Grace Tully and Harry Hopkins. Enjoying a relatively quiet weekend, the guests played gin rummy while Roosevelt told "endless stories." Whenever a message arrived, the president read it and handed it over to Hopkins, who decided whether it needed immediate attention. The next weekend Bob spent at Shangri-la was, as he put it, "all work and activity, with Generals and Admirals arriving, conferring and departing in great haste." No wives were allowed this time, but Sam Rosenman joined the group to help with the following week's dedication address for the new Bethesda Naval Hospital, two fireside chats, a Labor Day statement, and "a vitally important message to Congress on stabilization." [101] Lynn Fontanne wrote Jane and Wilfrid in December, "Bob is still working night and day, hardly taking any time off to sleep." His *tic douloureux* was "going most of the time full blast." [102]

War business took precedence over everything else as December 1942 brought another internal crisis between the OWI and the OSS. In a directive to the Joint Chiefs of Staff, Roosevelt had approved of the OSS's involvement in disseminating both "black" and "white" propaganda. Seeing this as a territorial issue, Elmer Davis and Bob protested that such a change would bring the military into their civilian-controlled area. After two months of hearing Bob and Davis threaten to resign, Roosevelt canceled the directive and placed the OSS under the control of military intelligence, where it would largely contribute to covert operations and "black" propaganda. Then in Executive Order 9312 of March 9, 1943, he guaranteed the OWI control over foreign propaganda activities to disseminate information—that is, "white" propaganda. In the event of military operations, the agency was to coordinate with the Joint Chiefs, the Department of War, and the Navy Department and to work under their control.

Elmer Davis proved an effective leader of the OWI, but, like Bill Donovan, he had trouble accepting Bob's freewheeling, autonomous work style and his wholesale support of Roosevelt. Hence, while Bob was off in Europe and North Africa on OWI business, Davis began to ruminate about his role in the agency. Bob's trip followed on the heels of Roosevelt and Churchill's meeting in Casablanca in which they declared that only an unconditional surrender on Germany's part could bring the conflict to an end. In light of the war conference, Bob and his British propaganda colleagues planned coordinated efforts in broadcasting and leafleting. He then traveled on to North Africa to evaluate the broadcasting situation there and make recommendations for reorganization and expansion. While he was away, his sister Cynthia died on March 27, 1943. Hers was a sad but expected departure, one that combined grief in her survivors with relief that her suffering was over.

Upon his return in late April, Bob discovered that Elmer Davis had finally recognized that he had little authority over the area of foreign propaganda. Wanting the agency to be less partisan, he insisted that New Deal political messages come to a stop. In fact, "liberalism" soon became a taboo subject. When outspoken congressmen accused the agency of being favorable toward communist policies in Poland and of being too soft on the Soviet Union, Davis took note. The OWI, he responded, was simply echoing the U.S. position that the Soviet Union was a friendly Allied power. Nevertheless, after the German government accused the Soviets of having executed ten thousand Polish army officers in 1939 and piling their bodies in a mass grave in the Katyn Forest, the OWI was unsure how to respond. Because of the criticism from Congress about its supposedly pro-Soviet stance, the agency chose not to contradict the Nazis' charge, but neither did it condemn the Soviets or extend sympathy to the Poles. This neutral position created more criticism because it still seemed to favor the communists. For several weeks Bob sarcastically lamented that he had to listen while Republicans in Congress insisted that he was "engaged in Communist plots and was getting Fourth-Term votes [for Roosevelt] among The Turks and The Lapps and The Tibetans." [103]

A different sort of problem arose after Mussolini's reign came to an end on July 25, 1943. Although the Fascist Party was still in control of Italy, Roosevelt and Churchill decided to back away from their original demand for an unconditional surrender in favor of a negotiated peace. At the time, Bob was at Shangri-La with Roosevelt and Elmer Davis was unavailable, so James Warburg, the highest-ranking official in New York City that weekend, issued instructions that the Voice of America was to announce the news about Mussolini's fall. Unaware of the change of position at the White House, Warburg utilized a commentary by Samuel Grafton of the *New York Post* announcing King Victor Emmanuel's appointment of Field Marshall Pietro Badoglio to replace the Fascist leader. Not known for his diplomacy, Grafton referred to Victor Emmanuel III as "the moronic little king who has stood behind Mussolini's shoulder for twenty-one years."[104] The broadcast was aired six times and heard by millions around the globe. Roosevelt's anger about this lack of judgment was palpable, but he, like Bob, placed the blame on an unknown staff member in New York. As the head of the Overseas Branch, Bob apologized to the president and the secretary of state, "explaining that we had momentarily 'got off the beam' and assuring him we were now back on it," but as he soon realized, the mishap "was the beginning of a situation" that would result in his removal.[105]

For Elmer Davis, the "moronic little king" incident was simply an extension of long-term internal problems of authority and control. In an earlier episode, Bob had accused Davis of foisting a man named Ben Stern upon the Overseas Branch. Stern had applied to Bob for a job and been turned down. He then went to Davis, who hired him. Bob accused Davis of "overriding . . . my authority and my judgment," an action he felt "unworthy" of him. "Well—of course there are internal politics in any organization, and I think you should pay more attention to their importance," Bob chided. "You were appointed to your job by the President, and I was appointed to my job by the President. But that does not give you dictatorial powers over all of OWI nor does it give me dictatorial powers over a part of OWI."[106]

Davis, however, did feel that he had the right to make decisions concerning all of the OWI, both domestic and foreign, and he instinctively knew that if he did not exert his authority, he ran the risk of losing his place. Therefore, he set about to restructure the organization with the intention of pushing Bob, Warburg, Johnson, and Barnes either into the background or out of the agency altogether. In November 1943 Davis appointed CBS executive (and best man at his wedding) Edward Klauber to replace Milton Eisenhower, who was resigning as associate director of the OWI. Bob and Eisenhower had a congenial relationship, so his leaving to take a position as president of Kansas State College was a blow. Klauber, however, was not only Davis's friend and ally but also was known for being a tough executive who felt no qualms about getting rid of personnel with whom he did not see eye to eye. Soon after he started work, Klauber paid a two-day visit to the New York office and reported back to Davis that it needed some cleaning up. Bob responded with an angry letter. "I cannot and shall not stand for any interference with or abrogation or undercutting of my authority as Director of Overseas Operations, or of those to whom I delegate authority," he told Davis. If he was investigated and proved incompetent, he should be replaced. Otherwise, he resented Davis's "trying to attack and disrupt" his office, especially after all the successes which it had had.[107]

While Elmer Davis was collecting the proof he needed to demote Bob, Wallace Carroll and other top men in the London OWI office resigned because the New York office consistently ignored their requests. Davis noted that New York often ignored his requests as well. Upon hearing several of these complaints, Bob knew that his days at the OWI were numbered. As he wrote to James Warburg, he was aware that Davis, Klauber, and others felt he was "a notably worthy and noble fellow—and an effective pleader on both ends of Pennsylvania Avenue—and (of course) a cracking good playwright—but that I'm so hopelessly inept as an administrator or executive that under me are our good friends, Anarchy and Chaos, each in a neat box on the Civil Service Chart." He realized that from Davis's point of view, he had "inadequate control over the Overseas Branch and therefore sterner and more vigilant authority must be set up in Washington."[108]

In January 1944 Elmer Davis announced his plans to overhaul the Overseas Branch. First and foremost, Bob was "to make no assignments of personnel and to dispatch no persons overseas" without his "express consent."[109] Not wishing to rile or insult Roosevelt by getting rid of Bob, he recommended that he be made director of propaganda and information, meaning that while he would be responsible for developing propaganda policy, a new executive director reporting directly to Davis would take over daily operations of the branch. Bob protested Davis's proposal, and arguments shot back and forth between New York and Washington and within Washington. Roosevelt asked for details, and Davis provided them, getting testimony from several OWI staff that they systematically disregarded Bob's orders and acted on their own. Davis then accused the office of being cliquish, poorly organized, and generally anarchic. In turn, Bob pointed out to the president the office's overall excellent and productive record. Of course, Roosevelt truly felt himself between a rock and a hard place. He had appointed Davis and respected his leadership; yet Bob had become a valued friend. So when on February 2 Davis and Bob reported to the White House, Roosevelt reprimanded them both for their childish behavior, which had gotten so far out of hand that the press was having a field day with it. He instructed the two to report to the Cabinet Room, the same place where Bob worked on his speeches, and not to come out until they had resolved their differences.

It took three days of meetings, but in the end Bob capitulated. "In order to promote harmony of operation and to avoid misunderstanding," the two announced that Davis would be in charge of all OWI operations and that Bob would be under him.[110] The director of the Overseas Branch was no longer to act as an independent entity but rather would report directly to Davis and carry out his orders. As for the immediate future, Bob was to take a brief trip to London to finalize "the expanded psychological warfare operations in consultation with military authorities and representatives of other Allied governments."[111] After his return, he would continue directing the Overseas Branch, but from the Washington office. James Warburg, Joseph Barnes, and Edd Johnson were forced to resign, as Davis had wished for some months. Edward W. Barrett, associate editor of *Newsweek*, was hired, supposedly to work under Bob, but in actuality he assumed all of Bob's duties. The public announcement was simply a face-saving action. As one reporter noted: "Mr. Sherwood lost finally. And having lost, where does he stand now? The answer is: Right where he was. He still is serving as head of the overseas branch, and is about to go to London, briefly, to step up psychological warfare from the OWI office there."[112]

Bob left for England soon after he and Davis announced their settlement, arriving there on February 10, 1944. Although he was dismayed over what was essentially a demotion and over the firings of Warburg, Barnes, and Johnson, he was not unhappy to be in London. He always felt that the heart of the Overseas Branch should be overseas and not in Washington or New York, and he now had the opportunity to work within that office. Also, Alfred Lunt and Lynn Fontanne were in England, performing his reconceptualized *There Shall Be No Night*. Ever since the play had closed after its December 18, 1941, performance in Rochester, Minnesota, because the Russians were now allies and the play's anti-Soviet message was therefore inappropriate, the Lunts had wanted Bob to rewrite it so they could take it to England. Fontanne was most concerned to do something in support of her original homeland, and Lunt and she decided to move there for the duration of the war. In the fall of 1943 the Lunts approached him about a rewrite, and Bob agreed, deciding to reset the story in Greece from 1938 through 1940, the year that nation experienced invasions by Italy, and 1941, when the Germans invaded. Since Italy had surrendered to the Allies on September 8, 1943, and declared war on Germany on October 13, the changes seemed timely and likely to be popular with audiences.

The new *There Shall Be No Night* was essentially the same as the original except for the altered character and place-names and some added passages of outright war propaganda. With his love for the history of Greece and its democratic origins, Bob could not help inserting some of his feelings as expressed in *Acropolis*. Dave Corween's opening radio broadcast had a very similar sound to Bob's Voice of America scripts: "Hello, America. This is Athens. I am speaking to you from Greece—a little country, but an eternally great one, which is at peace and intends to remain at peace . . . —one sight of the Parthenon, or the Acropolis, has restored some measure of faith. Here at least is proof that the human race can achieve perfection, and that this achievement can endure, through all the centuries, in spite of everything." [113] In the new version, the Axis powers were much more of a presence than the Soviets had been previously. Uncle Leonithas (formerly Waldemar) speaks of Mussolini's unfounded charges of "ruthless unprovoked Greek bombing outrages on Italian troops in Porto Edda," of Mussolini "and Herr Hitler . . . now conferring in Florence," and of the incongruousness of Japanese diplomats attending a performance in Athens of Puccini's *Madame Butterfly*. [114]

Lest the British or Americans forget, Bob emphasized the message of democracy's birth in Greece. As Dave remarks: "A Sophocles or a Euripides might find the right words to describe this tragedy. I am sorry that I can not. This war is very far away from you who are at home and safe and comfortable in the United States. But some of us Americans who are here cannot help remembering that the very roots of our freedom were grown here in the soil of Greece, and if those roots are torn up and destroyed, perhaps something within us will wither and will die." [115] Especially propagandistic was the scene in the schoolhouse where Karilo (formerly Kaarlo) recites a passage from Lord Byron's poem "The Isles of Greece" containing these lines:

> The mountains look on Marathon—
> And Marathon looks on the sea;
> And musing there an hour alone,
> I dream'd that Greece might still be free. [116]

Karilo then lectures his comrades on democracy—its precepts of class equality, its openness to immigration, its love of beauty and wisdom, and its eternal meaning and existence in the hearts of people everywhere throughout time.

The Lunts were thrilled with the play and most grateful for Bob's rewriting it and for helping them get to Great Britain. The war route required a twenty-day ocean crossing to Lisbon and then a British Overseas Airways flight to London. Neither Lunt commented that the air route was the same one that Leslie Howard had taken when his plane was shot down by the Germans three weeks earlier. Soon after arriving the Lunts cast the play, staying in constant communication with Bob about changes they wished to make. They also took time to visit the de Glehns and Great Enton and reported back that both were doing well. The new version of *There Shall Be No Night* opened on November 1, 1943, in Liverpool, then played Oxford, Newcastle, and Edinburgh. Finally it reached London on December 15, and Londoners, like audiences in the other cities, loved it. As Lunt later told Bob: "They laugh in *all* the right places, they cry in *all* the right places, and are as still as mice in *all* the right places & then on top of that there's an ovation at the end of *every* performance—Heaven we call it."[117]

One incident in particular illustrates the Lunts' continued adherence to their belief that the show must go on no matter what. In London the cast and crew were used to hearing bombs and sirens going off outside the theater during performances, but on one particular night, a "buzz bomb" hit a target very close to the theater. This new German V-1 rocket missile was particularly frightening because it was not dropped from a plane but shot from a site farther away, so there was no forewarning. People recognized it by its buzzing sound, but it was often too late to take cover. During this particular attack, Fontanne was on stage while Lunt was waiting for his cue in the wings. When the bomb hit, as she described it, "I found myself somehow on the other side of the stage." The scenery was "buckling like sails in a high wind, things were falling." Fontanne looked around for Lunt. "There he was," she recalled, "pushing a canvas wall up with one hand and starting to make his entrance." Next, the fire curtain began to come down, and Fontanne heard Lunt shout for the stage manager to raise it. "Like a shot it went up and then he turned to me and curious as it may seem, the precise line he had to speak in the script at that moment was, 'Are you all right, darling?'" The audience, "which had sat as silent as the grave all during the crashing . . . burst right out in cheers and stood up and kept on and on, really holding up the play much longer than the buzz bomb."[118] Meanwhile, the force of the blast had blown Terence Morgan, the young actor playing Philip (formerly Erik), right out the stage door. He, too, managed to clean the dust off his uniform and reappear on stage in time for his next line.[119] The German attack continued throughout the performance, lending the play an eerie reality.

There Shall Be No Night ran through June 30, 1944, giving Bob the opportunity to see it and to consult with the Lunts several times. It closed after a buzz bomb damaged the London theater, tragically killing a member of the air force who was purchasing tickets at the time. The Lunts then took it back out on tour for a month. During the play's run in London, Bob received a letter from the Greek king's private secretary offering him the crown's admiration for his portrayal of its subjects' "heroism and sacrifice," and the Lunts gave a special performance to benefit the Greek Red Cross.[120] An amusing incident occurred between Bob and Prime Minister Winston Churchill when Bob arrived in London carrying a letter from Roosevelt to the prime minister. One day Churchill invited him to lunch at 10 Downing Street, where "Winnie" announced several times that he had liked Bob's play, *The Night Shall Fall*. Bob sensed it would be impolitic to correct the British leader, but he could barely hold back his laughter when Churchill suggested a new scene to take place after the 1939 Nazi invasion of Czechoslovakia. "I want to know what those people thought and said about that," he told Bob.[121]

Bob's main job in London was not as a playwright and producer but as a propagandist, and he never took his eyes off that task. Although his original assignment had been to make a brief visit to England and then return to the United States as an underling, Bob chose to remain in London through September 15 so he could witness the D-Day invasion and its aftermath, the plans for which he and only a few others knew about in advance. With Italy out of the war and the Soviets regaining their own land and agreeing to a strong offensive, the time was right for opening an aggressive second front to split the German war effort in half. Most of Bob's work in England revolved around the preparation for this Allied invasion. During that period the OWI carefully planted warnings and innuendos in the press aimed at Germany. A *New York Daily News* article on May 1, for example, announced that ABSIE had begun its pre-invasion broadcasts to Europe, alerting the "conquered people" that "their day of liberation" was "not far distant." It quoted Bob as saying, "And now they will really learn what overwhelming force can be. Great Russian armies attacking from the East; great Allied armies and navies attacking from the West and South will end forever the shameful chapter of Nazi tyranny."[122] Although the date of the invasion was not definite, Bob and the OWI prepared "a suitable number of psychological warriors, equipped with mobile printing presses, broadcasting and public address units, movie films for liberated cinemas, etc." for immediate use.[123]

The week before D-Day, June 6, 1944, was a tense time in the London office. In order to relieve some of his stress, Bob attended a small party at the London flat of CBS broadcaster Charles Collingwood. Lunt and Fontanne were there as well as journalist Ernie Pyle and John Mason Brown, then serving as a lieutenant in the U.S. Army, who remembered "only that, starved as I was for theatre and book talk, the evening stood out for me as a blissful oasis." Someone requested that Bob perform his well-known number "The Red, Red Robin." With his signature hat and cane, he sang and danced and impelled everyone else in the room to bob, bob, bob along with him. Brown recalled this as different from his usual rendition:

> That night it was more than for fun that he did it. It was in agony. He was not merely dead panning his way through an absurd routine. Like his own hoofer in *Idiot's Delight* . . . he was dancing in a world where bombs were falling and mass annihilation would soon begin. . . . I have never seen a face more filled

with sorrow or tortured with compassion than was Mr. Sherwood's as he went grimly, fearfully through his number this spring evening when England was in glorious bloom and the youth of Britain and America and their allies was also gathered in full bloom on the south coast. . . . Mr. Sherwood, you see, knew . . . and had long known the backstage secrets of the highest echelons of what was then history-in-the-making. For a sensitive and imaginative man such knowledge must have been an oppressive load to carry.[124]

On June 5, Bob had dinner with the Lunts. Fontanne was upset because he had brought an army helmet and a gas mask with him, and she thought he might be planning to do something dangerous. He assured her he was not. After dinner he joined others in the OWI office who, once there, were not permitted to leave. As Bob told Madeline, "That all night vigil was a mighty strange experience." Since the city was blacked out, they could not see the planes, but they heard the "roar of the bombers overhead," signaling that everything was going as scheduled.[125] Throughout the attack, the OWI monitored the German news service and radio, while at the same time ABSIE did its own broadcasting to those in occupied Europe. "In this fighting," it proclaimed, "the great forces striking from Britain . . . will require the cooperation of you, the freedom-loving patriots of Europe. . . . We beg that you will heed [these] friendly words—and that you will listen to the Allied radio for further advice and instructions from the Supreme Allied Commanders. . . . [T]he cause of the United Nations [a term adopted by the Allies in January 1942]—is marching forward to victory." [126] The entire event was "weird and wonderful" to Bob, who had lived through other invasions, but who told his wife that "this one had a real sense of the Apocalypse about it. The sound of those waves of bombers overhead—and sunrise behind St. Paul's cathedral—and the sight of bombed London" were almost indescribable. "The main thing," he assured Madeline, was that "the end of this war is in sight and then I come home for good (and I mean good)." [127]

Within the next two months Soviet troops marched on Finland (a German ally during the war), then began a large offensive which on July 24 led to their liberation of the first of the concentration camps, at Majdanek, Poland. In mid-July Bob traveled close to the Allied front lines from Normandy (where he saw Arch, a young Sherwood relative) to Casablanca, Algiers, Naples, and Rome. He also arrived in Paris in time to see General Charles de Gaulle and his new government march victoriously down the Champs Élysée. While he traveled, he heard of the death of his brother Phil's son Philby in an air crash and tried unsuccessfully to visit young Lyd Sherwood in Italy. He was upset when he did not hear from Little Mary for weeks at a time and by the news that Mary Brandon had her lawyers hunting him down in an unsuccessful attempt to get him to pay half her income taxes.

On September 12 Roosevelt asked Harry Hopkins to wire Bob, who was still in Paris, to come home and help with his unprecedented fourth reelection campaign. The timing was perfect in terms of Bob's making a decision on what to do about the OWI. Just two days before, Elmer Davis had written to say that Bob was not to work for the agency and Roosevelt at the same time, as this could prove "injurious to OWI interests."[128] Apparently, congressmen had been criticizing Bob for writing speeches for Roosevelt while taking money to work for the OWI. Davis stood by him, telling reporters that Bob had been in Europe for seven months, working about seventy hours a week, and had only very occasionally helped out the president. With all this in his mind, a week after his return home, Bob resigned his position with the OWI.

In his resignation letter, Bob took stock of his OWI work. The Overseas Branch now counted over five thousand employees in the United States, Great Britain, Ireland, Sweden, the Soviet Union, France, Luxembourg, Belgium, Switzerland, Spain, Portugal, Italy, North Africa, South Africa, Equatorial Africa, Egypt, Syria-Lebanon, Turkey, India, Burma, China, Australia, and the Central Pacific. The agency still controlled and operated more than thirty radio transmitters in the United States and a number in other places and broadcast more than 3,400 radio programs a week in over fifty languages and dialects. Its "radio-photo" network was the first ever established on a global basis for transmitting photographs worldwide. The branch had successfully dropped millions of leaflets from aircraft, distributed motion pictures all over the world, and worked "in closest cooperation" with the army, navy, and State Department. Bob had no doubt that it would also meet with success in Japan, and at the close of the war would provide "well-trained men and women . . . to help peoples in liberated areas to reestablish their own free press and free radio."[129]

On September 25 Elmer Davis wrote that he was "sorry" to accept Bob's resignation but that he sincerely appreciated his "conviction" that he could be of "greater public service in private life."[130] While the public record indicates that Bob left in order to work on Roosevelt's campaign, Bob informed the president of a different truth in a letter which stated that "the attempts to settle the differences between Elmer and me have failed." To stay on, he felt, "would harm the war effort."[131] Before Bob left the OWI, however, he submitted an extensive report to Davis on his recommendations for reducing OWI's overseas operations after Germany's defeat. The report indicated that although Bob believed that his work was an essential part of the war effort, after the fighting was over, the airwaves should be returned to the people of the liberated nations. If not, the work of the Voice of America and other media would become unwelcome. He told Davis, "Government sponsored propaganda in any form is looked upon with suspicion and abhorrence by the peoples of the liberated countries." The United States needed to be "most scrupulous" in "setting a good example" in terms of respecting other people's rights to freedom of expression. "Ours should be a long-range program, unobtrusively cultivating good will," he added. Consultants and experts were valuable in helping nations such as France restart their press, radio, cultural, and educational institutions, but in all cases, the nationals should be in charge. In addition, it was important for OWI workers to stay out of the politics of the nations they were to help. "If one government is overthrown, and a new one comes into power, we must be in a position to assure the new authorities that we are there to accord them the same friendly cooperation and service that we accorded their predecessors." [132] Of great cultural interest was the Nazi confiscation of art treasures, which Bob felt should be publicized at great length.

Bob noted that whereas in countries such as Norway, Denmark, Holland, and Belgium, where more stable governments would welcome the OWI, in nations in "the Russian orbit" such as Poland or Czechoslovakia, only time would tell how the agency could be most effective. In Greece, Albania, and Yugoslavia, where governments might not at first be well disposed toward the United States, the OWI should work largely as a service organization, "with most rigorous abstention from all forms of political partisanship." In the case of those nations which had sided with Germany, the U.S. government would have to proceed carefully. During the seven months that Bob was in Europe, he had ensured that all but one of the networks in Germany's satellite nations came over to the side of the OWI. With this done, the agency's job was "no longer a preparatory one; it is a complement to actual military operations, convincing the Germans of the certainty and completeness of their defeat." The OWI, Bob felt, should not bother spending money on neutral nations such as Spain, Portugal, Sweden, Switzerland, and Turkey, which would probably not cooperate in the effort against Japan. The Soviet Union, however, presented an entirely different issue. Bob recommended that the OWI go ahead "with our present modest plans . . . in the hope that American information activities there may develop and continue." [133] Most important, however, was that staff and efforts needed to be moved immediately to Asia, where the war showed no signs of letting up.

Bob also addressed "the moral (but tangible) factor of the legitimacy of the term 'Voice of America.'" Since he had been the one who coined the term, he was "prepared to defend its legitimacy under war conditions." As the war wound down in Europe, however, he felt that it was "patently dishonest to describe as the 'Voice of America' broadcasts which are subject to rigid control by directives approved by the State Department and the Joint Chiefs of Staff." Those offices were not, in his opinion, "qualified to interpret the Voice of America—which is, eternally, many voices." With the free flow of information from one country to another being reinstated, "it would become increasingly apparent to the discerning listener that the U.S. Government controlled broadcasts were telling no more than a carefully selected part of the truth." Instead, the government should perhaps create "a permanent American information service" which could reciprocate with other nations around the globe, but ABSIE should "go out of business" as rapidly as possible.[134]

And so Robert Sherwood left the official employ of the U.S. government and returned to the private world of speechwriting for the president. Roosevelt, of course, was happy to have him back in his corner, as his opponent Thomas E. Dewey, the Republican governor of New York, was running an energetic and aggressive campaign. Bob reported to work just a few days before Roosevelt was scheduled to speak before the powerful Teamsters Union, the speech he had chosen to spark off his short but effective official campaign. Sam Rosenman and Harry Hopkins warned Bob that they were worried about the president's spirits, as he seemed to be physically weaker, more tired, and somewhat lethargic. In addition, there was much gossip and concern about his health. When Bob himself saw Roosevelt for the first time in eight months, he was "shocked" by the change in his appearance. He later recalled that he was "unprepared for the almost ravaged appearance of his face." With his coat off, his shirt collar looked too large for his "emaciated neck." After a few minutes of conversation, however, Bob found his own and others' fears "groundless." Roosevelt, to Bob, "seemed to be more full of good humor and of fight than ever."[135]

Rosenman, Hopkins, and Bob considered the Teamsters Union speech to be one of the greatest campaign speeches that Roosevelt ever gave. He delivered this and most subsequent speeches sitting down, as his steel braces had become too painful for standing and his leg and hip muscles had become frail. The audience—friendly and enthusiastic—was the right one for him to initiate this new practice. By this time, people had come to accept his disability and did not expect him to play the role of a physical superhero. Thomas Dewey had made the unfortunate mistake of ridiculing Roosevelt as tired and old, and so the president began this speech by humorously reflecting on the past four years, noting that he was "actually four years older—which is a fact that seems to annoy some people." He continued with several attacks on Dewey and the Republicans: their misrepresentations and their policies which differed so much from his own. He praised the workers of the nation and defended labor actions, saying that "since Pearl Harbor only one-tenth of one per cent of man-hours have been lost by strikes."[136] The audience cheered.

The president also amused his listeners with his defense of his dog, Fala. The previous July, Roosevelt had made a visit to Hawaii and Alaska. During his campaign some Republican congressional naysayers circulated a rumor that on the way home, the pooch was inadvertently left behind in Alaska and that Roosevelt had spent millions of the taxpayers' dollars having him returned aboard a naval destroyer. Fala, Roosevelt claimed, had "not been the same dog since" he heard these nasty allegations. The president was "accustomed to hearing malicious falsehoods" about himself and his family, he said, but he felt that he had "a right to resent, to object to libelous statements about my dog."[137] Although many commentators credited the Fala story to the wisecracking Robert Sherwood, Bob actually had nothing to do with it.

Because of the war and his poor health, Roosevelt did not carry on a rigorous campaign in terms of giving speeches. After the Teamsters Union appearance, he took four weeks off from campaigning except for a radio address. Toward the end of October, Bob and Rosenman accompanied him to New York, Philadelphia, and Chicago and to his final roundup speech in Boston on November 4. Bob later recalled how, during the week before the election, he and four other men, including Rosenman and Hopkins, each put five dollars in a pool estimating Roosevelt's electoral vote. Bob guessed that he would win with 484. Rosenman won, having guessed 431; the president actually received 432. Election night found the usual Roosevelt friends and supporters at Hyde Park waiting for the results. As Roseman wrote, "By this time the procedure had become somewhat routine."[138] Roosevelt, however, had enjoyed it, telling Bob it was a great satisfaction to have had him along during this "happy, fighting" electoral campaign.[139] Now that the voting was over, the administration could get back to winning the war.

After the election campaign, Bob had more time to spend at home with Madeline and Posie, now ninety. But whereas he might have thought his war days were over and that it was time to return to his writing, he was wrong, for in January 1945 Secretary of the Navy James Forrestal asked him if he would go on a naval operation in the Pacific to give him some advice on the welfare and recreational facilities for the men of the fleet. Bob conferred with Roosevelt, who agreed that the assignment would be worthwhile, especially if he would attempt to visit General Douglas MacArthur while he was in the

Philippines. The president wanted Bob to find out MacArthur's views on the eventual occupation of Japan. This was certainly a step up in his responsibilities to the president, the kind of task that Harry Hopkins might have performed had he not been ill. Bob did not tell Madeline and Posie that he would be observing combat personnel in action, nor that his salary was to be only a per diem of twenty-five dollars.

Bob left Washington on January 31, 1945, and flew to Guam, where he visited with Admiral Chester W. Nimitz, chatting and fishing. He then flew to Ulithi, where he boarded the aircraft carrier *Bennington*, one of twenty carriers making up the fleet known as Task Force 58 which was on its way to attack Japan. Bob's guide was Lieutenant James Britt, who accompanied him through all of the 37,000 miles he covered until his return to Washington on March 19. On February 10 the *Bennington* sailed from Ulithi with Bob and journalist Ernie Pyle on board. They cruised northeastward, passing to the east of the Marianas and the Volcano Islands. From a distance of within fifty miles, Bob witnessed strikes against Tokyo on February 16 and 17. The ship then left the Honshu coast and cruised southward, striking at Chichi Jima en route. On February 19 Bob observed the first U.S. landings on Iwo Jima, a mere four days before the U.S. Marines raised the flag there. On February 25 he was back near Tokyo and on March 1 near Okinawa. On March 4 the force returned to Ulithi. In the past Bob had experienced army life, but during these three and a half weeks he saw what life in the navy was like. As he wrote to Victor Samrock and Bill Fields at the Playwrights' Company, it was "a revelation & an inspiration to get a real load of the Navy."[140] Fortunately, Bob's only war injury came when he smashed his watch in heavy seas. He witnessed no attacks by the Japanese.

The next phase of Bob's trip was a flight from Guam to the Philippines aboard a transport plane which carried a large cargo of blood for the wounded. His plane arrived in Manila, where MacArthur had only recently achieved victory over the Japanese. The general was known for avoiding any official from Washington, D.C. Bob recalled, "It was reported that even generals from the War Department on inspection tours were being refused permission to enter the Philippine theater and those who did were as carefully chaperoned as if they were attempting to visit the Russian Front." The only reason Bob could figure out for MacArthur's willingness to meet with him was that he was "an obscure and relatively inoffensive civilian." In fact, Bob spent nearly three hours in two sessions with the general at his headquarters "in the awful, heart-rending desolation of Manila" and came away feeling inspired by his "remarkably liberal" ideas.[141] Perhaps Roosevelt's letter of introduction was the key that opened MacArthur's door to Bob, for in it Roosevelt referred to him as "my old friend" who was "largely responsible for the organization of our psychological warfare activities in this war." Bob's objective on this visit was to "bring home to the American people, and to the peoples of Allied Nations, the vital importance of the continued operations in the war against Japan." [142]

Bob arrived back in Washington, D.C., on March 19 and reported immediately to Secretary of the Navy Forrestal. Five days later he visited Roosevelt and informed him that he felt that MacArthur was the ideal choice for military governor of Japan. He also told the president that he had been "shocked" by the inaccuracy of information that the general and his staff had about "high policy in Washington." Bob felt there were "unmistakable evidences of an acute persecution complex at work. To hear some of the staff officers talk, one would think that the War Department, the State Department, the Joint Chiefs of Staff—and, possibly even the White House itself—are under the domination of 'Communists and British Imperialists.'" In spite of this, from a military point of view, things were "magnificent." MacArthur had spoken about his views on Japan and the postwar plans. If the Japanese military as well as the emperor were destroyed, the result would be a "spiritual vacuum and opportunity for the U.S. to introduce new concepts." The Japanese would fear and respect the United States for its defeat of their nation, and this would make them accept the United States as the "great influence in future developments in Asia." [143]

After speaking with Roosevelt, Bob met Madeline at the Carlton Hotel. To her he confided that the president was "in much worse shape" than he had ever seen him before. Roosevelt seemed "unnaturally quiet and ever querulous," and never before had Bob found himself in the position of carrying on most of the conversation. When he left the White House, he felt "profoundly depressed." [144] Bob saw the president again at the end of March and then had further contact with him while he worked in New York on a draft of a speech Roosevelt was to deliver on Thomas Jefferson Day, April 13. Bob sent his copy to Warm Springs, Georgia, where Roosevelt was supposed to be resting while revising it. While he was awaiting suggested changes, he received the shocking news on April 12 that Roosevelt had died suddenly. He described in his diary how he had been returning to his home at 25 Sutton Place at around 5:55 P.M. when "a blonde lady burst out of an apartment on the ground floor and asked, 'Have you heard the news?'" To Bob she looked "bewildered and bemused" as he inquired what news she meant. He thought perhaps the war in Germany had ended. "The President is dead," she told him. He could only think to ask: "What President? The President of what?" He walked closer to her "as though I were grilling her, like a District Attorney." She responded,

"President Roosevelt—it—it just came on the radio." Bob thought she must be crazy, as she did not seem the type who would care about Roosevelt. He went up in the elevator, found a note from Madeline telling him that she was resting, and then turned on the radio. "The terrible, unbelievable thing was true." Bob could not bear to tell his wife. "The shock was awful," he remembered, but in the end "merciful."[145]

Throughout the night, Bob worked on remarks that Paul Hollister of CBS had requested. Read over the air by Thomas Chalmers the next day, they expressed Bob's personal grief. "To those of us who knew and loved President Roosevelt—as a good, warm-hearted friend—the greatest memory we hold today is the memory of his indomitable good humor—his indomitable courage—his love for our country, his faith in our country." He wrote of Roosevelt's optimism, noting that even in the days after Pearl Harbor and throughout the still unended war, the president had never spoken of "disaster" and never had the "jitters." He continued:

> He was a good man. He was a decent man. He was a friendly, patient, supremely tolerant man. I never saw him lose his temper with anyone who was working for him and working for our country. I never saw him be mean to anyone, or inconsiderate of anyone. I have seen him goaded and insulted and driven beyond what seemed to me the limits of human endurance, but I have never seen him be anything less than great under pressure. I have never in my life known anyone to be so consistently kindly, so downright sympathetic and understanding. I confess that I feel very sad at the thought that he will not live to realize his dearest dream: to see the fruition of his tremendous plans.[146]

Bob's hero was dead. After he delivered the speech copy, read the newspapers, and spoke with Harry Hopkins on the phone, he sat down and wept. "The shock had passed, & its protection removed, & I felt defenseless, & I started to cry," he confided in his diary. "I tried hard to control myself, but I couldn't stop the tears. All I could think of was that that lovely, kind, good, great person had been struck down at the moment when he and we were so close to the goals he had fought for, so gallantly and with such great vision, against such terrible opposition, at home & abroad."[147]

On Saturday April 14, as Bob noted "eighty years to the day" after John Wilkes Booth assassinated Abraham Lincoln, he and Madeline attended Roosevelt's funeral in the East Room of the White House.[148] After a brief ceremony led by the Episcopal bishop of Washington, Bob and Madeline went with Harry Hopkins to his home in Georgetown. Hopkins had flown in from Rochester, Minnesota, where he was being treated for hemochromatosis caused by his chronic intestinal problems. He and Bob talked at length about Roosevelt and the new president, Harry S Truman, while Hopkins lay pale and ill on his bed. That night the funeral train left for Washington. Bob remembered it as the same one he had traveled on with Roosevelt during his presidential campaigns. Even the crew was the same. The next morning the burial service was held in the rose garden at Hyde Park. Bob stood silently watching and thinking. "I am sure of one thing," he later wrote. "Although crippled physically and prey to various infections, he was spiritually the healthiest man I have ever known. He was gloriously and happily free of the various forms of psychic maladjustment which are called by such names as inhibition, complex, phobia. His mind, if not always orderly, bore no traces of paralysis and neither did his emotional constitution and his heart was certainly in the right place."[149]

Roosevelt's death meant the end of his World War II service for Bob. Although he admired Harry Truman, there was no place in the new president's administration for Robert Sherwood. From their home in New York, the grieving Bob and Madeline quietly applauded Benito Mussolini's murder on April 28 and Adolf Hitler's suicide on April 30. On May 8, V-E (Victory in Europe) Day, Bob celebrated, but not in the way exemplified by the photographs of people dancing, singing, and kissing in Times Square. Back in March, Bob had warned the president that he would be very opposed to a V-E Day, especially one that would turn into a "nation-wide orgy." He thought it more suitable that the end of the war in Europe be noted with "prayer rather than hilarity."[150] In May he made his feelings known in an article for *Colliers* titled "I Am Passing Up V-E Day." In the form of a letter to a hypothetical friend named Pete, he wrote that people were forgetting that "there are an awful lot of shots to be fired against Japan." Besides, what were the victors to do with the 150 million Germans and Japanese who had survived the war, and "how are we going to relieve all the hunger and dispel all the poison they have spread throughout the world and all the hatred they have generated?" He described what he had heard from an army friend about the liberation of the Nazi concentration camps—the gas chambers and mass graves. He talked about the Filipino resistance to the Japanese, the destruction of people and property, the amount of humanitarian work to be done, concluding, "I don't see how we can be particularly happy at the prospect of the long and tough and vital job that lies ahead of us before this war is really won."[151]

On August 6, 1945, a U.S. B-29 bomber dropped an atomic bomb on Hiroshima, Japan, followed on August 9 by one on Nagasaki. Five days later, on August 14, the Japanese surrendered, and World War II came to an end. Bob was both "overwhelmed by the suddenness of the ending of the war against

Japan" and relieved that the fighting had finally ceased.[152] As he noted in his diary, he heard of Japan's surrender through radio reports from Okinawa and Manila. "I was at both places five months ago. Oh, God—the end of all the long unutterable horror."[153] Robert Sherwood had survived two world wars. Once again he found himself a veteran. His next job was to express those concerns which he had been unable to put into words when he completed his service in World War I: the problems facing returning veterans, the need to honor those who put their lives on the line or who died in the war, and the propagation of patriotic pride, which he no longer believed was a cause of war or an expression of greed. He once again turned to his pen and typewriter to send his message out to the world. In this, he found both success and failure.

9

Changing the Message

LIKE A NUMBER of men of his generation, Robert Sherwood had taken two turns at war which resulted in vastly different postwar experiences. A private in the trenches during World War I, he returned home to the common global disillusionment over the declared aim of that struggle: to make the world safe for democracy. His anger and disappointment resulted in a drastic shift from supporting militarism to embracing pacifism. Perceiving World War II as a battle against tyrannical fascism, however, cast things in an entirely different light. Being appointed by the president of the United States to head the Overseas Branch of the Office of War Information, and then acting as his emissary to General Douglas MacArthur, put Bob in the highest echelons of civilian participation in the war. In addition, from his perspective, the struggle did indeed result in the restoration of democracy in many war-torn countries. Seeing the liberation of the concentration camps, France returned to the French, and the ejection of the Japanese from the Philippines was enough for Bob to feel that his sacrifice in World War II was well warranted.

The great irony for him, however, was that while his disappointment in the post–World War I era resulted in his becoming a successful playwright and screenwriter, his sense of satisfaction at the end of World War II led to a decline in his productivity. His immediate major postwar successes included the screenplay for the film *The Best Years of Our Lives* and the historical biography *Roosevelt and Hopkins*. The play *The Rugged Path* was a failure, however, while the musical *Miss Liberty* met with only moderate success. Other scripts such as *On the Beach* and *The Twilight* simply ended up in his closet or in the "unproduced" file of the Playwrights' Company. While a constant stream of articles on foreign policy and popular culture and almost weekly book reviews kept a steady income flowing into the Sherwood home, in general, the postwar years were a time of frustration and creative failure. The basic problem was that Bob had gone through a career change. As his British propaganda colleague Sir Robert Bruce Lockhart noted: "During the war years, he moved from the literary coterie, in which he had hitherto worked, into the political world. Like many people in war-time, he became a changed man." When Lockhart saw Bob in 1951, it struck him that he was "still absorbed in politics, and I felt instinctively that the political bug had gone deep into his system and was interfering with his literary career." [1]

Before Franklin Roosevelt's death, rumors in Washington, D.C., and speculation among his friends indicated an expectation that the president would reward Bob for his service by naming him librarian of Congress. Roosevelt's death, however, abruptly ended Bob's political career. The loss of savings from the Joe Burden affair and the reduction of his annual income to approximately eight thousand dollars now made it urgent that Bob return to his writing in order to earn a living. During the war, Madeline had been forced to go to secretarial school and take a position in Brooklyn, and her accusation in May 1945 that for the past five years Bob had been "a poor provider" pained him deeply. [2] Rather than allowing himself a readjustment period, Bob tried his hardest to recapture his prewar life. Besides returning to work, he visited his mother every day. Together, he and a joyful Madeline planned for a renovation of their 25 Sutton Place apartment, and in 1946 the two resumed their tradition of spending summers at Great Enton. He also tried to pay more attention to his daughter. In 1942 Little Mary had become engaged to an army medic she had met only twice. Like so many similar impetuous commitments made during the war years, the relationship fell apart as soon as the two were reunited. Then, in early March 1946, she announced her engagement to Edgar Stillman Jr., or "Bud," as he was called, a young man she had recently met at a party in Manhattan. The two were wed that fall. Initially, Bob and Madeline were thrilled with Little Mary's new husband. As her father told her (with a slap at her mother), their marriage did not sound "like the kind of happiness that is compounded of delirium. Nothing is more fatal to the durability of love than infantilism. . . . [Y]ou can take my word for it with the assurance that I know from past experience what I'm talking about." [3] Their pleasure faded soon after, though, when they realized that the two fought a great deal, and when Bud turned out to have communist leanings.

Bob's natural course was to return to his career in the theater and the work of the Playwrights' Company. Yet his decision to do so was riddled with ambivalence and negativity, which in turn affected his ability to craft creative and successful works. In general, the Broadway theater community saw a small rise in the number of productions toward the end of the war, from seventy-two during the 1940–41 season to eighty-three during the 1944–45 season, but this was nothing in comparison to the lively theater scene of the 1920s. With the advent of television soon after the war's end, people preferred to stay in at night and save money. In 1941 Bob had written a short piece, "The Dwelling Place of Wonder," for *Theatre Arts* magazine. Contrary to his

former professions of great love for the theater, he spoke of his disillusionment. In actual practice, he said, he was no longer a theater "fan": "I dislike to
work in the theatre and I dislike to go to the theatre. The theatre is too expensive, too unrewarding, and above all, too damned uncomfortable. If I want
stimulation, I greatly prefer to read. If I want diversion, I prefer the movies."
These were startling words indeed from a man who claimed to be "itching
all over with a desire to write a new play." Why, then, did he continue his
theater work? As he explained, the art form, with all its faults, was "still the
best possible place in which to express my most profound convictions." The
church was too dogmatic for this believer and films too tightly controlled by
large commercial interests. The theater, however, allowed him to speak in his
own creative voice and to continue his proselytizing. "A great play," he noted,
"is a great inspiration, and its performance is a kind of revivalist meeting." [4]

By 1949, however, Bob could see that the new popularity of television had
created tremendous problems for the theater. Except for Arthur Miller and
Tennessee Williams, most playwrights were "weary veterans" who could not
give Broadway the "transfusions of new blood" it needed. [5] Because of their
lucrative rewards and wider exposure, new talent tended to prefer writing
for film or television. Eugene O'Neill, Lillian Hellman, Maxwell Anderson,
S. N. Behrman, and Elmer Rice were still writing plays, but after the war
the public wanted to hear new voices. Where were they? "The theatre," Bob
noted in 1952, "remains what it has always been—a temple of faith, faith in
the dignity of man, and such a temple requires youth to keep its lamps lit." [6]

Another problem which Bob identified was the high cost of producing
plays. Inflation had so spiraled after the war that he was "horrified to discover
how the costs of everything had multiplied." As a result, it was barely possible
to profit from writing plays. He told an audience of theater professionals that
in the twelve years since writing *There Shall Be No Night* in 1940, he had
earned "less than nothing" from his investments in his own or others' plays.
Between 1946 and 1949 the Playwrights' Company had produced only six
shows. "If any of you had invested a dollar in each of the six . . . productions,"
he observed, "you would have ended up with a financial loss," owing not to
mismanagement but to the "fabulous expense of a road tour and to the uncertainty of finding audiences outside of New York." His conclusion was that
investing in the theater was "a game strictly for suckers or for idealists." [7]

Because of the war and the high costs of theatrical production, his own
play *The Rugged Path*, which opened in November 1945, was the first presentation by the Playwrights' Company since January of the previous year.
Within the next three and half months the company mounted Elmer Rice's
Dream Girl, which had a good run of 348 performances and nineteen weeks

on the road, and Maxwell Anderson's *Truckline Café,* a dismal failure that lasted all of thirteen performances. The 1946–47 season proved to be more auspicious. Anderson's *Joan of Lorraine,* starring Ingrid Bergman, ran for 199 performances and Elmer Rice's opera of *Street Scene* for 148. Then almost an entire year passed before Anderson's *Anne of the Thousand Days* broke through for 288 performances and a ten-week tour, followed by guest writer Garson Kanin's five-performance flop, *The Smile of the World.* Another nine months passed before the Maxwell Anderson–Kurt Weill musical *Lost in the Stars,* based on the South African novelist Alan Paton's *Cry the Beloved Country,* opened for a successful run of 281 performances and a fourteen-week tour. Then another void of fourteen months fell upon the company.

The Playwrights' Company barely managed to survive its many ups and downs during the 1940s. The early death of Sidney Howard in 1939 continued to affect the group. The war also had a devastating effect. Bob's absence was sorely felt, as was Maxwell Anderson's when he left for the front to help boost military morale. When the four remaining playwrights reconvened in 1945, they were faced with yet another crisis: Sam Behrman had decided to withdraw his membership because he found that his own goals and needs no longer matched those of the company. Never a man interested in the business of producing, Behrman wanted his next play to be handled by the Theatre Guild because at the time he felt the Playwrights' Company simply could not provide the support he required. It deeply disturbed him when John Wharton announced that their agreement prohibited such an arrangement, and his partners refused to bend the rules in this case. At the age of fifty-two, Behrman wrote the group, he found "the amount of creative work one can get out of oneself . . . limited." To have had to spend much of the previous six months on "managerial problems—without even the result of getting my play on" was too much for him.[8]

Bob was shocked to receive Behrman's letter. He thought that when the group discussed the situation earlier in the year, it had been agreed that Behrman would revise his play, and then the company would find a star performer and discuss "the whole production set-up." Bob himself offered to help out as long as the government did not call him back for service. He suggested that perhaps Behrman had not been clear enough in explaining his reasons for preferring the Theatre Guild to act as his producer. Nevertheless, Bob respected Behrman's choice: "Sam is an artist," he told his colleagues. "He is the only one who can determine what are his 'personal professional aims and needs,' and also what are his personal interests. If he feels that the Playwrights' Company is an 'entity' which has become 'of itself intractable,' and that he will find more tractability in the Theatre Guild, then that is his decision, and he must make it." Yet Bob could not help revealing his disappointment. He had always felt that even if another producer made a better offer, out of loyalty to the company the playwright concerned should turn it down. Although it saddened Bob greatly to lose Behrman, he felt that if his friend could no longer work within the company's structure, then the "painful fact" was that "his only way out" was to resign.[9]

Maxwell Anderson wished that Behrman could have his way and remain in the Playwrights' Company as well. For him, the organization had been formed "to serve the interests of the members," and the group needed to be "flexible enough" to meet any situation. Anderson still loved the company, "no matter what happens," and he wanted to see it "grow, prosper, and take in more territory." He considered the entire issue "small" and easily solvable. Let Sam Behrman have an outside producer.[10] When he realized that his was the minority opinion, he threatened to leave as well. "It's a quarrel over who should control the destiny of a playwright's play," he explained, "the playwright or the company. I say the playwright should control—even when he's wrong."[11]

It took Behrman over six months to make his final decision, but he handed in his resignation in December. "I can well imagine that you're in a mood of deep discouragement," Bob wrote him. "But I have the urgent feeling that now more than ever those of us who have something to say must keep on trying to find the way to say it and to command attention."[12] The rest of the company, still hoping to find some resolution, held off on making Behrman's resignation public until June 1946. In the end, however, they had to face the inevitable. Behrman was gone, and he was sorely missed. That summer Maxwell Anderson wrote him: "Nothing reconciles me to losing you from the company except the news . . . that you have finished one play and started another. If resigning has that effect on you, you should do it often."[13] Almost five years after Behrman's departure, Bob approached him about rejoining the company on his own terms. "Believe me, we should love to have this happen," he wrote. "I am sure that an arrangement could be made whereby your plays could be produced by any other management, as you wished, as long as the Company had some kind of interest in them, and that you would be free of all obligation to or responsibility for any other plays produced by the Company. What we want is the benefit of your company."[14] Three months later Behrman turned down the offer. "I need not tell you what it means to me that you all want me back," he wrote Bob. "It warms my heart." The years with the Playwrights' Company were "some of the happiest" that he had ever had, and he felt "a strong emotional drive" to rejoin. Yet because of his fatigue and fear of what that involvement might mean in terms of physical effort, he decided to "resist" their request.[15]

Luckily, Maxwell Anderson never followed up on his threat to resign. Nevertheless, lawyer John Wharton worried that with two of the five playwrights out of the picture, the company could no longer survive. "We asked people to invest money on the assumption that profits and losses would be averaged over five playwrights' manuscripts," he argued. "It would seem to me that we would at least have to get their consent to continue with only three." The best solution he could come up with was "a complete reorganization of the company, dissolving the present corporation and setting up some kind of new enterprise which would give all the members more freedom of action."[16] The problem was temporarily solved when Kurt Weill was voted in as a member shortly after Behrman's departure, thereby somewhat filling in the ranks. His work with the company, however, was cut short by his death on April 30, 1950.

While Sam Behrman agonized over his inability to do creative work while part of the Playwrights' Company, Bob too suffered writer's block but never entertained the slightest thought of leaving his partners. A week before Roosevelt's death in April 1945, Bob began writing a new play which he tentatively called *On the Beach*. It was to be the story of a U.S. journalist in Germany in the spring of 1945 and his conversations with others who are as happy as he is to see the Nazis defeated. The play was to include characters drawn from the groups Bob had worked with during the war—propagandists, writers, and broadcasters. From the start, the script went nowhere. "It looks like a warming up after five years of no practice," he noted in his diary, "but at least it seems to have some vitality even if it proves to be crap."[17] Ignoring the trauma he had suffered after returning from World War I, Bob seems to have believed that picking up his prewar life where he had left it would be no trouble at all. This was not the case. Reflecting on the amount of work it had taken to produce the final draft of *There Shall Be No Night*, he wrote: "I wonder if I'll be able to pour anything like the same amount into this one. I don't seem to feel tremendously interested now."[18]

In less than a week, Bob had so completely lost his focus on the play that he could not even bring himself to read over the forty-two pages he had written of act one. He made no further progress with *On the Beach*, though parts of it were enfolded into his next effort, *A Medal of Honor*, or *The Rugged Path* as it was finally titled. From May 21 through June 15, 1945, he worked steadily on the script in spite of constant attacks of *tic douloureux*. His physician prescribed Seconal to ease the pain, but the medication made him feel groggy during the day, slowing down his usual quick writing pace. Still, within three weeks he had a rough draft, and by August 14 he had Garson Kanin's promise to direct, and Hollywood superstar Spencer Tracy had expressed interest in using the play as his first starring vehicle on Broadway.

The idea for *The Rugged Path* had its roots in Bob's visit to the Philippines, where he had been "tremendously moved" by the "loyalty and bravery" of the Filipinos.[19] They were "the salt of the earth," he felt, and Americans should "never forget it and never stop honoring them for what they have done in this war. Nor should we ever stop being proud of the part that we have played in helping them to fulfill their passionate desire for freedom." As he wrote in his article "Our New Western Frontier," the Filipinos had "upheld American values of democracy" through their indigenous guerrilla network, which transmitted information about their Japanese occupiers to the U.S. military. Particularly noteworthy was their aid in helping submarines and surface vessels break through the Japanese naval blockade to deliver food and ammunition to Mindanao and other islands. It was essential for the United States to "help them out" before they came to believe the Japanese and German propaganda that Americans were nothing but "money grubbing materialists."[20]

Bob recounted that when he had reached Bataan aboard a U.S. naval vessel, the Filipino people "began to come down out of the hills where they'd been hiding out. . . . They wanted to welcome us. They wanted to give us everything they had—the women and children and old people wanted to work for us, even though they were half-starved—the men wanted to fight with us. . . . Believe me . . . when we saw those Filipino people, and when we saw what . . . had been done to them, we knew what we'd been fighting for all these years." Bob had seen plenty of destruction in his visits to Europe, but for him Manila was "the most shocking sight" of all. "It's not only the physical wreckage," he wrote, "which is just about complete—it's the evidence, which you can see and hear and smell everywhere, of the horrible, savage ferocity which the [Japanese] visited upon this lovely place and its lovely people."[21] Just as *There Shall Be No Night* was written to honor Finnish and then Greek resistance, so *The Rugged Path* was meant to instruct the public about the invaluable work and courage of both the Filipino resistance fighters and the U.S. military, who had aided each other during the war. Bob also used the play to justify his prewar interventionist position for which critics had rebuked him. However clear his intentions were to himself, crafting the drama and then producing it proved problematic.

The Rugged Path tells the story of Morey Vinion, a reporter and editor on a small-town newspaper published by his brother-in-law, George Bowsmith Jr.

The play opens in 1940 with a scene in the White House, where Morey, an obviously influential and passionate journalist, is speaking with the president and his military aide about his articles on British popular opinion after the Blitz. The action quickly moves to Morey's affluent suburban home, where his wife, Harriet, expresses her concern that he seems restless and vaguely dissatisfied with his life. He then reports to the newspaper office, where his efforts to have a young Jewish reporter, Gil Hartnick, sent to Europe to cover the war are rejected because the young man appears to be a leftist. When Morey volunteers for the assignment, his distraught wife claims that he has become too "personally involved instead of being just an American reporter." As she tells her brother, "This Spring, when the Germans went into Greece—whenever they bomb London—you'd think they were invading him."[22]

In a local bar, Morey and Gil discuss U.S. neutrality as the Germans mass on the Polish border to attack the Soviet Union. Morey questions Gil's position that the United States should support Lend-Lease aid to the Soviets. "Sure, Morey," Gil responds, "you know what the isolationists will be saying. They'll be screaming for the President to send Lend-Lease to Hitler to stop the Red Menace. It won't only be America First. It will be all the silver shirts and the Christian mobilizers—all of our native Fascists."[23] In response, Morey assigns Gil to write an editorial on Winston Churchill's speech begging for aid to the Soviets. So incensed are the paper's editors and advertisers over this seemingly alarmist, pro-communist article that Gil is fired. While other customers at the bar tout neutrality and isolationist beliefs, Gil tells Morey that he has enlisted in the marines. Morey wistfully responds that he wishes he could go with him.

In the final scene of act one, Morey's announcement that he has joined the navy reflects the motivation that impelled Bob himself into active participation in World War II: "The thing is that history has brought us all to a Great Divide, and everyone of us has got to make his own decision—whether to try to stay put, or to turn back, or to push on over the ridge into the unknown. . . . I'm tired of being merely someone who stands by and watches. I want to be part of something. . . . I want to find out whether there really is anything in the world worth fighting for and dying for."[24] For Bob, playing a role in World War II had been the one way to figure out if the ideals that had led him into World War I were valid. He could no longer tolerate staying home, reading the newspapers, and writing plays. Only personal experience could help him find the answers to his entire interwar quest. As Elmer Rice noted, Bob had "a sense of moral obligation to devote his talents to the service of humanity [which] is evident in his public activities; it recurs again and again in his plays. . . . [W]e see the dilemma of a man torn between his personal desires and his compulsion to pursue an unselfish course." [25]

Act two takes an abrupt shift of direction. Set in June 1944 in the South Pacific, the action begins on the destroyer *Townsend,* where Morey has taken the job of ship's cook, an idea he got from Alfred Lunt, who in 1943 threatened to enlist as a cook in the merchant marine if Bob could not arrange for him and Fontanne to take *There Shall Be No Night* to England. As Morey cooks and converses with the crew, he reflects on the news that Gil Hartnick has been killed in action on one of the Pacific islands and wonders if the United States is really worth the cost of so many lives. His train of thought is broken off when the destroyer is attacked and all on board are ordered to abandon ship. Back home, Morey's family receives word that he is missing, but in actuality he is very much alive. Saved by Gregorio, a Filipino guerrilla, he is in a camp headed by a U.S. colonel named Rainsford, who is working with the Filipinos to resist the Japanese occupation. Rainsford, a former prisoner of war on Bataan, tells Morey that this is just one in a chain of camps reporting Japanese movements to General Douglas MacArthur, and in fact he is expecting a U.S. submarine to drop off arms and equipment, the first supplies since 1942. Morey can help to unload the cargo and then leave with the submarine. Morey wants to do more, however, and offers to help Querin, the Filipino radio operator (and Ph.D.), assemble the guerrillas' crudely made hand grenades. Querin tells Morey: "This fighting out here—it may seem childish, amateurish, to one who has seen war on the European scale. The majority of these guerrillas are not professional soldiers—they're not mature politically—they're simply people who love freedom so passionately that they will die for it." [26] Morey confesses that this is the kind of war he wants to be in, one with a cause and a faith. "I am no longer impressed by the power of the pen," he tells Querin. "For years I wrote about what was coming. I tried to tell what I had seen and heard and felt. I wrote my heart out. But it did no good." [27]

In Rainsford and Querin and the rest of the Filipino freedom fighters, Morey has found "rugged, crazy idealists" like those who had originally founded the United States. "And what this has meant to me," he tells Querin, "is beyond measurement, beyond expression. It's a revival of the spirit—a restoration of faith—the discovery of life. You don't get these things free, Doctor. And I don't want to go back until I'm sure I've paid for them." Again, Morey's words reflect Bob's transformation from embittered pacifist to impassioned interventionist when he adds: "I've resigned from the role of prophet. But it's hard for me to believe that we can forget—that we can ever slip back into the old complacency, the old suicidal selfishness. But—God forgive me if I'm turning into an optimist."[28] In an effort to put his new-found spirit into action, Morey prepares to lead his self-named Task Force Zero in an attack against the Japanese so that the U.S. submarine can drop off the desperately needed supplies. Before the attack, he gives his band of fighters a pep talk in which he relates meeting Roosevelt and reflecting that the lamp hanging over the main entrance of the White House was the "last light that is left shining anywhere on earth." The metaphorical lamp, he believes, will "restore the light to guide the tortured people out of the darkness."[29] This image and the speech surrounding it repeat the words Sam Rosenman recalled Bob speaking the night after the Japanese attack on Pearl Harbor. In the end, Morey is killed in the attack on the Japanese, and the play ends with Harriet at the White House accepting the Medal of Honor for her husband's bravery and turning it over to Querin to take back to the Philippines.

The Rugged Path received mixed reviews from both critics and friends. Burns Mantle claimed that Bob originally had two different plays in mind—one about influential journalists and the other a soldier's "search for understanding as to what the whole blooming mess was about, and why he was mixed up in it." In spite of its run of only eighty-one performances, Mantle felt that it was "an interesting, frequently eloquent and always honest report on several vitally important aspects of a democracy at war."[30] Some critics, however, had tired of Bob's using the stage as a political platform. As producer Arthur Hopkins declared: "No playwright should be given as much power as Bob has been given. It distracts him from his true vocation—writing plays."[31] In other words, he was sacrificing drama to promote his own agenda. As the reviewer in Time magazine noted, "The hero is sometimes protagonist, sometimes symbol, sometimes Robert E. Sherwood." Indeed, "the play as a whole is a tangled Sherwood Forest of Ideas."[32] John Wharton of the Playwrights' Company perceived an "inexplicable aura of failure" about the play. By Wharton's count, Bob was using the theme of "a man leading a full life who becomes obsessed with the belief that he must give more of himself to a worthy public cause" for the third time, after Abe Lincoln in Illinois and There Shall Be No Night, but here it simply did not work. "Sherwood knew something was amiss," he later wrote. "He never fooled himself. But this time he couldn't find the way to fix it."[33] Indeed, Bob himself termed the play "formless and messy and soggy." The trouble, he rationalized, was that he had tried to write it "too soon and too quickly" after leaving his war service.[34]

Even though the script for The Rugged Path was weak, a larger problem presented itself in the form of Spencer Tracy, the Hollywood star who took on the role of Morey. From the start, Tracy seemed skittish about appearing on stage, afraid of what the critics might think of him. Members of the Play-wrights' Company wondered why he had accepted the role when anything he played on film turned into gold. Bob told Victor Samrock that the actor was suffering from "a terrible sense of conscience" over the fact that he had made three separate offers to go overseas with the USO or the OWI, but each time reneged on the commitment and never rescheduled. Bob went so far as to tell Samrock that in one instance, Tracy had "ended up in a padded cell in Chicago, suffering with the DTs after an alcoholic binge."[35] Taking the role of Morey was a way of relieving the shame he felt for not having contributed even a small share of his time to the war effort.

In mid-August 1945 Bob and the play's director, Garson Kanin, began casting and approving set designs. Kanin, still a captain in the army, had just returned from Paris, so for both him and Bob, the war experience was fresh in their minds, a factor that may have been a sore spot for the sensitive Tracy. At first the rehearsals went through the usual honeymoon period of excitement and camaraderie. Spencer Tracy was friendly and cheerful to all, especially Victor Samrock, whom he invited to dinner at least twice a week in his suite at the Waldorf-Astoria hotel. Tracy's lover, the Hollywood star Katharine Hepburn, was usually there, as well as his brother Carroll, who served as Tracy's manager. Samrock, who had the responsibility of drawing up the actor's contract, had drafted the usual terms, but Tracy was reluctant to sign it, and Bob did not insist that he do so.

Two days before rehearsals began, Tracy asked Samrock to redraft the contract to include a guarantee of 25 percent of the profits. Samrock told him that this was not possible, as the actor had not invested any of his own money in the venture. Later that same day Carroll confronted Samrock, tell-ing him, "Well, if you can't agree to Spencer's request, then you better get somebody else." Samrock explained that stars performing in Playwrights' Company productions had "always" invested money "for their share of the profits."[36] He later recalled feeling that Tracy's behavior was "some form of Hollywood blackmail" which New York theater people did not practice. Denied the terms he wanted, Spencer Tracy decided to quit the play. Greatly disappointed, Bob broke up the cast, announcing that the Playwrights' Com-pany would regroup and produce it the next year. No sooner was this done than Tracy changed his mind and showed up for rehearsal. This on again, off again commitment to the production continued throughout tryouts and its short run on Broadway. Tracy was heard to say more than once: "What am I doing here? I'm a big star in Hollywood."[37]

The Rugged Path previewed at the National Theatre in Washington, where it held a special Friday matinee performance for Harry Truman, three hundred of his guests, and veterans from the Walter Reed Army Medical Center and Bethesda Naval Hospital. Then it traveled to Providence and Boston, where again Tracy threatened to leave but did not. Instead, he demanded rewrites. In addition, the stress on him was apparently so great that he missed a couple of performances in Boston because of illness—though not due to drinking. Bob, meanwhile, endured almost constant attacks of *tic douloureux*, sometimes on the left side of his face but more frequently on the right. Frustrated by Tracy's behavior and sympathetic to Bob's suffering, Samrock sent Tracy a telegram quoting two sentences directly from the script: "Dear Spencer. History has brought us to the great divide. Each one of us must make his own decision whether to stay here or turn back or push on over the ridge into the unknown." [38]

Although he personally received good reviews in Boston, Tracy was concerned about the mixed response to the play itself and again threatened to quit. Only after he spent half the night negotiating with Bob, Elmer Rice, and Garson Kanin did he return to the play with the assurance that Bob would complete rewrites that would satisfy him. Finally, on November 10, the weary and tense cast opened the show at the Plymouth Theatre in New York. In general, Tracy's reviews were very good, including that of Wolcott Gibbs, who wrote in the *New Yorker* that it was "hard to imagine what the play would have done without him." [39] Yet the star still complained, even in public, where his comments could only hurt ticket sales. Samrock later blasted Tracy for making negative statements at every press conference, "knocking the production, saying things like, 'I don't know how long I'll be able to stay in the play. The play is no good. Sherwood should rewrite it.'" [40]

Once the play had opened on Broadway, Bob felt it was both impractical and undesirable to do more rewriting. He was also disappointed and discouraged. This was not the experience he had wished for his return to the theater. No other actor had ever treated him or his work with such disrespect. In December, Tracy, anxious to return to his lucrative career in Hollywood, announced that he was definitely leaving the show on January 5. Bob, who was in Los Angeles working on the screenplay for *The Best Years of Our Lives*, sent a telegram saying: "I certainly realize it is not pleasant to be playing to any empty seats whatsoever, but I also cannot feel there is any excuse for announcing closing. . . . We are still the biggest legitimate gross in town." [41] Bob was right. Ticket sales during the last two weeks of December and the first in January topped over $20,000 each week. Tracy agreed to stay on until January 19 after Bob urged him to do so in consideration of their professional reputations, and in the hope of ending the debacle "with mutual respect and not in an atmosphere of such uncertainty and shabby gossip." [42] As Victor

Samrock later recalled, Bob believed that the play would have been a great success if Spencer Tracy had not spent so much time sabotaging it. He sincerely believed that it would have run at least a year on Broadway and made "a fortune" on the road.[43]

Samrock remained upset. He felt that Tracy had purposely painted him and Bob as villains because he could not face up to his own bad behavior. As he wired Bob in Hollywood, "Still feel that we should have been able to do better by you."[44] He was so angry, in fact, that he boldly announced to Bob that he was "not worried about Spencer's innermost feelings" and had no intention of assuaging the star's "soul-searching doubts."[45] Tracy insisted more than once that Samrock announce that the play was closing because of poor business, but he refused to do so, saying the public deserved to know that it was closing because the lead actor was abandoning the production. In fact, for nine of the show's ten-week run the house was 90 percent full and the play grossed $208,937. But because it had to close earlier than it might have had Tracy stayed, it lost the Playwrights' Company over $68,000, 25 percent of that being a personal loss for Bob.[46]

The newspapers had a field day with Spencer Tracy's defection. He gave several interviews, in each one attacking the play and its alleged poor business. Bob was particularly upset by a comment from Luella Parsons, a popular Hollywood gossip columnist, who wrote that the Playwrights' Company had sought out Tracy because it was "aware of the weakness of the Sherwood script and therefore had to get a big star name to carry it." "My God," he wrote Samrock. "The irresponsibility of the press! Any conclusion to which any fool on a newspaper may jump can be printed as a statement of fact without any checking or verification."[47] Samrock felt that the company had to "admit that we have had, to put it mildly, an erratic and highly unstable star." Nevertheless, to protect its prestige, he felt that the company should take no further action. "The fact will stand for a long time that we were able, chiefly through your efforts," he wrote Bob, "to prop up a very insecure individual who, fortunately or otherwise, happens to be a good actor."[48] Bob agreed that they should just let the uproar come to a quiet end, but he wondered if the actor might learn a lesson from the experience: that "nobody loves a quitter."[49]

On January 13, 1946, Laurence Schwab, a columnist for the *Miami Daily News*, lambasted Tracy for deserting *The Rugged Path* in such an unprofessional manner. He charged the actor with dishonesty and disloyalty to the cast and crew, concluding, "And if I ever see our hero on the screen again, making that Big Sacrifice for his palsy-walsy in the fifth reel, I am afraid I shall regurgitate."[50] Schwab's column unleashed the as yet unexpressed anger seething within the breast of William Fields, the company's press representative, who on January 18 whipped off a venomous letter to that "phony" Spencer Tracy. "There should be something decidedly wrong with a system that would permit you to forever get away with your spurious philanthropies, fake liberalism and grim little didoes," he wrote. Tracy's unconscionable defection had left 250 people unemployed, and in the process he had "maliciously slandered and gossiped about Gar[son] Kanin and Bob Sherwood, both of them better men than even Metro Goldwyn Mayer can ever succeed in making you." Not yet finished, Fields continued, "Your whole record is a sorry one of intimidating and browbeating people—actors and others—who are on a lower economic level than yourself." He ended, "It's about time, Buster, that you read a bad notice and heard the truth—for a change."[51] On this happy note, Fields made innumerable copies of Schwab's column and sent them to drama editors, critics, and other journalists across the country.

Victor Samrock wrote Bob that even before he left the production, Tracy was heard to mutter, "Where did I go wrong?" Although Tracy promised to try to sell the movie rights as soon as he returned to Hollywood, Samrock did not believe one word, telling Bob, "I mention this solely for the record."[52] Bob, who still believed in *The Rugged Path*, "bitterly" regretted the "initial mistake" he had made "when I first put my faith, and the fruits of long labors, in one who has proved, over and over again, that he possesses the morals and scruples and integrity and human decency of a louse." The experience, he told Samrock and Fields, was one he wished he could forget quickly, but it had produced "an ugly kind of poison which spread to all of us" and was difficult to shake.[53]

It was not solely Spencer Tracy's fault that *The Rugged Path* proved a failure. Granted, his undermining the production was a huge factor in its demise, but Tracy was also the main attraction, and an added draw was the occasional presence of Katharine Hepburn in the audience. Given its weak script, even with a different star the play would most likely have met an equally early demise. The fact that it failed may also have been a reflection on the times. Audiences wanted to forget the war, at least its tragedies. Bob had begun writing *The Rugged Path* before the conflict ended, but by the time it was produced, most of the fighting forces had returned home, and Americans were looking forward to happier, more prosperous times. Revisiting this particular dark story so soon after the fact may have been unappealing to audiences. In fact, the same fate that greeted *The Rugged Path* also greeted Harry Brown's drama *A Sound of Hunting*, another realistic look at U.S. military men and a journalist at war, this time set in a burned-out house in Italy. The play opened the same month as *The Rugged Path* and, though critically acclaimed, closed after only twenty-three performances. The more successful World War II plays took a less tragic approach to dramatizing the war, including William Wister Haines's 1947 *Command Decision,* which dealt with pilots, though none were sent off to combat during the play, and Thomas Heggen and Joshua Logan's 1948 *Mister Roberts,* a comedy about life on a naval destroyer.

There is no doubt that the entire experience surrounding *The Rugged Path* was a blow for Bob. It had not been easy for him to return to writing plays after having had such an important role in the Roosevelt administration. He found writing it a "far more constant work and worry" than anything he had done in the theater "in a very long time." He had spent "morning, noon, and night" at it.[54] In addition, writing for the theater remained less profitable than he would have wished it to be; in fact, the writing and production period almost amounted to doing volunteer work. So, despite his preferences, he had to turn his eyes toward Hollywood once again. In 1944, while working on Roosevelt's reelection campaign, Bob had been offered two lucrative motion picture contracts, one for $100,000 and another for "Name Your Own Price."[55] At the time he was too busy and too involved in politics to follow up on either. After his efforts in Washington ended, however, he committed himself to working for Samuel Goldwyn on a screenplay of MacKinlay Kantor's story (and then book), *Glory for Me,* which was retitled for the screen *The Best Years of Our Lives.* A project that Bob at first felt no compulsion to become involved with, it would become one of the three works that gave him his "greatest satisfaction"—the other two being *Abe Lincoln in Illinois* and *There Shall Be No Night.*[56]

The history of *The Best Years of Our Lives* began when Samuel Goldwyn read a story by the London-based war correspondent MacKinlay Kantor in *Time* magazine about readjustment problems facing a group of marines returning from the war. What a great idea for a film, he told Kantor in a meeting in Los Angeles: "Returning soldiers! Every family in America is part of this story. When they come home, what do they find? They don't remember their wives, they've never seen their babies, some are wounded—they have to readjust."[57] Goldwyn signed the author to develop the story and a screenplay treatment, but Kantor got carried away and produced a 434-page novel in verse form which was unusable as a film but was published on its own as *Glory for Me.* Goldwyn then put the idea on hold until director William Wyler spied the treatment in Goldwyn's collection of unproduced work and read it. A veteran himself, Wyler was so excited by the piece that he provided the jolt of enthusiasm Goldwyn needed to make a commitment. Together they decided that Bob was the best person to take on the task of turning *Glory for Me* into a film.

Bob's initial reaction to the story was negative. As he told Goldwyn and Wyler when he visited Hollywood in the summer of 1945, he found Kantor's emphasis on the veterans' isolation and their "bitterness against civilians, whom they considered slackers and idlers who had just sat back and enjoyed life," too depressing. Bob felt that World War II had been a communal experience shared by the entire nation, and he agreed to work on the film only if he could change the script so that the soldiers realize that those on the home front "also had a tough time and so would they as civilians."[58] Kantor was very amenable to Bob's making revisions, and on August 14, while working on *The Rugged Path*, he signed the contract to write *The Best Years of Our Lives*. As difficult as he found writing the play, he discovered that after not having scripted a film in years, he was equally rusty in that area. "It was not long after starting work," he later recalled, "that I realized fully the blighting effect of five years in government service." There was a big difference between writing "entertainment" and writing "Memoranda, Minutes, Directives and Aides Memos." The "slowness" of his progress made him "ashamed," for he knew that other veterans had been through experiences "even more soul-searching than my own." To get himself over the hump, he read and studied scripts such as *It Happened One Night* and *Mr. Deeds Goes to Town* and watched innumerable old and new films, "more . . . than I had seen in the previous ten years."[59]

A mere two weeks after signing the contract, Bob had second thoughts about reliving any form of postwar trauma and wrote Goldwyn that he thought they should drop the project. "This is entirely due to the conviction that, by next Spring or Fall, this subject will be terribly out of date," he noted. By the time the film came out, cities all over the country would be filled to overflowing with healthy veterans who had already "passed through the first stages of readjustment" and would feel resentful of the "small minority . . . afflicted with the war neuroses." Bob recalled that when he, Goldwyn, and Wyler first spoke together, the director had expressed the hope that the film would prevent "a lot of heart-aches and even tragedies" among returning veterans, but within a month of their conversation, the war in Japan had suddenly ended, leading to an earlier demobilization than the filmmakers had planned on. Therefore Bob urged them to save their money, sincerely believing that the film "will be doomed to miss the bus."[60]

But Goldwyn and Wyler definitely wanted to continue, so, although he was reluctant, Bob started writing. After a couple of months, when he had completed over two hundred pages, he ripped them up and started over again. Goldwyn, Bob later related, remained "patient, though suffering," and Bob himself was "spent."[61] He suggested they try another screenwriter, but

Goldwyn persuaded him not to give up. Once again, Bob fed a sheet of paper into his typewriter. As he worked, he hit on the answer to his problems. If he set the main storyline after the end of the war, emphasized one romance, and made the other stories "more incidental," the plot made more sense. Also, he wanted the characters to be more optimistic, to feel that they shared a common experience. "Very important to the story," he wrote Goldwyn, "is the general atmosphere of a small city in which all kinds of people not only the veterans have a tough job adjusting themselves to the circumstances of a new world which must develop under the hope or the threat inherent in such revolutionary developments as atomic powers." The essence of the film, therefore, shifted from Kantor's saga of three isolated and bitter veterans to one of national postwar adjustment in which "the whole country and the whole world of people face the necessity of finding a way to live at peace with each other." [62]

After *The Rugged Path* opened in late November, Bob made plans to leave for Hollywood to finish the screenplay. Goldwyn, sensitive to his agonies over the writing process, offered the hospitality of his estate, where Bob and Madeline resided in a separate guest cottage and Bob wrote in a guestroom in the main house. The tension over the script and the difficulties with *The Rugged Path* inflamed his *tic douloureux*, but he kept working even when the codeine he took to quiet the pain resulted in some drowsiness. He appreciated the lodgings, good food, and attentive service, though at times he felt that he was "living in the circumstances of a permanent story conference." [63] During the final two weeks he went over "every syllable and every bit of business" with William Wyler and his assistant, Lester Koenig. Unlike in his previous film experiences, Bob found that Goldwyn and Wyler were willing to work with him "on equal terms," as was done in the theater. This, he felt, was the key to the film's high quality. [64] In April, 1946 Bob wrote to Goldwyn and Wyler: "One thing that amazes me is that the story seems to flow along so smoothly and so naturally that it looks as if it had been extremely easy to write. . . . That same quality of smoothness and ease must be continued through to the finish." [65]

Bob submitted the final script on April 9. Shooting began six days later and lasted for one hundred days. Goldwyn had promised Bob that there would be no changes in the final script, and he kept that promise, not allowing Wyler to alter even one line. When the Production Code Administration suggested a few minor changes, they were ignored, and the censors simply backed off. By the end of their collaboration, Goldwyn, Wyler, and Bob had produced a film that ran two hours and forty-eight minutes. At its release in November, Bob joked, "If it is a success, it will be a formidable blow against the menace of the double-feature—for the picture itself is so long . . . that it will be difficult for an exhibitor to crowd another feature into the same program, and the title, *The Best Years of Our Lives*, is so long that there won't be room for any more electric light bulbs on the marquee." He added on a further humorous note that it was "good" to be back in films, "a relatively stable enterprise, rather than . . . the Government which is less so."[66]

The Best Years of Our Lives tells the story of three World War II veterans—Fred Derry, an air force bombardier who wins a Medal of Honor for bravery; Al Stephenson, an army sergeant who is drafted at the age of forty, leaving behind a wife and two teenagers; and Homer Parrish, a seaman who suffers a severe injury. In *Glory for Me*, Homer comes home a "spastic" whose left side is twisted, his speech impaired, and who is unable to stop drooling.[67] Bob and Wyler decided to change the injury because it would not work well on the screen, seeming either "phoney" or "too grotesque to watch."[68] Instead, they chose to cast a non-actor, veteran Harold Russell, a young man who had lost both his hands six inches above the wrists in a dynamite accident. Russell, who used steel hooks controlled by a shoulder harness and manipulated by elastic bands, had appeared in an army documentary made to aid amputees adjusting to similar disabilities. An optimistic and genial man, the veteran was ideal for the job and was soon entertaining the other actors by opening beer cans, lighting matches, and performing numerous tasks which seemed impossible to do without hands and fingers.

In the film, the three veterans return to their hometown, Boone City, in the same transport plane, and as the story evolves, their lives become intertwined. True to his intention, Bob centered the tale on the love story between Al's daughter Peggy and Fred. Fred's adjustment problem is that before the war he was a soda jerk, and returning to that mundane role after having been a bombardier, a captain, and a war hero causes great trauma. He also discovers that the woman he had rushed to marry just before going off to war has been running around with other men and is not particularly interested in him anymore. He tries to make a go of the marriage, but she leaves him. Since he has fallen in love with Peggy, the divorce is a godsend. Eventually, Fred finds work with a company that turns scrap metal from jet fighter planes into material for prefab housing; he also finds a new optimism with Peggy. Fred's story illustrates how the return of veterans meant more competition in the job market and added to the immediate postwar unemployment problem. As one resentful civilian character in the film comments, "No one's job is safe with all these servicemen crowding in."[69] While it was true that within ten days of the war's end, 1.8 million people were laid off from war production jobs, the millions of veterans received little preferential treatment in job placement—except when competing with women and minority men, who were summarily dismissed without any consideration of past performance or need. Added to the temporary employment crisis were skyrocketing prices and inflation, but in a relatively short time this slump evolved into a period of boom and prosperity.

The character of Al Stephenson had been a banker before leaving for the war. Upon his return he finds himself promoted, but he is restless in his job. He wants to use the bank's resources to help veterans obtain loans but is told that the bank will do so only if the applicants have proper collateral. He also has trouble adjusting at first to his family. He is unsure of his relationship with his wife and children, and this uncertainty, combined with memories of his war experiences and his unhappiness at work, leads him to drink. Again, everything works out in the end, as Al persuades the bank to institute a loan program for veterans, becomes more assertive in seeing that the GI bill promising financial help is used effectively, and reestablishes himself as a loving husband and father.

Finally, there is Homer, understandably depressed that he has come home so damaged that even sympathetic neighbors and children in the street stare at him. He believes that his sweetheart, Wilma, only feels pity for him and cannot possibly love him, but even more heart-wrenching is that he sees himself as unworthy of her. Wilma tries to convince him otherwise, but it is not until Homer shows her the apparatus that controls his hooks and how defenseless he is without it, and her unexpectedly loving response, that he realizes she is devoted to him for life. The film ends with an optimistic moral—that the United States is a compassionate nation whose people embrace their veterans, and that together they can move the country forward into greater, more peaceful times.

At the end of *Glory For Me*, MacKinlay Kantor included a strong message about putting an end to class and race prejudice in the United States. Bob also included a political statement in his version of the story, one that echoed his deeply felt urgency about the need for world peace after the atomic bombings of Hiroshima and Nagasaki. The bombings held a dark foreboding for him, especially when in July 1946 the United States tested a more powerful weapon that obliterated the Bikini atoll in the Pacific from the face of the earth. Early the next year Bob wrote: "No one can feel smug in the presence of the atomic bomb. Man created this fearful force, but he is not inclined to stand up to God and boast, 'Look at the miracle which *I* have wrought!' Rather he seeks desperately for divine assurance that he will not be destroyed by his own gigantic achievement." It was important for people to realize that "the force" which destroyed Hiroshima and Nagasaki must not be duplicated.

Individuals as well as nations had to accept the responsibility of being "their brother's keeper," for the only hope for the world was "in the brotherhood of man." [70]

In a January 1949 article for the *Atlantic Monthly*, Bob continued to express his fear of the effects of radioactivity on all life on earth and his anger that the military seemed unconcerned that there was currently "no antidote for bomb poisoning, no defenses against the atomic bomb." At the time he wrote the article, the Soviet Union had not yet tested its first atomic weapon, which it did that October. Still, Bob worried about such an event: "We do not want to drop so much as one bomb on the Russian people any more than we want them to drop one on us. Because the first one will be the period at the end of civilization." [71] In *The Best Years of Our Lives*, the danger is identified by Al Stephenson's teenage son Rob, who asks his father if, when he was in Hiroshima, he noticed any effects of radiation on the survivors of the bombing. "Should I have?" Al queries. Rob then explains how atomic energy, radiation, radar, jet propulsion, and guided missiles have combined to poison the atmosphere. In another scene, the fear of nuclear arms development is echoed by Butch, Homer's bar-owning uncle, who tries to comfort his nephew about the future by sarcastically assuring him, "Everything will be fine unless there's another war and then everyone will be blown to bits the very first day." [72]

Bob was one of the first public personalities to speak out against nuclear weapons, but he was not alone. Although popular opinion generally supported the attacks against Japan, the traditional peace organizations uniformly expressed their dismay over the use of the atomic bomb and their concern for the future. [73] The Fellowship of Reconciliation, the Catholic Worker movement, the War Resisters League, and the Women's International League for Peace and Freedom all issued public statements. The most influential piece of writing, however, was John Hersey's article (and then book) *Hiroshima*, which first appeared in the *New Yorker* on August 31, 1946. The article presented graphic descriptions of the bombing and its effects on the residents of Hiroshima. It was harrowing reading that awakened many to the realities of atomic devastation and radiation poisoning. Even scientists, many of whom had worked on the Manhattan Project which created and assembled the bomb, organized groups and published articles cautioning governments about the possibility of destruction facing the earth. *The Best Years of Our Lives* expressed Bob's strong desire for a period of domestic and international peace. Most people who saw the film noted only its message about the immediate postwar national situation and its celebration of the end of the fighting, completely ignoring the two brief mentions of atomic testing. But they loved what they saw.

Samuel Goldwyn dedicated $400,000 to advertising, touting *The Best Years of Our Lives* as a serious, sophisticated artistic creation. Theaters picked up on this message, some requiring patrons to reserve seats for the performance of their choice. The film officially previewed in New York on November 22, 1946, where reactions were unanimously positive. After a private screening at the Goldwyns', Ethel Barrymore, Gregory Ratoff, Hedda Hopper, Cole Porter, and George Cukor sent Bob a joint telegram stating, "This is the American motion picture at its best and Sherwood at his best."[74] Goldwyn received a letter from General Omar Bradley of the U.S. Army expressing his gratitude for a preview shown at the Pentagon and saying that the film would be a great aid to building an "even better democracy" in the nation. A Louisiana representative in Congress took the floor and announced that *The Best Years of Our Lives* should be "required seeing for every American." The reviewer for *Time* magazine called it "a sure fire hit . . . with good taste, honesty, wit—and even a strong suggestion of guts."[75]

The film proved to be the most lucrative of Bob's career. Within the first year it grossed close to $10 million, making it second only to *Gone With the Wind* in U.S. sound film profits. It also attracted large audiences in Australia, Brazil, France, England, and Japan. Award after award came in. It won seven Academy Awards, including one for Bob for best screenplay. Harold Russell received an Oscar for best supporting actor and an additional special award for his representation of disability on film, the first time in history that the actor portraying the disability was himself disabled. In addition to being named best picture of the year at the Oscars, *The Best Years of Our Lives* was honored by the New York Film Critics and the Hollywood Foreign Correspondents Association (the Golden Globe) and in film industry ceremonies in England, France, Belgium, and Japan. Posie's favorite award was Bob's screenwriting Oscar, which he brought to her apartment as soon as he received it.

Just before *The Best Years of Our Lives* opened, Samuel Goldwyn asked Bob if he would adapt Robert Nathan's story *The Bishop's Wife* for the screen. This light romantic Christmas love triangle involving a bishop, his wife, and a handsome angel was also nominated for best film of the year, though it did not win the Academy Award. Still, its popularity helped to fund Bob's less successful theatrical work. Posie, who loved her son's theater work above all else he did, was ecstatic when he announced to her in the autumn of 1946 that he was thinking "a lot about a new play. (Thank God!)"[76] The play that he wrote, however, led to nothing but frustration. Bob's intention was to say something about the militarization and international tensions of the postwar world in order to highlight what he perceived as the powerful gains of communist aggression and tyranny. In Europe, for example, the end of the war had resulted in the division of the continent into Eastern (communist) and Western (capitalist) spheres. Germany itself was divided, and within East Germany, the city of Berlin was divided as well. That city became the hub of tensions between the Soviet Union and the United States, Great Britain, and France, becoming a concentrated area of militarization, espionage, and confrontation. As Bob watched these divisions forming, his hopes for global peace and democracy faltered.

By 1947, when Bob wrote *The Twilight*, the Cold War was well under way. Certainly, Winston Churchill's "Iron Curtain" speech, which depicted the Soviet-influenced areas of Europe as being under a dictatorship equal to or worse than the Nazis', fueled this ideological conflict, which was fought through the nuclear arms race, economic competition, proxy wars throughout the world, and propaganda campaigns, including Bob's creation, the Voice of America. This Cold War, which lasted until the Soviet Union's demise in 1991, had, in Bob's opinion, been created by Soviet aggression against the innocent, democratic West. His response was to glorify the ideology he believed he had fought for rather than to criticize the postwar world, as he had done in 1917. He did not return to isolationism but rather urged that the United States should immediately take on the responsibility of "bolster[ing] the economy of other regions of this earth" so that the "seed of Fascism and of war" would not take hold, and doubt, fear, mistrust, and greed would be rendered extinct: "We must fight them and conquer them as they may appear anywhere on the surface of this earth; we must fight them and conquer them as they may appear within ourselves," he wrote.[77] He was convinced that the Russian people wanted friendship with America and, before the success of the Chinese revolution in 1949, that China would be the best ally in Asia in building trade and peace in the area; but he warned that power-hungry demagogues might subvert the people's desires. He was most disappointed in the factions and world tensions which appeared after the war, and in this mood of discouragement he wrote *The Twilight*, a play destined never to reach the stage.

The Twilight is a political fantasy about Steven, "a modern army or navy flier or civilian," whose plane crashes off the coast of a small island in the Ionian Sea. He is rescued by Lyrith, the half-mortal daughter of Aphrodite and Ganymede, whose superior, Ares, grants Steven the ability to see these gods, who would normally remain invisible to him, but who also removes his memory of mortal life. Steven and Lyrith fall in love, but Steven cannot stop wondering who he is, how he got to the island, and what his relationship is to the planes he sees flying overhead. Ares becomes curious about Steven's modern world and decides to take on mortal form to see it for himself. The comments he makes on his return echo Bob's opinions about modern warfare: "I saw instruments of war whereby one frail man could destroy an entire army or a great fleet with one touch of his finger." Ares is convinced that humans are "literally hurling themselves to destruction." He tells of "imaginary lines" that divide nations, of munitions and troops stationed on these "lines," and of "unfriendly, suspicious men bearing arms" who demand to see people's passports and visas, and demand to know their race, religion, and political beliefs.[78] Steven, meanwhile, cannot quell his curiosity whenever he sees a plane. Finally, he calls out to one and is rescued, taking a mortalized Lyrith along with him.

In April, Bob sent selections from the play to Alfred Lunt and Lynn Fontanne, who sadly informed him that it was horrible. Fontanne wrote: "I have been thinking . . . and cannot find anything wrong—*except* the most important . . . thing that makes or breaks and that is *no story no situations no drama—no tears*—and not enough laughter to cover. For my particular taste, I must have some of all."[79] Bob tried again, but he seemed somewhat hesitant, even unsure of his work, wanting to keep it "quiet and private" until he could "get some idea whether or not it stinks."[80] It did. In July the pair reiterated their criticism. Bob replied, "I imagine you were both pretty much embarrassed, not to say pained, by that episode, but, what the hell?" The three of them had been through great times and hard times together, and Bob appreciated their candor. "Any soft soap" from them would have been "patronizing and insulting."[81] Still, the Lunts felt sickened by their doubts, especially since they themselves could not think of any constructive way to improve the story. "You see," Lunt wrote Bob, "you are completely original and unpredictable and that is why we find it so impossible to discuss this particular matter. I constantly feel a fool, and a very silly fool at that. We have always been happier in your plays, than any others, and that includes Shaw and Shakespeare, and *I do hope the next one we do will be yours.*"[82] From that moment, *The Twilight* was a dead issue, although writing was not.

Throughout his years of working on *The Rugged Path*, *The Best Years of Our Lives*, *The Bishop's Wife*, and *The Twilight*, Bob never got over the loss of Franklin Roosevelt, and constantly found ways to honor his memory. In mid-1945 he established the Roosevelt Memorial Committee (later Foundation) to raise funds to support Sam Rosenman and Arthur Schlesinger Jr.'s work of classifying and publishing Roosevelt's papers and to write a biography of him. He was at Hyde Park when it was officially opened to the public, and he wrote innumerable recollections about Roosevelt for various publications. Bob worked steadily on his Roosevelt projects through the end of the decade. One of the many people planning to write a biography of Roosevelt was Harry Hopkins. His work never came to fruition, however, for Hopkins died less than a year after Roosevelt, on January 29, 1946, leaving behind an immense amount of material. Within a couple of weeks of his death, Hopkins's widow, Louise, asked Bob if he would consider completing Hopkins's book as a token of friendship and to preserve Hopkins's memory. Bob agreed, not knowing that Hopkins had not written one word of his proposed biography.

Harry Hopkins's forty filing cabinets and innumerable boxes filled with papers were moved to New York, where Bob, along with Hopkins's assistant Sidney Hyman, who had already spent eight months putting the papers in order, got to work. For the next two and a half years, Bob worked on *Roosevelt and Hopkins: An Intimate History*, a project that became the story of Roosevelt and Hopkins's work together. Obviously, during its writing, Bob accomplished little in the worlds of theater or film. As he recalled once the book was completed: "I don't know whether I would have had the courage to take that job on if I had known what it was going to be like. It was every day and all day, seven days a week. I couldn't think about anything else. But I must admit it was endlessly exciting all the way through."[83] Certainly, the Playwrights' Company members were not thrilled by Bob's new project, for it meant that no new potential blockbuster would be coming out of his typewriter. It was also during this busy and trying time that Posie died. The family, except for Little Mary, who was pregnant, attended the funeral service on January 22, 1948, at St. George's Episcopal Church on East Sixteenth Street. Bob later wrote Alfred Lunt: "I thought I was perfectly reconciled to my mother's death at the age of ninety-three, but when it happened, I found that I was crying at the thought of all the things I had done that I shouldn't have done, and all the things I had left undone that I should have done."[84] Little Mary, Lyd, Ros, Phil, and Arthur all felt a great emptiness in their lives. For Bob, it was a hole he could never fill, but he carried on with his work nonetheless.

Unlike several other biographies of Roosevelt being written at the time, Bob's had the blessing of those in the highest positions. President Truman sent him a letter offering any assistance he needed. "In fact, you were a witness to many of the developments," he noted, "which it is now your duty to chronicle."[85] Bob completed innumerable interviews and received documents and advice from many former government appointees, military leaders, and foreign dignitaries. The British cabinet offices extended their cooperation in obtaining records of certain conferences. The only restriction placed on him was by Winston Churchill, who insisted that Bob get his permission to quote verbatim any document he had written. Churchill's chief concern was that he was writing his own book at the time and did not want the two to conflict. He was also perturbed because Bob, who had carte blanche to use anything in Hopkins's papers without consulting anyone, was including private conversations between U.S. and British diplomats which Hopkins had noted down while attending meetings. Bob tried his best to allay the former prime minister's worries about his exposing diplomatic confidences. He visited Churchill at his manor home and spent three hours alone with him. The statesman showed him his goldfish, his swans, his thoroughbred mare, and his paintings. Bob gave him an advance copy of the book as a courtesy. Churchill then issued a list of requested deletions, some of which Bob accepted and others not. When Bob returned home, Churchill called him several times to check facts and offer his opinions. Because he did not have Bob's private unlisted phone number, he called the porter of his apartment building. When summoned to the phone, Bob instructed the man to say that he was not at home. He later explained that since it was two in the morning in England, Churchill would be "in too bad a mood after stewing all evening to have a productive conversation."[86]

Roosevelt and Hopkins was published on October 10, 1948, and became an instant success. It is an immense volume of close to one thousand pages of detailed history from the New Deal through Hopkins's death, complete with entire letters and documents as well as Bob's personal recollections. For admirers of Roosevelt and World War II history buffs, the book is fascinating reading. For scholars, it has become a mainstay in researching the Roosevelt years. For the average reader, however, it is often tough going, a book so full of detail that it is almost overwhelming. The reviews at the time were generally positive, especially those written by Bob's wartime colleagues. Granted, Archibald MacLeish felt that the book was "much too long. As a biography, it is too much like a history; and as a history; it is too much like a biography. Its documentation overwhelms the narrative." But "when all this has been put down—it will still be true that Sherwood's book is not only one of the important books of the last decade but one of the few books of which it can be said with certainty that it is essential to an understanding of the time."[87] Joseph Barnes, an OWI alumnus, wrote in the *New York Herald Tribune* that the book was "the longest . . . yet written about the political strategy of the war. It is also, by all odds, the best."[88] Even Elmer Davis added his opinion: "Sherwood . . . was an official member of the White House staff; he wrote a book that is a pleasure to read; and not the least of his merits is that being a playwright, professionally concerned with exploring the complexities of character, he knows enough about it to know how much he does not know. . . . [H]e merely sets down the record—all of the record." [89]

Bob received his fourth Pulitzer as well as the Gutenberg, Bancroft, and *Saturday Review of Literature* Book of the Year prizes for *Roosevelt and Hopkins*. Harvard University presented him with an honorary doctor of literature degree and Bishop's University a doctor of civil laws. To top it off, in December 1949 he was elected to membership in the American Academy of Arts and Letters. As columnist Leonard Lyons reported: "The *Roosevelt and Hopkins* book already has won several prizes, and at each prize ceremony Sherwood is called upon to take a drink. 'If the book wins any more prizes,' said Sherwood in Toots Shor's [restaurant] yesterday, 'I may wind up in a drunkard's grave.'"[90] The book was sold or serialized in Canada, France, England, the Netherlands, Norway, Germany, Sweden, Italy, Spain, the Philippines, Japan, Greece, South Africa, and Israel. "The reception of my book has been bewildering to me," Bob remarked in early 1949. "I had no idea that it would reach so large an audience so soon. It certainly proves that the soul of Franklin Delano Roosevelt goes marching on."[91]

Bob's family was not as enthusiastic as the public even after *Roosevelt and Hopkins* had been number one on the national best-seller list for nearly two months. "Have you ever heard of a more incredibly weird circumstance than this one," he wrote his uncle Wilfrid, "in which these sweet, generous people still cannot bear to accept the thought that I disgraced the family name by associating myself with That Man in the White House?"[92] Early in the project, he had joked that one of his great joys in working on the book was "the thought of what will happen to the blood pressure of my brother Arthur when he reads it," but he had not expected only silence from him after its great success.[93] His aunt Jane praised him to the skies, but she was the only one. Bob gave Lydia, aging and hard of hearing, a copy with a sentimental inscription. She in turn issued another of her backhanded compliments, saying that while she thought the book "tremendous & remarkable," she was a "slow reader" and it would take her forever to get through it.[94] Bob's sad wish was that Harry Hopkins could have seen it. "I hope," he wrote Elmer Davis, "Harry Hopkins got word of the official citation [the Pulitzer committee] gave my book, saying that it was a record of patriotic and unselfish service to the people, illustrated by an eminent example."[95]

Bob was next offered a contract to write a biography of the British statesman Lloyd George, but he turned it down. Not only would he have had to rely on Winston Churchill for access to certain documents, but also he wanted to get back to his theater work. For his next project, he continued in his mode of celebrating the nation by teaming up with his friend and hero

Irving Berlin on the musical *Miss Liberty*. Bob was new to musical theater as a writer but not as a fan. He had been attending musicals throughout his life and had written several vaudeville-type skits in his youth. But musical theater had evolved into something quite different from what it had been in the early twentieth century. In 1943 Richard Rodgers and Oscar Hammerstein had a breakthrough hit with their musical *Oklahoma!* which set a new model for other musicals to follow—an integrated production in which story, music, and dance all operated together to move the plot forward. In 1927 Jerome Kern's *Showboat* had used this form, as had the 1935 production of George Gershwin's *Porgy and Bess*. After *Oklahoma!* came on the scene, however, the most profitable and popular musicals generally had an integrated story and score.

Oklahoma! was followed by Leonard Bernstein, Betty Comden, and Adolph Green's 1944 *On the Town*, Rodgers and Hammerstein's 1945 *Carousel*, Alan J. Lerner and Frederick Lowe's 1947 *Brigadoon*, and Cole Porter's 1949 *Kiss Me Kate*. Needless to say, the competition was stiff, but Irving Berlin had written the highly popular *Annie Get Your Gun* in 1946, so he was eminently up to the task. Apparently, Bob had approached Berlin many times over the span of their friendship to collaborate on a musical. As one article reported, "Berlin had listened to 'let's do a show together' talk from Sherwood at least once a year for the past twenty years and had come to look upon it as a nervous habit of his friend."[96] But to Bob, Berlin was "one of the supreme heroes of the world," and he wanted to repeat on a larger scale the experience he had had with the composer during the staging of "Puttin' On the Ritz" in *Idiot's Delight*.[97] As for Berlin, with eighteen successful Broadway scores under his belt, he was eager to work with this newcomer to the musical comedy scene who had such a tremendous reputation in theater, film, government service, and now biographical writing. It was Bob's idea to write the script around the story of the Statue of Liberty, explaining that during one of his wartime crossings to Europe on the *Queen Mary* with fifteen thousand recruits, he had been "deeply moved . . . [and] greatly impressed by the emotion that sight of the statue generated among these soldiers." When he later saw Berlin in England, he told him about his idea. "Who better to set it to music than the composer of 'God Bless America,'" he thought, "himself an immigrant who came to this country in 1893 at the age of five with his Russian parents?"[98]

Berlin suggested that the two of them invite Moss Hart to join their team as co-producer and director. Hart, a Pulitzer Prize–winning playwright also known for his musical theater direction, eagerly joined the project. Each of the three raised $250,000 to fund the show, then released a large portion of their shares to their respective companies or associates, in Bob's case the

Playwrights' Company, which also took on many of the business responsibilities. [99] Victor Samrock became the general manager and William Fields the press representative.The underlying plot for *Miss Liberty* hinges on the mythical competition for newspaper readers between James Gordon Bennett of the *New York Herald* and Joseph Pulitzer of the *New York World*. As a ploy to lure customers, Bennett sends his novice reporter Horace Miller to Paris to find the model for Frédéric-Auguste Bartholdi's Statue of Liberty. In the artist's studio, Horace snaps a photograph of a young woman in the statue's pose, but unbeknownst to him, she is not Liberty's model; Bartholdi's mother is. Horace innocently wires Bennett that he has found the model, Monique DuPont, and the publisher arranges for him to bring her and her grandmother as her chaperone to the United States, where they are lavishly celebrated. Pulitzer eventually discovers and publishes the truth. Although Horace faces a jail sentence and Monique and her grandmother deportation, Pulitzer saves them from both. Monique and Horace are then free to plan a happy life together. Interspersed is a love triangle involving Horace, Monique, and Horace's reporter friend Maisie. The play ends with Monique dressed as Miss Liberty singing the words to Emma Lazarus's poem engraved on the base of the statue, "The New Colossus" ("Give Me Your Tired Your Poor") to the tune of a beautiful Irving Berlin hymn.

Taking a good-natured swipe at Rodgers and Hammerstein, Bob told a reporter that what he liked most about working on *Miss Liberty* was that it had "no social significance, no symbolic ballet, and practically no resemblance to historical fact." [100] After working so long on *Roosevelt and Hopkins*, he felt tremendous relief not to have to worry about historical accuracy. By May 13, 1949, he had written the book and Berlin enough songs that the fifty-five actors, singers, and dancers could go into rehearsal. It was a huge endeavor, and Bob found it difficult to write dialogue because he constantly heard the songs "pounding in my brain, heart and throat." [101] He also found the exact timing required between dialogue and song difficult to adjust to. As he told his sister Ros, who had made a small investment in the production: "Every scene has to be put together like a watch. You haven't got time to spend several pages of manuscript establishing a character by a series of seemingly chance remarks, unobtrusive revelations. You have to sock it over." Collaborating on a musical was "incredibly complex." [102] By early June, Bob noted that working on *Miss Liberty* had become "time-consuming and distracting." [103] In addition to struggling with the writing, he was consumed by attacks of *tic douloureux* which were so bad that he had to take medication constantly. The painkillers on top of his usual drinks at lunch made him so drowsy that at times he seemed "drunk," according to Berlin's daughter Mary Ellin Barrett.[104]

His discomfort was so great, in fact, that he could not always remain in the theater, leaving Berlin and Hart to work on the rewrites. Allyn Ann McLerie, who played Monique, recalled: "When Sherwood did deign to attend rehearsals, it was painfully apparent to the cast members that he had been drinking heavily. At one point he broke into song, not one of Berlin's hits, but 'When the Red, Red Robin comes Bob, Bob, Bobbin' Along.'. . . Everything was sad. Everything was bad." [105]

On June 13 *Miss Liberty* opened in Philadelphia. Even though the reviews were generally negative, the entire four-week run was sold out. Bob, who had become overly protective and sensitive about his script and had refused to allow any changes, finally bent to the needs of the play. He stopped mixing alcohol and pain medications and began rewrites, but still, the musical did not improve. After seeing a performance in Philadelphia, John Wharton commented, "Well, I guess when three of the biggest men in the theatre make a mistake it's got to be one of the biggest mistakes ever seen." [106] Nonetheless, the company left Philadelphia with a $175,000 profit to pour into the New York production. The advance sale was huge—half a million dollars—and the public in general enjoyed the show, especially the Berlin tunes, though the critics felt it to be mediocre at best. Three months earlier another Rodgers and Hammerstein smash, *South Pacific*, had hit Broadway. Compared to it, *Miss Liberty* was mere fluff, a weak musical with poorly integrated components and too many long, boring spoken scenes. Brooks Atkinson described its July 15 opening as "disappointing"; Ward Morehouse called it a "sharp disappointment"; and Richard Watts Jr., "only pretty fair." Robert Sylvester of the *News* felt that perhaps the critics and public had "expected too much" from the illustrious team of writers, whereas the less sympathetic *Variety* critic simply said that it was "something of a clinker . . . [with] an overly-plotty book, undistinguished score, insufficient comedy and merely adequate performances." [107]

Miss Liberty lasted 308 performances, largely because of its huge advance sales and the popularity of its songs. "Let's Take an Old Fashioned Walk," "Only for Americans," "Just One Way to Say I Love You," "Homework," and "Give Me Your Tired Your Poor (Hymn)" all became huge sellers, especially for school choral groups, which bought the sheet music in volume. In addition, soon after it opened, ninety-eight singles and three albums of the show's tunes were recorded. In December 1949 the Playwrights' Company reported weekly profits ranging from $5,000 to $9,000. [108] In six weeks on the road, however, the show lost about $25,000 and signaled to Bob "the ultimate kick in the pants" and "fatal damage to any chance of a movie sale." [109] The work, he told Jane, had cost him "much in blood, toil, sweat & tears." Irving

Berlin blamed him for his first Broadway failure, and as a result, Bob felt no great ambition to start anything new. "Writing the Roosevelt and Hopkins book, on top of five years of government service, really took it out of me, and it's damned hard for me to summon enthusiasm for a career on Broadway. I may end up in Hollywood, God help me."[110] In fact, after *Miss Liberty*, all ventures slowed down dramatically for Robert Sherwood. As he entered the 1950s, his creativity diminished greatly, as did his health. Still, he persisted in trying to express himself through plays, films, and articles.

10

The Message Is Lost

ROBERT SHERWOOD spent the last six years of his life split between two worlds. He received a constant stream of honors for his work as a playwright and biographer despite being stuck in the quicksand of writer's block. Although he tried several times to compose a play or film that would once again capture the nation's heart, he was continually unsuccessful. Meanwhile, he enjoyed politics and campaigned for Herbert H. Lehman for the U.S. Senate, Franklin D. Roosevelt Jr. for Congress, and Adlai Stevenson for president, and won awards as a spokesman for human rights. At times, the tug between being a creative writer on the one hand and, on the other, working on political campaigns and commenting on world affairs seemed to be won by the political forces. Through it all, whether working for politics or his art, whether for a profit or none, Bob used the written word to advance his ideas. He told one of his admirers: "The only valid suggestion that any veteran writer can give to people just starting to write is this: Write—morning, noon and night—write anything and everything that you can think of and in any form that seems to be available. You may meet with persistent and unbearable discouragement, and you may end up in the poorhouse or in potter's field, but the only way to be a writer is to be one." [1] If he was anything, Robert Sherwood was indeed a writer, one who had survived one of the most trying political periods in U.S. history—that is, until the Cold War.

In some ways, the Cold War was a shocking and confusing development for Bob, a sad end to his hopes for a world of peace and freedom. No longer able to fit his old ideals into yet another modern political situation, he spent his final years speaking for the contradictory positions of world peace and militarism. Especially frightening to him were two events that took place in 1949: the testing of the Soviet Union's first atomic bomb and the victory of Mao Zedong's communist revolution in China. The latter he blamed on the once infallible Franklin Roosevelt for postponing a decision "on an enduring Chinese policy until it was too late" to save the Asian nation from the "Reds." [2] Although the Soviet Union and China differed in many aspects of their ideologies, Bob agreed with the assessment among Western nations that whether "red" or "yellow," they amounted to one monolithic communist menace.

Like the U.S. leadership in general, Bob had developed into a "cold warrior," one who despised communism in any form. Whereas earlier in his life he had looked upon the Bolshevik experiment as a positive attempt to improve the lives of the common people, he grew to believe that in practice, communist governments threatened the right to peace, prosperity, and individualism. The one hope for humankind, he felt, was the United Nations. To this end, he aided Eleanor Roosevelt in the wording of the "Preamble for the Declaration of Human Rights." He also wrote the introduction for U.N. Secretary General Trygve Lie's book *Peace on Earth*, calling the United Nations "the tangible, workable expression of man's highest aspirations." In Bob's view, whereas wars had been fought for both noble and ignoble reasons, the people of the world had finally achieved some understanding of these myriad causes. Therefore, the postwar world offered a new opportunity. "World peace can be achieved and the human race has no valid excuse for not proceeding to its achievement," he wrote. "But as Eleanor Roosevelt said not long ago, this task can never be completed by weaklings. It can only be done by men and women who are strong in faith and in knowledge and in purpose." [3]

Bob was one of a number of people who jumped on the world government bandwagon as the only means to avoid a nuclear holocaust. What this called for in real terms was a restructured, democratically run United Nations with the authority to legislate and mediate global affairs. U.S. government leaders and writers whom Bob admired were spokespeople for the movement, including Senator J. William Fulbright, novelist Thomas Mann, and Norman Cousins, the editor of the *Saturday Review of Literature*. The United World Federalists, under whose auspices Bob spoke several times, was the most prominent of the world government organizations, claiming 46,775 members and 720 chapters in the United States in 1949. World Government Week was celebrated in nine states in 1949, and that same year, ninety-one members of Congress introduced a resolution supporting the concept as the "fundamental objective" of U.S. foreign policy. [4]

Bob had favored some type of world government since before World War II, when he came out in favor of the creation of an Atlantic Union, a federation limited to the nations of western Europe, Canada, and the United States which could serve as a model for future global unity. When in April 1949 the North Atlantic Treaty Organization (NATO) was formed as a security measure against the Soviet Union, Bob was wary. NATO was not in any way a "first step toward world government—and peace." Indeed, it was just the opposite and would most likely be "interpreted as a ganging up—a purely defensive measure inspired by fear of Russia." Furthermore, NATO could backfire, exacerbating the arms race and supplying the Russians with "a terrific propaganda weapon—the same weapon that Hitler used so effectively—

the cry that they are being encircled." If through NATO the West appeared to be forming some kind of "exclusive" club "with the inevitable implication of Jim Crow restrictions," it would defeat the purpose of creating a government "of and by and for all of the peoples of our one world." [5] The one glitch in Bob's worldview was that there was no room for communism. Hence, the Korean conflict of 1950–1953 put another crimp in his campaign for world government.

After World War II, Korea, which had been a colony of Japan for many years, was divided into North and South. North Korea came under the influence of the Soviets and South Korea under that of the United States. The initial plan was that once the two Koreas had established their own governments, each of the victor nations would retreat. Of course, this scenario did not take into account self-determination for Koreans, who generally scorned the idea of a divided state. In June 1950 communist North Korea, in an effort to unite the country, invaded the South. This sparked a war that involved U.N. troops, which were drawn largely from the United States and under U.S. leadership, since the United Nations did not have its own military police. The looming threat during the Korean conflict was that of an altercation between the United States and the People's Republic of China, which bordered Korea. When U.S. planes bombed bridges and troops crossed the Yalu River into China, war appeared imminent.

Although the Soviet Union paid little attention to the events in Korea and offered the North only the smallest amount of aid, the U.S. government used the episode to propagandize against both the Soviets and the Chinese. Most people in the United States came to see the conflict as one instigated by the USSR even though it was Chinese aid that the North Koreans most relied on. Since American men were being drafted into the military to fight in Korea, the war was no small issue for the nation. In 1951 Bob lamented the "countless thousands—Americans, British, Koreans, Chinese," who had been killed and the many thousands of other "innocent people" who had been "rendered homeless." He thought he knew exactly whom to blame for the fiasco and how to prevent any such future wars: the Korean conflict was "simply" the fault of "the masters of the Soviet Union," who were "carrying on the work of Hitler, Mussolini and the Japanese war lords." The one way to stop such "international gangsters," he argued, was to strengthen the United Nations "to the point where it will become a real World Government." [6] This world government would presumably be a Western-oriented capitalist system which would in some unspecified way put an end to communism and thereby open the floodgates to world peace. In Korea it supposedly would lead to non-communist reunification.

The Korean hostilities did not officially end until July 1953, when an armistice was signed which basically set the borders between North and South close to where they had previously been. The death toll, however, was staggering for such a short conflict. U.S. casualties totaled 54,246 dead and 103,284 wounded, while nearly 5 million Koreans and other Asian nationals perished, 3 million of them civilians. In October of the previous year, Bob had reiterated his belief that "there can be no doubt that this brutal action was ordered by the Communist Czars in Moscow" as the "first step in a calculated campaign to conquer the world."[7] His job, then, was to use his pen in the war against communism. Under the auspices of the Committee on the Present Danger, which he helped to create, Bob expressed his belief that it was "plain insanity" for the United States to put all of its efforts into fighting communism in Asia when the clearest "danger" was to leave the Soviets free to overrun Europe, the oil-rich Middle Eastern nations, and Africa, with its great supply of uranium. Furthermore, overloading Asia with U.S. military forces would lead to an abandonment of those airbases in other nations from which the United States and its allies could "most efficiently attack Russian military and industrial centers."[8] In a surprising reversal of his postwar warnings against atomic weapons, Bob added his voice in support of U.S. nuclear development as a defensive measure. "Enduring peace and the improvement of world order," he stated in the code words of nuclear weapons proponents, could come about only if Western Europe and the United States maintained strong military forces that could "inflict major damage on Russia's strategic centers."[9]

The U.S. testing of the hydrogen bomb in 1952 followed by continuous aboveground testing in the Pacific Ocean confused the obviously conflicted Robert Sherwood. Whereas, on the one hand, he thought of himself as a nuclear pacifist (that is, one who opposed nuclear weapons development and the concept of nuclear war), on the other, he had to forgo his beliefs if he was to insist on protecting democracy against any seemingly oppressive tyrant. He continued to embrace the elements of Roosevelt's New Deal philosophies when he asserted: "That we are in a death struggle against Communism is only part of the truth. . . . We are in a struggle with all the forces of ignorance and fear, of tyranny and poverty and disease, physical and spiritual, that make war possible—and as long as war is possible, the human race will remain enslaved in a perpetual reign of terror." Although "we" would all feel safer if the Soviet Union were "dead," in the process "we could all too easily eliminate ourselves, and civilization itself."[10]

Once again using images he had painted in *The Petrified Forest* and *There Shall Be No Night*, Bob stressed that if the West were not unified in its efforts to rid the world of the causes of war, its people would become "easy victims for the men of the jungle, armed with clubs, advancing on their own two feet." Therefore, all must work to achieve a "world of peace and prosperity, of dignity and harmony, of enlightenment and hope in the sight of God." In the end, Bob preached a mixed Cold War message of wanting peace but seeing no way for the nation to disarm as long as communism continued to spread its evil poison. "I wish I could," he wrote. "But the dreadful fact is that, under present circumstances, we must be stronger and stronger, and stronger, ad infinitum. But for God's sake, let us never forget that world disarmament is the ultimate goal." [11]

The threat of communism was quite real to Bob, and he spoke constantly of his fear that the "red menace" would spread throughout the world, leaving the United States isolated. In effect, he was still living the antifascist struggle of World War II. Like the government of the United States, he simply substituted for the Axis threat one from Russia and China. Yet in actuality, the nation was well protected from any foreign clashes. Tensions in Eastern Europe which exploded in Hungary, Czechoslovakia, and East Germany in the late 1940s, the Korean conflict, and even the French struggle with the Vietnamese, which was largely funded by the United States, did not threaten the country. What did harm the nation, however, was the anticommunist hysteria fostered by Senator Joseph R. McCarthy of Wisconsin. Although McCarthyism got its official start in February 1950, when the senator made a speech in Wheeling, West Virginia, claiming he had proof that the State Department was teeming with communists, fears of ideological infiltration of the nation dated back to World War I and its accompanying Red Scare, which never really ended. During the 1920s and 1930s there was continual suspicion surrounding the activities of the U.S. Communist Party, labor activists, civil libertarians, and pacifists, which quieted down when the Soviet Union became a World War II ally. After the war, however, and the advent of the Cold War, domestic political intolerance moved to the forefront of government activity.

Unfortunately for those supporting peace, President Harry Truman was a true cold warrior, as was Dwight D. Eisenhower, who took office in 1953. In 1947 Truman ordered investigations of more than 3 million federal employees to discover whether they were loyal to the U.S. government or, presumably, to the Soviets. Three years later, workers whom the FBI determined to present some sort of security risk were fired. The difficulty was that the label "security risk" often had no basis. A person who drank too much or was homosexual or had signed a peace petition in the 1930s could lose his or her job. Once McCarthy came on the scene, the hysteria grew. The House

Committee on Un-American Activities (HUAC) beefed up its investigations, and among those brought before it were many Hollywood and Broadway personalities. Will Geer, Zero Mostel, Elia Kazan, Lillian Hellman, Dashiell Hammett, Charlie Chaplin . . . the list was endless. A group of screenwriters and directors known as the "Hollywood Ten" went to prison because they refused to "name names." Of every development that took place in the early 1950s, the Red Scare was the one Bob hated the most. To him, this anticommunist crusade was just as bad as communism itself, for it infringed upon the most sacred right of all: freedom of speech.

Bob's first mention of the Red Scare came in 1947, when he heard rumors that *The Best Years of Our Lives* was being described as "Communist propaganda." At the time, he felt no personal threat and decided to say nothing until his accusers publicly announced their "fantastic absurdity," at which time he would "fight it and discredit them." From his viewpoint, the purpose of red-baiting Hollywood figures was to "put the fear of God" into them so there would "never again . . . be any Communist (i.e. New Deal) propaganda on the screen." He noticed that film projects such as *The Senator Was Indiscreet* and *Born Yesterday,* which portrayed "crooked Senators," were either abandoned or altered so that government officials appeared uncorrupted. "All of which means," he noted, "that we're so terrified of the Communist Police state that we're imitating it. We cannot permit any 'diversionist tendencies' from the strict Party (Republican) Line." [12] For Bob, the Red Scare was similar to Stalin's purge of the Soviet government. Anyone who had been a staunch Democratic follower of Franklin Roosevelt had to be disposed of.

Bob simply could not tolerate any infringement on people's free speech and individual liberties. In 1946 he became upset when the popular young singer Frank Sinatra came under attack for speaking out on civil rights and freedom of speech and for performing consistently with racially integrated bands. Sinatra, a staunch Roosevelt man, spoke passionately against racism and xenophobia, giving thirty "Racial Tolerance" speeches in 1945 alone. As a result, the FBI accused him of being a communist and earmarked him for investigation. Bob considered Sinatra one of his young heroes and noted that "in times of national peril, [he] suddenly discovered that he is a Citizen, possessed of certain unalienable rights and of certain solemn responsibilities." For speaking out "against intolerance and injustice, against bigotry and prejudice and special privilege—fights for freedom and for the fundamental concept of equality under the law," he was being persecuted. [13]

Almost as an echo to the Sinatra controversy, in 1946 Bob sought the support of producers and writers in a boycott against the National Theatre in Washington, D.C., which would not allow African Americans to attend performances. Ever since the theater's segregationist policy had prohibited blacks from attending the 1938 preview of *Abe Lincoln in Illinois*, Bob had wanted to take action. With the postwar civil rights movement just gaining steam, he and Elmer Rice took a stand on behalf of the theater community that declared in part, "Racial discrimination is as anachronistic as it is offensive."[14] Actors Equity followed by demanding that employment contracts forbid segregation. As a result of the National Theatre's refusal to change its policy, no professional touring company would perform in the nation's capital. The theater's owner, Marcus Heiman, then converted the building into a segregated movie house, but by 1952 he had to give in to public and economic pressure and integrate.

Its pursuit of show business personalities gave HUAC its greatest media attention, but no one was safe from McCarthyism. The FBI investigated every lead it received on people who had had any ties with leftist, labor, pacifist, or liberal causes, and the resulting blacklists meant job losses for many—from blue-collar workers to professionals. Bob protected as many people as he could. In October 1950 he wrote in support of Isador Lubin, a member of Roosevelt's staff, stating that Lubin had in no way tried to "prejudice" Bob about any issue, least of all communism.[15] Next was Anna Rosenberg, appearing before the Senate Armed Services Committee in connection with her appointment as assistant secretary of defense. The poor woman had the misfortune to share a surname with Julius and Ethel Rosenberg, who had been arrested for conspiracy to commit espionage for allegedly passing atomic secrets to the Soviets. The Rosenbergs received the death sentence and were executed in 1953. With regard to Anna Rosenberg, Bob attested, "I have known her well for years and know she is violently opposed to Communism." Indeed, he noted in language her accusers could relate to, she had a "remarkably acute awareness of the tactics of the Communists in this country and of their serious danger to our national security."[16] Toward the end of the Red Scare, in 1954, he responded to a query from President Eisenhower about J. Robert Oppenheimer, the scientist who had headed the Manhattan Project but who later came under scrutiny for his leftist affiliations in the 1930s. Bob noted that whereas Oppenheimer may have been guilty of "political naivete in some phase of his career," it would be "dreadful" to think that McCarthy's "carnival" might put an end to his contributions to the nation.[17] In the end, Oppenheimer lost his top security clearance, thereby becoming a pariah in the nuclear weapons program.

In a speech before the Freedom Forum of the Anti-Defamation League, Bob attacked Eisenhower's secretary of state John Foster Dulles for firing John Paton Davis, a member of the Foreign Service who had been investigated eight times before being let go, and Edward Corsi, a "liberal" Republican whom Eisenhower had appointed to work with a select group of refugees from Europe. In his attack on Dulles Bob asked: "Just when did we resolve that the rights of the individual American citizen should be subordinated and indeed destroyed by some undocumented interpretation of what some official tells us is national security? . . . At what point in our history did the American people resolve that they must be protected by such unconstitutional, un-democratic, unrepublican, star-chamber procedures?" If the nation's security meant the elimination of civil liberties, then "our national security is not worth defending." Bob was incensed by what he described as a "heartless, soulless, callous tyranny," the likes of which the nation's founders had fought against. Had the United States become just an imitator of the USSR and China? "It is an ironic fact," he noted, "that whenever you study the motives and objectives of some so-called 'patriotic' organization, or group—which wraps itself in the Constitution and urges a 'return to our constitutional form of government'—you will observe that this organization seeks to preserve our Constitution by amending it, distorting it, disemboweling it." Prevent-ing authorities such as Paul Hoffman, an adviser to President Eisenhower, from giving a speech because the American Legion deemed his sponsor, the American Civil Liberties Union, unacceptable was "silliness" which could be compounded into "mania" and then into "totalitarian tyranny—the very destruction of our constitutional system." [18]

Even the Playwrights' Company was unable to evade repercussions from the Red Scare. Elmer Rice and a group of other dramatists formed an orga-nization early in the 1950s to produce well-known plays for television. The contract the group signed gave them control over the script, production, cast-ing, and other elements of each presentation. Rice began casting his play, *Counsellor-at-Law*, only to discover that six of the actors he had suggested for the starring role had been the targets of unsubstantiated accusations printed in *Red Channels: The Report of Communist Influence in Radio and Television* (1950) and *Counterattack*, a red-baiting periodical created by three former FBI agents. The studio would not clear Rice's choices, so he resigned rather than be a party to blacklisting. As he declared publicly: "I have repeatedly denounced the men who sit in the Kremlin for judging artists by political standards. I do not intend to acquiesce when the same procedure is followed by political commissars who sit in the offices of advertising agencies or busi-ness corporations." In this particular case, the sponsor, the Celanese Corpora-tion, backed down, and, as Bob pointed out, "deserve[s] honor for creating a precedent by repudiating black-listing." [19]

Soon after this episode, Rice proposed a resolution committing the Authors

League of America to defend any writer barred from work because of being listed in *Red Channels*. Maxwell Anderson, however, did not support the resolution because it "refused to discriminate between innocent and guilty."[20] This great divergence of opinion created an uproar within the Playwrights' Company. Like Bob, Rice was a free speech advocate, but Anderson felt that there were indeed communists and other radicals whose rhetoric called for the overthrow of the U.S. government, even if their actions proved otherwise. He supported the work of HUAC and did not want anything to do with protecting those who were guilty of adhering to the communist line. It hurt Rice that "two such wholehearted believers in democracy" as Anderson and him should be so "diametrically opposed" on such a fundamental issue. He understood that Anderson thought of communists as criminals and had no quarrel with his expressing his own opinion. Nevertheless, as he pointed out to his old friend, there was no law in the United States barring the Communist Party or membership in it. Neither the House, the Senate, nor the Supreme Court had addressed the issue in terms of the law; all the Senate had done was to establish HUAC in the hope of perhaps passing some kind of "remedial legislation." Rice told Anderson that he also had no great love for communists, but he had "a deep devotion to the principles of the Bill of Rights and to the Anglo-American system of law."[21]

Rice also objected to Anderson's sanctioning *Red Channels*, pointing out that the report took its information directly from California's Tenney Committee, a local version of HUAC, which had listed numbers of people who had ever had their names attached to liberal causes. "I am cited thirteen times," he noted, "pretty good for a guy who has openly been attacking Soviet imperialism and the principles of the American Communist Party, for years and years." He added with some glee that "a certain Maxwell Anderson; Hollywood Writers' Mobilization, 1945; Sponsor, National Council for Soviet-American Friendship, 1948," was also cited.[22] Rice himself was condemned for being on the board of directors of the American Civil Liberties Union, for being a member of the National Institute of Arts and Letters, for having signed a congratulatory telegram to the Moscow Art Theatre on its fiftieth anniversary, and other arts-related ventures.

Anderson responded to Rice that he had never accused anybody of being a communist, but he "reserv[ed] the right" to choose his associates and to steer clear "of what looks to me like traitorous company." The Communist Party, he demurred, was indeed criminal, as its intention to overthrow the government of the United States was, according to the Constitution, treasonous. "Every Communist Party member is pledged to just such a conspiracy and deserves to be treated as a traitor." To Anderson, the Communist Party was nothing more than "an international Ku Klux Klan" devoted to the "extirpation of all human rights and liberties among nonmembers and the destruction of all governments which it does not control." In a tone of friendly disagreement, he concluded, "The heart of our argument, of course, is that you believe our local Communists to be acceptable citizens while I believe them to be enemy agents, engaged in wrecking us from within." He clearly believed that the "over-whelming" evidence was on his side and that Rice needed to wake up to that fact.[23]

In a letter to John Wharton, who was concerned that Anderson approved of HUAC's and *Red Channels'* presumption of guilt until proven innocent, Anderson responded that of course under the law all were innocent until proven guilty, but "in all private human relations, there are no rules of evidence and men and women usually decide as whim and prejudice and a superficial examination of facts convince them." In terms of the actors and writers who had lost jobs because they had been accused of supporting communism, Anderson felt that producers had the right to employ only those "who they believe are likely to bring a return in sales or prestige." If a producer was a "fellow traveler," then he also had the right to employ "reds and fellow travelers . . . as it suits his fancy."[24] Anderson could not see that the practices of the government during the era of McCarthyism was negatively influencing people's decisions. To him, the two issues were absolutely separate.

At this point Bob entered the discussion. He wanted Anderson to understand that whether as a result of government policy or private opinion, a person's "livelihood, career, and morale" should not be subject to "suspicion, false inference, and misunderstanding." If Anderson did not want to associate with someone whose behavior he felt was potentially subversive, he had the responsibility of gathering evidence to substantiate his accusation before taking any action which might harm that individual. The difference between himself and Anderson, as Bob saw it, was that Anderson believed "in an unrestrained individualism that gives anyone the right to discriminate against people collectively, or by categories," whereas Bob believed "in a collective responsibility that demands that people should be judged as individuals." To illustrate this difference, Bob pointed out that if Anderson did not want to associate with African Americans, he had the right to do so, but when Marcus Heiman insisted on maintaining racist policies at the National Theatre, that was "against the public interest and in violation of the United States Constitution." Fear, hatred, "suspicion, intolerance and wholesale condemnation of people by categories" could only spell trouble for a democracy. Above all, free speech, even if it advocated the abolition of democracy, had to be protected. "I think that the greatest internal threat to our society is the growing tendency to penalize people for their doctrines," he cautioned Anderson. "Once we set our feet in that path we are marching straight toward totalitarianism."[25]

Although Bob was not personally accused of any wrongdoing during the Red Scare, he had his own fears for Little Mary and Bud Stillman, who moved within alleged communist circles. Bob complained to his sister that he often received letters from his son-in-law that were "utterly raving and incoherent," especially when Bud read of Bob's work with the Committee on the Present Danger.[26] Nervous about McCarthyism, in 1951 Bob warned his daughter about the dangers of being "girdled" by the "Communist Party line." He found her politics especially disconcerting since she was now the mother of two—Joseph, born in 1948, and Madeline in 1950. Bud and Little Mary, Bob felt, had let themselves become "dominated by doctrines which are deliberately calculated to promote wholesale hatred and suspicion, cynicism and fear." So disturbed was he by Bud's outspokenness that Bob avoided having any sort of political discussion with him because he did not like to see "someone of whom I am deeply fond frothing at the mouth."[27]

Little Mary was rightfully angry at her father's insulting comments. She accused him of knowing "next to nothing" about her life since 1946 and of charging her with being some kind of "communist dupe or fellow traveler." She denied being either of those things; she simply had an intense interest "in communal life as it is in the kibbutz in Israel." She did not believe that her desire to try collective living could be equated with "being hopelessly tied down by the party line." Once she had begun her defense, her anger quickly escalated. "I think it a justified reaction," she told him, "to be annoyed at being told what I am, how awful my life is, that I'm doomed, etc., by someone I've seen 3 times in 10 months, and who takes no apparent interest in seeing me, my husband, or my children." She complained that Bob and Madeline appeared "totally bored" with them whenever they visited.[28]

Bob wanted to be a more attentive father, but he had always been a busy man. And of course he had a somewhat low opinion of Bud's personal and political influence on Little Mary. When the couple asked if he would allow his name to be used as a sponsor for a conference of the Emergency Civil Liberties Committee, Bob told them no. He belonged to the American Civil Liberties Union, but the two groups were not affiliated, and he could not trust any group Bud recommended. He was also smarting over the fact that his daughter had had several miscarriages, and he blamed Bud for being irresponsible and uncaring toward her. When in 1955 Little Mary told him that all was not well in her marriage, Bob wrote to his aunt Jane: "This news aroused mixed emotions in me. I'm afraid that boy requires the tender offices of a psychiatrist."[29]

In fact, the purposely distant father chose to ignore the fact that his daughter, like her mother, was an alcoholic and a drug user. Depressed by her addiction, her constant arguments with Bud, and the institutionalization of her developmentally disabled daughter, one day Little Mary simply walked out on Bud, leaving Joe in his custody. In the long run, she remained attached to her father in a weird and angry sort of way, seemingly wanting to test his affection for her. She also remained close to the rest of her Sherwood family, noting with sorrow the death of Bob's brother Arthur and his uncle Wilfrid in 1951 and his aunt Lydia in 1952. After Wilfrid's death, a frail and aging Jane decided to remain in England, where she died in 1961.

Bob's artistic response to McCarthyism was a free speech project which attacked European communism, not the Red Scare at home. With director Elia Kazan he created the film *Man on a Tightrope,* which was released the same year as another, fairly inconsequential film he wrote, *Main Street to Broadway.* Bob found the Kazan partnership deeply meaningful. Kazan, considered one of the greatest stage and film directors of his time, had known Bob through their relationships with the Theatre Guild and the New York theater community. Early in his career Kazan was recognized as a leftist and had for a time been a member of the Communist Party. As an actor with the socially conscious Group Theatre, he had performed in the productions of Clifford Odets's pro-labor *Waiting for Lefty* and the Paul Green–Kurt Weill antiwar piece *Johnny Johnson.* Therefore it came as quite a shock when the popular director appeared before HUAC as a friendly witness in January 1952, answering every question the committee put to him about his membership in the Communist Party between the summer of 1934 and the spring of 1936. When he returned for a second session of queries, he told the members he had decided that the correct action for him to take was to "name names." His identification of eight members of the Group Theatre and a few officials of the Communist Party made him anathema to many on Broadway and in Hollywood.

In spite of his hatred of McCarthyism, Bob still admired Kazan's talents. He also needed an interesting, profitable project. So in the summer of 1952, when Kazan asked if he would write the screenplay for a film based on a true story by Neil Paterson about a troupe of East German circus performers who had executed a successful "escape . . . through the Iron Curtain," Bob eagerly agreed. He and Kazan then made a trip from Munich to Nuremberg, visiting refugee camps full of Eastern Europeans who had arrived in the West with little but the clothes on their backs. Bob noted: "The great majority are Czechs, but there are also Poles, Hungarians, Roumanians, Bulgarians and even some Russians. There is no barbed wire around them. They are technically free to go as they please, but they have no place to go. They have their churches in wooden shacks and they can worship as they please—but they have no reason for faith in the future." [30] Bob and Kazan interviewed refugees whose stories of resistance against both the Nazis and the communists cemented Bob's belief that the two systems could be equated.

In Passau, Bob, Kazan, and their official government escorts met Carl Sembach, the proprietor of the Circus Krone, who exposed the visitors to the world of the circus, a world that Bob had loved since he was a boy. He gleefully jotted down his impressions of the one-ring show, complete with tigers, polar bears, brown bears, and a hippopotamus "who sits at a café table and eats salad served to him by a clown dwarf." [31] What struck him most was that neither nationality nor political beliefs played a role in being a circus performer. All that mattered was competence. Kazan agreed. He later stated that the circus was "a good image for democracy. It has room for all kinds, it has need for all kinds. It must have humor, surprise, irreverence or it dies. Fantasy also; but based on realism; muscles, eyes, knowledge of danger. Also, of course, it has to have discipline, responsibility or it dies. Without these, anarchy!" [32]

Man on a Tightrope, which was released in 1953, was a true Cold War–era, anticommunist film, a piece of propaganda of which the Office of War Information or its successor, the U.S. Information Agency (USIA), would have been proud. Set in 1952 Czechoslovakia, it tells the story of the Cirkus Černik, a poor one-ring traveling affair trying to survive in its communist-controlled nation. Throughout the film, the performers are spied on by plainclothes policemen, informed on by traitors from within, harassed by government officials, and threatened with imprisonment. Černik, the manager, was formerly the owner of the troupe until it became "nationalized . . . like everything else," he tells the police. Before that, the circus had been under his family's ownership for two generations or more. He is not used to being ordered around with regard to his art. When government police accuse the circus performers of glorifying France because one act involves waving a French flag and questions if a Chinese performer is "of the Chinese republic or one of the lackeys of the defeated fascist regime," Černik responds that the man probably has no idea what he is: "He's a juggler. Circus people aren't like other people. The only religion . . . and the only nationality we have is the circus. We have no politics. We have no home but the circus." [33]

Bob's script attacked the censorship he felt was implicit in a communist-controlled country. In *Man on a Tightrope*, the government demands that the circus change its acts so that they attack the West and praise the East. Therefore, a violent and brutal clown should represent Wall Street imperialism and his victim should be an African American worker. Černik makes the change, but the audience does not find it funny, so he undoes it. For this he is fined and threatened with charges of treason, and even with having the circus liquidated. Černik finally decides to make a run for the border with the entire circus troupe. He tells his close friends to prepare, and in a dramatic border crossing complete with a homemade bomb and a truck crashing through the gate, they make their break. Although Černik dies in the escape, the film closes with a shot of the circus troupe traveling down the road to freedom.

Man on a Tightrope received mixed reviews and was not much of a success at the box office. In Kazan's eyes, the fault was Bob's. "I didn't think the script was very good," he later recalled. "Sherwood, a brilliant and wonderful man, was exhausted at the end of his life." Kazan felt that the love story was particularly weak and found much of the discussion between the government commissar and Černik "schematic." But the director could not change the script because, as was his custom, Bob insisted that none of his writing be altered, and producers caved in to this demand. "Sherwood had prestige and power," Kazan noted, "and he had his rights." Still, Kazan felt that "many scenes were embarrassing . . . just statements of politics, rather flat New Deal statements which, by 1952 . . . in the context of a little circus, seemed absurd." In the end, he claimed, "I do believe that if I had had a young writer and worked three months more on it, I could have made a helluva good picture." [34] Bob also recognized the weakness of his script, commenting after the film's opening that he was "slightly disappointed." Instead of acknowledging that he now needed help with his writing, he rationalized that had he been present during the actual filming in Bavaria, "I could have done some things here and there to make the narrative flow more smoothly." [35] In spite of the film's failure, it received a special prize from the Senate of Berlin at the 1953 Berlin International Film Festival, more a political than an artistic recognition.

Nothing could prevent Robert Sherwood from plying his craft. Articles, speeches, filmscripts, and book reviews all kept him clacking away at his typewriter. Indeed, in spite of his declining productivity, he continued to receive accolades for his work. In 1951 he was elected to honorary membership in the Mark Twain Society and was honored on television with a "Toast of the Town" segment on the popular *Ed Sullivan Show*, which featured scenes of his work performed by Alfred Lunt, Montgomery Clift, Raymond Massey, Helen Hayes, and James Mason. The next year he received an award from the Association of Founders and Friends of Roosevelt College. In 1953 Canada's Black Watch Regiment, in which he had served during World War I, offered him honorary membership in the Officers' Mess, which he happily accepted, and in 1955 he received the World Brotherhood award from the Jewish Theological Seminary of America. This ongoing recognition, however, caused its own problems. If he was so accomplished, why could he not complete a top-notch play or film? The question was simply unanswerable, and Bob's decline continued to affect all those around him.

In 1949 Bob's friend Philip Barry died, leaving behind an unfinished script, *Second Threshold*. Barry had worked on the play for eleven years, completing four drafts of it. Naturally his wife wished to see it produced, so she asked Bob to take on the task of making any necessary revisions, which he did. In the end, he felt that he had not created anything new; "in the nature of carpentry," he had completed the final work as "a labor of love" rather than through "a sense of professional obligation." [36] The play opened in New York on January 2, 1951, and ran for 126 performances—not a great success. As a result, the other members of the Playwrights' Company, which had an investment in the show, grew concerned about the steady decline in the quality of Bob's writing. By the end of 1950 they were down to just three playwrights, none of whom was producing great scripts. Bob himself did not complete a producible play until 1955 with *Small War on Murray Hill*. So severe was the situation that soon after Kurt Weill's death in April 1950, John Wharton once again wrote to the three remaining playwrights, expressing his concern that the company might not be able to survive economically. Bob's response reflected his deep connection with the institution and its importance in his life. As he grew older, he had no desire to strike out on his own, he said, searching for producers and collaborators who would not know him as intimately as the Playwrights' Company team. "If there were no Playwrights Co.," he wrote Elmer Rice, "I can't believe that I'd have any interest left in working in the theatre." [37]

To save the company, Wharton approached Roger L. Stevens, a wealthy real estate mogul and novice theatrical producer who was as interested in the creative process as he was in raising funds. He was immediately approved for full membership, the first time the playwrights had welcomed someone specifically to raise money. Besides giving the company a financial boost, Stevens added personal clout as well. As Wharton put it: "To the vast majority of unsung and underpaid theatre workers, anyone with as much as $10,000 in the bank was considered rich. In their minds, a man who could buy the Empire State Building [as Stevens had] must have money enough to pay off the national debt." [38] Stevens's effect on the company was to make it into a more commercial venture, which was in part good. Victor Samrock and William Fields, who had both been removed from the full-time payroll, were put back on staff. Stevens also linked the group with two other corporations—Whitehead-Stevens, Inc., and Producers Theatre, Inc.—both involving Robert Whitehead, another prominent producer. As a result, the Playwrights' Company lost some of its own profit to other stockholders and investors and eventually lost much of its collective and creative nature as well.

John Wharton once stated that if Bob had decided to become an independent producer in 1951, he would have been tremendously successful because he had a network of backers and an innate sense for good scripts, even though he seemed unable to write one himself. It was Bob who recommended playwright Robert Anderson for membership in the company. Anderson's 1953 *Tea and Sympathy* was a huge success, playing 712 performances on Broadway followed by a forty-seven-week tour. Other Playwrights' Company successes from 1950 to 1955 included Jan de Hartog's *The Fourposter*, with 632 performances and forty-two weeks on the road; Samuel Taylor's *Sabrina Fair*, with 318 performances; Jean Giraudoux's *Ondine*, with a moderate 156 performances; Maxwell Anderson's *The Bad Seed*, with 334 performances and thirty-one weeks on tour; Tennessee Williams's *Cat on a Hot Tin Roof*, with 694 performances and thirty-three weeks on the road; and Giraudoux's *Tiger at the Gates*, with 217 Broadway performances. Of these, *The Bad Seed* was the only one written by an original member of the company.

In 1950, after the excitement surrounding *Roosevelt and Hopkins* and *Miss Liberty* had died down, Bob began another play he at first called *Girls With Dogs* and then *The Seventh Floor*. The plot revolved around life in an apartment house in Chicago; the characters included a neurologist who wants to "analyze the chemistry of hatred . . . the prevailing disease," his "bolshevik" priest brother, a neighbor who is accused of collaborating with the Nazis but says he can live with anyone, and a woman who runs a "bordello" on the seventh floor.[39] Bob was convinced that the play delved deeply into the modern hypocrisy of men who purported to be moral examples to the public but who practiced immoral behavior in private. As he described it, his main character, Paul, the neurologist, seeks "to retreat into research out of disgust with cannibalism and follies of modern man" but is faced with the "extremely earthy problem" of the brothel in his apartment house.[40]

John Wharton noted that *Girls With Dogs/The Seventh Floor* "was quickly consigned to that limbo from which it never should have come."[41] During the period of its creation, the people who cared intimately about Bob knew he was stuck, but they all remained hopeful that he would turn the corner and come up with something new. Because they were so terribly worried about him, all those who read the script tiptoed around the truth that the play was simply no good. Upon reading an early revision Wharton commented that although "thematically" the play left him "completely confused," this version was still "infinitely superior to the first from a dramaturgical standpoint."[42] In general, Wharton believed that Bob had lost the ability to write "certain scenes called 'obligatory scenes'; the author has set the stage for some kind of confrontation for which the audience waits eagerly; the scene between Hamlet and his mother is world famous. Bob simply could not write these scenes any more."[43] Nor could he develop a theme and carry it through to its logical conclusion. Maxwell Anderson read the play twice, each time gently suggesting extensive rewrites.[44] Elmer Rice also tried to be encouraging, re-marking that there were "several vivid characters, some very good situations, and needless to say, a lot of entertaining dialogue." Still, he had "some grave reservations" about the play as a whole. Neither the central character nor the plot seemed very well developed. As a good colleague, he pointed out the "miracles" Bob had performed in the rewriting of *There Shall Be No Night* and felt sure he would accomplish the same thing in this situation.[45]

Early on in the writing process, Bob once again approached Alfred Lunt and Lynn Fontanne about a collaboration. Unsure of the play's quality but sensitive to Bob's plight and unwilling to hurt his feelings as they had done with *The Twilight*, throughout March and early April 1950 the couple skirted the issue, making short comments about the improvements in the script and their pleasure in "its vitality its originality & the very fact that you are writing for the theatre again."[46] But by mid-April, Lunt had to admit that although he enjoyed the dialogue, he felt that "the play as a whole is still on the meager side," especially in its "non interesting" characters.[47] Bob, however, could not see any problems. On April 25 he wrote Lunt that he felt very good about *Girls With Dogs* and was waiting "in an increasing sweat of anxiety" for some word from Genesee Depot.[48] Finally, Lunt sent the inevitable hurtful let-ter. Bob told Victor Samrock that it was "pretty damned annoying . . . some lame explanations of why he had delayed over two weeks in reading the new script." Lunt apparently criticized the weak character development and then "ended the letter abruptly."[49]

Although he found the criticism disturbing, Bob kept plugging away. He approached Garson Kanin about possibly directing, but Kanin declined in a long letter full of comments, saying that in the end he just did not "really get it. I don't know *for sure* what it's about, what it means, the point it is mak-ing, or why it is called *Girls With Dogs*."[50] Film producer and friend Joseph Mankiewicz claimed to love the play but not the main character, Paul, who for Bob represented the essence of the work. Mankiewicz felt that as soon as Paul entered, "everything becomes routine."[51] Ignoring Mankiewicz's com-ments, Bob moved ahead with planning the production, approaching John

Van Druten as another possible director. Van Druten declined. Eventually, Bob just gave up. *Girls With Dogs/The Seventh Floor* was going nowhere, and he needed to earn, not lose, money. As it was, he owed the Playwrights' Company over $7,000, $5,000 of which he could repay within a month, but that still left him over $2,000 in arrears.

By January 1952 Bob had another script almost completed. Titled *The Better Angels*, it revolved around incidents in Salt Lake City, in the Utah territory, in 1860 and 1861, just before the Civil War. Bob wrote the play because of his interest in the Mormons as a "minority" group: "This is the eternal story of the minority that is oppressed, persecuted, hounded from pillar to post, driven out of one home to another and finally finds its home in a remote wilderness and there achieves freedom and independence and power in its own area and then promptly begins to persecute any new minority that appears in that area."[52] The plot follows the lives of Colonel Stephen Doery of the U.S. Army Corps of Engineers, who is in Utah to survey routes for the Transcontinental Railroad; Zaccheus Trumbull, the Mormon leader he boards with; Charlotte Lambaux, a French widow; and Isaiah, a Jewish peddler. Recycling many of the ideas Bob had successfully expressed in previous plays, the men debate war, nationality, and religion. Zaccheus's son, Nephi, tells Stephen that Mormons consider themselves to be "in a different country—with a bigger breed of men and the only true religion."[53] Zaccheus backs him up, predicting that the Union will be split and civil war "shall be poured out on the faithless people."[54] The war will not be their problem, however, as Utah is a territory and its residents not yet citizens. Through various experiences, Stephen comes to understand that Utah is a theocratic state, where Brigham Young rules like a monarch and the church dictates everything. Charlotte, who is not a Mormon, is being strong-armed to convert and marry Nephi, and Isaiah is treated as the eternal outsider. In the end, Charlotte asks Stephen to help her escape to California, but he chooses to leave for the South to fight for the Confederacy. His choice, so common among Bob's military characters, is made because he is "a soldier."[55] He and Charlotte go their separate ways.

Once again, Bob had written a bad play, and in his heart, he knew it. As he told reporter Seymour Peck in an interview about *The Better Angels*, he had recently seen a revival of *The Road to Rome*, a play he had not revisited since the late 1920s, and was surprised at how well it stood up. "I confess," he said, "I thought it was pretty darned good. In fact, I had a sort of rueful feeling—'Why can't I write like that now?'"[56] John Wharton concurred. The plot for *The Better Angels* meandered around into nothingness. Bob felt that he had written a historical play with "a certain implied application to

the present age," as Arthur Miller would do most successfully the following
year with *The Crucible*.[57] Neither the message nor the plot, however, clearly
implicated McCarthyism. In the meantime, Bob continued to revise *The Better Angels*. By June, the Playwrights' Company had earmarked November 1
as the tentative date to start rehearsals, with Joshua Logan as co-producer
and director. But Logan was too involved with the musical *Wish You Were
Here* to start the project on time, and Bob was called to Hollywood, where he
made some much-needed cash with *Main Street to Broadway* and then *Man
on a Tightrope*. Next the elections of 1952 interrupted production plans, as
Bob was working on Adlai Stevenson's presidential campaign. By December
the play was still not done, and money had become so tight that Bob and
Madeline made the decision to put Great Enton up for sale. For the past two
years, he wrote Jane, the couple had had to borrow money to support themselves while living there. It would be cheaper for them simply to rent a flat
in London for the two months of each year they hoped to spend in England.
It took until July 1954 to sell the place, but Bob and Madeline left it empty
so they would not have to maintain a staff and pay for anything other than
basic maintenance.

Next Bob got waylaid by television and again put *The Better Angels* on
hold. He signed a lucrative contract with NBC for $100,000 (equal to over
$700,000 in 2005) to write four original one-hour plays each year for four
years.[58] He had already given approval for adaptations of *Abe Lincoln in Illinois* and *The Petrified Forest*, which had appeared on network television.
In addition, Bob took on more article writing. In the summer of 1953, while
he and Madeline were in England, he wrote various pieces, the most arduous being a series on the coronation of Queen Elizabeth II. By the time he
finished the assignment, he had to admit that "thrilling as it was, I have had
my fill of Coronations and I'm glad to think there will never be another while
I'm alive." Worst of all was having to get up at 4:30 in the morning, "encase"
himself in "white tie and tails," and then spend eight hours straight in a tiny,
cramped space observing the ceremony.[59] By the end of the year, however, he
had been able to complete a television script. Called *The Backbone of America*,
it was a satire of modern American advertising, but as Bob wrote Jane, it was
"roasted by some of the better critics."[60] One called it "a disappointing start
in the Playwrights Series," while another said that while it had "some nice
little satire and some nice little comedy," basically there was "nothing great
about it." The fifty-six-minute work lacked drama and was "as obvious as
apple pie."[61] The network figures, however, showed that over 12 million TV
sets were tuned to it, and viewers liked it very much.

The next year, 1954, Bob's second, much more successful one-hour play written specifically for TV, *Diary* was aired. The story centers on Jack, a small-time criminal who kills a policeman in a shootout, and Susie, a young runaway from suburban Massachusetts who falls in love with him and as a result meets an early death. As one reviewer noted, despite being "a little drawn out and unnecessary," it was "otherwise just about perfect." [62] Still, Bob was not enamored of writing for television and by January 1955 began to take steps to cancel the contract. By then, only two of the five scripts he had written had been produced. Even though NBC was enthusiastic about the other three, the network had not moved forward on staging them, leaving Bob frustrated and unhappy. Yet television had its advantages. As Bob noted, it proved an unexpected boon for the theater, for it nurtured that element which was most needed—new playwrights. "Most, if not all, of these young playwrights," he wrote, "would not have been able to practice their craft and, at the same time, keep on eating had it not been for television and, in many cases, radio as well." [63]

Nineteen fifty-five, the final year of Robert Sherwood's life, was just as busy and just as frustrating as the preceding few. While continuing to craft articles about politics and the theater, he struggled with the quality of his creative writing. The two major works of political opinion he wrote took on a new form for Bob—depressing, futuristic predictions. The first, "The USSR versus the US (Operation Eggnog)—Confidential," was a mock report on a nuclear war, supposedly begun in Yugoslavia in 1952. By 1954, as envisioned in the piece, the USSR has "disintegrated," followed by "the vast area from the Baltic to the Bering Straits and the China Sea disrupt[ing] in anarchy, with new states emerging, as if they were moons shot off from a molten planet. Some of these states have begun to achieve identity as independent republics; others bear more resemblance to the baronies of feudal times; others have relapsed into oriental satrapies." The fault, of course, rests squarely in the hands of the Russians, who have undermined the desire of the "western democracies" for "peace and friendship" after World War II. [64]

The first nation to use atomic weapons in the war is the United States, and even though the Soviet Union retaliates, its output never matches that of its attacker. In addition to causing chaos in the Soviet Union and Eastern Europe, the war also sparks internal strife, "fomented and supported by the Chinese Reds," in "Burma, Malaya, Indo-China, Indonesia and the Philippines." The Chinese then grab up South Korea and the island of Hokkaido in Japan. Seeing the Soviets self-destruct, and fearful that atomic bombs will be used on them, the Chinese eventually back down and negotiate a settlement with the United Nations. The war ends with the "Denver Declaration," which moves the nations toward negotiations and, perhaps, world government. Bob ended the article: "But no one can yet tell how resolution of the greatest problems of all is progressing throughout the world; the prevention of further catastrophe, the realization of the aspirations of every man on earth to live among his neighbors in freedom and in dignity and in peace, the will to save our human race from suicide and restore it to the fulfillment of the will of God." [65]

The second article predicted nuclear disaster unless nations agreed on disarmament: "If this objective is not achieved by 1980—long before 1980—then we may as well write 'FINIS' to the human story." Bob was convinced that the world had already reached "the ultimate in the capacity for mutual destruction," and his one hope was that a final, third world war would never come to fruition. He himself had great "confidence" in the future, largely, he claimed, because he believed that "God created 'man' in His own image" and that was what allowed for people to "progress and to reach for immortality." He could not believe that the human race would deliberately destroy itself, although he did believe that certain power-hungry men could bring about the end of the world. "The issue is sheer survival," he mused. "If we retain the capacity that has been shown over and over again through all the centuries, we shall survive. If we have lost it, we will never know what hit us." Even though there was great risk involved, the United States had to take the lead in negotiating disarmament and in the establishment of international controls to ensure and monitor it. If not, the world "may be blasted . . . into radio-active rubble." [66]

That vague construct "peace" was never far from Bob's thinking. In 1955 it still represented an abstract ideal of a world free of violence, with all civil liberties guaranteed to people everywhere. This dream remained a fantasy from the past, however, because his strong feelings of hatred toward communism in any of its variations left Bob unable to detach himself from the militaristic ideology of the cold warriors. In this state of mind he wrote *Small War on Murray Hill*, a sweet, romantic historical comedy with some similarities to *The Road to Rome*. Like that earlier play, *Small War on Murray Hill* involves a beautiful young wife whose influence prevents an experienced military leader from achieving his war aims. In the case of this new play, Bob's antiwar message is mixed with support for the patriotic cause of U.S. independence and liberty.

The play is set in 1776 in New York City, where General Sir William Howe is intent on destroying Israel Putnam's colonial troops before they can join up with George Washington's in Harlem Heights. After crossing the East River from Brooklyn to Manhattan, Howe and his aide, Lieutenant Lord Frederick Beckenham, stop to rest at the home of the Quaker and loyalist businessman Robert Murray and his wife, Mary. Unbeknownst to her husband, Mary is not only a supporter of the revolution but an informal spy who passes on to the colonial army information she gathers from her husband's offhand remarks. In this trio of Howe, Robert, and Mary there are echoes of Fabius Maximus, Hannibal, and Amytis of *The Road to Rome*. While Robert is away on business, Mary wines, dines, and has sex with Howe in order to stall him from attacking and to allow Putnam's troops to sneak away north. In the end, Howe suspects that he has been hoodwinked, but his attraction to Mary is so great that he merely makes light of it. When Robert returns, he of course suspects nothing.

Compared to the acerbic wit in *The Road to Rome*, the comments on war and peace in *Small War on Murray Hill* seem almost innocuous. Throughout the play there are references to Bob's persistent themes: that war is unnecessary; that if reason held sway, nations (and people) would not have to resort to violence. As Howe expresses it to Mary, "I'm sure that if common sense had prevailed, I should not be here, enforcing His Majesty's will at the point of a bayonet."[67] In response, she asks him if he believes this to be a "good war." "My dear lady," he exclaims, "no war is a good war—because no war is necessary. This one, especially, is a tragic folly." As a professional soldier (just like Hannibal), he simply has to "hold the responsibility—and I shall fight as hard, and as bitterly, and as brutally as I know how."[68] General Graf Von Donop of the mercenary Hessian troops is also a professional. As he tells Howe, he sees no reason for war other than as a job: "Patriotism should have no place in the conduct of war. And no more does your English conception of what you call 'sportsmanship.'"[69]

The difference between Amytis of *The Road to Rome* and Mary is that the latter sees a cause to fight for: liberty, independence, and basic freedoms. Howe asks Mary, "Is it worth it to endure starvation, hardship, leading to violent death—to redress wrongs which time itself could remedy?"[70] Bob himself favored nonviolent methods to achieve freedom, but he recognized from his World War II experience that violence can sometimes be necessary. So Mary tells Howe, "You showed me that the war is all tragic folly, but that you must fight it as hard and as bitterly and as brutally as you know how."[71] Besides having his characters debate whether war is necessary or not, Bob also mildly addresses his old idea that greed is the fuel for all wars. Samuel Judah, Mary's neighbor and fellow independence supporter, tells Mary, "It seems to me that if you dig into the roots of all the wars—or at least most of them—that have afflicted mankind, all of your channels of research will lead you back to one word: greed." For Bob, the exceptions were the antifascist struggles of the World War II era and the war against communism. Echoing the hymn in *Miss Liberty*, Bob has Samuel Judah express his dream of what an independent nation would be: "I am looking forward to a country which, if it can go ahead on its own—its own momentum—could prosper to a fabulous extent, an unlimited extent; and could provide a home for the homeless—a refuge, a haven, and—sanctuary."[72]

Before completing his revisions of *Small War on Murray Hill*, Bob spent three months writing and traveling for Michael Todd's planned film adaptation of Leo Tolstoy's novel *War and Peace*. Though disappointed when the venture fell through, Bob enthusiastically returned to his work on the play. For the first time in fifteen years, he told Roger Stevens, he was "in the extraordinary position of having nothing to work on except my own play—no movies, no television, no politics."[73] Hence, he was able to deliver his final draft of *Small War on Murray Hill* to the Playwrights' Company on July 19. He had hoped that Alfred Lunt might agree to direct it, but because of health problems and other commitments, he turned down the offer, although he loved the play. "It's exquisite," he wrote Bob after reading a draft in March, "& I hope the word will not offend—*redolent* with charm. *And* my dear Bob *every* character is *real* truly real. . . . In fact the whole thing is a triumph—it's like an American flag waving in a gentle breeze—a mighty pretty sight & I must say the Union Jack looks pretty too."[74] But Bob was tired and, as he soon discovered, ill as well. Before going ahead with choosing a director, cast, and designers, he and Madeline planned a brief vacation in Sun Valley, Idaho, where they had the loan of Averell Harriman's vacation home.

Just before leaving, however, Bob suffered "an unusual kind of stomach ache," as he told the Lunts. He persuaded Madeline to go on ahead while he had a few medical tests. Much to his surprise, the doctor informed him that "for years" he had been going around with a "diseased gall bladder which is stuffed to the gills with mineral formations."[75] He was told that since he was in no imminent danger, he should have a good time on vacation and then come back for a scheduled operation on August 17. Bob caught up with Madeline in Sun Valley, whose beautiful vistas and mysterious character gave him new ideas for a revision of *The Better Angels,* which he figured he could have ready for a possible production the next year. Idaho offered the "complete peace and quiet, health and relaxation" that he needed. As he wrote Victor Samrock, he hated to leave the place, as there were "no social obligations whatsoever."[76]

Three days after he returned to New York on August 9, Bob suffered such excruciating pain that he was rushed to Doctor's Hospital, where he required an emergency gallbladder operation followed by two weeks of recuperation. By the time he returned home, he had lost forty pounds and remained a bit shaky. Almost immediately, he left for ten quiet days of what he termed "lethargy and indolence" at Averell Harriman's home at Sands Point, Long Island.[77] Then, after being assured that he was completely cured, he returned to his daily ritual of lunch, along with a drink or two, at Dinty Moore's or Toots Shor's. Edna Ferber, who had had the same operation fourteen years earlier, advised Bob to avoid any exertion. He responded that he was happy to do so. In fact, the avoidance of banquets, luncheons, awards ceremonies, and other social gatherings put him in a "happy mood," so much so, in fact, he told Ferber that he had "decided never to recover from this lovely condition." In early October, however, he suffered "such an attack of violent nausea" as he had not experienced since World War I. The doctor assured him that it was only a common virus ("all viruses are now common") and not related to the operation. Soon he felt better, though again "a shade shaken."[78]

Also, beginning in late September, he suffered another long siege of *tic douloureux*. Every day Bob had two or three attacks. He noted in his diary that this bout was "the worst" he had ever experienced "for frequency," and his "consumption of dope" was "appalling."[79] Over the years he had tried all sorts of treatments for his headaches and even considered an operation at Johns Hopkins Hospital. The procedure was a simple one that involved cutting the affected nerve at a point in the cheek between the eye and ear, but since in his case the pain was on both sides of his face at different times, the doctors warned that he could suffer partial facial paralysis. He chose to try medications instead. Early in the 1950s a doctor recommended thiamin chloride tablets, which offered some relief. Then he was switched to Theragran vitamin pills, which, as he told a fellow sufferer, were "powerless to stop the pain" but may have increased his resistance to the attacks. Now he turned once again to the "emergency remedies" he always carried with him— Empirin, codeine, Demerol, Seconal, and "even a few morphine tablets."[80]

Throughout October, Bob saw a physician almost every day, sometimes remaining at home because the pain was so severe and continuous. On October 22, in a period of seven hours, he took four Seconals and four codeine pills, and when the pain still persisted, he resorted to "of all things Absorbine Jr.," a "counter-irritant" lotion that dulled the pain enough so that he could sleep.[81] Two days later he recorded in his diary that his "consumption of dope" must be a "record," and noted: "Workless days of drugged drowsiness, aching eyes. How long, O Lord?" After continual attacks between 1:50 and 4:05 in the morning, the pain subsided, but he then took more drugs to ensure that he could get some sleep. Still, at 6:35, the torture began again. "Terribly sleepy—difficult to get up," he wrote. "Demoral fixed this one quickly."[82] After six weeks, the attacks took a brief break.

Meanwhile, Bob tried in every way he could to move forward on the production of *Small War on Murray Hill*, but his headaches and general ill health made casting problematic. As a result, on November 2 he informed the Playwrights' Company that it might be necessary to postpone the play until the next fall's season. Elmer Rice noticed that his friend "looked gaunt and haggard."[83] Four days later the "*tic* pains" began again, though not as severely as the previous month. More frightening were "the heart flutterings and falterings," which sent him running for the codeine bottle.[84] He came to the conclusion that it was heartburn, but as a precaution, on November 7 he visited his physician. After taking his blood pressure and listening to his heart, the doctor assured him that all was well but arranged an appointment for him to see a heart specialist on November 23. Bob never made that appointment. For a week he staggered through a sleepless combination of sharp headaches, painkillers, and weak attempts to continue working.

In an effort to improve his health, Bob and Madeline made plans to sail for England early in December. Perhaps the sea voyage would be good for him, and while in England he could find an actor to play the lead in *Small War on Murray Hill* and complete revisions on *The Better Angels*. On November 9 he had lunch with Little Mary and seven-year-old Joe, then went to see a performance of the new musical *Damn Yankees*, which, true Yankee fan that he was, he loved. On November 11 he again attempted to write, but noted in his diary, "Have many ideas, but the minute I try to work, I feel dead."[85] It became more difficult for him to summon the energy to do anything, as his body rebelled against every effort. Still, no one anticipated the major heart attack that, on November 14, would kill him within hours. He was only fifty-nine years old.

Bob's sister Ros wrote Jane de Glehn: "The infected gall bladder pulled him down, but this heart attack came out of the blue. What a terrible shock it has been and what a time of anguish!"[86] Madeline was in a state of shock, but she did not allow her private feelings to show in public. She chose not to have an open coffin or visitations in the funeral parlor but instead opened her and Bob's home for two days to the approximately eighty visitors who joined her there and talked. Little Mary, who had become close to Bob, Madeline, and Mary after her separation from Bud Stillman, was especially grief-stricken. Although they had had their difficulties, her father had been the one stable factor in her troubled life. Jane de Glehn, who was too frail even to consider traveling to New York, described the news of her nephew's death as "quite a physical shock as well as the grief."[87] She later attended a memorial held for him in England but could not bring herself to speak to anyone, her sorrow was so great.

Funeral services were held on a depressingly rainy November 16 at St.

George's Episcopal Church, the same family church where Bob had bid farewell to his mother. The Reverend Edward O. Miller led the services, while a choir of forty voices sang hymns. More than five hundred people attended, including some of the biggest names in show business and politics. Of course, Bob's family and the surviving members of the Playwrights' Company were there in full force, and so were Bob's political friends Sam Rosenman and Averell Harriman. Other celebrities included Bob's co-creators and friends: Irving Berlin, Joshua Logan, Gilbert Miller, Robert Whitehead, Raymond Massey, Edna Ferber, Edward R. Murrow, Samuel Goldwyn, and of course Alfred Lunt and Lynn Fontanne. Even Marc Connelly, who occasionally had lunch with Bob, came to pay his respects. Maxwell Anderson wrote the eulogy, which Alfred Lunt delivered. It was an unemotional piece of writing which Ros thought suffered from having been written too hastily. She told Jane that it was "one of those things that didn't quite come off as he meant it." [88] In actuality, Anderson was so distraught that he found it "difficult to write or talk about" Bob's death. [89]

After the funeral, friends gathered in Bob and Madeline's apartment. Toots Shor set up a buffet and bar and sent over a couple of waiters to serve the guests. About a hundred people dropped in for what Quentin Reynolds described as a "very animated, not depressing" affair. Madeline kept herself busy greeting people, seeing that they had food and drinks, and emptying ashtrays. Guests shared anecdotes about Bob, all "pleasant . . . that evoked chuckles, not tears." Samuel Goldwyn, Reynolds noted, told everyone that the previous week he and Bob had talked about a new project on the life of Thomas Jefferson. "The deal was all set. Now Sam said he had about decided to abandon it. 'Who in hell else knew Jefferson but Bob?' Goldwyn said seriously." Joe DiMaggio, one of Bob's special Yankee heroes whom he often met at Toots Shor's, attended the funeral and the apartment gathering afterwards. "He doesn't drink, you know," Reynolds wrote, "but when he heard that Bob had died he sat up most of the night getting blind with Toots" and then hired a horse-drawn carriage and told the driver to circle Central Park while he thought about Bob. [90] Meanwhile, Averell Harriman and Sam Rosenman complained that Maxwell Anderson's eulogy had ignored Bob's political side, only mentioning his work in the theater. As Harriman told Reynolds: "Look around the apartment. Maybe a third of those here are from the theatre. But there are judges and politicians with whom Bob worked during the FDR days. There are sports writers and saloon keepers—all part of Bob's life." [91]

Madeline received hundreds of letters of sympathy, but perhaps the most moving came from her sister-in-law Ros. "You have been the perfect woman for him," Ros wrote. "You have understood him, nurtured him, loved him and brought him to a glorious maturity he never would have achieved without you. What can anyone ask?" [92] The others expressed a mix of personal anguish and professional admiration. Thornton Wilder, Mayor Robert F. Wagner, Irene Mayer Selznick, Leonard Lyons, Herbert Lehman, and Brooks Atkinson were but a few who praised Bob's talent and commented on their grief that the nation had lost one of its literary and political treasures. More personal messages came from those who had worked or played with him. Elmer Rice told Madeline that he had made a donation to the NAACP in Bob's name to honor his passing. Grace Tully, Franklin Roosevelt's secretary, expressed her "great sense of personal loss of a dear friend and a great American." [93] Adlai Stevenson felt the loss deeply, wiring Madeline: "I am heartbroken. This is one of the saddest days in my life." [94] Toots Shor credited Bob's friendship with "any good" he had ever done in the world because Bob "showed me how to be decent to everybody." [95] Perhaps Sam Behrman summed up everyone's feelings best when he wrote, "In a unique way, Sherwood combined [a] sense of fun with the most inexorable determination and self-discipline in behalf of any cause he believed to be right." [96] Behrman considered him "one of the most remarkable and admirable men I have ever known. His integrity was inviolable; on any question of principle he would be burned at the stake rather than abdicate an inch." [97]

Epilogue

MANY PEOPLE gathered to honor Robert Sherwood after his death. ANTA, of which he had been one of the creators and presidents, held a memorial to him on November 29 which attracted more than three hundred people. A host of theater people spoke, among them Sam Rosenman, Moss Hart, and Elmer Rice, and the newsman Charles Collingwood. The Dramatists Guild established a yearly award to be given in Bob's memory to a Columbia University student in the Theatre Arts Division of the School of the Arts. The Fund for the Republic, of which Bob was the director at the time of his death, established the Robert E. Sherwood award for television programs that addressed issues of "liberty and justice."[1] In the second year of its existence the Ford Foundation funded the prize, allocating $20,000 for the best network drama, $20,000 for the best network documentary, and $15,000 for the best program in either class presented by an independent station. Finally, the Hasty Pudding Institute of Harvard University dedicated a lounge and fireplace in his name.

The Playwrights' Company discussed several possibilities for honoring Bob, ranging from participating in television presentations of his work to following through on the productions of *Small War on Murray Hill* and *The Better Angels*. Over the next few years condensed versions of *The Petrified Forest, Abe Lincoln in Illinois, There Shall Be No Night*, and *Waterloo Bridge* appeared on television from time to time. *The Better Angels* eventually fell by the wayside, but the company, with Madeline's support, went ahead with its production of *Small War on Murray Hill*. Garson Kanin eagerly took on the task of co-producing and directing the play, which finally went into rehearsals in the fall of 1956, a year after Bob's death, opening on Broadway on January 3, 1957, to mediocre reviews. Robert Coleman of the *Daily News* called it "amiable but small" and not "top-shelf Sherwood." He found the experience "a bit disappointing."[2] John McClain of the *Journal American* agreed. For him, the play was "regretfully . . . disappointing" in its light-hearted consideration "of war and its mixed motives."[3] Brooks Atkinson of the *New York Times* called it a "little anecdote from the American Revolution . . . missing [Bob's] humor—the drollery and geniality of his earliest plays."[4] Finally, Walter F. Kerr of the *Herald Tribune* summed up what most reviewers and audience members felt: "He never quite came back to the brisk, colorful, ironic, bumptious, sometimes savage and sometimes funny world of the practical theater; the theater that is a satisfying end in itself. . . . [T]hat ship that could once be swung freely and with a sort of laughter was permanently hung on the wall; the satirist had turned quietly reflective."[5] *Small War on Murray Hill* lasted only twelve performances, a grave disappointment to all those who had loved and respected Robert Sherwood. Madeline wrote to the Lunts: "I believe it deserved a better fate, but what can one do? It's expensive to keep going, and, as you well know, it's impossible to nurse a play along these days." Madeline felt that the critics had expected "too much" from Bob, and that had the play been written by "some little-known author," the reviews would have been "different."[6]

The Playwrights' Company never recovered from the impact of Bob's death. As John Wharton put it: "The Company disintegrated at an astonishingly rapid pace. It was a remarkable example of what can happen to a group of people when the leadership changes."[7] With Bob at the helm, the organization truly was a playwrights' company; with Roger L. Stevens leading the effort, it became just another producing venture—and not a very successful one at that. Of the twenty-seven plays produced after Bob's death, only five ran for more than 200 performances: Jean Anouilh's *Time Remembered*; Samuel Taylor and Cornelia Otis Skinner's *The Pleasure of His Company*; Alec Coppel's *The Gazebo*; Peter Shaffer's *Five Finger Exercise* (with a substantial run of 337 performances and twenty-nine weeks on the road); and, the company's final production, Gore Vidal's *The Best Man,* a major success that ran for 520 performances and had a twenty-week tour. Although *The Best Man* was a solid hit, it was during its run that the company filed a certificate of dissolution on June 30, 1960, less than five years since Bob's death and a year after Maxwell Anderson's.

Madeline, despite showing great control and fortitude following Bob's death, was of course deeply grieved. For some time she concentrated on answering the hundreds of condolence letters that arrived and then paid careful attention to the production of *Small War on Murray Hill* and other plans being made to honor Bob and potentially revive his plays. To an even greater degree, she had to deal with her emotional turmoil and with very practical concerns as well. As Ros wrote to Jane, Madeline "worshiped [Bob] and he adored the ground she walked on."[8] But Bob had experienced so many ups and downs in his financial fortunes that Madeline found herself in need of drastically cutting expenses. Within three months of his death, she moved out of their large Sutton Place apartment to a smaller one at 29 East Sixty-fourth Street. Ros noted, "It has been a big chore for her and an awful wrench to leave her old home where she has lived with Bob for 18 years." Although Madeline had "bad cold feet" about the move, Ros felt it was helpful for her to keep busy and to get away from "that big, lonely apartment." Madeline's friends admired her courage, but Ros knew it was only a front. "Her whole behavior has been marvelous beyond words," she told Jane, "but she is a terribly afflicted, sad, lonely woman."[9]

Bob's death seems to have brought Madeline closer to the Sherwoods, whom she sought out "in a way she has never done before," noted Ros, but she chose to shun Little Mary, refusing even to give her a memento from Bob's desk. Madeline had "loads of good friends" who kept a constant watch over her, taking care not to leave her alone for too long a time and inviting her to join them for dinner or entertainment. Ros felt confident that she would "gradually work herself into a new life," but she worried about her "none too robust" finances. "Filthy lucre was not a part of the great legacy Bob has left behind," she noted.[10] Still, Madeline owned his unproduced works and many of the others, and perhaps these would ensure her a steady income. To her final days, Madeline Sherwood took care of her husband's affairs, ensuring that his legacy would be available to future scholars and artists by donating his papers to the Houghton Library at Harvard University. She died on Bob's birthday, April 4, 1989.

Little Mary was the most tragically affected by her father's death. By September 2, 1956, she was in New York Hospital with a nervous breakdown and a bad attack of alcohol-induced jaundice. Under a psychiatrist's care, she continued treatment in a sanatorium after her release from the hospital. In December of the same year, the young woman, like her father before her, spent six weeks in Reno obtaining a divorce. It seemed to her aunt Rosamund that the "intense unhappiness of her wretched marriage" and her "complete lack of maturity" and "finally, the loss of her father who was her bulwark" had all compounded to cause her "to fly into a thousand pieces." Ros blamed Bud for the "terrible things" he had done to Little Mary's "mind and soul." She felt that "his crazy theories and violent hatreds" had "kept Mary's mind in an unhealthy turmoil" throughout their ten years of marriage.[11] Little Mary struggled with her psychological problems and her addictions for the next six years. During that time she remarried, becoming Mary Sherwood Elms. That marriage, too, ended in divorce. So despondent was she about the breakup that on Christmas Day 1962 she slashed her wrists with a razor and was found dead in her Manhattan apartment.

Robert Sherwood himself fell out of history. Although several of his plays and films, and of course *Roosevelt and Hopkins*, are still well known, people do not associate them with a man by the name of Robert Emmet Sherwood.

The Best Years of Our Lives, Abe Lincoln in Illinois, The Petrified Forest, Waterloo Bridge, The Bishop's Wife, and *Rebecca* appear regularly on cable television. Yet his strongest political works, in particular *The Road to Rome, Idiot's Delight,* and *There Shall Be No Night,* are hardly known at all. Perhaps the problem for Robert Sherwood was that the loss of his ability to frame a message to fit the times killed his writing career, or perhaps his denigration of his own pacifist plays drove them into oblivion. From 1927 to 1940 his plays spoke to the political concerns that most deeply affected his audiences—the desire for peace, no matter the cost to the rest of the world, and then the fear that fascism would spread from Europe to infect American shores. After World War II, Bob was politically confused. He still entertained a longing for the end of war and a socially just world, but he got caught in the Cold War trap of equating communism with Nazism and lost his way in his writing. By the time he tried to include some sort of antiwar message in *Small War on Murray Hill,* his ideas had become dated. The nuclear arms race and Cold War confrontations around the globe had frightened the public, and there was little room for generalities about peaceful coexistence, although there was still some opportunity to speak out against the effects of nuclear testing.

It would have been interesting to see what might have happened if Robert Sherwood had survived into even the earliest years of the Vietnam War. In 1954, after the French defeat at Dienbienphu, he called the ensuing Geneva conference a "dismal failure" in its purpose of ensuring peace and democracy in the region.[12] At that moment he seemed to be awakening to the reality of U.S. Cold War imperialism. By the next year he feared that U.S. involvement in places like Vietnam, Korea, and China would exacerbate the possibility of war because the government felt the need to "prove that our mighty nation is not a 'paper tiger.'" Bob felt "inarticulate frustration" over the Eisenhower administration's policies. "One gets the impression," he said, "that there is an impenetrable iron curtain between the White House and the thinking world."[13] In the 1960s, when the antiwar voice was raised to its loudest pitch in the nation's history, how would Robert Sherwood have reacted? Would he have been one of the first to publicly protest U.S. involvement in Vietnam, as his 1955 statement might indicate? Would the antiwar movement once again have inspired his creative voice and pushed him in new directions? Or would he have toed the Cold War line, which held that Vietnam was just one more domino in danger of falling to communist tyranny? We will, of course, never know the answers to these questions, but one thing we can be sure of—Robert Sherwood would have been right in the middle of the debate.

Notes

Abbreviations

AS	Arthur Sherwood Sr.
AW	Alexander Woollcott
b.	box
CS/CST	Cynthia Sherwood; after marriage Cynthia Sherwood Townsend
EFP:Smithsonian	Emmet Family Papers, 1792–1989. Archives of American Art, Smithsonian Institution
FDR	Franklin Delano Roosevelt
f.	folder
HGARC/BU	Howard Gotlieb Archival Research Center, Boston University
HH	Harry Hopkins
HHU	Houghton Library of Harvard University
HUA	Harvard University Archives
JE/JED	Jane Emmet; after marriage Jane Emmet de Glehn
L/F	Alfred Lunt and Lynn Fontanne
LFE	Lydia Field Emmet
MBS	Mary Brandon Sherwood
MHS	Madeline Hurlock Sherwood
mr	microfilm reel
MSJr	Mary Sherwood (daughter)
NAC,O	National Archives of Canada, Ottawa
n.d.	no date
NYPL/42nd Street	New York Public Library, Forty-second Street
NYPL/LC	New York Public Library for the Performing Arts, Lincoln Center
PCA/AMPAS	Production Code Administration Records, Academy of Motion Picture Arts and Sciences
PPC	Playwrights Producing Company
PS	Philip Sherwood
RES	Robert Emmet Sherwood
RosS	Rosina Emmet Sherwood (Posie)
SCH:UCB	Sidney Coe Howard Papers, The Bancroft Library, University of California, Berkeley
SHSW	The State Historical Society of Wisconsin, Madison

SNB   S. N. Behrman
WD   William Donovan

Prologue

1. RosS to LFE, June 1901, MS Storage 275, b. 1, RES:HHU.

2. Quoted in Susan Zeiger, "Finding a Cure for War: Women's Politics and the Peace Movement in the 1920s," *Journal of Social History* 24 (Fall 1990): 69–86.

1. Being an Emmet and a Sherwood

1. Information on Thomas Addis Emmet and Robert Emmet culled from Helen Landreth, *The Pursuit of Robert Emmet* (New York: McGraw Hill, 1948); John Chartres Molony, *Ireland's Tragic Comedians* (1935; reprint, Freeport, N.Y.: Books for Libraries Press, 1970); R. W. Postgate, *Dear Robert Emmet* (New York: Vanguard Press, 1932); and W. E. Vaughan, ed., *A New History of Ireland,* vol. 5, *Ireland under the Union, I (1801–70)* (Oxford: Clarendon Press, 1989).

2. Grenville Temple Emmet Jr., interviewed in *The Emmet Video* by Nancy B. Doyle, Jon Child, and Marian L. Schwartz, 1988, EPF:Smithsonian.

3. Information on the Emmet family's background derived from "Tales of Old New York," mr4754, ser. 1, b. 1, EFP:Smithsonian; *The Emmet Video*; and Donald Roper, "Thomas Addis Emmet," in *American National Biography,* ed. John A. Garraty and Mark C. Carnes, 24 vols. (New York: Oxford University Press, 1999), 7:501–502.

4. See Thomas Addis Emmet, *The Emmet Family, with some incidents relating to Irish history and a biographical sketch of Prof. John Patten Emmet, M.D., and other members* (New York: Bradstreet Press, 1898).

5. Cited in Landreth, *Pursuit of Robert Emmet,* 352; and Postgate, *Dear Robert Emmet,* 250.

6. Grenville Temple Emmet Jr. in *The Emmet Video.*

7. Information on Elias Boudinot derived from "Boudinot Family History," typescript, mr4754, ser. 1, b. 1, EFP:Smithsonian; and H. James Henderson, "Elias Boudinot," in Garraty and Carnes, *American National Biography,* 3:243–245. The "Boudinot Family History" typescript is not very accurate, however.

8. Cited in Henderson, "Elias Boudinot," 244.

9. Information on the Sherwood family's background derived from M. E. W. Sherwood, *An Epistle to Posterity: Being Rambling Recollections of Many Years of My Life* (New York: Harper and Brothers Publishers, 1897); and Joann E. Castagna, "Mary Elizabeth Wilson Sherwood," in Garraty and Carnes, *American National Biography,* 19:828–829.

10. RES to Robert H. Sherwood, September 30, 1954, bMSAm1947, f. 1507, RES:HHU.

11. RES, "Remarks at Kent School," typescript, November 16, 1954, bMSAm1947, f. 2255, RES:HHU.

12. M.E.W. Sherwood, *Epistle to Posterity*, 57.

13. RES to the Honorable Hugo L. Black, May 21, 1945, bMSAm1947, f. 990, RES:HHU.

14. RES, "Remarks at Kent School."

15. Background on Posie's siblings derived from primary sources: Martha J. Hoppin, *The Emmets: A Family of Women Painters* (Pittsfield, Mass.: Berkshire Museum, 1982); Daniel Martin Dumych, "William Le Roy Emmet," in Garraty and Carnes, *American National Biography*, 7:503–504; and Jeanne Madeline Weimann, *The Fair Women* (Chicago: Academy Chicago, 1981).

16. Background information on William Jenkins and Julia Colt Pierson Emmet derived from William Le Roy Emmet, *The Autobiography of an Engineer* (Albany, N.Y.: Fort Orange Press, 1931.)

17. Unsigned, "Of Interest: Rosina Emmet Sherwood," *International Institute Bulletin* (March 1950), mr4754, ser. 1, b. 1, EFP:Smithsonian.

18. For information on Candace Wheeler, see Anthea Callen, *Women Artists of the Arts and Crafts Movement, 1870–1914* (New York: Pantheon Books, 1979).

19. RosS to William Le Roy Sherwood, January 17, 1881, mr4755, ser. 3B, b. 1, EFP:Smithsonian.

20. RosS to Philip Sherwood, August 2, 1882, mr4755, ser. 3B, b. 1, EFP:Smithsonian.

21. Background information on the Women's Building derived from Weimann, *The Fair Women*.

22. Ibid., 262.

2. Born to Be a Ham

1. RosS to JED, April 5, 1939, mr4763, ser. 3B, b. 6, EFP:Smithsonian.

2. RosS to LFE, 1901, MS Storage 275, b. 1, RES:HHU.

3. RosS diary, 1903, mr4754, ser. 2, b. 1B, EFP:Smithsonian.

4. JE to LFE, September 10, 1897, mr4755, ser. 3B, b. 2, EFP:Smithsonian.

5. JE to LFE, December 20, 1897, mr4755, ser. 3B, b. 2, EFP:Smithsonian.

6. RosS to LFE, January 11, 1898, mr4755, ser. 3B, b. 2, EFP:Smithsonian.

7. RosS to LFE, May 5, 1897, MS Storage 275, b. 1, RES:HHU.

8. RosS diary, 1899, mr4754, ser. 2B, b. 1, EFP:Smithsonian.

9. JE to LFE, February 3, 1898, mr4755, ser. 3B, b. 2, EFP:Smithsonian.

10. JE to RosS, March 15, 1898, mr4756, ser. 3B, b. 2, EFP:Smithsonian.

11. RES, "'Deers and wild pings in a wood' drawing, at 3 yrs and 11 months," MS Storage 275, b. 1, RES:HHU.

12. RES drawing, n.d., MS Storage 275, b. 1, RES:HHU.

13. RosS to LFE, 1904, MS Storage 275, b. 1, RES:HHU.

14. Gretchen Finletter, *From the Top of the Stairs* (Boston: Little, Brown, 1946), 225.

15. LFE to Julia Colt Emmet, July 25, 1904, mr4756, ser. 3B, b. 2, EFP:Smithsonian.

16. RosS to Julia Colt Emmet, 1904, MS Storage 275, b. 1, RES:HHU.

17. RosS to Julia Colt Emmet, 1903, MS Storage 275, b. 1, RES:HHU.

18. RosS to Julia Colt Emmet, July 5, 1904, MS Storage 275, b. 1, RES:HHU.

19. RES, "The Show," typescript, March 1, 1955, bMSAm1947, f. 2162, RES: HHU.

20. "The Original Schoolroom, 1908," photo, www.fayschool.org/about_history4 .html.

21. RosS to LFE, April 28, 1904, MS Storage 275, b. 1, RES:HHU.

22. LFE to Julia Colt Emmet, April 6, 1905, mr4757, ser. 3B, b. 3, EFP:Smithsonian.

23. RosS to Julia Colt Emmet, January 19, 1906, mr4758, ser. 3B, b. 3, EFP:Smithsonian.

24. Julia Colt Emmet to JED, October 5, 1906, mr4758, ser. 3B, b. 3, EFP:Smithsonian.

25. RosS to Julia Colt Emmet, November, 1907, MS Storage 275, b. 1, RES: HHU.

26. Julia Colt Emmet to JED, July 3, 1905, mr4757, ser. 3B, b. 3, EFP:Smithsonian.

27. Julia Colt Emmet to LFE, April 12, 1905, mr4757, ser. 3B, b. 3, EFP:Smithsonian.

28. LFE to JED, June 23, 1905, mr4757, ser. 3B, b. 3, EFP:Smithsonian.

29. RosS to Julia Colt Emmet, August, 1907, mr4758, ser. 3B, b. 3, EFP:Smithsonian.

30. RES to RosS, 1908, MS Storage 275, b. 2, RES:HHU.

31. RosS to Julia Colt Emmet, November, 1907, MS Storage 275, b. 1, RES: HHU.

32. RosS to CS, n.d., mr4759, ser. 3B, b. 3, EFP:Smithsonian.

33. RosS to Julia Colt Emmet, n.d., mr4759, ser. 3B, b. 3, EFP:Smithsonian.

34. RosS to Julia Colt Emmet, November, 1907, MS Storage 275, b. 1, RES:HHU.

35. Finletter, *From the Top of the Stairs*, 221.

36. Ibid.

37. Ibid., 223.

38. See Allen Woll, *Black Musical Theatre: From Coontown to Dreamgirls* (1989; reprint, New York: Da Capo Press, 1991).

39. Finletter, *From the Top of the Stairs*, 229.

40. Ibid., 230.

41. Ibid.

42. Ibid., 232.

43. RosS to LFE, September, 1909, mr4759, ser. 3B, b. 3, EFP:Smithsonian.

44. Julia Colt Emmet to JED, November 3, 1907, mr4759, ser. 3B, b. 3, EFP: Smithsonian.

45. RES, "Ode on the Wedding," n.d., MS Storage 275, b. 1, RES:HHU.

46. "A Brief History of Milton Academy," www.milton.edu/about/pages/history .asp. Account of Sherwood's experience at the school based on primary sources and John Mason Brown, *The Worlds of Robert E. Sherwood: Mirror to His Times, 1896–1939* (1962; reprint, New York: Harper & Row, 1965).

47. "Marks" episode related ibid., 61–63.

48. RES cited ibid.

49. RosS to LFE, n.d., mr4759, ser. 3B, b. 4, EFP:Smithsonian.

50. RES, "Prologue," in *Milton Orange and Blue* 22, no. 1 (October 1913), MS Storage 275, b. 1, RES:HHU.

51. RES Milton Academy transcript, 1912–1914, RES Records:HUA.

52. RES cited in Brown, *Worlds*, 65.

3. From Soldier to Pacifist

1. RosS to LFE, "Friday, 1914," mr4759, ser. 3B, b. 4, EFP:Smithsonian.

2. RosS to LFE, n.d., mr4759, ser. 3B, b. 4, EFP:Smithsonian.

3. AS to Henry A. Yeomans, March 27, 1915, RES Records:HUA.

4. Henry A. Yeomans to RES, March 29, 1915, RES Records:HUA.

5. RosS to Henry A. Yeomans, April 2, 1915, RES Records:HUA.

6. B. S. Hurlbut to RES, June 4, 1915, RES Records:HUA.

7. AS to B. S. Hurlbut, July 26, 1915, RES Records:HUA.

8. F. S. Cowley to Professor H. C. Bierwirth, December 22, 1915(?), RES Records: HUA.

9. AS to Henry A. Yeomans, December 28, 1915, RES Records:HUA.

10. AS to B. S. Hurlbut, May 31, 1916, RES Records:HUA.

11. RES, "Remarks at Kent School," typescript, November 16, 1954, bMSAm1947, f. 2255, RES:HHU.

12. RosS to Helena (Nelly) Phelps, April 17, 1917, mr4759, ser. 3B, b. 4, EFP: Smithsonian.

13. RosS to LFE, n.d., mr4759, ser. 3B, b. 4, EFP:Smithsonian.

14. RosS to Henry A. Yeomans, February 11, 1917, RES Records:HUA.

15. Arthur Sherwood Jr. to C. C. (Pete) Little, March 22, 1917, RES Records:HUA.

16. LFE to Mrs. W. J. Emmet, April 4 and 5, 1898, mr4756, ser. 3B, b. 2, EFP: Smithsonian.

17. AS to LFE, April 26, 1898, mr4756, ser. 3B, b. 2, EFP:Smithsonian.

18. Russo-Japanese War story told by John Mason Brown, *The Worlds of Robert E. Sherwood: Mirror to His Times, 1896–1939* (1965; reprint, New York: Harper and Row, 1962), 24.

19. RES Drawing Books, 1907, MS Storage 275, b. 1, RES:HHU.

20. Cited in Brown, *Worlds*, 93.

21. "Lyons Den" column, *Boston Herald*, June 24, 1951, clipping, RES Biography File:HUA.

22. "Lyons Den" column, *Boston Herald*, April 4, 1950, clipping, RES Biography File:HUA.

23. RES, "Convocation Afterthoughts," handwritten notes, ca. 1950, bMSAm1947, f. 2233, RES:HHU.

24. AS to Mr. Cram, July 17, 1917, RES Records:HUA.

25. Attestation Paper, RES, Personnel Records:NAC,O.

26. Medical Record, RES, Personnel Records:NAC,O.

27. RosS to JED, January 17, 1918, mr4759, ser. 3B, b. 4, EFP:Smithsonian.

28. F. Maurice Child, clipping, n.d., MS Storage 275, b. 2, RES:HHU.

29. RosS to LFE, n.d., mr4759, ser. 3B, b. 4, EFP: Smithsonian.

30. Thomas Dinesen, *Merry Hell! A Dane with the Canadians*, translated from Danish (London: Jarrolds Publishers, 1930), 71.

31. F. Maurice Child to CS, February 21, 1918, MS Storage 275, b. 2, RES:HHU.

32. RES, "Convocation Afterthoughts."

33. RosS to LFE, n.d., MS Storage 275, b. 1, RES:HHU.

34. PS to RosS, March 8 [no year], mr4759, ser. 3B, b. 4, EFP: Smithsonian.

35. Dinesen, *Merry Hell!*, 102.

36. RES, "Convocation Afterthoughts."

37. RES to AS, April 6, 1918, MS Storage 275, b. 2, RES:HHU.

38. Dinesen, *Merry Hell!*, 109.

39. Letter to Editor of the *Tribune*, June 12, 1918, MS Storage 275, b. 2, RES: HHU.

40. RES to LFE, September 11, 1918, typescript letters and extracts, MS Storage 275, b. 2, RES:HHU.

41. Thomas Dinesen to JED, October 30, 1957, MS Storage 275, b. 2, RES: HHU.

42. RES to RosS, June 21, 1918, typescript letters and extracts, MS Storage 275, b. 2, RES:HHU.

43. Unsigned article, "King's Tallest Soldier Here," *Boston Herald*, February 17, 1919, clipping, MS Storage 275, b. 2, RES:HHU.

44. RES to RosS, June 21, 1918, typescript letters and extracts, MS Storage 275, b. 2, RES:HHU.

45. RES to RosS, n.d., typescript letters and extracts, MS Storage 275, b. 2, RES:HHU.

46. RES to RosS, n.d., typescript letters and extracts, MS Storage 275, b. 2, RES:HHU.

47. Dinesen, *Merry Hell!*, 126.

48. Article XXIIIa of the Second Hague Peace Conference agreements cited in L. F. Haber, *The Poisonous Cloud: Chemical Warfare in the First World War* (Oxford: Clarendon Press, 1986), 19.

49. Medical Case Sheet, RES, Personnel Records:NAC,O.

50. Cited in Colonel G. W. L. Nicholson, *Canadian Expeditionary Force, 1914–1919 (Official History)* (Ottawa: Queen's Printer and Controller of Stationery, 1962), 389.

51. Ibid., 398.

52. RES to RosS, n.d., typescript letters and extracts, MS Storage 275, b. 2, RES: HHU.

53. RES to RosS, n.d., typescript letters and extracts, MS Storage 275, b. 2, RES: HHU.

54. RES to RosS, n.d., typescript letters and extracts, MS Storage 275, b. 2, RES: HHU.

55. Brown, *Worlds,* 119.

56. RES to RosS, August 26, 1918, typescript letters and extracts, MS Storage 275, b. 2, RES:HHU.

57. LFE to JED, January 21, 1919, mr4760, ser. 3B, b. 4, EFP:Smithsonian.

58. Casualty Form, Active Service and Medical Case Sheet, RES, Personnel Records:NAC,O.

59. Medical History of an Invalid, RES, Personnel Records:NAC,O.

60. Thomas Dinesen to JED, October 30, 1957, MS Storage 275, b. 2, RES: HHU.

61. Medical History of an Invalid, RES, Personnel Records:NAC,O.

62. RES to CST, August 26, 1918, MS Storage 275, b. 2, RES:HHU.

63. Cited in Nicholson, *Canadian Expeditionary Force,* 424.

64. Cited ibid., 400.

65. RES to RosS, n.d., typescript letters and extracts, MS Storage 275, b. 2, RES: HHU.

66. RES to PS, September 15, 1918, MS Storage 275, b. 2, RES:HHU.

67. RES to RosS, November 18, 1918, typescript letters and extracts, MS Storage 275, b. 2, RES:HHU.

68. RES to RosS, November 15, 1918, typescript letters and extracts, MS Storage 275, b. 2, RES:HHU.

69. Ibid.; RES, preface to *Waterloo Bridge* (New York: Charles Scribner's Sons, 1930), xxi.

70. RosS to LFE, 1919, MS Storage 275, b. 1, RES:HHU.

71. LFE to JED, January 21, 1919, mr4760, ser. 3B, b. 4, EFP:Smithsonian.

72. All related in RosS to MSJr, October 1928, MS Storage 275, b. 2, RES:HHU. This letter, written to RES's daughter when she was only five, may have been meant for posterity, or else RosS misdated it.

73. Medical Records, RES, Personnel Records:NAC,O.

4. Life after the War

1. RosS to LFE, April 5, 1919, mr4760, ser. 3B, b. 4, EFP:Smithsonian.

2. RES to Norman Cousins, July 7, 1949, bMSAm1947, f. 1065, RES:HHU.

3. RosS to LFE, 1919, MS Storage 275, b. 1, RES:HHU.

4. LFE to JED, November 17, 1920, mr4760, ser. 3B, b. 4, EFP:Smithsonian.

5. RES to Nathaniel Benchley, January 4, 1955, bMSAm1947, f. 978, RES:HHU; also in Robert Benchley Papers, HGARC/BU.

6. RES quoted in Nathaniel Benchley, foreword to *Robert Benchley* (New York: McGraw-Hill, 1955), xiii–xiv.

7. RES, "Remarks at Kent School," typescript, November 16, 1954, bMSAm1947, f. 2255, RES:HHU.

8. RES to Nathaniel Benchley, January 4, 1955, bMSAm1947, f. 978, RES:HHU; also in Robert Benchley Papers, HGARC/BU.

9. RES, "The Wanderings of a Column Hound," *Vanity Fair* 13, no. 7 (October 1919): 67. (The magazine made errors in the numbering of its issues. I have followed the numbering on the title page.)

10. RES, "The Blood Lust on Broadway," *Vanity Fair* 13, no. 9 (December 1919): 69.

11. RES, "If Shakespeare Were on Broadway," *Vanity Fair* 14, no. 2 (April 1920): 59, 108.

12. SNB, "Old Monotonous: Robert E. Sherwood," in *The Suspended Drawing Room* (New York: Stein and Day, 1965), 138–139.

13. Barry Day, ed., *Dorothy Parker In Her Own Words* (Lanham, Md.: Taylor Trade Publishing, 2004), xiii (RES), 17 (Dorothy Parker).

14. Ibid., 17.

15. Background information on the Algonquin Round Table culled from Margaret Case Harriman, *The Vicious Circle: The Story of the Algonquin Round Table* (New York: Rinehart, 1951), and James R. Gaines, *Wit's End: Days and Nights of the Algonquin Round Table* (New York: Harcourt Brace Jovanovich, 1977).

16. RES to Nathaniel Benchley, January 4, 1955, bMSAm1947, f. 978, RES:HHU; also in Robert Benchley Papers, HGARC/BU.

17. Quoted in Day, *Dorothy Parker In Her Own Words*, 33–34.

18. Quoted in Robert E. Drennan, ed., *The Algonquin Wits: Bon Mots, Wisecracks, Epigrams, and Gags* (1968; reprint, New York: Citadel Press Books, 1985), 121.

19. Quoted in Day, *Dorothy Parker in Her Own Words*, 38.

20. Background information of theater history derived from Mary C. Henderson, *The City and the Theatre: The History of New York Playhouses* (New York: Back Stage Books, 2004); Bernard Hewitt, *Theatre U.S.A.: 1665 to 1957* (New York: McGraw-Hill, 1959); Garff B. Wilson, *Three Hundred Years of American Drama and Theatre: From "Ye Bear and Ye Cubb" to "Hair"* (Englewood Cliffs, N.J.: Prentice-Hall, 1973).

21. RES and Samuel P. Sears, *Barnum Was Right*, n.d., bMSAm1947, f. 1728, RES: HHU.

22. RES and Samuel Powers Sears, *Barnum Was Right* (music/lyrics), 1920, NYPL/LC.

23. Quoted in Donald Elder, *Ring Lardner* (New York: Doubleday, 1956), 283–285.

24. Quoted in John Mason Brown, *The Worlds of Robert E. Sherwood: Mirror to His Times, 1896–1939* (1962; reprint, New York: Harper and Row, 1965), 211.

25. RES, *Robert E. Sherwood: Film Critic—The Best Moving Pictures of 1922–23,* reprint ed. (New York: Revisionist Press, 1974), vii.

26. Information on the history of the silent film culled from Richard Koszarski, *An Evening's Entertainment: The Age of the Silent Feature Picture, 1915–1928* (Berkeley: University of California Press, 1990), and Wilson, *Three Hundred Years of American Drama.*

27. Quoted in E. R. Hagemann, "An Extraordinary Picture: The Film Criticism of Robert E. Sherwood," *Journal of Popular Film* 1, no. 2 (Spring 1972): 81.

28. RES, "The Silent Drama" column, *Life* 80, no. 2090 (November 23, 1922): 24.

29. Quoted in Hagemann, "An Extraordinary Picture," 92.

30. RES, "The Silent Drama" column, *Life* 80, no. 2083 (October 5, 1922): 22.

31. RES, *Best Moving Pictures of 1922–23,* 70.

32. RES, "The Higher Education on the Screen," *Vanity Fair* 13, no. 5 (February 1920): 67.

33. Ibid.

34. RES, "The Silent Drama" column, *Life* 77, no. 2003 (March 24, 1921): 432.

35. RES, "The Silent Drama" column, *Life* 77, no. 2013 (June 2, 1921): 812.

36. RES, "The Silent Drama" column, *Life* 80, no. 2075 (August 10, 1922): 24.

37. RES, "The Silent Drama" column, *Life* 88, no. 2302 (December 16, 1926): 24.

38. RES, "The Silent Drama" column, *Life* 86, no. 2250 (December 17, 1925): 26.

39. RES, "The Silent Drama" column, *Life* 89, no. 2312 (February 24, 1927): 26.

40. RES, "The Silent Drama" column, *Life* 89, no. 2310 (January 30, 1927): 24.

41. RES, "The Silent Drama" column, *Life* 86, no. 2249 (December 10, 1925): 24–25.

42. RES, "The Silent Drama" column, *Life* 86, no. 2250 (December 17, 1925): 26.

43. RES, "The Silent Drama" column, *Life* 83, no. 2158 (March 13, 1924): 26.

44. RES, "The Silent Drama" column, *Life* 89, no. 2318 (April 7, 1927): 26.

45. RES, "The Silent Drama" column, *Life* 83, no. 2168 (May 22, 1924): 24.

46. Charles DeBenedetti, "The $100,000 American Peace Award of 1924," *Pennsylvania Magazine of History and Biography* 98, no. 2 (April 1974): 224–249.

47. "Winners of War Prize Contest," *Life* 83, no. 2166 (May 8, 1924): 10.

48. Untitled notice, *Life* 83, no. 2167 (May 15, 1924): 24.

49. "*Life's* Question Contest Winner to Question #1," *Life* 85, no. 2208 (February 26, 1925): 10.

50. "*Life's* Question Contest," *Life* 85, no. 2210 (March 12, 1925): 12.

51. RES, "The Silent Drama" column, *Life* 85, no. 2214 (April 9, 1925): 26.

52. RES, "The Silent Drama" column, *Life* 91, no. 2360 (January 26, 1928): 26.

53. Information on the background of censorship in the films culled from Koszarski, *An Evening's Entertainment*, 198–210.

54. Ibid., 206–207.

55. RES, "The Cinema Primer" column, *Life* 78, no. 2024 (August 11, 1921): 20.

56. RES, "The Silent Drama" column, *Life* 80, no. 2070 (July 6, 1922): 24.

57. RES, "The Silent Drama" column, *Life* 82, no. 2140 (November 8, 1923): 24.

58. RES, "The Silent Drama" column, *Life* 90,no. 2346 (October 20, 1927): 30.

59. RES, "Notice to Presidential Possibilities!" *Life* 83, no. 2151 (January 24, 1924): 6.

60. RES, "We Want Doheny!" *Life* 83, no. 2157 (March 6, 1924): 7.

61. RES (signed *Life*), "For President: Will Rogers," *Life* 91, no. 2377 (May 24, 1928): 3.

62. RES to Homer Croy, March 17, 1952, bMSAm1947, f. 1073, RES:HHU.

63. Will Rogers, "Prohibition and Farm Relief," *Life* 91, no. 2379 (June 7, 1928): 9.

64. RES to Homer Croy, March 17, 1952, bMSAm1947, f. 1073, RES:HHU.

65. Unsigned piece, *Life* 92, no. 2401 (November 9, 1928): 5.

66. RES, "The Silent Drama" column, *Life* 79, no. 2050 (February 22, 1922): 22.

67. RES, "The Silent Drama" column, *Life* 79, no. 2057 (April 7, 1922): 24.

68. Ibid.

69. RES, "The Silent Drama" column, *Life* 79, no. 2058 (April 13, 1922): 22.

70. RES, "The Silent Drama" column, *Life* 87, no. 2263 (March 18, 1926): 28.

71. The film is sometimes listed as *Lucky Lady*. The working title was *Lady Luck*. Information on *The Lucky Lady* and *Oh, What a Nurse* obtained from the American Film Institute database at www.afi.com.

72. RES, "The Silent Drama" column, *Life* 82, no. 2134 (July 19, 1923): 24.

73. RES, "The Silent Drama" column, *Life* 83, no. 2157 (March 6, 1924): 26.

74. RES, "The Silent Drama" column, *Life* 88, no. 2286 (August 26, 1926): 26.

75. RES, "The Silent Drama" column, *Life* 88, no. 2291 (September 30, 1926): 24.

76. RES, "The Silent Drama" column, *Life* 90, no. 2347 (October 27, 1927): 24.

77. RES, "The Movies" column, *Life* 92, no. 2393 (September 14, 1928): 24.

78. RES, "The Movies" column, *Life* 92, no. 2395 (September 28, 1928): 22.

79. RES, "The Silent Drama" column, *Life* 85,no. 2204 (January 29, 1925): 26.

80. RES, "The Silent Drama" column, *Life* 81, no. 2009 (January 25, 1923): 24.

81. RES to SCH, December 15, 1928, b. 7, Robert E. Sherwood folder, SCH: UCB.

82. RES to Maurice and Frida Child, May 9, 1943, bMSAm1947, f. 1041, RES: HHU.

83. RES to McCready Huston, July 2, 1926, bMSAm1947, f. 1242, RES:HHU.

84. R.H.D. of the Frank A. Munsey Company to O. K. Liveright, n.d., MS Storage 275, b. 2, RES:HHU.

85. RES, "Extra! Extra!," in *The Best Short Stories of 1926 and the Yearbook of the*

American Short Story, ed. Edward J. O'Brien (New York: Dodd, Mead, 1926), 237–243.

86. Julie Goldsmith Gilbert, *Ferber: A Biography* (New York: Doubleday, 1978), 314.

87. RES to Edna Ferber, February 7, 1927, U.S. Mss 98AN, b. 1, Edna Ferber Papers:SHSW.

5. Writing Plays for Peace

1. RES, "Remarks at Kent School," typescript, November 16, 1954, bMSAm1947, f. 2255, RES:HHU.

2. RES, *The Queen's Husband* (New York: Charles Scribner's Sons, 1928), xvii.

3. Unsigned cartoon, *Boston Post*, January 16, 1939, clipping, MS Storage 275, b. 2, RES:HHU.

4. RES, *The Road to Rome* (New York: Charles Scribner's Sons, 1927), xli, xlii.

5. Ibid., 36.

6. Ibid., 23.

7. Ibid., 89.

8. Ibid., 113.

9. Ibid., 35.

10. Ibid., 145.

11. Ibid., 42.

12. Ibid., 123–124.

13. Ibid., 63.

14. *The General Pact for the Renunciation of War* (Washington, D.C.: Government Printing Office, 1928).

15. RES, *The Road to Rome*, 154.

16. Edward Sheldon to RES, n.d., mr4760, ser. 3B, b. 5, EFP:Smithsonian.

17. LFE to JED, n.d., mr4760, ser. 3B, b. 5, EFP:Smithsonian.

18. LFE to JED, February 3, 1927, mr4760, ser. 3B, b. 5, EFP:Smithsonian.

19. Quoted in John Mason Brown, *The Worlds of Robert E. Sherwood: Mirror to His Times, 1896–1939* (1962; reprint, New York: Harper and Row, 1965), 220.

20. Percy Hammond, "The Theaters" column, *New York Herald Tribune*, February 1, 1927, 20.

21. Alexander Woollcott, *New York World*, February 1, 1927, cited in Barnard Hewitt, *Theatre U.S.A.: 1665 to 1957* (New York: McGraw-Hill, 1959), 368.

22. Unsigned review of *The Road to Rome*, *New Republic*, March 9, 1927, MS Storage 275, b. 2, RES:HHU.

23. Brooks Atkinson, "The Play" column, *New York Times*, February 1, 1927, 24.

24. Robert Benchley, "Life Drama" column, *Life*, 89, no. 2311 (February 17, 1927): 19.

25. Burns Mantle, ed., *The Best Plays of 1926–27 and the Year Book of the Drama in America* (New York: Dodd, Mead, 1927), 153.

26. John Gassner, ed., *Twenty-Five Best Plays of the Modern American Theatre: Early Series* (New York: Crown Publishers, 1949), 294.

27. RES, *The Road to Rome*, ix.

28. Ibid., xvi.

29. Ibid., xxvi.

30. Ibid., xxxix.

31. RosS to JED, May 21, 1928, mr4760, ser. 3B, b. 5, EFP:Smithsonian.

32. RosS to JED, August 17, 1928, mr4760, ser. 3B, b. 5, EFP:Smithsonian.

33. RES to RosS, 1929, MS Storage 275, b. 2, RES:HHU.

34. RosS to JED, April 12, 1929, mr4760, ser. 3B, b. 5, EFP:Smithsonian.

35. RES to George Abbott, March 19, 1949, bMSAm1947, f. 916, RES:HHU.

36. See Ring W. Lardner, *The Love Nest and Other Stories* (New York: Charles Scribner's Sons, 1926), 3–27.

37. RES, *The Love Nest* (typescript), 1926, NCOF folder, NYPL/LC.

38. Ibid., 9

39. Ibid., 21.

40. Brooks Atkinson, "The Play" column, *New York Times*, December 23, 1927, 17.

41. Robert Benchley, "Life Drama" column, *Life* 90, no. 2356 (December 29, 1927): 21.

42. Robert Benchley, "Life Drama" column, *Life* 91, no. 2359 (January 19, 1928): 21.

43. Quoted in Donald Elder, *Ring Lardner* (Garden City, N.Y.: Doubleday, 1956), 237.

44. RES quoted in Jonathan Yardley, *Ring: A Biography of Ring Lardner* (New York: Random House, 1977), 322.

45. RES, *The Queen's Husband* (New York: Charles Scribner's Sons, 1928), 61.

46. Ibid., 51.

47. Ibid., 90.

48. Ibid., 40.

49. Ibid., 115.

50. Ibid., 105.

51. Ibid., 107.

52. Ibid., 110.

53. Ibid., 116.

54. Percy Hammond, *New York Herald Tribune*, January 26, 1928, 14.

55. Brooks Atkinson, "The Queen's Husband," *New York Times*, January 26, 1928, 17.

56. Robert Benchley, "Life Drama" column, *Life* 91, no. 2362 (February 9, 1928): 19.

57. Unsigned, untitled review, *Toronto Daily Star*, February 16, 1932, MS Storage 275, b. 2, RES:HHU.

58. RES, *The Queen's Husband*, xv.

59. Ibid., xvi.

60. Ibid., xvii.

61. Ibid., xix.

62. RES, "Footnote to a Preface," typescript, *Saturday Review of Literature Anniversary Issue*, July 7, 1949, bMSAm1947, f. 2081, RES:HHU.

63. RES to SCH, March 16 and April 13, 1929, BANC MSS70/185z, b. 7, Robert E. Sherwood folder, SCH:UCB.

64. RES, *Waterloo Bridge* (New York: Charles Scribner's Sons, 1930), xxiii.

65. Ibid., 66.

66. Ibid., 131.

67. Ibid., 130.

68. Ibid., 19.

69. Ibid., 13.

70. Ibid., 44.

71. Ibid., 155.

72. Ibid., 61.

73. Brooks Atkinson, "The Play" column, *New York Times*, January 7, 1930, 29.

74. Arthur Ruhl, "Waterloo Bridge" review, *New York Herald Tribune*, January 7, 1930, 24.

75. RES to SCH, January 15, 1930, BANC MSS70/185z, b. 7, Robert E. Sherwood folder, SCH:UCB.

76. RES, *There Shall Be No Night* (New York: Charles Scribner's Sons, 1941), xiv.

77. RES to Charles Poletti, February 13, 1949, bMSAm1947, f. 1432, RES:HHU.

78. Ibid.

79. RES, *This Is New York* (New York: Charles Scribner's Sons, 1931), ix.

80. Ibid., 38.

81. RosS to JED, December 1, 1930, mr4761, ser. 3B, b. 5, EFP:Smithsonian.

82. Brooks Atkinson, "This Is New York," *New York Times*, November 29, 1930, 21.

83. Percy Hammond, "The Theaters" column, *New York Herald Tribune*, November 29, 1930, 10.

84. RosS to JED, December 10, 1930, mr4761, ser. 3B, b. 5, EFP:Smithsonian.

85. RES, "Radio Speech by Robert E. Sherwood Delivered November 5, 1934, for Mobilization for Human Needs," typescript, bMSAm1947, f. 2182, RES:HHU.

86. RES quoted in SNB, *People in a Diary: A Memoir* (Boston: Little, Brown, 1972), 73.

87. Ralph Straus, "Unending Crusade," *Sunday Times* (London), September 18, 1932, clipping, mr4765, ser. 4E, b. 7, EFP:Smithsonian.

88. RES, *Marching as to War*, typescript, 1927, act 1, 18, 35, bMSAm1947, f. 1755, RES:HHU.

89. Ibid., act 1, 39.

90. Ibid., act 2, 16–17.

91. Ibid., act 3, 29.

92. RES, *The Virtuous Knight* (New York: Charles Scribner's Sons, 1931), 228.

93. Ibid., 250.

94. Ibid., 253.

95. Ibid., 234.

96. Ibid., 251.

97. RES, *There Shall Be No Night*, xiv–xv.

98. RES, *Reunion in Vienna* (New York: Charles Scribner's Sons, 1932), vii.

99. Ibid., ix.

100. Ibid., xiv.

101. Ibid., xvi.

102. Ibid., 31.

103. Ibid., 162.

104. Background information on Alfred Lunt and Lynn Fontanne derived from primary sources and two biographies: Jared Brown, *The Fabulous Lunts: A Biography of Alfred Lunt and Lynn Fontanne* (New York: Atheneum, 1988), and Margot Peters, *Design for Living: Alfred Lunt and Lynn Fontanne, A Biography* (New York: Alfred A. Knopf, 2003).

105. RES quoted in RES, "The Lunts," in *The Passionate Playgoer: A Personal Scrapbook,* ed. George Oppenheimer (New York: Viking, 1958), 80.

106. Alfred Lunt to RES, January 7, 1933 (probably), Mss622, b. 5, f. 16, L/F: SHSW.

107. Lawrence Langner, *The Magic Curtain: The Story of a Life in Two Fields: Theatre and Invention by the Founder of the Theatre Guild* (New York: E. P. Dutton, 1951), 253–254.

108. RES cited in Ward Morehouse, "The Potomac after Dark," *New York Sun,* October 8, 1938, clipping, bMSAm1449, f. 1523, AW:HHU.

109. Richard Lockridge and Gilbert W. Gabriel quoted in Brown, *The Fabulous Lunts,* 199–200.

110. Brooks Atkinson, "Reunion in Vienna," *New York Times,* November 17, 1931, 31.

111. Arthur Ruhl, "The Theaters" column, *New York Herald Tribune,* November 17, 1931, 16.

112. Burns Mantle, ed., *The Best Plays of 1931–32 and the Yearbook of the Drama in America* (New York: Dodd, Mead, 1932), vii.

113. Alfred Lunt to RES, June 23, 1932, Mss622, b. 5, f. 16, L/F:SHSW.

114. Alfred Lunt to RES, January 7, 1934, Mss622, b. 5, f. 16, L/F:SHSW.

115. RES to Alfred Lunt and Lynn Fontanne, May 7, 1935, Mss622, b. 5, f. 16, L/F: SHSW.

116. Cited in Brown, *The Fabulous Lunts,* 197.

117. RES, *The Oxford Accent,* typescript, ca. 1932, act 1, 7, bMSAm1947, f. 1759, RES:HHU.

118. RES, *Afterglow,* typescript, 1932, scene 10, 71, bMSAm1947, f. 1726, RES: HHU.

119. Ibid., 74.

120. Ibid., 76.

121. Ibid., 77.

122. Ibid., 78.

123. RES quoted in Collie Small to RES, February 11, 1949, bMSAm1947, f. 750, RES:HHU.

124. RES, *Acropolis,* typescript, 1932, act 1, 4, mrZC-52, NYPL/LC.

125. Ibid., act 1, 27.

126. Ibid., act 2, 11.

127. Ibid., act 3, 15.

128. RES, *There Shall Be No Night,* xix.

129. W. A. Darlington, "Acropolis," *Daily Telegraph,* November 24, 1933, clipping, bMSAm1947, f. 2411a, RES:HHU.

130. "Acropolis," *Morning Post,* n.d., clipping, bMSAm1947, f. 2411a, RES:HHU.

131. M. Willson Disher, "Acropolis," *Daily Mail,* and unsigned review, *Daily Sketch,* n.d., clippings, bMSAm1947, f. 2411a, RES:HHU.

132. JED to LFE, November 24, 1933, mr4761, ser. 3B, b. 5, EFP:Smithsonian.

133. Edward Sheldon to RES, April 1934, bMSAm1947, f. 739, RES:HHU.

134. Jo Mielziner to RES, December 16, 1935, bMSAm1947, f. 569, RES:HHU.

135. Langner, *The Magic Curtain,* 237.

136. RES to SCH, August 6, 1931, BANC MSS70/185z, b. 7, Robert E. Sherwood folder, SCH:UCB.

137. Comparisons to 2005 dollar amounts throughout this book are taken from "The Inflation Calculator," www.westegg.com/inflation/, accessed August 6 and 9, 2006.

6. Marriage, Divorce, and *The Petrified Forest*

1. John Mason Brown, *The Worlds of Robert E. Sherwood: Mirror to His Times, 1896–1939* (1962; reprint, New York: Harper and Row, 1965), 170.

2. Marc Connelly, *Voices Offstage: A Book of Memoirs* (New York: Holt, Rinehart and Winston, 1968), 120.

3. "Robt. E. Sherwood Weds Miss Brandon," *New York Times,* October 30, 1922, 15.

4. RosS to JED, November 25, 1922, MS Storage 275, b. 1, RES:HHU.

5. LFE to JED, October 10, 1923, mr4760, ser. 3B, b. 4, EFP:Smithsonian.

6. Quoted in Brown, *Worlds,* 225.

7. Barry Day, ed., *Dorothy Parker In Her Own Words* (Lanham, Md.: Taylor Trade Publishing, 2004), 43.

8. For consistency, and to avoid confusion, I will retain "Little Mary" throughout this book.

9. MBS to LFE, October 1923 (probably), mr4760, ser. 3B, b. 4, EFP:Smithsonian.

10. RES, "Brother Preble Catches the Spirit," *Life* 86, no. 2248 [Christmas number] (December 3, 1925): 25–26.

11. LFE to JED, December, 1926, mr4760, ser. 3B, b. 5, EFP:Smithsonian.

12. LFE to JED, February 14, 1927, mr4760, ser. 3B, b. 5, EFP:Smithsonian.

13. Brown, *Worlds*, 226.

14. RES to AW, April 27, 1930, bMSAm1449, f. 1522, AW:HHU.

15. RES to SCH, March 16, 1929, BANC MSS70/185z, b. 7, Robert E. Sherwood folder, SCH:UCB.

16. RosS to JED, May 15, 1931, mr4761, ser. 3B, b. 5, EFP:Smithsonian.

17. LFE to JED, February 3, 1927, mr4760, ser. 3B, b. 5, EFP:Smithsonian.

18. RosS to JED, November 16, 1931, mr4761, ser. 3B, b. 5, EFP:Smithsonian.

19. RosS to JED, April 13, 1932, mr4761, ser. 3B, b. 5, EFP:Smithsonian.

20. LFE to JED, March 5, 1932 (probably), mr4761, ser. 3B, b. 5, EFP:Smithsonian.

21. LFE to JED, 1905, mr4757, ser. 3B, b. 3; RosS to JED, August 27, 1931, mr4761, ser. 3B, b. 5; LFE to JED, March 24, 1932, mr4761, ser. 3B, b. 5, EFP:Smithsonian.

22. LFE to JED, March 24, 1932, mr4761, ser. 3B, b. 5, EFP:Smithsonian.

23. RosS to JED, April 13, 1932, mr4761, ser. 3B, b. 5, EFP:Smithsonian.

24. LFE to JED, March 24, 1932, mr4761, ser. 3B, b. 5, EFP:Smithsonian.

25. RosS to RES, n.d., MS Storage 275, b. 1, RES:HHU.

26. RosS to JED, March 30, 1933, mr4761, ser. 3B, b. 5, EFP:Smithsonian.

27. LFE to JED, July 7, 1933 (probably), mr4761, ser. 3B, b. 5, EFP:Smithsonian.

28. RosS to RES, n.d., MS Storage 275, b. 1, RES:HHU.

29. LFE to JED, January 16, 1934, mr4761, ser. 3B, b. 5, EFP:Smithsonian.

30. Ibid.

31. Brown, *Worlds*, 221–222.

32. Ibid., 230.

33. "Lyon's Den" column, *Boston Herald*, December 7, 1949, clipping, Harvard University Clippings:RES file, HUA.

34. RosS to JED, January 18, 1934, MS Storage 275, b. 2, RES:HHU.

35. LFE to JED, January 16, 1934, mr4761, ser. 3B, b. 5, EFP:Smithsonian.

36. Ibid.

37. RosS to JED, January 18, 1934, MS Storage 275, b. 2, RES:HHU.

38. LFE to JED, January 26, 1934, mr4761, ser. 3B, b. 5, EFP:Smithsonian.

39. RosS to JED, February 1, 1934, mr4761, ser. 3B, b. 5, EFP:Smithsonian.

40. Lynn Fontanne to AW, February 5, 1934, bMSAm1449, f. 543, AW:HHU.

41. LFE to JED, March 16, 1934, mr4761, ser. 3B, b. 5, EFP:Smithsonian.

42. LFE to JED, April 16, 1934, mr4762, ser. 3B, b. 5, EFP:Smithsonian.

43. LFE to JED, May 10, 1934, mr4762, ser. 3B, b. 5, EFP:Smithsonian.

44. RES, "Six Weeks in Reno," typescript, bMSAm1947, f. 1981, RES:HHU.

45. Ibid.

46. RES to Geoffrey Kerr, May 12, 1934, MS Storage 275, b. 2, RES:HHU.

47. RES, "Six Weeks in Reno."

48. RES to Geoffrey Kerr, May 12, 1934, MS Storage 275, b. 2, RES:HHU.

49. RosS to JED, May 18, 1934, mr4762, ser. 3B, b. 5, EFP:Smithsonian.

50. LFE to JED, May 24, 1934, mr4762, ser. 3B, b. 5, EFP:Smithsonian.

51. LFE to JED, May 31, 1934, mr4762, ser. 3B, b. 5, EFP:Smithsonian.

52. RosS to JED, June, 1934 (probably), mr4762, ser. 3B, b. 5, EFP:Smithsonian.

53. RosS to PS, November 14, 1934, mr4762, ser. 3B, b. 5, EFP:Smithsonian.

54. SNB, *The Suspended Drawing Room* (New York: Stein and Day, 1965), 144.

55. RES to Ward Morehouse, May 27, 1948, bMSAm1947, f. 1377, RES:HHU.

56. RES, *There Shall Be No Night* (New York: Charles Scribner's Sons, 1941), xx–xxi; RES, *The Petrified Forest* (New York: Charles Scribner's Sons, 1935), 63.

57. RES, *The Petrified Forest*, 8.

58. Ibid., 9.

59. Ibid., 15.

60. Ibid., 21.

61. Ibid., 30, 62, 65.

62. RES quoted in "The Author," typescript, n.d., *Abe Lincoln in Illinois* file, PPC:NYPL/42nd Street.

63. RES, *The Petrified Forest*, 99.

64. Ibid., 132.

65. Ibid., 156.

66. Ibid., 113–114.

67. Ibid., 52.

68. Ibid., 118.

69. Ibid., 136.

70. Ibid. 143.

71. Ibid., 130.

72. Brooks Atkinson, *Broadway Scrapbook* (New York: Theatre Arts, 1947), 10–11.

73. Richard Watts and Gilbert Gabriel quoted on book jacket of RES, *The Petrified Forest*.

74. Burns Mantle, ed., *The Best Plays of 1934–35 and the Year Book of the Drama in America* (New York: Dodd, Mead, 1935), 115.

75. Eleanor Flexner, *American Playwrights: 1918–1938* (New York: Simon and Schuster, 1938), 278.

76. John Howard Lawson, *Theory and Technique of Playwriting* (1936; reprint, New York: Hill and Wang, 1960), 142–145.

77. Brown, *Worlds*, 319.

78. RES diary, January 20, 1936, 89M-66(b), b. 1, RES:HHU.

79. RosS to JED, February 8, 1935, mr4762, ser. 3B, b. 5, EFP:Smithsonian.

80. Federal and New York State Income Tax Reports, calendar years 1929–1934, Marc Connelly Papers:HGARC/BU.

81. RosS to JED, March 28, 1935, mr4762, ser. 3B, b. 5, EFP:Smithsonian.

82. JED to LFE, April 3, 1935, mr4762, ser. 3B, b. 5, EFP:Smithsonian.

83. RosS to JED, n.d., mr4762, ser. 3B, b. 5, EFP:Smithsonian.

84. LFE to JED, April 18, 1935, mr4762, ser. 3B, b. 5, EFP:Smithsonian.

85. RES to AW, May 6, 1935, bMSAm1449, f. 1522, AW:HHU.

86. RES to L/F, May 7, 1935, Mss622, b. 5, f. 16, L/F:SHSW.

87. RES to RosS, June 21, 1935, MS Storage 275, b. 2, RES:HHU.

88. LFE to JED, April 7, 1935, mr4762, ser. 3B, b. 5, EFP:Smithsonian.

89. RosS to JED, December 16, 1935, mr4762, ser. 3B, b. 5, EFP:Smithsonian.

90. RosS to JED, December 25, 1935, mr4762, ser. 3B, b. 5, EFP:Smithsonian.

91. LFE to JED, December 26, 1935, mr4762, ser. 3B, b. 5, EFP:Smithsonian.

92. RES diary, January 18, 1936, 89M-66(b), b. 1, RES:HHU.

93. RES, *There Shall Be No Night*, xxi.

94. RES diary, February 6, 1936, 89M-66(b), b. 1, RES:HHU.

7. From Pacifist to Soldier

1. RES diary, January 18, 1938, 89M-66(b), b. 1, RES:HHU.

2. "Didactic Dramas: Antiwar Plays of the 1930s," http://historymatters.gmu.edu/d/5164, accessed November 22, 2005.

3. For detailed information and analysis of these seven plays, see Richard G. Scharine, "'The War that is to Begin Tomorrow Night': American Anti-War Drama in the 1930s," *Journal of American Drama and Theatre* 2, no. 1 (Winter 1990): 27–37.

4. RES to Walter Kerr, June 21, 1955, bMSAm1947, f. 1277, RES:HHU.

5. RES to Ward Morehouse, May 27, 1948, bMSAm1947, f. 1377, RES:HHU.

6. Alfred Lunt to RES, July 18, 1935, Mss622, b5, f. 16, L/F:SHSW.

7. RES, *Idiot's Delight* (1935; reprint, New York: Charles Scribner's Sons, 1936), 124.

8. Ibid., 107.

9. RES diary, January 25, 1936, 89M-66(b), b. 1, RES:HHU.

10. LFE to JED, February 11, 1936, mr4762, ser. 3B, b. 6, EFP:Smithsonian.

11. RES, *Idiot's Delight*, 103–104.

12. "Idiot's Delight Solitaire," http://www.solitairecentral.com/id.html, accessed April 18, 2004.

13. RES, *Idiot's Delight*, 106.

14. Ibid., 79–80.

15. Ibid., 12–13.

16. Ibid., 54.

17. Ibid., 60.

18. Ibid., 14.

19. Ibid., 84.

20. Ibid., 73.

21. Ibid., 82.

22. Ibid., 105.

23. Ibid., 152.

24. Ibid., 45–46.

25. Ibid., 130.

26. RES diary, January 21, 1936, 89M-66(b), b. 1, RES:HHU.

27. RES, *Idiot's Delight*, 121.

28. Ibid., 162.

29. RES, *There Shall Be No Night*, xxii; RES, *Idiot's Delight*, 60–61.

30. RES, *Idiot's Delight*, 123.

31. RES, *There Shall Be No Night*, xxi.

32. RES, *Idiot's Delight*, 189–190.

33. Ibid.

34. RosS to JED, December 25, 1935, mr4762, ser. 3B, b. 5, EFP:Smithsonian.

35. RES diary, February 3, 1936, 89M-66(b), b. 1, RES:HHU.

36. RES to SCH, February 8, 1936, BANC MSS70/185z, b. 7, Robert E. Sherwood folder, SCH:UCB.

37. RES diary, January 3, 1936, 89M-66(b), b. 1, RES:HHU.

38. RES to Alfred Lunt, February 3, 1936, Mss622, b. 5, f. 16, L/F:SHSW.

39. RES diary, March 16–19, 1936, 89M-66(b), b. 1, RES:HHU.

40. RES diary, March 24, 1936, 89M-66(b), b. 1, RES:HHU.

41. RES diary, March 25, 1936, 89M-66(b), b. 1, RES:HHU.

42. Brooks Atkinson cited in Bernard Beckerman and Howard Siegman, eds., *On Stage: Selected Theatre Reviews from the New York Times, 1920–1970* (New York: Arno Press in cooperation with Quadrangle/New York Times Book, 1973), 176.

43. Percy Hammond, review of *Idiot's Delight*, clipping, MS Storage 275, b. 2, RES:HHU.

44. John Anderson, Gilbert Gabriel, Richard Lockridge, John Mason Brown, and Robert Garland, reviews of *Idiot's Delight*, clippings, MS Storage 275, b. 2, RES:HHU.

45. Cited in Howard Stein, "Joseph Wood Krutch: A Rare Critic," *Columbia: The Magazine of Columbia University* (Summer 2000): 43.

46. Frances Marion, *How to Write and Sell Film Stories*, reprint ed. (New York: Garland Publishing, 1978), 232.

47. G.S., Memorandum Re: Pioneer Pictures, March 25, 1936, *Idiot's Delight* folder, PCA:AMPAS.

48. Frederick Herron letter quoted in Gregory D. Black, *Hollywood Censored: Morality Codes, Catholics, and the Movies* (New York: Cambridge University Press, 1994), 283.

49. Frederick L. Herron to Joseph I. Breen, May 7, 1937, *Idiot's Delight* folder, PCA:AMPAS.

50. RES diary, May 1, 1937, 89M-66(b), b. 1, RES:HHU.

51. RES to RosS, May 5, 1937, MS Storage 275, b. 2, RES:HHU.

52. Joseph I. Breen to Frederick L. Herron, May 13, 1937, *Idiot's Delight* folder PCA:AMPAS.

53. Hunt Stromberg to Joseph I. Breen, June 23, 1937, *Idiot's Delight* folder, PCA:AMPAS.

54. Joseph I. Breen to Louis B. Mayer, August 26, 1938, *Idiot's Delight* folder, PCA: AMPAS.

55. Ruth Vasey, *The World According to Hollywood, 1918–1939* (Madison: University of Wisconsin Press, 1997), 192.

56. RES to L/F, March 25, 1939, Mss622, b5, f. 16, L/F:SHSW.

57. RES diary, February 13, 1938, 89M-66(b), b. 1, RES:HHU.

58. RES to Walter Kerr, June 21, 1955, bMSAm1947, f. 1277, RES:HHU.

59. RES diary, January 3 and February 5, 1937, 89M-66(b), b. 1, RES:HHU.

60. RES diary, October 19, 1937, 89M-66(b), b. 1, RES:HHU.

61. RES diary, November 19, 1937, 89M-66(b), b. 1, RES:HHU.

62. RES diary, November 3, 1937, 89M-66(b), b. 1, RES:HHU.

63. Information on *tic douloureux* found on http://www.webmd.com and http://www.health-alliance.com, both accessed January 14, 2006.

64. Quoted in Julie Goldsmith Gilbert, *Ferber: A Biography* (New York: Doubleday, 1978), 147.

65. RES diary, April 29, 1938, 89M-66(b), b. 1, RES:HHU.

66. RES diary, April 2, 1937, 89M-66(b), b. 1, RES:HHU.

67. RES diary, November 17, 1937, 89M-66(b), b. 1, RES:HHU.

68. RES, *Abe Lincoln in Illinois* (1937; reprint, New York: Charles Scribner's Sons, 1939), 189.

69. RES diary, January 2, 1937, 89M-66(b), b. 1, RES:HHU.

70. Edd Johnson, "Sherwood Tells Why He Wrote *Lincoln*," *World Telegram*, October 29, 1938, 6, MS Storage 275, b. 2, RES:HHU.

71. "The Author," typescript, n.d., b. 3, PPC:NYPL/42nd Street.

72. RES, "The Silent Drama" column, *Life* 83, no. 2154 (February 14, 1924): 24.

73. Johnson, "Sherwood Tells Why He Wrote *Lincoln*," 6.

74. "The Author," typescript, n.d., b. 3, PPC:NYPL/42nd Street.

75. RES to RosS, May 5, 1937, MS Storage 275, b. 2, RES:HHU.

76. RES, "Remarks at Kent School," typescript, November 16, 1954, 2, bMSAm1947, f. 2255, RES:HHU.

77. RES diary, December 6, 1937, 89M-66(b), b. 1, RES:HHU.

78. RES diary, December 30, 1937, 89M-66(b), b. 1, RES:HHU.

79. RES diary, May 26, 1936, 89M-66(b), b. 1, RES:HHU.

80. RES diary, January 9, 1937, 89M-66(b), b. 1, RES:HHU.

81. RES diary, March 22, 1938, 89M-66(b), b. 1, RES:HHU.

82. RES diary, March 12, 1937, 89M-66(b), b. 1, RES:HHU.

83. RES diary, October 31, 1937, 89M-66(b), b. 1, RES:HHU.

84. RES diary, October 7, 1937, 89M-66(b), b. 1, RES:HHU.

85. RES diary, October 10, 1937, 89M-66(b), b. 1, RES:HHU.

86. RES diary, March 11, 1938, 89M-66(b), b. 1, RES:HHU.

87. RES diary, March 14, 1938, 89M-66(b), b. 1, RES:HHU.

88. RES diary, March 18, 1938, 89M-66(b), b. 1, RES:HHU.

89. RES diary, March 19, 1938, 89M-66(b), b. 1, RES:HHU.

90. RES diary, March 27, 1938, 89M-66(b), b. 1, RES:HHU.

91. RES, *Abe Lincoln in Illinois*, 250.

92. RES diary, September 19, 1938, 89M-66(b), b. 1, RES:HHU.

93. RES diary, September 21, 1938, 89M-66(b), b. 1, RES:HHU.

94. RES to SCH, May 4, 1936, BANC MSS70/185z, b. 7, Robert E. Sherwood folder, SCH:UCB.

95. RES diary, March 9, 1936, and January 8, 1937, 89M-66(b), b. 1, RES:HHU.

96. RES diary, February 28, 1937, 89M-66(b), b. 1, RES:HHU.

97. RES diary, March 9, 1937, 89M-66(b), b. 1, RES:HHU.

98. RES diary, March 10, 1937, 89M-66(b), b. 1, RES:HHU.

99. RES diary, November 5, 1937, 89M-66(b), b. 1, RES:HHU.

100. RES diary, January 2, 1938, 89M-66(b), b. 1, RES:HHU.

101. RES diary, January 3, 1938, 89M-66(b), b. 1, RES:HHU.

102. RES diary, August 12, 1938, 89M-66(b), b. 1, RES:HHU.

103. RES, *There Shall Be No Night*, xxiii.

104. RES to LFE, February 4, 1938, MS Storage 275, b. 2, RES:HHU.

105. RES, *Abe Lincoln in Illinois*, 35.

106. Ibid., 75.

107. Ibid., 77.

108. Ibid., 106.

109. Ibid., 138.

110. Ibid., 139–140.

111. Ibid., 183–184.

112. Elmer Rice, *Minority Report: An Autobiography* (New York: Simon and Schuster, 1963), 374.

113. SNB, *People in a Diary: A Memoir by S. N. Behrman* (Boston: Little, Brown, 1972), 215–217.

114. RES to SNB, March 10, 1938, b. 18, f. 8, SNB:NYPL/42nd Street.

115. "Agreement," April 12, 1938, USMssIAN, b. 1, f. 1, PPC:SHSW.

116. RES to Lucius Beebe, n.d., USMssIAN, b. 3, f. 6, PPC:SHSW.

117. Quoted in Ward Morehouse, "The Potomac after Dark," *New York Sun*, October 8, 1938, clipping, bMSAm1449, f. 1523, AW:HHU.

118. Brooks Atkinson, *Broadway Scrapbook* (New York: Theatre Arts, 1947), 94–97.

119. Reviews by Sidney B. Whipple, October 17, 1938; Burns Mantle, October 17, 1938; and Heywood Broun, October 18, 1938, clippings, MS Storage 275, b. 2, RES: HHU.

120. John Mason Brown cited in Burns Mantle, ed., *The Best Plays of 1938–39 and the Year Book of the Drama in America* (New York: Dodd, Mead, 1939), 32.

121. Comments by Sidney B. Whipple, October 17, 1938, and Burns Mantle, October 17, 1938, clippings, MS Storage 275, b. 2, RES:HHU.

122. To Stockholders of PPC, June 21, 1939, b. 18, f. 8, SNB:NYPL/42nd Street.

123. Quoted in Blanche Wiesen Cook, "Women and Peace: The Legacy," *Ms.* 16, no. 1 (Winter 2006): 42.

124. Quoted in Harriet Hyman Alonso, *Peace as a Women's Issue: A History of the U.S. Movement for World Peace and Women's Rights* (Syracuse: Syracuse University Press, 1993), 138.

125. RES to Archibald MacLeish, May 24, 1940, bMSAm1947, f. 1348, RES: HHU.

126. RES, "Outline of Plan for National Theatre Activities," December 11, 1939, bMSAm1947, f. 1985, RES:HHU.

127. RES diary, May 31, 1938, 89M-66(b), RES:HHU.

128. RES, *There Shall Be No Night*, xxv–xxvi.

129. RES diary, April 13, 1939, 89M-66(b), RES:HHU.

130. RES diary, April 5, 1939, 89M-66(b), RES:HHU.

131. RES diary, April 7, 1939, 89M-66(b), RES:HHU.

132. JED to LFE, April 8, 1939, mr4763, ser. 3B, b. 6, EFP:Smithsonian.

133. RES diary, May 13, 1939, 89M-66(b), RES:HHU.

134. RES diary, August 22, 1939, 89M-66(b), RES:HHU.

135. RES diary, August 31, 1939, 89M-66(b), RES:HHU.

136. LFE to JED, July 20 and 21, 1939, mr4763, ser. 3B, b. 6, EFP:Smithsonian.

137. RosS to JED, August, 1939 (probably), mr4763, ser. 3B, b. 6, EFP:Smithsonian.

138. RES diary, November 30, 1939, 89M-66(b), RES:HHU.

139. RES diary, December 11, 1939, 89M-66(b), RES:HHU.

140. William L. White's December 25, 1939, radio address reprinted in *New York Herald Tribune*, June 9, 1940, MS Storage 275, b. 2, RES:HHU.

141. RES diary, January 13, 1940, 89M-66(b), RES:HHU.

142. RosS to JED, February 13, 1940, mr4763, ser. 3B, b. 6, EFP:Smithsonian.

143. RES, *There Shall Be No Night*, xi.

144. Cited in Jared Brown, *The Fabulous Lunts: A Biography of Alfred Lunt and Lynn Fontanne* (New York: Atheneum, 1988), 291.

145. RES, *There Shall Be No Night*, xi.

146. Ibid., xxvi.

147. Ibid., xxvii.

148. Ibid., xxviii.

149. Ibid., 149–150.

150. Ibid., xxix–xxx.

151. Ibid., 20.

152. Ibid., 22.

153. Ibid., 49.

154. Ibid., 86.

155. Ibid., 89.

156. Ibid., 99–100.

157. Quoted in Alonso, *Peace as a Women's Issue*, 138.

158. Maxwell Anderson to RES, n.d., bMSAm1947, f. 27, RES:HHU.

159. Quoted in Patricia Bosworth, *Montgomery Clift: A Biography* (New York: Bantam Books, 1978), 78.

160. Cited in Brown, *The Fabulous Lunts*, 292.

161. Ibid.

162. L. A. Sloper, *Christian Science Monitor*, April 2, 1940, MS Storage 275, b. 1, RES:HHU.

163. Brooks Atkinson, "Sherwood and the Lunts," *New York Times*, May 5, 1940, sec. 10, 1.

164. Richard Lockridge, "The New Play," clipping, MS Storage 275, b. 2, RES: HHU.

165. Gilbert Kanour, clipping, MS Storage 275, b. 2, RES:HHU.

166. Richard Watts Jr., clipping, MS Storage 275, b. 2, RES:HHU.

167. Burns Mantle, *The Best Plays of 1939–40 and the Yearbook of the Drama in America* (New York: Dodd, Mead, 1940), vi.

168. AW to Lynn Fontanne, June 12, 1940, bMSAm1947, f. 1714, RES:HHU.

169. L/F to AW, December 30, 1940, bMSAm1449, f. 551, AW:HHU.

170. Quoted in Brown, *The Fabulous Lunts*, 293.

171. Felix Frankfurter to RES, April 23, 1940, bMSAm1947, f. 300, RES:HHU.

172. RES royalties, US MssiAN, b. 3, f. 6, PPC:SHSW.

173. RES to Herbert Hoover, May 10, 1940, bMSAm1947, f. 1228, RES:HHU.

174. Sidney B. Whipple, "Sherwood Play Is Picked by Pulitzer Group," *New York World-Telegram*, May 6, 1941, clipping, mr4764, ser. 3B, b. 6, EFP:Smithsonian.

175. Unsigned clipping, "Author Holds It Writers' Duty to Warn America of Naziism," May 3, 1940, bMSAm1947, f. 2411a, RES:HHU.

176. RES, "Stop Hitler Now!" ad, *New York Post*, June 10, 1940, bMSAm1947, f. 2411a, RES:HHU.

177. William Allen White to RES, June 14, 1940, bMSAm1947, f. 877, RES: HHU.

178. RES to William Allen White, June 17, 1940, bMSAm1947, f. 1621, RES: HHU.

179. Unsigned clipping, "Roosevelt Praises 'Stop Hitler' Move," *London Evening Standard*, June 12, 1940, bMSAm1947, f. 2411a, RES:HHU.

180. Lynn Fontanne to AW, July 31, 1940, bMSAm1449, f. 550, AW:HHU.

181. *New York Times Magazine*, July 7, 1940, clipping, bMSAm1947, f. 2411a, RES: HHU.

182. RES, "Radio Speech to Canada and the British Empire," typescript, August 25, 1940, bMSAm1947, f. 2189, RES:HHU.

183. Editorial, *Toronto Daily Star*, July 13, 1940, clipping, bMSAm1947, f. 2411a, RES:HHU.

184. "Sherwood Assails Ford, Lindbergh," *New York Times*, August 26, 1940, clipping, bMSAm1947, f. 2411a, RES:HHU.

185. Walter Winchell, "On Broadway," n.d., clipping, bMSAm1947, f. 2411a, RES:HHU.

8. Sherwood and Roosevelt

1. Paul Green, *Johnny Johnson* (music by Kurt Weill), in *Five Plays of the South* (New York: Hill and Wang, 1963), 100.

2. RES, "The Responsibilities and Opportunities Attached to Leadership in a Democracy," typescript speech delivered at Milton Academy, April 28, 1954, bMSAm1947, f. 2249, RES:HHU.

3. RES, *Roosevelt and Hopkins: An Intimate History* (1948, 1950; reprint, New York: enigma books, 2001), 4.

4. Ibid., 168.

5. RES to HH, July 30, 1940, bMSAm1947, f. 1232, RES:HHU.

6. LFE to JED, July 3, 1940, mr4763, ser. 3B, b. 6, EFP:Smithsonian.

7. RosS to JED, July 21, 1940, mr4763, ser. 3B, b. 6, EFP:Smithsonian.

8. JED to LFE, May 20, 1940, mr4763, ser. 3B, b. 6, EFP:Smithsonian.

9. RES to HH, July 16, 1940, bMSAm1947, f. 1232, RES:HHU.

10. RosS and AS quoted in Collie Small to RES, February 11, 1949, bMSAm1947, f. 750, RES:HHU.

11. RES, *Roosevelt and Hopkins*, 179.

12. Samuel I. Rosenman, *Working with Roosevelt* (New York: Harper and Brothers, 1952), 8.

13. RES, *Roosevelt and Hopkins*, 179.

14. Ibid., 207.

15. Ibid., 209.

16. Ibid.

17. Ibid., 210.

18. RES to Ernest Brandenburg, October 1, 1948, bMSAm1947, f. 111, RES:HHU.

19. FDR quoted in Ernest Brandenburg, "The Preparation of Franklin D. Roosevelt's Speeches," *Quarterly Journal of Speech* 35, no. 2 (April 1949): 214, bMSAm1947, f. 111, RES:HHU.

20. Rosenman, *Working with Roosevelt*, 233.

21. Ibid., 234.

22. Ibid., 232.

23. Ibid., 240.

24. FDR, "Campaign Speech, Madison Square Garden, New York City," October 28, 1940, in Basil Rauch, ed., *The Roosevelt Reader: Selected Speeches, Messages, Press Conferences, and Letters of Franklin D. Roosevelt* (New York: Rinehart, 1957), 258–267.

25. Rosenman, *Working with Roosevelt*, 240.

26. FDR, "Campaign Address at Boston, Massachusetts," October 30, 1940, in

FDR, *The Public Papers and Addresses of Franklin D. Roosevelt with a Special Introduction and Explanatory Notes by President Roosevelt, 1940 Volume: War—and Aid to Democracies* (New York: Macmillan, 1941), 514–524.

27. RES, *Roosevelt and Hopkins*, 196.

28. FDR, "Campaign Address at Cleveland, Ohio," November 2, 1940, in *Public Papers, 1940*, 544–553; Rosenman, *Working with Roosevelt*, 252.

29. Rosenman, *Working with Roosevelt*, 253.

30. RES, "Hyde Park Revisited," typescript for *New York Times Magazine*, April 9, 1950, bMSAm1947, f. 2091, RES:HHU.

31. Rosenman, *Working with Roosevelt*, 254.

32. Quoted in "Lyons Den" column, *Boston Herald*, December 25, 1955, RES: HUA.

33. Elmer Rice, *Minority Report: An Autobiography* (New York: Simon and Schuster, 1963), 402.

34. RES, *Roosevelt and Hopkins*, 201.

35. "People of the Week," editorial, *New York Daily News*, December 14, 1944, clipping, MS Storage 275, b. 2, RES:HHU.

36. Unsigned clipping, n.d., bMSAm1947, f. 1445, RES:HHU.

37. RES to John Gunther, November 7, 1949, bMSAm1947, f. 1194, RES:HHU.

38. Ibid.

39. RES to Ed Sullivan, November 14, 1951, USMss111AN, b. 1, f. 9, Ed Sullivan Papers:SHSW.

40. SNB, *People in a Diary: A Memoir by S. N. Behrman* (Boston: Little, Brown, 1972), 224.

41. Rosamund Sherwood to RES, November 7, 1940, 89M-66(b), b. 2, RES: HHU.

42. Behrman, *People in a Diary*, 225.

43. RES to L/F, November 13, 1940, Mss622, L/F:SHSW.

44. MHS to RosS, September 14, 1942, MS Storage 275, b. 2, RES:HHU.

45. RES, *Roosevelt and Hopkins*, 220.

46. Lynn Fontanne to AW, March 19, 1941, bMSAm1449, f. 551, AW:HHU.

47. RES diary, February 1, 1941, 89M-66(b), b. 1, RES:HHU.

48. RES diary, February 2, 1941, 89M-66(b), b. 1, RES:HHU.

49. RES diary, March 16, 1941, 89M-66(b), b. 1, RES:HHU.

50. Ibid.

51. RosS to JED, March 20, 1941, mr4764, ser. 3B, b. 6, EFP:Smithsonian.

52. RosS to JED, April 14, 1941, mr4764, ser. 3B, b. 6, EFP:Smithsonian.

53. John Wharton to SNB, April 28, 1941, b. 18, f. 10, SNB:NYPL/42nd Street.

54. RES quoted in Henry R. Luce, *The American Century* (New York: Farrar and Rinehart, 1941), 80, 86, 89.

55. RosS to JED, May 8, 1941, mr4764, ser. 3B, b. 6, EFP:Smithsonian.

56. FDR, "President Franklin Delano Roosevelt Radio Address Announcing the Proclamation of an Unlimited National Emergency, 'We Choose Human Freedom,'"

May 27, 1941, http://www.usmm.org/fdr/emergency.html, accessed February 8, 2006.

57. LFE to JED, June 4, 1941, mr4764, ser. 3B, b. 6, EFP:Smithsonian.

58. RES to RosS, June 20, 1941, MS Storage 275, b. 2, RES:HHU.

59. Background information on RES and his propaganda work informed by Clayton D. Laurie, *The Propaganda Warriors: America's Crusade Against Nazi Germany* (Lawrence: University Press of Kansas, 1996); Holly Cowan Shulman, *The Voice of America: Propaganda and Democracy, 1941–1945* (Madison: University of Wisconsin Press, 1990); and Allan M. Winkler, *The Politics of Propaganda: The Office of War Information, 1942–1945* (New Haven: Yale University Press, 1978).

60. RES to FDR, July 12, 1941, bMSAm1947, f. 1468, RES:HHU.

61. FDR quoted in RES to WD, July 12, 1941, bMSAm1947, f. 1101, RES:HHU.

62. RES to WD, July 12, 1941, bMSAm1947, f. 1101, RES:HHU.

63. Ibid.

64. RosS to JED, July, 1941, mr4764, ser. 3B, b. 6, EFP:Smithsonian.

65. Slim to RES, July 21, 1941, USMssIAN, b. 3, f. 6, PPC:SHSW.

66. RES, "The Front Line Is in Our Hearts," typescript for *Ladies' Home Journal*, August 1941, bMSAm1947, RES:HHU.

67. RES, November 20, 1941, bMSAm1947, bMSAm1947, f. 2180, RES:HHU.

68. RES to Edward P. Lilly, December 4, 1945, bMSAm1947, f. 1314, RES:HHU.

69. RES to HH, December 17, 1941, bMSAm1947, f. 1232, RES:HHU.

70. RES to Edward P. Lilly, December 4, 1945, bMSAm1947, f. 1314, RES:HHU.

71. RES cited in Winkler, *Politics of Propaganda*, 28–29.

72. FDR, "War Message to Congress," December 8, 1941, in *The Roosevelt Reader*, 300–301.

73. Quoted in Rosenman, *Working with Roosevelt*, 310.

74. JED to LFE, December 11, 1941, mr4764, ser. 3B, b. 6, EFP:Smithsonian.

75. LFE to JED, December 11, 1941, mr4764, ser. 3B, b. 6, EFP:Smithsonian.

76. RosS to JED, December 10, 1941, mr4764, ser. 3B, b. 6, EFP:Smithsonian.

77. RosS to JED, January 1, 1942, mr4764, ser. 3B, b. 6, EFP:Smithsonian.

78. RosS to JED, January 15, 1942, mr4764, ser. 3B, b. 7, EFP:Smithsonian.

79. RES to WD, February 13, 1942, bMSAm1947, f. 1101, RES:HHU.

80. RES to WD, n.d., bMSAm1947, f. 1101, RES:HHU.

81. RES to HH, February 24, 1942, bMSAm1947, f. 1232, RES:HHU.

82. RES to HH, March 9, 1942, bMSAm1947, f. 1232, RES:HHU.

83. Cited in Winkler, *Politics of Propaganda*, 77.

84. Ibid.

85. Quoted in John Houseman, *Front and Center* (New York: Simon and Schuster, 1979), 24.

86. Quoted ibid., 34.

87. RES to Edward P. Lilly, December 4, 1945, bMSAm1947, f. 1314, RES:HHU.

88. Houseman, *Front and Center*, 35.

89. Ibid., 41.

90. FDR to RES, June 13, 1942, bMSAm1947, f. 694, RES:HHU.

91. RES to Edward P. Lilly, December 4, 1945, bMSAm1947, f. 1314, RES:HHU.

92. RES to HH, December 9, 1942, bMSAm1947, f. 1232, RES:HHU.

93. "Silhouette: Robert Emmet Sherwood," unsigned article in *The English-Speaking World*, 217–223, n.d., MS Storage 275, b. 2, RES:HHU.

94. RosS to JED, November 28, 1942, mr4764, ser. 3B, b. 7, EFP:Smithsonian.

95. RES to Edward P. Lilly, January 9, 1947, bMSAm1947, f. 1314, RES:HHU.

96. RES to Rex Stout, July 6, 1943, bMSAm1947, f. 1541, RES:HHU.

97. Included with FDR to RES, n.d., bMSAm1947, f. 694, RES:HHU.

98. Text of Japanese flier, 1942, bMSAm1947, f. 1232, RES:HHU.

99. RES, "Footnote to a Preface," typescript for *Saturday Review of Literature Anniversary Issue*, July 7, 1949, bMSAm1947, f. 2080, RES:HHU.

100. Unsigned London newspaper clipping, n.d., mr4766, ser. 10A, b. 8, EFP:Smithsonian.

101. RES, "F.D.R. at Shangri-la," typescript, December 2, 1953, bMSAm1947, f. 2144, RES:HHU.

102. Lynn Fontanne to JED and Wilfrid de Glehn, December 18, 1942, Mss622, b. 3, f. 1, L/F:SHSW.

103. Quoted in MHS to RosS, November 24, 1943, MS Storage 275, b. 2, RES:HHU.

104. Quoted in Laurie, *Propaganda Warriors*, 177.

105. RES to Edward W. Barrett, June 11, 1953, bMSAm1947, f. 966, RES:HHU.

106. RES to Elmer Davis, June 14, 1943, bMSAm1947, f. 1089, RES:HHU.

107. RES to Elmer Davis, November 24, 1943, bMSAm1947, f. 1089, RES:HHU.

108. Quoted in Winkler, *Politics of Propaganda*, 106.

109. Elmer Davis to RES, January 8, 1944, bMSAm1947, f. 219, RES:HHU.

110. Document signed by RES and Elmer Davis, February 5, 1944, bMSAm1947, f. 2445, RES:HHU.

111. Davis/RES agreement, February 7, 1944, cited in Winkler, *Politics of Propaganda*, 109.

112. Unsigned, "People of the Week," n.d., MS Storage 275, b. 2, RES:HHU.

113. RES, *There Shall Be No Night* (Greece version), act 1, scene 1, typescript, 1943, bMSAm1947, f. 1830, RES:HHU.

114. Ibid.

115. Ibid., act 3, scene 1.

116. Ibid., act. 3, scene 2.

117. Alfred Lunt to RES, August 24, 1944, Mss622, b. 5, f. 16, L/F:SHSW.

118. Quoted in Jared Brown, *The Fabulous Lunts: A Biography of Alfred Lunt and Lynn Fontanne* (New York: Atheneum, 1988), 311.

119. Episode cited in George Freedley, *The Lunts* (New York: Macmillan, 1958), 77.

120. P. Metaxas to RES, March 2, 1944, bMSAm1947, f. 567, RES:HHU.

121. Quoted in MHS to RosS, March 20, 1944, MS Storage 275, b. 2, RES: HHU.

122. Unsigned article, "ABSIE Warns Patriots to Await Signal," *New York Daily News*, May 1, 1944, p. M1, MS Storage 275, b. 2, RES:HHU.

123. RES, "Preface for *The New Yorker War Pieces*," typescript, n.d., bMSAm1947, f. 2053, RES:HHU.

124. John Mason Brown, review of *Roosevelt and Hopkins* for *Saturday Review*, typescript, n.d., bMSAm1947, f. 124, RES:HHU.

125. Quoted in MHS to RosS, July 8, 1944, MS Storage 275, b. 2, RES:HHU.

126. RES, "Statement over A.B.S.I.E.—Top Secret," n.d., bMSAm1947, f. 2018, RES:HHU.

127. Quoted in MHS to RosS, July 8, 1944, MS Storage 275, b. 2, RES:HHU.

128. Elmer Davis to RES, September 10, 1944, bMSAm1947, f. 219, RES:HHU.

129. RES to Elmer Davis, September 22, 1944, bMSAm1947, f. 1089, RES: HHU.

130. Elmer Davis to RES, September 25, 1944, bMSAm1947, f. 219, RES:HHU.

131. RES to FDR, n.d., bMSAm1947, f. 1468, RES:HHU.

132. RES to Elmer Davis, "Confidential," September 20, 1944, bMSAm1947, f. 1089, RES:HHU.

133. Ibid.

134. Ibid.

135. RES, *Roosevelt and Hopkins*, 784.

136. FDR, "Campaign Speech to the Teamsters Union," September 23, 1944, in *The Roosevelt Reader*, 363–372.

137. Ibid.

138. Rosenman, *Working with Roosevelt*, 506.

139. FDR to RES, November 25, 1944, bMSAm1947, f. 694, RES:HHU.

140. RES to Victor Samrock and William Fields, February 17, 1945, USMss1AN, b.3, f. 7, PPC:SHSW.

141. RES, *Roosevelt and Hopkins*, 839; and RES to Senator Herbert Lehman, April 2, 1955, bMSAm1947, f. 1305, RES:HHU.

142. FDR to General Douglas MacArthur, January 20, 1945, bMSAm1947, f. 1305, RES:HHU.

143. RES to FDR, n.d. bMSAm1947, f1468, RES:HHU.

144. RES, *Roosevelt and Hopkins*, 841.

145. RES diary, April 12, 1945, 89M-66(b), b. 1, RES:HHU.

146. RES, "Remarks of RES on the Death of President Roosevelt," typescript, April 13, 1945, bMSAm1947, f. 761, RES:HHU.

147. RES diary, April 13, 1945, 89M-66(b), b. 1, RES:HHU.

148. RES, "The Shortest News Flash" for *Redbook Magazine*, typescript, January 8, 1951, bMSAm1947, f. 2101, RES:HHU.

149. RES, *Roosevelt and Hopkins*, 844.

150. RES to FDR, March 29, 1945, bMSAm1947, f. 1468, RES:HHU.

151. RES, "I Am Passing Up V-E Day" for *Colliers*, typescript, n.d., bMSAm1947, f. 2027, RES:HHU.

152. RES to Maurice Child, August 23, 1945, bMSAm1947, f. 1041, RES:HHU.

153. RES diary, August 14, 1945, 89M-66(b), b. 1, RES:HHU.

9. Changing the Message

1. Sir Robert Bruce Lockhart, *Friends, Foes and Foreigners* (London: Putnam–Richard Clay, 1957), 98, 103.

2. RES diary, May 22, 1945, 89M-66(b), b. 1, RES:HHU.

3. RES to Mary and Edgar Stillman Jr., November 11, 1946, MS Storage 275, b. 1, RES:HHU.

4. RES, "The Dwelling Place of Wonder," *Theatre Arts* (February 1941): 120–122, bMSAm1947, f. 2005, RES:HHU.

5. RES, "Footnote to a Preface," typescript for *Saturday Review of Literature Anniversary Issue,* July 7, 1949, bMSAm1947, f. 2080, RES:HHU.

6. RES, "Address before the New England Theatre Conference," typescript, October 4, 1952, bMSAm1947, f. 2241, RES:HHU.

7. Ibid.

8. SNB to John Wharton, RES, Elmer Rice, and Maxwell Anderson, May 5, 1945, USMssIAN, b. 1, f. 8, PPC:SHSW.

9. RES to SNB, Maxwell Anderson, Elmer Rice, and John Wharton, May 9, 1945, USMssIAN, b. 3, f. 7, PPC:SHSW.

10. Maxwell Anderson to RES, SNB, Elmer Rice, and John Wharton, May 24, 1945, USMssIAN, b. 1, f. 4, PPC:SHSW.

11. Maxwell Anderson to "Company," June 2, 1945, USMssIAN, b. 1, f. 4, PPC: SHSW.

12. RES to SNB, December 29, 1945, MssCol 248, b. 23, f. 12, SNB:NYPL/42nd Street.

13. Maxwell Anderson to SNB, August 1, 1946, MssCol 248, b. 1, f. 7, SNB: NYPL/42nd Street.

14. RES to SNB, April 6, 1950, bMSAm1947, f. 977, RES:HHU.

15. SNB to RES, July 19, 1950, bMSAm1947, f. 69, RES:HHU.

16. John Wharton to Maxwell Anderson, SNB, Elmer Rice, RES, and Victor Samrock, May 15, 1945, USMssIAN, b. 1, f. 2, PPC:SHSW.

17. RES diary, April 6, 1945, 89M-66(b), b. 1, RES:HHU.

18. RES diary, April 7, 1945, 89M-66(b), b. 1, RES:HHU.

19. RES to JED, May 2, 1945, MS Storage 275, b. 1, RES:HHU.

20. RES, "Our New Western Frontier," typescript, n.d., bMSAm1947, f. 2034, RES:HHU.

21. RES, "I Am Passing Up V-E Day," typescript of article for *Colliers,* n.d., bMSAm1947, f. 2027, RES:HHU.

22. RES, *The Rugged Path,* typescript, 1945, act 1, scene 2, 11, NCOF+(Sherwood, RE Rugged Path), NYPL/LC.

23. Ibid., act 1, scene 3, 23.

24. Ibid., act 1, scene 6, 46.

25. Elmer Rice, *Minority Report: An Autobiography* (New York: Simon and Schuster, 1963), 395.

26. RES, *The Rugged Path,* act 2, scene 10, 36.

27. Ibid., act 2, scene 10, 37.

28. Ibid., act 2, scene 10, 38.

29. Ibid., act 2, scene 11, 47.

30. Burns Mantle, ed., *The Best Plays of 1945–46 and the Yearbook of the Drama in America* (New York: Dodd, Mead, 1946), 308–309.

31. Arthur Hopkins quoted in SNB, *People in a Diary: A Memoir by S. N. Behrman* (Boston: Little, Brown, 1972), 227.

32. Reviewer cited in R. Baird Shuman, *Robert E. Sherwood* (New York: Twayne Publishers, 1964), 109.

33. John F. Wharton, *Life among the Playwrights: Being Mostly the Story of the Playwrights Producing Company, Inc.* (New York: Quadrangle/New York Times Book, 1974), 137.

34. RES to Jay Carmody, December 29, 1948, bMSAm1947, f. 1033, RES:HHU.

35. Victor Samrock quoted in Bill Davidson, *Spencer Tracy: Tragic Idol* (New York: E. P. Dutton, 1987), 95.

36. Victor Samrock to RES, September 17, 1945, USMssIAN, b. 48, f. 1, PPC: SHSW.

37. Davidson, *Spencer Tracy,* 96.

38. Victor Samrock to Spencer Tracy, October 16, 1945, USMssIAN, b. 48, f. 1, PPC:SHSW.

39. Quoted in Davidson, *Spencer Tracy,* 97.

40. Ibid.

41. RES to Spencer Tracy, December 12, 1945, USMssIAN, b. 48, f. 1, PPC: SHSW.

42. RES to Spencer Tracy, December 18, 1945, bMSAm1947, f. 1567, RES:HHU.

43. Victor Samrock quoted in Davidson, *Spencer Tracy,* 97.

44. Victor Samrock to RES, December 27, 1945, USMssIAN, b. 48, f. 1, PPC: SHSW.

45. Victor Samrock to RES, January 2, 1946, USMssIAN, b. 48, f. 1, PPC: SHSW.

46. "Statement of RES Account with *The Rugged Path* as of April 30, 1946," USMssIAN, b. 3, f. 7, PPC:SHSW.

47. RES to Victor Samrock, January 11, 1946, USMssIAN, b. 48, f. 1, PPC: SHSW.

48. Victor Samrock to RES, January 9, 1946, USMssIAN, b. 48, f. 1, PPC: SHSW.

49. RES to Victor Samrock, January 11, 1946, USMssIAN, b. 48, f. 1, PPC: SHSW.

50. Laurence Schwab, "Look Here, Now!" clipping, *Miami Daily News*, January 13, 1946, b. 6, PPC:NYPL/42nd Street.

51. William Fields to Spencer Tracy, January 18, 1946, b. 6, PPC:NYPL/42nd Street.

52. Victor Samrock to RES, January 21, 1946, USMssIAN, b. 3, f. 7, PPC:SHSW.

53. RES to Victor Samrock and William Fields, January 24, 1946, USMssIAN, b. 48, f. 1, PPC:SHSW.

54. RES to Samuel Goldwyn, October 6, 1945, f. 1181, RES:HHU.

55. William Herndon to RES, September 28, 1944, USMssIAN, b. 3, f. 7, PPC: SHSW.

56. "Interview for WNYE Program, 'On Stage,'" typescript, January 26, 1954, bMSAm1947, f. 2150, RES:HHU.

57. Samuel Goldwyn quoted in A. Scott Berg, *Goldwyn: A Biography* (New York: Alfred A. Knopf, 1989), 393. Background information on Goldwyn adapted from the same book.

58. RES to Samuel Goldwyn, January 10, 1951, bMSAm1947, f. 1181, RES:HHU.

59. RES, "Hollywood Revisited," typescript for *Sunday Times Magazine*, November 8, 1946, bMSAm1947, f. 2044, RES:HHU.

60. RES to Samuel Goldwyn, August 27, 1945, bMSAm1947, f. 1181, RES:HHU.

61. RES, "Hollywood Revisited."

62. RES to Samuel Goldwyn, October 6, 1945, bMSAm1947, f. 1181, RES:HHU.

63. RES to SNB, December 29, 1945, MssCol 248, b. 23, f. 12, SNB:NYPL/42nd Street.

64. RES, "Hollywood Revisited."

65. RES to Samuel Goldwyn and William Wyler, April 22, 1946, bMSAm1947, f. 1181, RES:HHU.

66. RES, "Hollywood Revisited."

67. MacKinlay Kantor, *Glory for Me* (New York: Coward-McCann, 1945), 14.

68. RES and William Wyler quoted in Berg, *Goldwyn*, 411.

69. RES, *The Best Years of Our Lives*, Samuel Goldwyn, 1946 (DVD: MGM Entertainment, 2000).

70. RES, "Will Atomic Fission Destroy God?" typescript, January 4, 1947, bMSAm1947, f. 2050, RES:HHU.

71. RES, "Please Don't Frighten Us," *Atlantic Monthly* (January 1949): 77–79, bMSAm1947, f. 2074, RES:HHU.

72. RES, *The Best Years of Our Lives*.

73. Background information on the antinuclear movement is given in great detail in Lawrence S. Wittner, *One World or None: A History of the World Nuclear Disarmament Movement through 1953* (Stanford: Stanford University Press, 1993).

74. Ethel Barrymore, Gregory Ratoff, Hedda Hopper, Cole Porter, and George Cukor to RES, October 29, 1946, bMSAm1947, f. 322, RES:HHU.

75. All quoted in Berg, *Goldwyn*, 419.

76. RosS to JED, October 30, 1946, MS Storage 275, b. 1, RES:HHU.

77. RES, "The Strength, the Might and the Glory," typescript, April 23, 1945, bMSAm1947, f.2022, RES:HHU.

78. RES, *The Twilight*, typescript, 1947, act 2, scene 5, 29, 31, bMSAm1947, f. 1824, RES:HHU.

79. Lynn Fontanne to RES, April 1947, Mss622, b. 5, f. 16, L/F:SHSW.

80. RES to L/F, June 2, 1947, Mss622, b. 5, f. 16, L/F:SHSW.

81. RES to L/F, July 26, 1947, Mss622, b. 5, f. 16, L/F:SHSW.

82. Alfred Lunt to RES, August 2, 1947, Mss622, b. 5, f. 16, L/F:SHSW.

83. Unsigned article, "Sherwood in New Role," clipping, *CUE*, June 18, 1949, 17, MS Storage 275, b. 2, RES:HHU.

84. RES to Alfred Lunt, June 12, 1955, Mss622, b. 5, f. 16, L/F:SHSW.

85. Harry S Truman to RES, May 23, 1946, bMSAm1947, f. 823, RES:HHU.

86. RES to Collie Small, February 11, 1949, bMSAm1947, f. 750, RES:HHU.

87. Archibald MacLeish, book review, n.d., clipping, bMSAm1947, f. 2411a, RES:HHU.

88. Joseph Barnes, *New York Herald Tribune Weekly Book Review*, October 24, 1948, clipping, bMSAm1947, f. 2411a, RES:HHU.

89. Elmer Davis, *Saturday Review of Literature*, October 23, 1948, clipping, bMSAm1947, f. 2411a, RES:HHU.

90. Leonard Lyons, "The Lyons Den" column, *Boston Herald*, May 5, 1949, clipping, bMSAm1947, f. 448, RES:HHU.

91. RES to David Stelling, January 28, 1949, bMSAm1947, f. 1530, RES:HHU.

92. RES to Wilfrid de Glehn, December 19, 1948, MS Storage 275, b. 2, RES:HHU.

93. RES to Edgar Stillman Jr., February 25, 1947, MS Storage 275, b. 1, RES:HHU.

94. LFE to JED, July 28, 1948, mr4765, ser. 3B, b. 7, EFP:Smithsonian.

95. RES to Elmer Davis, May 7, 1949, bMSAm1947, f. 1089, RES:HHU.

96. Unsigned article, "Sherwood in New Role," *CUE*, June 18, 1949, 17, clipping, MS Storage 275, b. 2, RES:HHU.

97. RES to Irving Berlin, October 26, 1938, bMSAm1947, f. 983, RES:HHU.

98. Harry Harris, "Robert E. Sherwood," *Miss Liberty*, program, June 19, 1949, USMssIAN, b. 50, f. 15, PPC:SHSW.

99. William Fields to Al Hine, July 17, 1949, b. 5, PPC:NYPL/42nd Street.

100. "Sherwood in New Role," 17.

101. RES to John Mason Brown, May 10, 1949, bMSAm1947, f. 1013, RES:HHU.

102. RES to Rosamund Sherwood, March 6, 1949, MS Storage 275, b. 2, RES:HHU.

103. RES to John Mason Brown, June 7, 1949, bMSAm1947, f. 1013, RES:HHU.

104. Mary Ellin Barrett, *Irving Berlin: A Daughter's Memoir* (New York: Simon and Schuster, 1994), 252.

105. Quoted in Laurence Bergreen, *As Thousands Cheer: The Life of Irving Berlin* (New York: Viking Penguin, 1990), 488.

106. Wharton, *Life among the Playwrights*, 186.

107. Brooks Atkinson, Ward Morehouse, Richard Watts Jr., Robert Sylvester, and Hobe Morrison quoted in Edward Jablonski, *Irving Berlin: American Troubadour* (New York: Henry Holt, 1999), 262.

108. Financial report, December 2, 1949, b. 1, "Correspondence 1940–1950" folder, PPC:NYPL/42nd Street.

109. RES to Rosamund Sherwood, October 20, 1950, MS Storage 275, b. 2, RES: HHU.

110. RES to JED, September 28, 1949, MS Storage 275, b. 2, RES:HHU.

10. The Message Is Lost

1. RES to Annette Saphire, December 31, 1945, bMSAm1947, f. 1492, RES: HHU.

2. RES, "An Examination of U.S. Foreign Policy Objectives in Relation to American Political and Moral Values, with Particular Reference to the Contemporary Situation," typescript, October 19, 1953, bMSAm1947, f. 2246, RES:HHU.

3. RES, intro. to Trygve Lie, *Peace on Earth* (New York: Heritage House, 1949), 2, 4.

4. Cited in Lawrence S. Wittner, *One World or None: A History of the World Nuclear Disarmament Movement through 1953* (Stanford: Stanford University Press, 1993), 70.

5. RES, "Excerpt from 'The Myth That Threatens the World,'" typescript, December 4, 1949, bMSAm1947, f. 2086, RES:HHU.

6. RES, "What America Means to Me," transcript, January 12, 1951, bMSAm1947, f. 2102, RES:HHU.

7. RES, "Introduction to Adlai Stevenson," typescript, October 15, 1952, bMSAm1947, f. 2130, RES:HHU.

8. Unsigned article, "Sherwood Urges Europe's Defense," *New York Times*, April 30, 1951, clipping, USMssIAN, b. 4, f. 1, PPC:SHSW.

9. RES, "Statement for the Committee on the Present Danger" typescript, n.d., bMSAm1947, f. 2122, RES:HHU.

10. RES, "The Responsibilities and Opportunities Attached to Leadership in a Democracy," typescript, April 28, 1954, bMSAm1947, f. 2249, RES:HHU.

11. Ibid.

12. RES to Edgar Stillman Jr., August 29, 1947, MS Storage 275, b. 1, RES: HHU.

13. RES Statement, February 15, 1946, bMSAm1947, f. 2180, RES:HHU.

14. Elmer Rice to RES, November 8, 1946, bMSThr380, f. 193–199, Elmer Rice Papers:HU.

15. RES Statement in Support of Isador Lubin, typescript, February 28, 1950, bMSAm1947, f. 2087a, RES:HHU.

16. RES to the Honorable Leverett Saltonstall, December 9, 1950, bMSAm1947, f. 1489, RES:HHU.

17. RES to Dwight D. Eisenhower, April 13, 1954, bMSAm1947, f. 1117, RES: HHU.

18. RES, "Individual Freedom and National Security," typescript, n.d., bMSAm1947, f. 2260, RES:HHU.

19. RES, intro. to Merle Miller, *The Judges and the Judged* (New York: Doubleday, 1952), 10, 14.

20. Laurence G. Avery, ed., *Dramatist in America: Letters of Maxwell Anderson, 1912–1958* (Chapel Hill: University of North Carolina Press, 1977), 254n1.

21. Elmer Rice to Maxwell Anderson, February 4, 1952, in John F. Wharton, *Life among the Playwrights: Being Mostly the Story of the Playwrights Producing Company, Inc.* (New York: Quadrangle/New York Times Book, 1974), 209–213.

22. Ibid.

23. Maxwell Anderson to Elmer Rice, February 13, 1952 in Avery, *Dramatist in America*, 254–256.

24. Maxwell Anderson to John F. Wharton, February 20, 1952, ibid., 257–259.

25. RES to Maxwell Anderson, February 25, 1952, bMSAm1947, f. 933, RES: HHU.

26. RES to Rosamund Sherwood, October 20, 1950, MS Storage 275, b. 2, RES: HHU.

27. RES to MSJr, April 5, 1951, MS Storage 275, b. 1, RES:HHU.

28. MSJr to RES, May 15, 1951, MS Storage 275, b. 1, RES:HHU.

29. RES to JED, January 30, 1955, MS Storage 275, b. 2, RES:HHU.

30. RES, "The Orphaned Fatherland," typescript, in RES to Leonard Lyons, July 1, 1952, bMSAm1947, f. 2128, RES:HHU.

31. Ibid.

32. Quoted in Richard Schickel, *Elia Kazan: A Biography* (New York: Harper-Collins Publishers, 2005), 275.

33. RES, *Man on a Tightrope*, Twentieth Century Fox, 1953 (Cable Network FXM, December 19, 2004).

34. Quoted in William Baer, ed., *Elia Kazan Interviews* (Jackson: University Press of Mississippi, 2000), 172.

35. RES to Paul Bonner Jr., June 5, 1953, bMSAm1947, f. 995, RES:HHU.

36. RES, preface (1951) to Philip Barry, *Second Threshold* (New York: Harper and Brothers, 1949), xiii.

37. RES to Elmer Rice, August 30, 1950 in Wharton, *Life among the Playwrights*, 197.

38. Ibid., 200.

39. RES, *The Seventh Floor,* typescript, 1951, act 1, scene 1; act 1, scene 3; act 2, scene 5, bMSAm1947, f1820, RES:HHU.

40. RES to John Wharton, May 11, 1951, bMSAm1947, f. 1618, RES:HHU.

41. Wharton, *Life among the Playwrights,* 188.

42. John Wharton to RES, March 17, 1951, bMSAm1947, f. 871, RES:HHU.

43. Wharton, *Life among the Playwrights,* 230.

44. Maxwell Anderson to RES, April 24, 1951, bMSAm1947, f. 27, RES:HHU.

45. Elmer Rice to RES, March 14, 1951, USMssIAN, b. 4, f. 1, PPC:SHSW.

46. Alfred Lunt to RES, March 22, 1951, Mss622, b. 5, f. 16, L/F:SHSW.

47. Alfred Lunt to RES, April 19, 1951, Mss622, b. 5, f. 16, L/F:SHSW.

48. RES to Alfred Lunt, April 25, 1951, Mss622, b. 5, f. 16, L/F:SHSW.

49. RES to Victor Samrock, April 28, 1951, USMssIAN, b. 4, f. 1, PPC:SHSW.

50. Garson Kanin to RES, June 6, 1951, bMSAm1947, f. 431, RES:HHU.

51. Joseph Mankiewicz to RES, July 15, 1951, bMSAm1947, f. 539, RES:HHU.

52. RES quoted in Seymour Peck, "Mr. Sherwood Discusses a Combine," *New York Times,* December 28, 1952, xi.

53. RES, *The Better Angels,* typescript, 1952, act 1, scene 1, 8, bMSAm1947, f. 1739, RES:HHU.

54. Ibid., act 1, scene 1, 21.

55. Ibid., act 3, scene 4, 29.

56. RES quoted in Seymour Peck, "Mr. Sherwood Discusses a Combine," *New York Times,* December 18, 1952, xi.

57. RES to Laurence Olivier, August 6, 1952, bMSAm1947, f. 1406, RES:HHU.

58. MHS to Lynn Fontanne, December 21, 1952, Mss622, b. 5, f. 16, L/F:SHSW.

59. RES to Paul Bonner Jr., June 5, 1953, bMSAm1947, f. 995, RES:HHU.

60. RES to JED, March 26, 1954, MS Storage 275, b. 2, RES:HHU.

61. Jack Gould review for *New York Times* and Milton R. Bass review for *The Berkshire Evening Eagle,* December 31, 1953, clippings, MS Storage 275, b. 2. RES:HHU.

62. John Crosby, review of *Diary, New York Herald Tribune,* clipping, MS Storage 275, b. 2, RES:HHU.

63. RES, "The New Breed," *New York Herald Tribune,* April 21, 1954, clipping, bMSAm1947, f. 2151, RES:HHU.

64. RES, "The USSR versus the US (Operation Eggnog)—Confidential," typescript, n.d., bMSAm1947, f. 2111, RES:HHU.

65. Ibid.

66. RES, "1980: No Alternative," typescript for *Fortune Magazine,* 1955, bMSAm1947, f. 2171, RES:HHU.

67. RES, *Small War on Murray Hill* (1955; reprint, New York: Dramatists Play Service, 1957), 33.

68. Ibid., 34.

69. Ibid., 12.

70. Ibid., 35.

71. Ibid., 57.

72. Ibid., 41–42.

73. RES to Roger Stevens, April 11, 1955, USMssIAN, b. 4, f. 1, PPC:SHSW.

74. Alfred Lunt to RES, March 24, 1955, Mss622, b. 5, f. 16, L/F:SHSW.

75. RES to L/F, July 20, 1955, Mss622, b. 5, f. 16, L/F:SHSW.

76. RES to Victor Samrock, August 1, 1955, USMssIAN, b. 50, f. 12, PPC: SHSW.

77. RES to Edna Ferber, August 30, 1955, bMSAm1947, f. 1140, RES:HHU.

78. RES to Edna Ferber, October 7, 1955, USMss98AN, b. 1, f. 6, Edna Ferber Papers:SHSW.

79. RES diary, October 13, 1955, 89M-66(b), b. 1, RES:HHU.

80. RES to Anne DeKohary, August 11, 1953, bMSAm1947, f. 1093, RES:HHU.

81. RES diary, October 22, 1955, 89M-66(b), b. 1, RES:HHU.

82. RES diary, October 24, 1955, 89M-66(b), b. 1, RES:HHU.

83. Elmer Rice, "A Personal Memoir," typescript, n.d., MS Storage 275, b. 2, RES: HHU.

84. RES diary, November 6, 1955, 89M-66(b), b. 1, RES:HHU.

85. RES diary, November 11, 1955, 89M-66(b), b. 1, RES:HHU.

86. Rosamund Sherwood to JED, November 20, 1955, mr4765, ser. 3B, b. 7, EFP: Smithsonian.

87. JED to Rosamund Sherwood, December 29, 1955, mr4765, ser. 3B, b. 7, EFP: Smithsonian.

88. Rosamund Sherwood to JED, November 29, 1955, mr4765, ser. 3B, b. 7, EFP: Smithsonian.

89. Maxwell Anderson to MHS, November 19, 1955, bMSAm1947.1, f. 6, RES: HHU.

90. Quentin Reynolds to John Gunther, n.d., 89M-66(b), b. 2, RES:HHU.

91. Averell Harriman quoted ibid.

92. Rosamund Sherwood to MHS, December 3, 1955, 89M-66(b), b. 2, RES: HHU.

93. Grace Tully to MHS, November 21, 1955, bMSAm1947.1, f. 66, RES:HHU.

94. Adlai Stevenson to MHS, November 15, 1955, bMSAm1947.1, f. 58, RES: HHU.

95. Toots Shor to MHS, November 15, 1955, bMSAm1947.1, f. 55, RES:HHU.

96. SNB to "Dear Sir," November 1955 (probably), MssCol 248, b. 23, f. 12, SNB: NYPL/42nd Street.

97. SNB, *People in a Diary: A Memoir by S. N. Behrman* (Boston: Little, Brown, 1972), 227.

Epilogue

1. Flier, n.d., bMSAm1947, f. 1716, RES:HHU.

2. Robert Coleman, review, *New York Daily Mirror,* January 4, 1957, clipping, MS Storage 275, b. 2, RES:HHU.

3. John McClain, review, *New York Journal American,* January 4, 1957, clipping, MS Storage 275, b. 2, RES:HHU.

4. Brooks Atkinson, review, *New York Times,* n.d., clipping, MS Storage 275, b. 2, RES:HHU.

5. Walter F. Kerr, review, *New York Herald Tribune,* n.d., clipping, MS Storage 275, b. 2, RES:HHU.

6. MHS to L/F, January 9, 1957, Mss622, b. 5, f. 16, L/F:SHSW.

7. John F. Wharton, *Life among the Playwrights: Being Mostly the Story of the Playwrights Producing Company, Inc.* (New York: Quadrangle/New York Times Book, 1974), 236.

8. Rosamund Sherwood to JED, November 20, 1955, mr4765, ser. 3B, b. 7, EFP: Smithsonian.

9. Rosamund Sherwood to JED, February 21, 1956, mr4765, ser. 3B, b. 7, EFP: Smithsonian.

10. Ibid.

11. Rosamund Sherwood to JED, December 5, 1956, mr4765, ser. 3B, b. 7, EFP: Smithsonian.

12. RES to Walter Lippman, May 3, 1954, bMSAm1947, f. 1317, RES:HHU.

13. RES to Walter Lippman, April 22, 1955, bMSAm1947, f. 1317, RES:HHU.

Bibliography

Archival Sources

Alexander Woollcott Papers, 1887–1943. Houghton Library, Harvard University. Cambridge, Mass.

Alfred Lunt and Lynn Fontanne Papers, 1838–1983. Archives Division, State Historical Society of Wisconsin, Madison.

Arthur Sherwood Jr. Student Records. Harvard University Archives. Cambridge, Mass.

Ed Sullivan Papers. Archives Division, State Historical Society of Wisconsin. Madison.

Edna Ferber Papers. Archives Division, State Historical Society of Wisconsin. Madison.

Elmer Rice Papers. Theatre Collection, Harvard University. Cambridge, Mass.

Emmet Family Papers, 1792–1989. Archives of American Art, Smithsonian Institution. Washington, D.C.

John Mason Brown Papers. Houghton Library, Harvard University. Cambridge, Mass.

Judah-Brandon Family Papers, 1820–1950. Manuscripts and Archives Department, Indiana Historical Society. Indianapolis.

Marc Connelly Archives. The Howard Gotlieb Archival Research Center, Boston University. Boston, Mass.

Moss Hart Papers. Archives Division. State Historical Society of Wisconsin. Madison.

Motion Picture Association of America, Production Code Administration Records. Special Collections, Margaret Herrick Library, Academy of Motion Picture Arts and Sciences. Beverly Hills, Calif.

National Board of Review of Motion Pictures Papers. Rare Books and Manuscripts Division, Astor, Lenox and Tilden Foundations, New York Public Library, Forty-second Street. New York.

Philip Sherwood Student Records. Harvard University Archives. Cambridge, Mass.

Playwrights Producing Company Papers. Archives Division, State Historical Society of Wisconsin. Madison.

Playwrights Producing Company Press Department Records. Rare Books and Manuscripts Division, Astor, Lenox and Tilden Foundations, New York Public Library, Forty-second Street, New York.

Robert Benchley Papers. The Howard Gotlieb Archival Research Center, Boston University. Boston, Mass.

Robert Sherwood Manuscripts. Fales Collection, Elmer Bobst Library, New York University. New York.

Robert E. Sherwood Papers. Houghton Library, Harvard University. Cambridge, Mass.

Robert E. Sherwood Papers. Theatre Collection, Harvard University. Cambridge, Mass.

Robert E. Sherwood Plays. Billy Rose Theatre Collection, Astor, Lenox and Tilden Foundations, New York Public Library for the Performing Arts, Lincoln Center. New York.

Robert E. Sherwood Student Records. Harvard University Archives. Cambridge, Mass.

Robert E. Sherwood World War I Personnel Records © Department of National Defence. Reproduced with the permission of the Minister of Public Works and Government Services Canada (2006).Library and Archives Canada/RG 150, Ministry of the Overseas Military Forces of Canada fonds/Canadian Expeditionary Force personnel files/Accession 1992–93/166/Box 8862–28, file 2075473. National Archives of Canada. Ottawa.

Sidney Coe Howard Papers. The Bancroft Library, University of California. Berkeley.

S. N. Behrman Papers. Rare Books and Manuscripts Division, Astor, Lenox and Tilden Foundations, New York Public Library, Forty-second Street. New York.

World Federalists Papers. Manuscripts Department, The Lilly Library, Indiana University. Bloomington.

Periodicals

Life, 1921–1929.
New York Herald (Tribune), 1927–1945.
New York Times, 1927–1945.
Vanity Fair, 1919–1920.

Robert E. Sherwood's Published Plays, Books, Short Stories, Screenplays, and Radio and Television Scripts

"Abraham Lincoln," *Cavalcade of America*, Presented by DuPont, February 13, 1940.

Abe Lincoln in Illinois. New York: Charles Scribner's Sons, 1937, 1939.

"Extra! Extra!" In *The Best Short Stories of 1926 and the Yearbook of the American Short Story*. Ed. Edward J. O'Brien. New York: Dodd, Mead, 1926. 237–243.

Idiot's Delight. New York: Charles Scribner's Sons, 1935, 1936.

Miss Liberty. New York: Samuel French, 1949, 1977. (Lyrics and Music by Irving Berlin; book by Robert Sherwood.)

Marco Polo. In *How to Write and Sell Film Stories* by Marion Frances. 1937. Reprint ed. New York: Garland Publishing, 1978.

The Petrified Forest. New York: Charles Scribner's Sons, 1934, 1935.

The Queen's Husband. New York: Charles Scribner's Sons, 1928.

Reunion in Vienna. New York: Charles Scribner's Sons, 1932.

The Road to Rome. New York: Charles Scribner's Sons, 1927.

Robert E. Sherwood: Film Critic—The Best Moving Pictures of 1922–23. 1923. Reprint ed. New York: Revisionist Press, 1974.

Roosevelt and Hopkins: An Intimate History. 1948, 1950. Reprint ed. New York: enigma books, 2001.

Small War on Murray Hill. New York: Dramatists Play Service, 1955, 1957.

There Shall Be No Night. New York: Charles Scribner's Sons, 1941.

This Is New York. New York: Charles Scribner's Sons, 1931.

Tovarich (by Jacques Deval; adapted by Robert E. Sherwood). New York: Random House, 1937.

Unending Crusade. London: W. Heinemann, 1932.

The Virtuous Knight. New York: Charles Scribner's Sons, 1931.

Waterloo Bridge. New York: Charles Scribner's Sons, 1930.

Robert E. Sherwood's Unpublished Plays, Screenplays, and Television Scripts

Acropolis (a play), 1932.

Afterglow (a play), 1932.

Barnum Was Right (a play), 1920. (Book and lyrics by Robert E. Sherwood; music by S. P. Sears.)

The Better Angels (a play), 1952.

Diary (a television script), 1954.

Girls With Dogs (also known as *The Seventh Floor*) (a play), 1951.

The Love Nest (a play), 1926.

Marching As to War (a play), 1927.

Milk and Honey (a play), 1934.

On the Beach (a play), 1945.

The Oxford Accent (a play), ca. 1932.

Rebecca (a film script), 1939.

The Rugged Path (a play), 1945.

There Shall Be No Night (a play; Greece version), 1943.

The Twilight (a play), 1947.

Films Viewed

Abe Lincoln in Illinois. Max Gordon Plays and Pictures Corp., 1940. TCM: viewed February 12, 2004.

The Adventures of Marco Polo. Samuel Goldwyn, 1938. VHS: Samuel Goldwyn Home Entertainment/HBO, n.d.

The Best Years of Our Lives. Samuel Goldwyn, 1946. DVD: MGM Entertainment, 2000.

The Bishop's Wife. Samuel Goldwyn, 1947. DVD: MGM Home Entertainment, 2001.

The Divorce of Lady X. Alexander Korda Films, 1938. VHS: Madacy Entertainment Group, 1997.

The Emmets: Portrait of a Family. Nancy B. Doyle, John Child, and Marian L. Schwartz, 1988. VHS: Smithsonian Institution.

The Ghost Goes West. Alexander Korda Films, 1935. VHS: Samuel Goldwyn Home Entertainment/HBO, n.d.

Goldwyn: The Man and His Movies. A Peter Jones Production. DVD: Samuel Goldwyn Foundation, 2001.

Idiot's Delight. Lowe's Incorporated/Metro Goldwyn Mayer, 1939. VHS: MGM/UA Home Entertainment Group, 1985.

Irving Berlin: An American Song. VHS: A&E Television Networks: Biography, 1999.

Jupiter's Darling. Metro Goldwyn Mayer, 1955. VHS: MGM/UA Home Entertainment Video and Turner Entertainment, 1992.

Man on a Tightrope. Twentieth Century Fox, 1953. FXM: viewed December 19, 2004.

Northwest Passage. Metro Goldwyn Mayer, 1940. TCM: viewed 2004.

The Petrified Forest. Warner Bros., 1936. VHS: Turner Entertainment, 2000.

Rebecca. Selznick International, 1940. Channel 13/PBS: viewed 2002.

Roman Scandals. Samuel Goldwyn, 1933. VHS: MGM Home Entertainment, 2000.

The Royal Bed. RKO Radio Pictures, 1931. VHS: VCI Entertainment, 1997.

The Scarlet Pimpernel. Alexander Korda/United Artists, 1934. DVD: Madacy Entertainment Group, 1998.

The Ten-Year Lunch: The Wit and Legend of the Algonquin Round Table. Aviva Slesin. VHS: Aviva Films NY Corp., 1986.

Thunder in the City. United Artists, Akos Tolnay/Alexander Esway, 1937. VHS: Madacy Entertainment Group, 1997.

Vaudeville. Rosemary Garner for "American Masters." DVD: Thirteen/WNET, KCTS/9 Television and Palmer/Fenster, 1997.

Waterloo Bridge. Metro Goldwyn Mayer, 1940. VHS: Warner Bros., 2000.

Waterloo Bridge. Universal, 1931. "Forbidden Hollywood Collection: Volume One." DVD: Turner Entertainment, 2006.

Selected Published Articles, Prefaces, Introductions by Robert E. Sherwood

NOTE: Robert E. Sherwood wrote innumerable articles, many of which are referred to in the text and are noted in the endnotes. Since most of them are in archival collections and in typescript form, they are not included in this bibliography.

Barry, Philip. *Second Threshold: A Play*. With revisions and a preface by Robert E. Sherwood. New York: Harper and Brothers, 1949, 1951.

Benchley, Nathaniel. *Robert Benchley*. With a foreword by Robert E. Sherwood. New York: McGraw-Hill, 1955.

Burnett, Whit. *This Is My Best: America's 93 Greatest Living Authors*. Includes "Robert E. Sherwood: The Election of Lincoln," with excerpt from *Abe Lincoln in Illinois*. Cleveland: World Publishing, 1942.

Devereux,, James P. S. *The Story of Wake Island*. With a preface by Robert E. Sherwood. Philadelphia: J. B. Lippincott, 1947.

Lie, Trygve, et al. *Peace on Earth*. With an introduction by Robert E. Sherwood. New York: Hermitage House, 1949 (copyright © United Nations).

Luce, Henry R. *The American Century*. With comments by Robert E. Sherwood. New York: Farrar and Rinehart, 1941.

Miller, Merle. *The Judges and the Judged*. With a foreword by Robert E. Sherwood. Garden City, N.Y.: Doubleday, 1952.

Oppenheimer, George, ed. *The Passionate Playgoer: A Personal Scrapbook*. Includes "The Lunts," 79–86. New York: Viking Press, 1958.

Webster, H. T. *The Best of H. T. Webster: A Memorial Collection*. With a preface/introduction by Robert E. Sherwood. New York: Simon and Schuster, 1953.

Other Sources

"Abe Lincoln in Illinois." In *Drama for Students*. Ed. David Galens and Lynn Spampinato. Vol. 11. Detroit: Gale, 2002. 1–20.

Adler, Selig. *The Isolationist Impulse: Its Twentieth-Century Reaction*. New York: Abelard-Shuman, 1957.

Allen, Devere. *The Fight For Peace*. Vol. 1. New York: Macmillan, 1930.

Alonso, Harriet Hyman. *Peace as a Women's Issue: A History of the U.S. Movement for World Peace and Women's Rights*. Syracuse: Syracuse University Press, 1993.

Anderson, Maxwell. *The Wingless Victory*. Washington, D.C.: Anderson House, 1936.

———. *Winterset*. New York: Dramatists Play Service, 1935, 1973.

———, and Laurence Stallings. *What Price Glory?* In *Famous American Plays of the 1920s*. New York: Dell Publishing, 1959.

Ashley, Sally. *F.P.A.: The Life and Times of Franklin Pierce Adams*. New York: Beaufort Books, 1986.

Atkinson, Brooks. *Broadway*. 1970, 1974. Revised ed. New York: Limelight Editions, 1990.

———. *Broadway Scrapbook*. New York: Theatre Arts, 1947.

Atkinson, D. Scott, and Nicolai Cikovsky Jr., eds. *William Merritt Chase: Summers at Shinnecock, 1891–1902*. Washington, D.C.: National Gallery of Art, 1987.

Avery, Laurence G., ed. *Dramatist in America: Letters of Maxwell Anderson, 1912–1958*. Chapel Hill: University of North Carolina Press, 1977.

Baer, William, ed. *Elia Kazan Interviews*. Jackson: University Press of Mississippi, 2000.

Barrett, Mary Ellin. *Irving Berlin: A Daughter's Memoir*. New York: Simon and Schuster, 1994.

Beckerman, Bernard, and Howard Siegman, ed. *On Stage: Selected Theatre Reviews from The New York Times, 1920–1970*. New York: Arno Press in cooperation with Quadrangle/New York Times Book, 1973.

Behrman, S. N. *Four Plays by S. N. Behrman*. New York: Random House, 1952.

———. "Old Monotonous: Robert E. Sherwood." In *The Suspended Drawing Room*. New York: Stein and Day, 1965. 137–165.

———. *People in a Diary: A Memoir by S. N. Behrman*. Boston: Little, Brown, 1972.

Berg, A. Scott. *Goldwyn: A Biography*. New York: Alfred A. Knopf, 1989.

Bergreen, Lawrence. *As Thousands Cheer: The Life of Irving Berlin*. New York: Viking Penguin, 1990.

Bernstein, Barton J. "The Quest for Security: American Foreign Policy and International Control of Atomic Energy, 1942–1946." *Journal of American History* 60, no. 4 (March 1974): 1003–44.

Bernstein, Matthew. *Controlling Hollywood: Censorship and Regulation in the Studio Era*. New Brunswick, N.J.: Rutgers University Press, 1999.

Berton, Pierre. *Vimy*. 1986. Reprint ed. Toronto: Anchor Canada, 2001.

Bhatia, Nandi. "Robert E. Sherwood." In *Dictionary of Literary Biography*. Ed. Bruccoli Clark Layman. Detroit: Gale, 2004. 313–325.

Black, Gregory D. *Hollywood Censored: Morality Codes, Catholics, and the Movies*. New York: Cambridge University Press, 1994.

Bolt, Ernest C., Jr. *Ballots before Bullets: The War Referendum Approach to Peace in America, 1914–1941*. Charlottesville: University Press of Virginia, 1977.

Bosworth, Patricia. *Montgomery Clift: A Biography*. New York: Bantam Books, 1978.

Brandenburg, Ernest. "The Preparation of Franklin D. Roosevelt's Speeches." *Quarterly Journal of Speech* 35, no. 2 (April 1949): 214–221.

Brown, Jared. *The Fabulous Lunts: A Biography of Alfred Lunt and Lynn Fontanne*. New York: Atheneum, 1986.

Brown, John Mason. *The Ordeal of a Playwright: Robert E. Sherwood and the Challenge of War*. New York: Harper and Row, 1970.

———. *Two on the Aisle: Ten Years of the American Theatre in Performance*. New York: W. W. Norton, 1938.

———. *The Worlds of Robert E. Sherwood: Mirror to His Times, 1896–1939*. New York: Harper and Row, 1962, 1965.

Bryan, J., III. *Merry Gentlemen (and One Lady)*. New York: Atheneum, 1985.

Cage, Nigel. *Battleground Europe: AARAS: Vimy Ridge*. 1996. Reprint ed. Barnsley, South Yorkshire: Pen and Sword Books, 2000.

Callen, Anthea. *Women Artists of the Arts and Crafts Movement, 1870–1914*. New York: Pantheon Books, 1979.

Chapman, John, ed. *The Burns Mantle Best Plays of 1949–1950 and the Year Book of the Drama in America*. New York: Dodd, Mead, 1950.

Chatfield, Charles. *The American Peace Movement: Ideals and Activism*. New York: Twayne Publishers, 1992.

———. *For Peace and Justice: Pacifism in America, 1914–1941*. Knoxville: University of Tennessee Press, 1971.

Clute, Penelope D. "The Plattsburg Idea." *New York Archives* 5, no. 2 (Fall 2005): 10–15.

Cole, Wayne S. *America First: The Battle against Intervention, 1940–1941*. New York: Octagon Books, 1953, 1971.

Connelly, Marc. *Voices Offstage: A Book of Memoirs*. New York: Holt, Rinehart and Winston, 1968.

Cook, Blanche Wiesen. "Women and Peace: The Legacy." *Ms.* 16, no. 1 (Winter 2006): 40–43.

Cook, Tim. *No Place to Run: The Canadian Corps and Gas Warfare in the First World War*. Vancouver: UBC Press, 1999.

Corbin, Richard, and Miriam Balf, eds. *Twelve American Plays: Alternate Edition*. New York: Charles Scribner's Sons, 1969, 1973.

Curti, Merle. *Peace or War: The American Struggle, 1636–1936*. New York: W. W. Norton, 1936.

Dallek, Robert. *Franklin D. Roosevelt and American Foreign Policy, 1932–1945*. New York: Oxford University Press, 1979.

Davidson, Bill. *Spencer Tracy: Tragic Idol*. New York: E. P. Dutton, 1987.

Dawley, Alan. *Changing the World: American Progressives in War and Revolution*. Princeton: Princeton University Press, 2003.

Day, Barry, ed. *Dorothy Parker In Her Own Words*. Maryland: Taylor Trade Publishing, 2004.

DeBenedetti, Charles. "The $100,000 American Peace Award of 1924." *Pennsylvania Magazine of History and Biography* 98, no. 2 (April 1974): 224–249.

———. *Origins of the Modern American Peace Movement, 1915–1929*. Millwood, N.Y.: KTO Press, 1978.

Deval, Jacques. *Tovaritch*. New York: Henry Holt, 1938.

Dilling, Elizabeth. *The Red Network: A "Who's Who" and Handbook of Radicalism for Patriots*. Chicago: By the Author, 1934.

Dinesen, Thomas, V. C. *Merry Hell! A Dane with the Canadians*. Translated from Danish. London: Jarrolds Publishers, 1930.

Divine, Robert A. *The Reluctant Belligerent: American Entry into World War II*. New York: John Wiley and Sons, 1965.

———. *Second Chance: The Triumph of Internationalism in America during World War II*. New York: Atheneum, 1967.

Doherty, Thomas. *Pre-Code Hollywood: Sex, Immorality, and Insurrection in American Cinema, 1930–1934*. New York: Columbia University Press, 1999.

Douglas, Ann. *Terrible Honesty: Mongrel Manhattan in the 1920s.* New York: Farrar, Straus and Giroux, 1995.

Drennan, Robert E., ed. *The Algonquin Wits: Bon Mots, Wisecracks, Epigrams, and Gags.* New York: Citadel Press Books, 1968, 1985.

Dusenbury, Winifred L. *The Theme of Loneliness in Modern American Drama.* Gainesville: University of Florida Press, 1960.

Elder, Donald. *Ring Lardner.* Garden City, N.Y.: Doubleday, 1956.

Elder, Glen H. *Children of the Great Depression: Social Change in Life Experience.* Chicago: University of Chicago Press, 1974.

Emmet, Thomas Addis. *The Emmet Family, with some incidents relating to Irish history and a biographical sketch of Prof. John Patten Emmet, M.D., and other members.* New York: Bradstreet Press, 1898.

———. *Memoir of Thomas Addis and Robert Emmet with Their Ancestors and Immediate Family.* 2 vols. New York: The Emmet Press, 1915.

Emmet, William Le Roy. *The Autobiography of an Engineer.* Albany, N.Y.: Fort Orange Press, 1931.

Evans, Elizabeth. *Ring Lardner.* New York: Frederick Ungar Publishing, 1979.

Fearnow, Mark. "The Meaning of Pictures: Myth and American History Plays of the Great Depression, or, Lincoln Died (So You and I Might Live)." *Journal of American Drama and Theatre* 5, no. 3 (Fall 1993): 1–15.

Ferrell, Robert H. *Peace in Their Time: The Origins of the Kellogg-Briand Pact.* New Haven: Yale University Press, 1952.

Finletter, Gretchen. *From the Top of the Stairs.* Boston: Little, Brown, 1946.

Flexner, Eleanor. *American Playwrights: 1918–1938.* New York: Simon and Schuster, 1938.

Freedley, George. *The Lunts.* New York: Macmillan, 1958.

Gaines, James G. *Wit's End: Days and Nights of the Algonquin Round Table.* New York: Harcourt Brace Jovanovich, 1977.

Gallati, Barbara Dayer. *William Merritt Chase.* New York: Harry N. Abrams in association with the National Museum of American Art, Smithsonian Institution, 1995.

Garraty, John A., and Mark C. Carnes, eds. *American National Biography.* New York: Oxford University Press, 1999. S.v. "Mary Elizabeth Wilson Sherwood" by Joann E. Castagna; "William Le Roy Emmet" by Daniel Martin Dumych; "Elias Boudinot" by H. James Henderson; "Thomas Addis Emmet" by Donald Roper.

Gassner, John, ed. *Twenty-five Best Plays of the Modern American Theatre: Early Series.* New York: Crown Publishers, 1949.

Gilbert, Julie Goldsmith. *Ferber: A Biography.* New York: Doubleday, 1978.

Green, Paul, and Kurt Weill. *Johnny Johnson.* In *Paul Green: Five Plays of the South.* New York: Hill and Wang, 1963.

Haber, L. F. *The Poisonous Cloud: Chemical Warfare in the First World War.* Oxford: Clarendon Press, 1986.

Hagemann, E. R. "An Extraordinary Picture: The Film Criticism of Robert E. Sherwood." *Journal of Popular Film* 1, no. 2 (Spring 1972): 81–104.

Harriman, Margaret Case. *The Vicious Circle: The Story of the Algonquin Round Table.* New York: Rinehart, 1951.

Hawes, William. *Filmed Television Drama, 1952–1958.* Jefferson, N.C.: McFarland, 2002.

———. *Live Television Drama, 1946–1951.* Jefferson, N.C.: McFarland, 2001.

Henderson, Mary C. *The City and the Theatre: The History of New York Playhouses.* New York: Back Stage Books, 2004.

Hewitt, Barnard. *Theatre U.S.A.: 1665 to 1957.* New York: McGraw-Hill, 1959.

Himelstein, Morgan Y. *Drama Was a Weapon: The Left-Wing Theatre in New York, 1929–1941.* New Brunswick, N.J.: Rutgers University Press, 1963.

Holmes, John Haynes, and Reginald Lawrence. *If This Be Treason.* New York: Macmillan, 1935.

Hoppin, Martha J. *The Emmets: A Family of Women Painters.* Pittsfield, Mass.: Berkshire Museum, 1982.

Houseman, John. *Front and Center.* New York: Simon and Schuster, 1979.

———. *Run-Through: A Memoir.* New York: Simon and Schuster, 1972.

Howard, Sidney. *The Ghost of Yankee Doodle.* New York: Charles Scribner's Sons, 1938.

———. *They Knew What They Wanted.* In *Famous Plays of the 1920s.* New York: Dell Publishing, 1959.

———. *Yellow Jack: A History.* New York: Harcourt, Brace, 1933.

"*Idiot's Delight.*" In *Drama for Students.* Ed. David Galens and Lynn Spampinato. Vol. 15. Detroit: Gale, 2002. 48–67.

Jablonski, Edward. *Irving Berlin: American Troubadour.* New York: Henry Holt, 1999.

Jonas, Manfred. *Isolationism in America: 1935–1941.* Ithaca: Cornell University Press, 1966.

Kantor, MacKinlay. *Glory For Me.* New York: Coward-McCann, 1945.

Kaufman, Beatrice, and Joseph Hennessey, eds. *The Letters of Alexander Woollcott.* London: Cassell, 1946.

Kennan, George F. *American Diplomacy: 1900–1950.* Chicago: University of Chicago Press, 1951.

Kennedy, David M., ed. *The American People in the Depression.* West Haven, Conn.: Pendulum Press, 1973.

Kirkendall, Richard S. *The United States, 1929–1945: Years of Crisis and Change.* New York: McGraw-Hill, 1974.

Koszarski, Richard. *An Evening's Entertainment: The Age of the Silent Feature Picture, 1915–1928.* Berkeley: University of California Press, 1990.

Kurtz, Michael L. *The Challenging of America, 1920–1945.* Arlington Heights, Ill.: Forum Press, 1986.

Landreth, Helen. *The Pursuit of Robert Emmet*. New York: McGraw Hill, 1948.

Langner, Lawrence. *The Magic Curtain: The Story of a Life in Two Fields, Theatre and Invention, by the Founder of the Theatre Guild*. New York: E. P. Dutton, 1951.

Lardner, Ring W. *The Love Nest and Other Stories*. New York: Charles Scribner's Sons, 1926.

Lasch, Christopher. *The New Radicalism in America: 1889–1963: The Intellectual As a Social Type*. New York: Alfred A. Knopf, 1966.

Laurie, Clayton D. *The Propaganda Warriors: America's Crusade against Nazi Germany*. Lawrence: University Press of Kansas, 1996.

Lawson, John Howard. *Theory and Technique of Playwriting*. New York: Hill and Wang, 1936, 1960.

Leff, Leonard J., and Jerald L. Simmons. *The Dame in the Kimono: Hollywood, Censorship, and the Production Code*. Lexington: University Press of Kentucky, 2001.

Leigh, Michael. *Mobilizing Consent: Public Opinion and American Foreign Policy, 1937–1947*. Westport, Conn.: Greenwood Press, 1976.

Leuchtenburg, William. *The Perils of Prosperity, 1914–1932*. Chicago: University of Chicago Press, 1958.

Lieberman, Joseph I. *The Scorpion and the Tarantula: The Struggle to Control Atomic Weapons, 1945–1949*. Boston: Houghton Mifflin, 1970.

Link, Arthur. *Wilson the Diplomatist: A Look at His Major Foreign Policies*. Baltimore: Johns Hopkins University Press, 1957.

Lockhart, Robert Bruce. *Friends, Foes, and Foreigners*. London: Putnam/Richard Clay, 1957.

Mantle, Burns, ed. *The Best Plays of 1926–27 and the Year Book of the Drama in America*. 1927. Reprint ed. New York: Dodd, Mead, 1947.

———. *The Best Plays of 1931–32 and the Year Book of the Drama in America*. New York: Dodd, Mead, 1932.

———. *The Best Plays of 1934–35 and the Year Book of the Drama in America*. 1935. Reprint ed. New York: Dodd, Mead, 1964.

———. *The Best Plays of 1935–36 and the Year Book of the Drama in America*. New York: Dodd, Mead, 1936.

———. *The Best Plays of 1936–37 and the Year Book of the Drama in America*. New York: Dodd, Mead, 1937.

———. *The Best Plays of 1938–39 and the Year Book of the Drama in America*. New York: Dodd, Mead, 1939.

———. *The Best Plays of 1939–40 and the Year Book of the Drama in America*. New York: Dodd, Mead, 1940.

———. *The Best Plays of 1945–46 and the Year Book of the Drama in America*. New York: Dodd, Mead, 1946.

McCoy, Donald R. *Coming of Age: The United States During the 1920s and 1930s*. Harmondsworth: Penguin Books, 1973.

Meade, Marion. *Dorothy Parker: What Fresh Hell Is This?* New York: Penguin Books, 1987, 1989.

Meserve, Walter J. *Robert E. Sherwood: Reluctant Moralist*. New York: Pegasus/Western Publishing, 1970.

Molony, John Chartres. *Ireland's Tragic Comedians*. 1935. Reprint ed. Freeport, N.Y.: Books for Libraries Press, 1970.

Mordden, Ethan. *Beautiful Mornin': The Broadway Musical in the 1940s*. New York: Oxford University Press, 1999.

Morrison, Charles Clayton. *The Outlawry of War: A Constructive Policy for World Peace*. Chicago: Willett, Clark and Colby, 1927.

Navasky, Victor S. *Naming Names*. New York: Viking Press, 1980.

Nelson, John K. *The Peace Prophets: American Pacifist Thought, 1919–1941*. Chapel Hill: University of North Carolina Press, 1967.

Nicholson, Colonel Gerald W. L. *Canadian Expeditionary Force, 1914–1919: Official History of the Canadian Army in the First World War*. Ottawa: Queen's Printer and Controller of Stationery, 1962.

Nolan, Paul T. *Marc Connelly*. New York: Twayne Publishers, 1969.

O'Donnell, Patrick. *Operatives, Spies, and Saboteurs: The Unknown Story of the Men and Women of WWII's OSS*. New York: Free Press, 2004.

Parker, Dorothy. *Dorothy Parker: Complete Stories*. New York: Penguin Books, 1995.

Paschall, Rod. *The Defeat of Imperial Germany, 1917–1918*, 1989. Reprint ed. New York: Da Capo Press, 1994.

Perrett, Geoffrey. *America in the Twenties: A History*. New York: Simon and Schuster, 1982.

Peters, Margot. *Design for Living: Alfred Lunt and Lynn Fontanne: A Biography*. New York: Alfred A. Knopf, 2003.

"The Petrified Forest." In *Drama for Students*. Ed. David Galens and Lynn Spampinato. Vol. 15. Detroit: Gale, 2002. 192–210.

Pisano, Ronald G. *A Leading Spirit in American Art: William Merritt Chase*. Seattle: University of Washington Press, 1983.

Postgate, R. W. *Dear Robert Emmet*. New York: Vanguard Press, 1932.

Radosh, Ronald, and Allis Radosh. *Red Star Over Hollywood: The Film Colony's Long Romance with the Left*. San Francisco: Encounter Books, 2005.

Rauch, Basil, ed. *The Roosevelt Reader: Selected Speeches, Messages, Press Conferences, and Letters of Franklin D. Roosevelt*. New York: Rinehart, 1957.

Renshaw, Patrick. *Franklin D. Roosevelt*. London: Pearson/Longman, 2004.

Rice, Elmer. *Judgment Day*. New York: Coward-McCann, 1934.

———. *Minority Report: An Autobiography*. New York: Simon and Schuster, 1963.

———. *Street Scene*. In *Famous Plays of the 1920s*. New York: Dell Publishing, 1959.

Richter, Donald. *Chemical Soldiers: British Gas Warfare in World War I*. Lawrence: University Press of Kansas, 1992.

Romasco, Albert V. *The Poverty of Abundance: Hoover, the Nation, the Depression*. New York: Oxford University Press, 1965.

Roof, Katherine Metcalf. *The Life and Art of William Merritt Chase*. New York: Charles Scribner's Sons, 1917.

Roosevelt, Franklin D. *The Public Papers and Addresses of Franklin D. Roosevelt with a Special Introduction and Explanatory Notes by President Roosevelt. 1940: War and Aid to Democracies.* New York: Macmillan, 1941.

———. *Roosevelt's Foreign Policy, 1933–1941: Franklin D. Roosevelt's Unedited Speeches and Messages.* New York: Wilfred Funk, 1942.

Rosenman, Samuel I. *Working with Roosevelt.* New York: Harper and Brothers, 1952.

Russett, Bruce M. *No Clear and Present Danger: A Skeptical View of the U.S. Entry into World War II.* New York: Harper and Row Publishers, 1972.

Sahu, N. S. *Theatre of Protest and Anger.* Delhi: Amar Prakashan Publishers, 1988.

Sarris, Andrew. *"You Ain't Heard Nothin' Yet": The American Talking Film: History and Memory, 1927–1949.* New York: Oxford University Press, 1998.

Scharine, Richard G. " 'The War That Is to Begin Tomorrow Night': American Anti-War Drama in the 1930s." *Journal of American Drama and Theatre* 2, no. 2 (Spring 1990): 27–37.

Schickel, Richard. *Elia Kazan: A Biography.* New York: HarperCollins Publishers, 2005.

Schwartz, Jordan A. *The Interregnum of Despair: Hoover, Congress, and the Depression.* Urbana: University of Illinois Press, 1970.

Shannon, David. *Between the Wars: America, 1919–1941.* Boston: Houghton Mifflin, 1979.

Shaw, George Bernard. *Arms and the Man.* New York: Penguin Books, 1898, 1958.

Shaw, Irwin. *Bury the Dead.* New York: Random House, 1936.

Sherwood, M. E. W. *An Epistle to Posterity: Being Rambling Recollections of Many Years of My Life.* New York: Harper and Brothers, 1897.

Shivers, Alfred S. *The Life of Maxwell Anderson.* New York: Stein and Day Publishers, 1983.

Shulman, Holly Cowan. *The Voice of America: Propaganda and Democracy, 1941–1945.* Madison: University of Wisconsin Press, 1990.

Shulman, R. Baird. *Robert E. Sherwood.* New York: Twayne Publishers, 1964.

Sklar, George, and Albert Maltz. *Peace on Earth.* New York: Samuel French, 1934.

Smith, Harry W. "An Air of the Dream: Jo Mielziner, Innovation, and Influence, 1935–1955." *Journal of American Drama and Theatre* 5, no. 3 (Fall 1993): 42–54.

Sontag, Raymond J. *A Broken World, 1919–1939.* New York: Harper and Row Publishers, 1971.

Sova, Dawn B. *Forbidden Films: Censorship Histories of 125 Motion Pictures.* New York: Facts on File, 2001.

Stein, Howard. "Joseph Wood Krutch: A Rare Critic." *Columbia: The Magazine of Columbia University* (Summer, 2000): 42–45.

Summers, Anthony, and Robbyn Swan. *Sinatra: The Life.* New York: Alfred A. Knopf, 2005.

Travers, Tim. *The Killing Ground: The British Army, the Western Front, and The Emergence of Modern War, 1900–1918.* 1987. Reprint ed. Barnsley, South Yorkshire: Penn and Sword Books, 2003.

Vasey, Ruth. *The World According to Hollywood, 1918–1939.* Madison: University of Wisconsin Press, 1997.

Vaughan, W. E., ed. *A New History of Ireland.* Vol. 5. *Ireland under the Union, I (1801–70).* Oxford: Clarendon Press, 1989.

Wainscott, Ronald H. *The Emergence of the Modern American Theater, 1914–1929.* New Haven: Yale University Press, 1997.

Waldau, Roy S. *Vintage Years of the Theatre Guild: 1928–1939.* Cleveland: Press of Case Western Reserve University, 1972.

Wattenberg, Richard. "'Old West'/New 'West': The New Frontier in Sherwood's *The Petrified Forest* (1934) and Saroyan's *The Time of Your Life* (1939)." *Journal of American Drama and Theatre* 1, no. 2 (Fall 1989): 17–33.

Weimann, Jeanne Madeline, *The Fair Women.* Chicago: Academy Chicago, 1981.

Wertheim, Albert. *Staging the War: American Drama and World War II.* Bloomington: Indiana University Press, 2004.

Wharton, John F. *Life Among the Playwrights: Being Mostly the Story of the Playwrights Producing Company.* New York: Quadrangle/New York Times Book, 1974.

Williams, Jeffery. *Byng of Vimy: General and Governor General.* 1983. Reprint ed. Barnsley, South Yorkshire: Penn and Sword Books, 1992.

Wilson, Garff B. *Three Hundred Years of American Drama and Theatre: From "Ye Bear and Ye Cubb" to "Hair."* Englewood Cliffs, N.J.: Prentice-Hall, 1973.

Wiltz, John E. *From Isolation to War, 1931–1941.* Arlington Heights, Ill.: Harlan Davidson, 1968.

Winkler, Allan. *The Politics of Propaganda: The Office of War Information, 1942–1945.* New Haven: Yale University Press, 1978.

Wittner, Lawrence S. *One World or None: A History of the World Nuclear Disarmament Movement through 1953.* Stanford: Stanford University Press, 1993.

———. *Rebels Against War: The American Peace Movement, 1933–1983.* Philadelphia: Temple University Press, 1989.

Woll, Allen. *Black Musical Theatre: From "Coontown" to "Dreamgirls."* 1989. Reprint ed. New York: Da Capo Press, 1991.

Yardley, Jonathan. *Ring: A Biography of Ring Lardner.* New York: Random House, 1977.

Zeiger, Susan. "Finding a Cure for War: Women's Politics and the Peace Movement in the 1920s." *Journal of Social History* 24 (Fall 1990): 69–86.

Websites

www.afi.com. Information on *Oh, What a Nurse* and *The Lucky Lady.* American Film Institute. Accessed October 9, 2005.

www.askart.com/artist/S/rosina_emmet_sherwood.asp?ID=16983. "Rosina Emmet Sherwood." Accessed January 18, 2005.

www.fayschool.org/about_history4.html. Fay School photo, "The Original Schoolroom, 1908." Accessed March 4, 2005.

www.fayschool.org/about_history5.html. Fay School photo, "The School Code, 1908." Accessed March 4, 2005.

www.fdrlibrary.marist.edu/psf/box37/t335d01.html. FDR to Winston Churchill, February 7, 1944. Accessed January 29, 2006.

www.health-alliance.com. "*Tic Douloureux.*" Accessed January 14, 2006.

http://historymatters.gmu.edu/d/5164. "Didactic Dramas: Antiwar Plays of the 1930s." Accessed November 22, 2005.

www.hoosiergrovemuseum.com/tillie/wool01.html. Rosina Emmet Sherwood, "Wool Gathering," in *Harper's Second Reader.* Accessed February 25, 2005.

www.ibdb.com. "Internet Broadway Data Base: Robert E. Sherwood, Mary Brandon." Accessed May 20, 2006.

www.imdb.com. "Internet Movie Data Base: Robert E. Sherwood." Accessed October 26, 2005.

www.jssgallery.org/Paintings/The_Fountain_Villa_Torlonia_Frascati.html. "Wilfrid and Jane de Glehn. Accessed January 18, 2005.

www.milton.edu/about/pages/history.asp. "A Brief History of Milton Academy." Accessed March 4, 2005.

http://silentladies.com/BHurlock.html. "Madeline Hurlock." Accessed December 30, 2005.

www.solitairecentral.com/id.html. "Idiot's Delight Solitaire." Accessed April 18, 2004.

http://www.usmm.org/fdr/emergency.html. FDR, "President Franklin Delano Roosevelt Radio Address Announcing the Proclamation of an Unlimited National Emergency, 'We Choose Human Freedom,' May 27, 1941." Accessed February 8, 2006.

www.webmd.com. "*Tic Douloureux.*" Accessed January 14, 2006.

www.westegg.com/inflation/. "The Inflation Calculator." Accessed August 6 and 9, 2006.

Acknowledgments

IN THE SUMMER of 1990 I attended a National Endowment for the Humanities Summer Seminar for College Teachers. The topic, "American Playwrights, 1920–1980," was of tremendous interest to me, as I had always had a love for the theater and as an undergraduate had majored in it and in English and American literature. Life plays funny tricks on people, and in a move that surprised everyone who knew me, after fifteen years of teaching English, I changed paths and became a historian. The NEH seminar was my first effort toward bringing my two disciplines together. The wonderful seminar leader, Howard Stein, then chair of the Theatre Program of the Oscar Hammerstein Center for Theatre Studies at Columbia University, suggested that as a historian writing about peace movements, I might find Robert E. Sherwood an interesting subject. He was absolutely correct.

Ten years passed after that intense summer of reading, discussing, and attending plays before I revisited Sherwood in any serious manner. During those years I wrote three books and several articles, but none on Sherwood. I did read his many plays, however, and started searching out his films. In the end, I decided to write this book, a blend of my two disciplines and loves—history and theater. In 2004 I applied for a National Endowment for the Humanities Research Fellowship, and once again, Howard Stein played a key role in my life as one of my referees. I am most grateful to the NEH for both the summer seminar and the year-long research fellowship for the 2005–6 academic year. I am also extremely grateful to Howard Stein, who stuck with me through this entire process. He not only read every chapter of this book in its first draft form but also commented on them and raised important questions for me to consider while making revisions. He also told me many interesting theater history stories that made this journey even more of a joy than it already was. I consider myself truly fortunate to have him in my life.

I also extend my appreciation to the PSC-CUNY research award program for two grants which allowed me release time for research and writing, travel funds, and photo reproduction. I am grateful to the City College of New York for granting me a year-long sabbatical during the 2005–6 academic year. For other support at City College, I am grateful to Deans James Watts, Daniel Lemons, and Fred Reynolds.

I am indebted to Robert Sherwood's grandson Joseph Stillman for generously sharing his memories of Robert, Madeline, and Mary Sherwood and Mary Brandon, and for granting permission to quote from archival sources and publications and to use family photos.

Many thanks to the librarians and archivists in the following collections, who always made me feel as if I were the only person asking for help: the Houghton Library of Harvard University, the State Historical Society of Wisconsin, the Smithsonian Institution, the Harvard University Archives, the Harvard University Theatre Collection, the Indiana Historical Society, the Howard Gotlieb Archival Research Center of Boston University, the Margaret Herrick Library of the Academy of Motion Pictures Arts and Sciences, the New York Public Library at Forty-second Street, the New York Public Library for the Performing Arts at Lincoln Center, the Fales Collection of New York University, the National Archives of Canada in Ottawa, the Bancroft Library of the University of California at Berkeley, the Lilly Library of Indiana University, and the Interlibrary Loan area of the City College of New York library. I also thank the Eileen Darby Estate for granting permission to publish Darby's wonderful photograph which captured the tension, fatigue, and frustrations of producing *The Rugged Path*.

For their support throughout this project, I thank these friends and colleagues: Claudia Wilsch Case, Kathleen Dalton, and Melanie Gustafson, who read and commented on the manuscript; and Catherine Franklin, Gela Kline, Bonnie Anderson, Tom Sabia, Nancy Tomes, Susan Zeiger, Robert Rosenstone, John Chambers, Tony Rotundo, Doris Cintron, Alice Kessler-Harris, Anne Marie Pois, Aviva Slesin, and Darren Staloff. Thanks also to my 2004–5 City College history honors class for their input on various parts of this work during our year together.

This is my second book with the University of Massachusetts Press. I consider myself lucky to have Paul Wright as my editor. He has been a strong supporter of my work from the day we met several years ago. This book was one of the last that Paul took through the evaluation process before entering that delightful stage of life known as retirement. My thanks to him and my best wishes for many new adventures. I am also grateful to the press's director, Bruce Wilcox, who has been a constant voice of support; to managing editor Carol Betsch for her care and great sense of humor while overseeing the production process; and to others at the press who give so much to each and every book that comes their way.

A very special thanks to my stepson, Pablo Alonso, for venturing into the archives for the first time in his life and doing a top-notch job in obtaining copies of the papers on the censorship of Sherwood's films, especially *Idiot's Delight*. Also for their support of this project I thank Clara Hyman, Carolyn Beck, Miguel Alonso, Lucinda Alonso, Liza Korolova, and Victor Alonso. And to Joe, just for being.

Index

In subheadings, Robert Emmet Sherwood is referred to as RES.

HARRIET HYMAN ALONSO was born in Brooklyn, New York, and raised in the New York metropolitan area. She earned a bachelor's degree in English literature and dramatic arts and a master's degree in English language education from New York University, a master's in women's history from Sarah Lawrence College, and a doctorate in history from the State University of New York at Stony Brook. She was director of the Women's Center at Jersey City State College from 1987 to 1989 and taught history and women's studies at Fitchburg (Massachusetts) State College from 1989 to 1999. In 1992 the students at Fitchburg voted her Faculty Member of the Year. Alonso is currently chair of the Department of Interdisciplinary Arts and Sciences and professor of history at the City College of New York, City University of New York, and holds an appointment at the CUNY Graduate Center. She is a longtime member of the Peace History Society. Among her previous books are *The Women's Peace Union and the Outlawry of War, 1921–1942* (1989; 1997), *Peace as a Women's Issue: A History of the U.S. Movement for World Peace and Women's Rights* (1993), and the award-winning *Growing Up Abolitionist: The Story of the Garrison Children* (University of Massachusetts Press, 2002). Alonso received a National Endowment for the Humanities Research Fellowship for her work on Robert Sherwood.